AN AMERICAN PROBLEM

An American Problem

HOW THE COUNTRY BUILT—AND THE SUPREME COURT BROKE—THE VOTING RIGHTS ACT

MICHAEL G. MILLER

KEVIN T. MORRIS

PRINCETON UNIVERSITY PRESS
PRINCETON & OXFORD

Published by Princeton University Press
41 William Street, Princeton, New Jersey 08540
99 Banbury Road, Oxford OX2 6JX

press.princeton.edu

GPSR Authorized Representative: Easy Access System Europe - Mustamäe tee 50, 10621 Tallinn, Estonia, gpsr.requests@easproject.com

ISBN 9780691285504
ISBN (epub) 9780691295237
ISBN (PDF) 9780691285528

Library of Congress Control Number: 2026939827

British Library Cataloging-in-Publication Data is available

Editorial: David McBride and Abigail Corcelli
Production Editorial: Nathan Carr
Jacket/Cover Design: Chris Ferrante
Production: Erin Suydam
Publicity: James Schneider

Jacket/Cover Credit: Jacket images adapted from martinova4 / Shutterstock and the Voting Rights Act of 1965, courtesy of National Archives at Washington, DC.

This book has been composed in Arno

Printed in the United States of America

10 9 8 7 6 5 4 3 2 1

MIX
Paper | Supporting responsible forestry
FSC® C008955
FSC www.fsc.org

For the unnamed thousands who have given their lives for the right to vote

"With a country as with a person, 'What is man profited if he shall gain the whole world, and lose his own soul?' There is no Negro problem. There is no Southern problem. There is no Northern problem. There is only an American problem."

—PRESIDENT LYNDON JOHNSON'S SPEECH TO CONGRESS ON VOTING RIGHTS, MARCH 15, 1965

CONTENTS

LIST OF TABLES

LIST OF FIGURES

ACKNOWLEDGMENTS

WE MET in 2019, when we discovered, somewhat accidentally, that we were working more or less on the same research question. Kevin was a newly arrived researcher at the Brennan Center for Justice, and Michael had just spent a year there as a fellow, so we knew many of the same people. Late that year, we realized we were both circulating papers that sought to determine how *Shelby County v. Holder* had affected voter purges in formerly covered counties. We soon also realized two important truths: We are both committed to producing research in furtherance of transparent, participatory democracy, and we are stronger together than apart. Since that realization, we have been working collaboratively on the research that forms this book. It has been a long road, and we have incurred many debts along the way—both together and separately.

Several of our colleagues have worked directly with us on questions related to this book, either prior to our beginning it or along the way, as we produced a number of articles and working papers that advanced the research in the pages that follow. For this, we thank Jonathan Brater, Chris Deluzio, Catalina Feder, Bernard Fraga, Coryn Grange, Phoebe Henninger, Cora Henry, Arlyss Herzig, Marc Meredith, Peter Miller, Myrna Pérez, and Ian Shapiro.

Aspects of chapter 5 draw on the following article: Kevin T. Morris and Michael G. Miller, “Did *Shelby County v. Holder* Increase the Racial Turnout Gap?” *The Journal of Politics* 89, no. 3 (2027). Similarly, parts of chapter 9 draw on: Michael G. Miller, Kevin T. Morris, Ian Shapiro, and Coryn Grange, “The Disparate and Durable Effects of Mail Voting Restrictions: Evidence from Texas,” *The Journal of Politics* 89, no. 1 (2027). We thank the editorial staff at *The Journal of Politics* and the six anonymous reviewers who worked to improve those articles. Their advice ultimately shaped the direction of this book as well.

As various aspects of the research came together, we presented our work at a wide range of conferences and workshops. Parts of this project have been presented at several different meetings of the American Political Science

Association, the Midwest Political Science Association, the Southern Political Science Association, the Election Sciences, Reform, and Administration Conference, and the State Politics and Policy Conference. We also presented this work at the 2024 Brennan Center Turnout Gap Conference and the 2024 New Topics in Modern Electoral Research workshop at the University of Konstanz, along with talks at Loyola University Chicago, Reed College, the University of Massachusetts, Amherst, and Western Carolina University. We are grateful to the many discussants and participants in those panels whose comments shaped the project's direction. For their suggestions either as panelists or audience members, or for simply serving as soundboards for our ideas, we particularly want to thank Cameron Arnzen, Chris Clark, Conor Dowling, Donald P. Green, Paul Gronke, Jake Grumbach, Brian Hamel, Richard Hasen, Michael Herron, Jonathan Katz, Vlad Kogan, J. Morgan Kousser, Thad Kousser, Kate Krimmel, Martha Kropf, Peyton McCrary, Michael McDonald, Lia Merivaki, Justin Phillips, Richard Pildes, Michael Podhorzer, Enrijeta Shino, Daniel Smith, Nicholas Stephanopolous, Hannah Walker, and Ariel White.

Writing a social science book like this backed up by a full coterie of civil rights lawyers from the Brennan Center means we needed to work twice as hard. It also means the finished product is far better than it would have been otherwise. We are especially thankful for the years of conversations with (and buckets of red ink spilled by) Sean Morales-Doyle, Kareem Crayton, Eliza Sweren-Becker, Eileen O'Connor, Ben Nyblade, Yurij Rudensky, Myrna Pérez, Chelsea Jones, Peter Miller, Jasleen Singh, Andrew Garber, Leah Tulin, Kendall Verhovek, Alexandra Ringe, Brian Palmer, Wendy Weiser, and Michael Waldman. We are grateful for your firm belief in the importance of rigorous social science to the modern civil rights movement. Your collective faith that this book might have an impact beyond the halls of the academy have made the project immeasurably better.

For their able research assistance, we are grateful to Madeline Breeden, Aditi Chatradhi, Abigail Fleming, Cadence Gonzales, Coryn Grange, Emma Sherman-Hawver, Joseph Hennessy, Sarah Heppen, Sara Loving, Zoe Merriman, Lena Pothier, Julia Shimizu, Joyce Shin, Julia Spector, Kate Travis, and Noelia Wassaff.

At Princeton University Press, David McBride believed in this project immediately, and that early endorsement was incredibly meaningful. We thank him for his capable and efficient stewardship of this project as editor. Two anonymous reviewers also provided thoughtful, earnest comments that improved the project immensely.

Finally, we want to thank our partners, who have endured years of hearing us talk to them and each other about this book—and who ultimately read and commented on much of the manuscript. Michael thanks Michelle Tuma for being a sounding board and reader throughout the entire process. Kevin thanks Kelsey Swift for support throughout the project, and for always pushing him to think more theoretically. For better or worse, both Kelsey and Michelle have also become experts in preclearance along the way. Their support has been instrumental, and we could not have completed this work without their care and patience. We also want to acknowledge Ronald Tuma-Miller, a French bulldog who in his capacity as Assistant to the Authors (even though he napped through most of the writing) has graciously agreed to accept responsibility for any errors or omissions in the pages that follow, despite the immense efforts by the people named above to forestall our making them.

INTRODUCTION

AS AMERICA bound up its wounds after the Civil War, there was at least some reason to hope that a real democracy could be possible. The 13th Amendment settled the question of slavery once and for all. The 14th Amendment unambiguously granted citizenship to the formerly enslaved, creating a bulwark against judicial decrees that had sought to deny Black people—whether free or not—the protections thereof.[1] Finally, the 15th Amendment outlawed the denial or abridgment of voting rights "on account of race, color, or previous condition of servitude." Taken together, the Reconstruction Amendments (along with the 19th Amendment, guaranteeing voting rights to women in 1920) held great promise for bringing everyone into American democracy, regardless of their race.

Even so, the nation's original sin cast a long shadow. Many of the people who had perpetuated slavery retained power in the South and sought to maintain supremacy over newly freed Black citizens by any means necessary.[2] Even with federal troops still garrisoned in the former Confederacy—in part to secure civil rights for Black Americans—racial violence convulsed elections there. When those troops began pulling out as Reconstruction ended, Southern states gradually closed off civic life to their Black citizens. Segregation degraded public accommodations and education, and restrictive voting laws guaranteed that Black voters would find it all but impossible to even *register* to vote, much less to cast a ballot.

For nearly a hundred years, Black voters in much of the South were locked out of the political process. By any reasonable count, thousands were killed during this period for trying to claim their voting rights. Others chose to fight in the federal courts. For the most part, they found little relief from either judges or the United States Congress. During this postbellum century, the federal government largely looked the other way, refusing to enforce the Constitution or federal statutes that clearly empowered it to secure Black Americans' voting rights. The South had its way, and for four generations of Black Southerners, the promise of the 15th Amendment remained unfulfilled.

In the wake of World War II, the Civil Rights Movement offered the promise of moving America toward multiracial democracy. Its leaders certainly wanted racial equality on all fronts, but obtaining the vote was central among their concerns. If they were able to influence policy via the ballot box, civil rights advocates reasoned, they would be able to steer government toward their desired ends. In 1957 Martin Luther King Jr. made this case plain in a speech delivered in Washington, DC:

> Give us the ballot, and we will no longer have to worry the federal government about our basic rights.
>
> Give us the ballot, and we will no longer plead to the federal government for passage of an anti-lynching law; we will by the power of our vote write the law on the statute books of the South and bring an end to the dastardly acts of the hooded perpetrators of violence.
>
> Give us the ballot, and we will transform the salient misdeeds of bloodthirsty mobs into the calculated good deeds of orderly citizens. . . .
>
> Give us the ballot, and we will place judges on the benches of the South who will do justly and love mercy, and we will place at the head of the Southern states governors who have felt not only the tang of the human, but the glow of the Divine.[3]

Eight years later, after skillful maneuvering both as opinion makers and as lobbyists, King and his allies saw this ambition fulfilled. Enacted in 1965—almost exactly a century after the ratification of the 14th and 15th Amendments—the Voting Rights Act (VRA) finally made good on the Reconstruction Amendments' promise. The doors to American polling places were thrown open to all potential voters, regardless of their race. The new law empowered the federal government to oversee registration of Black voters immediately. Moreover, Section 2 of the VRA offered powerful ongoing protection against racially discriminatory voter suppression and the dilution of minority representation for voters nationwide.

The VRA also employed a novel approach to ensuring that problematic jurisdictions could no longer circumvent constitutional protections in the longer term. In tandem, Sections 4(b) and 5 of the VRA mandated that states and localities with a history of racial discrimination in their voting policies "preclear" with the federal government *any* changes to their election practices.

The preclearance condition effectively granted federal regulators active oversight of election administration in these areas and substantially reduced the need for the constant litigation that had historically slowed progress and frustrated civil rights advocates. Prior to the VRA, Black voters would have to prove discrimination on a case-by-case basis. Now the burden of proof was on jurisdictions to show that even facially innocuous changes would maintain racial equity in terms of ballot access and representation.

By any measure the Voting Rights Act was tremendously successful. Throughout the states of the former Confederacy, registration rates among Black voters surged nearly 20 percentage points in just three years, with the largest effects concentrated among the most egregious pre-VRA offenders.[4] In Mississippi, for instance, Black voter registration swelled to roughly 60% in 1968—up nearly ten times from the pre-VRA rate of just 6.7%.[5] In real terms, the VRA allowed more than a million Black Southerners to register and vote for the first time. Black participation in elections grew over the subsequent decades, reaching parity with white voters in 2008, when the first Black president was elected. Over the second half of the twentieth century, Congress extended the VRA's protections to other groups, eventually also protecting linguistic minorities as well. All the while, the Department of Justice (DOJ) and the federal judiciary maintained their vigilance over jurisdictions "covered" by the VRA's preclearance provisions, stopping laws whose effects were unlikely to be race neutral. This ongoing preclearance process was the linchpin of the VRA, allowing the federal government to ensure equal ballot access for all Americans. Until, suddenly, it was gone.

On June 25, 2013, by a 5–4 vote in *Shelby County v. Holder* (570 U.S. 529, 2013), the United States Supreme Court struck down Section 4(b) of the Voting Rights Act. That section contained the coverage formula that determined which parts of the country would be subject to the preclearance power of Section 5. The Supreme Court ruled that the coverage formula, conceived at the height of Southern efforts to disenfranchise Black voters, was antiquated and no longer reflected the covered jurisdictions' willingness to discriminate. The hypothetical federal preclearance power was left intact, but the list of jurisdictions required to preclear all their election changes was eliminated. The decision therefore effectively ended preclearance as well: If no jurisdictions were required to submit their laws for federal review, there was nothing DOJ examiners could do to stop problematic changes before they went into effect.[6]

In the wake of *Shelby County*, jurisdictions that formerly had to secure federal consent before changing election policies—comprising hundreds of counties across all or part of fifteen states—are free to do whatever they wish, constrained only by the threat of lawsuits. Stripped of the extraordinary power of Section 5, advocacy groups and the DOJ once again find themselves in a pre-1965 world in which litigation serves as the sole method of striking down policies that deny voters of color equal access to the ballot box. But even Section 2 of the VRA, which protects against discriminatory election policies nationwide and under which much of this litigation is brought, has been weakened in recent years. In 2024, for instance, the Court erected new, more restrictive barriers to bringing claims of racial discrimination in the drawing of electoral districts.[7]

The most far-reaching actions weakening Section 2 came in the 2021 case *Brnovich v. Democratic National Committee* (594 U.S. 647), and in the 2026 case *Louisiana v. Callais* (No. 24-109, slip op. (U.S. Apr. 29, 2026)). In *Brnovich*, the Court held that racially disparate voting rules do not necessarily violate Section 2 if the effects are "modest." This ruling necessarily means that fewer challenges alleging racial discrimination under Section 2 will succeed in the future. Litigators have apparently recognized this reality: In early 2025 *Bloomberg Law* reported a remarkable drop in cases citing Section 2 in the years since the *Brnovich* ruling.[8] Prior to *Shelby County*, voting rights litigators often referred to Section 5 as the shield that blocked discriminatory laws from ever being implemented and Section 2 as the sword used to strike down any such laws that *did* go into effect. And while Brnovich weakened Section 2's ability to strike down racially discriminatory laws making it harder to cast a ballot, *Callais* is likely to do the same thing for claims of racial vote dilution. Handed down in April 2026, *Callais* is likely to make proving that lawmakers discriminated against minority voters when drawing their maps more difficult than it has been in decades. In the words of Associate Justice Elena Kagan, *Callais* "renders Section 2 all but a dead letter." More than a decade after *Shelby County*, the shield is broken and the sword is dulled.

The hyperlocal nature of American election administration, virtually unique among developed democracies, further compounds efforts to find and halt problematic regulations. Countless policies—such as the siting of polling places or the drawing of school board districts—are developed at the county or even local level. Coupled with an ever-eroding capacity of local media in many areas of the country (and therefore fewer people asking questions about local governments' activity), the localized nature of election administration makes it functionally impossible for the DOJ or advocacy groups to even *know* about all the potentially problematic changes that jurisdictions have enacted since *Shelby County*. Even if they could know, resources for litigation are limited. City council district lines in a small town, even if drawn in a manner that dilutes the power of minority voters, may simply not make it through the triage process for election lawyers and interest groups looking to contest discriminatory election policies in the courts. In the wake of the *Shelby County* decision, then, efforts to protect minority voting rights are necessarily less centralized and are also likely to be both less expeditious and less effective than they were before the Court's decision.

If jurisdictions with a history of discriminating against minority voters began doing so again with federal oversight removed, we would expect substantial backsliding—or "retrogression"—of minority voting rights in the wake of *Shelby County*. That expectation guides the central line of inquiry in this book. For nearly fifty years, the VRA's preclearance procedure did its job, blocking policies that would burden minority voters—regardless of whether a given jurisdiction intended to do so. The VRA's victory over racial disenfranchisement was so total that it provided an opening for the *Shelby County* majority to posit that discriminatory election practices were a thing of the past. This assumption provides a testable proposition, and in the following chapters we engage a relatively simple overarching question: Has voting or representation become less racially equitable in jurisdictions formerly subject to preclearance since *Shelby County*?

Unfortunately, we find substantial evidence that they have. We show that *Shelby County* has been devastating for voting rights. Nearly everywhere we look and on every metric we can conceive, we find that the removal of federal preclearance has led to substantial backsliding in the extent to which minority voters enjoy equal representation and access to the ballot. Our examination of a wide range of state and local election actions—both those we are able to readily observe using data and those that to date have largely escaped media and scholarly attention—finds that they have materially undermined political representation for Americans of color. We estimate that hundreds of thousands of ballots have gone uncast by nonwhite Americans because of the forces unleashed by *Shelby County v. Holder*. And the effects of the decision appear only to be growing.

Our conclusions about the disastrous effects of the *Shelby County* decision shed light on broader processes at play in the American political system—and, specifically, on the implications of our highly federalized system of election administration. Fights like this one are hardly new; since its earliest days, there have been major disagreements about whether the decentralized nature of American electoral systems is a net positive. The lack of a single (federal) election administration is not without benefits.[9] However, this book makes plain that America's decentralized election oversight may also foster the proliferation of below-the-radar retrogressive policies.

In many ways, Section 5 offered a well-tailored balance to this federalism problem by ensuring federal oversight of a highly decentralized system. With this check on local autonomy gone, the system has deteriorated. And while the system might resist complete takeover by an antidemocratic regime, it also allows local actors to effect politics far beyond their home town. As political scientist Jacob Grumbach describes in *Laboratories Against Democracy*, "Antidemocratic interests need only to take control of a *state* government for a short period of time to implement changes that make it harder for their opponents to participate in politics *at all levels*—local, state, and national."[10] Our study of *Shelby County* both concurs with this conclusion and moves beyond it: While Grumbach rightly notes the importance of the 50 different state regimes, we argue that much of the backsliding is driven by actions taken at *even lower* levels—in the many thousands of counties and towns that are siting polling places, drawing school board districts, and maintaining voter rolls. The effects are all exacerbated by the decline of local media, making it harder than ever to track policy development among election administrators.

We trace the rise and fall of the Voting Rights Act, paying particular attention to how the demise of preclearance following *Shelby County* affected minority voting rights and the political power of minority voters. To understand the contemporary legal landscape around voting rights in the United States, however, we must first step back to examine the context in which the original 1965 Voting Rights Act was passed. In Part I, we therefore provide a political history of voting rights, moving more or less chronologically from the post–Civil War Reconstruction to 2013, when the Supreme Court decided the *Shelby County* case.

The Reconstruction Amendments did much in theory—and, until the end of Reconstruction in the late 1870s, in practice—to advance equal rights for minority citizens. However, as we explain in chapter 1, in the century after the Civil War, many state and local policies were designed to eliminate any hope of Black Americans gaining meaningful political power. While not a wholly Southern enterprise, these actions were heavily concentrated there. As the 19th century gave way to the 20th, Black Southerners found themselves shut out of equal public accommodations and prevented from registering to vote by a range of methods that were transparently contrived to circumvent the Reconstruction Amendments. Rather than use the new amendments to combat states' efforts to impede racial equality, the Supreme Court often acted as a willing enabler. Congress simply did nothing, and as the postwar century passed, the promise of true democracy in the Southern states flickered and died.

Things began to change after World War II, however, when Black veterans—fresh from a victory over the racist fascism of Nazi Germany—came home determined to claim their civil rights. With allies from across the United States, Black Southerners built one of the most effective social movements in the history of the world. Their collective action forced Congress to finally ensure that states fall in line. The late 1950s and early 1960s saw a flurry of congressional action shoring up protections for minority citizens' civil and voting rights, including the first federal civil rights laws passed in more than 80 years. The Civil Rights Acts of 1957 and 1960 gradually expanded the federal government's power to protect voting rights via litigation. The more robust Civil Rights Act of 1964 expanded federal regulatory capacity even more. The practical impact of these bills on voter access, however, ultimately proved negligible.

In 1965, in response to continued advocacy from civil rights leaders and the stewardship of President Lyndon B. Johnson, Congress finally faced the practical realities of ongoing minority voter disenfranchisement head-on. The VRA gave the federal government substantial power over states' election practices, and preclearance played the starring role. In passing it, Congress finally woke from its long slumber and showed itself willing to enforce the entire Constitution. Over time, the VRA would realize its potential as one of the most important pieces of legislation that Congress had ever enacted.

The 1965 version of the law was not Congress's final word on voting rights, however, nor was the VRA enacted without resistance from the states that would be subject to federal preclearance of their election practices. In chapter 2 we detail those challenges and how they led to the emergence of a new (and historically unlikely) ally for voting rights advocates: the US Supreme Court. In a series of decisions, the Court largely affirmed congressional authority to regulate state elections, upholding key elements of the VRA, including preclearance. Meanwhile, each time the VRA's required reauthorization came before Congress, its opponents failed in their efforts to hollow it out. To the contrary, the VRA only grew *stronger* over time, as reauthorizations expanded its scope. By the time the 2006 reauthorization rolled around, the VRA was barely even controversial, passing the Senate by a vote of 98–0. Its passage by such a wide margin would have been unthinkable just a generation before, and to many, voting rights looked more secure than ever.

One reason for the VRA's success was the vigor with which the Department of Justice enforced it. In chapter 3 we leverage unique data to better understand the VRA's scope. The DOJ maintained comprehensive records on covered jurisdictions' preclearance requests, which we use to provide a descriptive analysis of *where* the requests emerged (at the state, county, or local level), *what* jurisdictions wanted to change about their election policies, and *when* the requests were made. These data reveal not only how active the Department of Justice was when it came to preclearance but also how diffuse the requests that it processed were. The DOJ reviewed on average more than 400 individual submissions *every month*, containing an average of 851 proposed changes. The majority of these emerged not from highly visible state (or even county) policies but from local jurisdictions such as towns or utility districts. Although the DOJ rejected only about 0.1% of submissions in the later years of preclearance, we are able to glean information from the particular policies that jurisdictions proposed (and those that were rejected). These trends can tell us where to look for policy changes after *Shelby County* that may have been deemed problematic had they been subject to preclearance.

That information is important because chapter 4 reveals that as Congress grew increasingly comfortable with a robust Voting Rights Act, the opposite trend was taking hold at the Supreme Court. Fueled by years of appointments from Republican presidents, the Court was tacking undeniably to the right. The emerging majority looked askance at several aspects of the VRA; preclearance was among them. The coverage formula created two classes of states: those that had discriminated prior to 1972 (and were subject to preclearance), and those that had not and whose behavior with respect to election policies was constrained only by the threat of litigation. Absent evidence of ongoing racial disparities in turnout, these justices wondered whether the coverage classification could be justified. In *Shelby County*, after years of signaling a willingness to do away with the coverage formula, the justices finally made good. Underpinning their decision, as Chief Justice John Roberts wrote in the majority opinion, was a claim that while all agreed that racial disenfranchisement once haunted Southern elections, "things have changed." A dozen years since *Shelby County*, this is now a testable premise.

That point leads directly into Part II of the book, where we employ a range of data sources to determine the extent to which *Shelby County* has raised additional hurdles to voting or diluted the quality of representation for minority voters. Both the flow and the focus of this book changes in Part II in at least two important ways. First, we depart from the chronological organization of Part I; instead, each chapter in part II focuses on a particular aspect of the regulatory environment in the post–*Shelby County* era. We do not constrain these chapters to an examination of *just* the Voting Rights Act, nor do we consider election law changes *only* in formerly covered jurisdictions. Rather, we take a broad national look at the state of election regulation in the period since *Shelby County* was decided. We also do not claim to explore every possible research question in this area, as it is probably not possible for a single book to consider all changes to state and federal election laws over the past decade. Rather, Part II is an effort to address areas of high concern to political scientists, litigators, journalists, and the public.

Second, in Part II we shift the analytic approach, using novel data and advanced statistical techniques to identify the causal effects of ending preclearance. Freed of federal oversight, formerly covered jurisdictions were suddenly able to pursue various policies and other actions, including (but certainly not limited to) districting, voter purges, voter ID laws, and changes to mail ballot procedures. In Part II, we investigate the effects of these policies, as well as the extent to which the *totality* of the new policy environment that sprang up after *Shelby County* affected key outcomes.

By and large, we utilize an approach popular among social scientists called *difference-in-differences*. In effect, difference-in-differences asks whether outcomes for a group of units (such as counties, states, or individuals) to which something happened (or who receive a "treatment") differ relative to outcomes observed in units where no treatment occurred. Researchers leverage patterns over time in the two groups to draw conclusions about the effect of the treatment. We are, in short, looking for the *difference* between these groups in the *differences* they display in some outcome—such as turnout—over time.[11] At several points in Part II, this examination entails comparing jurisdictions subject to preclearance (the treated group) with jurisdictions that never had to submit changes for federal review (the control group) over a long period of time covering elections before *Shelby County* and after.

While this simplified description of our approach provides a decent explanation of how we proceed, it is also important to stress that the statistical methods we employ are considerably more complicated than merit explanation to a general reader. For instance, identifying which "untreated" units are the best comparisons for our treated units requires a great deal of care that exceeds the scope of a book intended for a broad audience. Nevertheless, we anticipate that many readers are still interested in the more statistically technical aspects of our analyses. We have therefore placed many of the details of our statistical models in the Methodological Appendix, which can be found online,* and where interested readers can learn much more about them.

At the same time, we present our findings in a way that all readers should find accessible, and we believe that our findings in Part II are important. For instance, in chapter 5, we examine trends in the racial turnout gap—that is, the difference in turnout between white and minority voters.[12] A high turnout gap indicates that white voters have turned out at higher rates than nonwhite voters, which is precisely the scenario that would have drawn attention from preclearance reviewers when Section 4(b) was in effect. We show that prior to *Shelby County*, the turnout gap in places covered by Section 4(b) and similar noncovered ones moved more or less in the same way; within both groups, the turnout gap tended to rise in some elections and decline in others. We might then assume that if *Shelby County* had not been handed down, the turnout gap in these two groups of counties would have continued to move in a similar manner. But, as our analysis reveals, that was not the case: Once *Shelby County* was handed down, the turnout gap grew much more quickly in places that were no longer protected by preclearance.

In other words, we find that the cumulative effect of changes that formerly covered jurisdictions made to their election laws after the Court's decision *caused* the turnout gap between white and minority voters to widen. It would be impossible for us to track every such change, but fortunately, that comprehensiveness is not necessary. Our methods are designed to capture the total impact of *all* changes to election policies nationally, so we do not need to point to a given policy in a given state to conclude that the widening turnout gap in formerly covered areas can be traced directly to *Shelby County*. We therefore argue that, contrary to claims that the justices made in rendering the *Shelby County* decision, there is still a tendency in the preclearance jurisdictions to enact policies that result in lower minority turnout.

In the remainder of part II, we investigate other particular areas of concern that have emerged in election administration since 2013. We are guided in these efforts by a recognition of Section 5's ability both to stop practices *known* to be discriminatory and to block new ways of discriminating against Americans

* https://press.princeton.edu/ISBN/9780691295237#resources

of color. For instance, Section 5 did not simply stop attempts to make casting ballots more difficult for minorities. It also blocked efforts to diminish the power of votes that *are* cast through tactics like racial gerrymandering that dilute voters' political power.

In chapter 6, we therefore detail the effects that *Shelby County* had in the 2020 redistricting cycle, which was the first in decades to be completed without preclearance. Since *Shelby County* was decided, federal courts have struck down maps in several formerly covered states because they failed to produce sufficient opportunity for minority voters to elect representatives of their choice. In a number of cases, the problematic congressional maps were used in at least one election cycle—often even after federal judges deemed them likely illegal. We discuss these cases in detail before proceeding to a causal analysis at the local level. There, we show that formerly covered municipalities began systematically annexing whiter, unincorporated areas after *Shelby County*, thereby diluting the political power of nonwhite voters in those communities.

In chapter 7, we examine the practice of voter list maintenance. Making it difficult to register to vote has been a tactic used to disenfranchise minority voters for decades; here, we show that *staying* on the rolls has become more difficult in the aftermath of *Shelby County*. We detail state-level policies that require people to present documentary proof of citizenship before they may register to vote. We describe how these efforts have prevented few noncitizens from voting, while disenfranchising thousands of otherwise eligible citizens. We also discuss illegal voter "purges" in formerly covered jurisdictions that might have been thwarted by preclearance. Finally, we show that the *Shelby County* decision led to formerly covered jurisdictions purging voters at significantly higher rates than noncovered ones.

In chapter 8, we trace the emergence of state-level voter identification policies that have been enacted since *Shelby County*. In a more granular analysis, we also drill down into Texas, where voter ID has been a hot-button and heavily litigated policy area. One result of that litigation has been the creation of administrative records that essentially provide a list of voters who attempted to vote in that state without ID that complies with the Texas voter ID law. In line with previous work, we find not only that minority voters are more likely to lack ID but that once they attempt to vote without ID, these voters tend to stay away from the voting booth for years—with effects concentrated more heavily among voters who cite an enduring hardship that prevents them from easily obtaining identification. These results should give pause to anyone claiming that the effects of voter ID laws are race neutral or trivial. While we do not find that an overwhelming number of Texans attempted to vote without identification, that state's voter ID law did affect minority voters more, and the effects on their subsequent voting behavior can be substantial and long-lasting.

Finally, in chapter 9, we consider the effects of restrictions that have been placed on mail voting, particularly in the wake of the so-called Big Lie, following the 2020 presidential election. Prior to 2020, white Americans were more likely than minority voters to cast their ballots by mail. This pattern shifted in 2020, and the racial polarization by vote mode perhaps made restricting access to mail ballots an attractive tactic to systematically impede nonwhite voters. Here again, we focus on a law in Texas that implemented new identification and signature requirements for absentee voters after 2020—and, in doing so, created a lot of administrative data that we can exploit to examine the effects of these changes. We show that the restrictions on mail voting in Texas, which would formerly have been subject to preclearance review, fueled higher rates of rejected mail ballots in the 2022 primary (the first election in which they were in effect). Worse, we also find that rejection rates of both mail ballot applications and mailed ballots were significantly higher among nonwhite voters, and that experiencing a rejection ultimately led substantial numbers of minority voters to sit the election out. This pattern—a seemingly race-neutral policy that ultimately created more substantial burdens for minority voters than their white fellow citizens—is exactly the sort of device that states used to shape the electorate before the Voting Rights Act.

On the whole, our analysis in part II offers little in the way of good news for voting rights advocates. Nor does it provide validation for the majority opinion in *Shelby County*, which confidently held that the ruling would not result in backsliding toward the days when local election officials wielded their power to disadvantage minority voters. Whether we examine the total universe of policies enacted after *Shelby County* or place various individual ones under a microscope, we find evidence that relative to white voters, ballot access is growing more difficult for minority voters since 2013—and representation of minority communities is more unsettled. The "American Problem," long kept in check by a strong federal law and vigorous administration, once again stalks voting rights.

PART I

The Voting Rights Act

A LEGAL AND POLITICAL HISTORY

1

Time of Justice

THE LONG RISE OF THE VRA

> When we got to the edge of the Edmund Pettus Bridge, Hosea looked down at the Alabama River. "John, can you swim?" he said. . . . "We're not going to jump," I said. "We're not going back. We're going to move forward." And that's what we did.
>
> —JOHN LEWIS[1]

BENJAMIN BRIM dug his fingers into the Louisiana mud and pulled himself forward. It was Easter Sunday, or maybe Monday; Brim had been passing in and out of consciousness for the past several hours, so it was hard to know for sure. He had been shot in the back of the head and again in the gut. Brim had done his best to play dead, but when he choked on the blood filling his mouth and coughed, his attackers had returned and shot him a third time. Miraculously, though, Brim was still alive. He crawled through the mud 20 yards at a time, moving slowly under cover of darkness and the now-driving rain, assuming the posture of a corpse if anyone came near. As he reached a ditch and covered himself with debris and branches, Brim thought he might escape and make it home to his wife and four children. Although he was gravely wounded, Brim's was a better fate than most of his comrades, who had numbered more than a hundred when the sun rose over the Grant Parish Courthouse in Colfax that morning of April 13, 1873.[2]

Benjamin Brim had lived in Louisiana his whole life. He was born into slavery and, after the Civil War, joined other freedmen asserting their newfound rights in the Reconstruction era. With the federal government's protection, Black Americans began organizing, voting, and running for office. In the span of a decade, some had been elevated from enslaved laborers to elected officials. For a moment, the South looked as if it could move toward a multiracial democracy.

That moment was fleeting. The expansion of Black political power was met everywhere with opposition, including violence. Southern counties regularly gerrymandered their districts and moved polling places to frustrate Black voters.[3] But the Ku Klux Klan, founded immediately after the Civil War, was a more ominous threat. The Klan perpetuated constant terrorism during the Reconstruction period, targeting Black newspapers and political organizations. Its members engaged in intimidation to dissuade Black residents from voting. When that failed, the Klan was willing to go further, using violence against as many as 10% of Black participants in Southern states' constitutional conventions.[4]

But the Klan was only one part of a political ecosystem in which white Democrats were perfectly willing to achieve their ends with political violence as the 1860s progressed. In one instance in Camilla, Georgia, a white mob led by the Mitchell County sheriff opened fire on a Black-led Republican political parade, ultimately killing about 20 people.[5] In New Orleans, city officials attacked a group of veteran freedmen outside Louisiana's 1866 constitutional convention, killing more than 30.[6] Worse, these events were hardly exceptional; they were part of a longer list of separate massacres perpetuated by white vigilantes that saw freedmen murdered in double-digit numbers in the 1860s.[7] In total, the Klan and its allies—many of whom were firmly embedded in the machinery of the state—fostered "a nameless terror" that constantly stalked Black citizens who dared to exercise their political rights.[8]

It was plain that the states could not be relied on to secure the rights of their newly free Black citizens. Radical Republicans in Congress were determined, therefore, to throw the weight of federal power behind the cause. They had outlawed slavery with the 13th Amendment to the U.S. Constitution in 1865. In 1868, Congress passed and the states ratified the 14th Amendment, which extended the protections of citizenship to all persons—regardless of whether they had been born free. The amendment also barred states from abridging Americans' "privileges and immunities" and from denying them due process of the law, regardless of their race. The 14th Amendment therefore undercut the Supreme Court's decision in *Dred Scott v. Sandford*, which held that Black Americans were not citizens and were therefore not guaranteed constitutional protections.[9] The architect of that opinion, Chief Justice Roger B. Taney, had died in 1864, but *Dred Scott* was a reminder that the courts—like the states—were not a steady partner when it came to ensuring equal rights.

Simultaneously, Congress worked to guarantee voting rights in particular. In 1867, it passed and then overrode President Andrew Johnson's veto of the Reconstruction Acts, which among other things required the states of the former Confederacy to allow Black men to vote before they could be readmitted to the Union (they would also have to ratify the 14th Amendment). In 1869 Republicans made an even stronger statement, passing the 15th Amendment on a party line vote with no Democrats in favor. Section 1 of the Amendment, ratified in 1870, banned the abridgment of citizens' right to vote "on account of race, color, or previous condition of servitude," and Section 2 granted Congress the power to enforce Section 1 "by appropriate legislation."

This constitutional amendment marked a significant change in the federal government's role in election administration. Prior to the ratification of the 15th Amendment, the Elections Clause of the Constitution gave states broad authority to determine the "Times, Places and Manner" of all elections;[10] Congress however could override these decisions with respect to *federal* (but not state or local) election administration. The 15th Amendment empowered Congress to protect minority voting rights in *all* American elections. In other words, until the passage of the 14th and 15th Amendments, the federal government had little role to play in elections to state and local offices. Now, Congress could intervene in the administration of these elections to eliminate racial disenfranchisement.

The same year the 15th Amendment was ratified, Congress responded to the murder of hundreds of freedmen in scores of politically motivated instances by passing the Enforcement Act and the Ku Klux Klan Act.[11] In tandem with each other, these laws empowered President Ulysses S. Grant's administration to combat the Klan's tactics. With these statutes, it became a federal crime to "by force, intimidation, or threat" abridge others' right to equal protection of the law or to prevent others from voting in a federal election, from being a party or witness in court, or from discharging the official duties of a public office.[12] Prosecuting the Klan for abridging Black Americans' civil rights, it was thought, would be more effective in federal court, outside the states' reach. Congress also empowered the president to use federal troops to enforce the law and to suspend habeas corpus if necessary to protect democratic institutions. If Southern Democrats and their Klan allies would not recognize freedmen's voting rights, these statutes clearly signaled that, at least in the early 1870s, Congress would commit significant federal power to the cause.

Colfax, in north central Louisiana near the boundary of Winn and Rapides Parishes, was a microcosm of both the Democratic-Klan alliance to subvert democracy in the South and the federal government's attempt to stop it. At the state level, Black and white voters had formed a coalition that managed to elect a generally pro-Reconstruction Republican Louisiana legislature in 1868, but not without conflict. Fraud tainted the results, with Democratic presidential candidate Horatio Seymour receiving more than 90% of the vote in 20 of Louisiana's 48 parishes (and more than 99% in 15), despite the fact that many of them had relatively high percentages of Black residents. This included Winn Parish, where Seymour tallied 94.3% of the vote. There and in bordering Rapides Parish, white vigilantes harassed Republicans with nocturnal visits in the weeks preceding the election.[13] On Election Day there were reports of "armed skirmishes" and ballot boxes being moved in an effort to intimidate Black voters.[14] Even so, on one plantation heavy Black turnout fueled a 72-point margin of victory for Republicans, leading white vigilantes to throw the ballot box into the Red River to negate the votes.[15] After the election, Hal Frazier, a pillar of the Black community whose property was used for political organizing, was murdered.[16]

William Smith Calhoun was a Republican state senator who owned a large plantation in the area. Although he and his family had long owned slaves in the area prior to the Civil War, Calhoun's views had evolved; by 1868 he was solidly pro-Reconstruction.[17] Thumbing his nose at Democrats after the 1868 election, Calhoun advocated for a new parish to be named after Republican president (and hero of the Union) Ulysses S. Grant. The parish would be carved out of Winn and Rapides and consisted largely of Calhoun's family plantation. The new Grant Parish was majority-Black, and Calhoun hoped it would provide a buttress against Democrats' antidemocratic machinations, affording his Black neighbors (nearly all of whom had once been enslaved by his family) the possibility of self-determination. The parish, with the tiny town of Colfax as its seat, was incorporated in March 1869.[18]

Calhoun's hopes for Grant Parish were no match for the disastrous 1872 Louisiana gubernatorial election. Former governor Henry Clay Warmoth had broken from the Republican Party, endorsing a fusion candidate, John McEnery, backed by the Liberal Republican and Democratic Parties.

Impropriety clouded the election's certification.[19] Warmoth's handpicked Returning Board (effectively the state board of elections) splintered into separate factions, reflecting the governor's mercurial politics. One side held that Republican William Pitt Kellogg won a fair victory, while the other certified a win for McEnery.[20] Both candidates held inaugurations, but a federal judge ruled for Kellogg and ordered federal troops to secure the statehouse for him.[21] This did not foil McEnery, who swore in appointees and established a shadow government. Uncertainty prevailed, and the possibility of still more election violence hung in the air.

In Colfax, Black and white Republicans dug in around the courthouse, a repurposed barn now serving as the center of Grant Parish government. Led by Black militia captain William Ward, the Republican contingent was fearful that Democrats would steal the parish seat in service to McEnery. With appointments from Kellogg in hand, they were resolved to defend their new county government even though they possessed mainly shotguns (a poor weapon at range), enough ammunition for just two shots per man, and a shoddy "cannon" that ultimately proved useless.[22] The Republican militia dug a shallow defensive trench around the courthouse and held the ground for several weeks until escalating violence in early April signaled that a major conflict was inevitable. By Easter Sunday, Ward and nearly every white Republican had departed the defenses, leaving it guarded by a wholly Black force of about 150 with practically no military experience among them.[23]

On the morning of April 13, 1873, a paramilitary force of 165 white men marched on the courthouse, determined to take it back for Democrats. They were mounted and carried rifles as well as a 4-pound cannon taken from a nearby steamship. That afternoon, following a brief parlay and a warning period, the battle commenced. The Republicans were almost immediately outflanked and took heavy artillery fire into their trench. The surviving Black defenders retreated to the courthouse, itself under heavy fire. The white forces promptly forced a Black prisoner to set the courthouse roof on fire. Choked by the smoke, Black militiamen waved a white flag of surrender. Several Black defenders began stacking their rifles inside the courthouse, preparing to leave the structure unarmed.[24]

When the Republicans emerged from the courthouse, however, they were met with a volley of fire. The attackers rushed forward with a fury, and two took friendly fire. Their wounds only enraged the white vigilantes more. The white mob surged ahead, killing several Black defenders in close combat. Many Black men retreated back to the burning courthouse, some hiding in the floor.[25] At least one chose to die there by fire rather than face the white men outside.[26]

The Democrats entered the courthouse, killing and taking dozens of Black militiamen prisoner. The prisoners were told they would be held until morning and then released, but their captors had no intention of letting them go. As the sun dipped below the horizon, it began to rain, and the white men started killing the wounded Black prisoners. Then they began peeling off the nonwounded in groups of two, leading them some distance away, and shooting them in the head.[27] Thirteen were hanged from a pecan tree. In the chaos, some Black defenders—among them Benjamin Brim—were able to escape, but most did not. By the time two militia colonels arrived from New Orleans the next morning with the doomed mission of heading off the conflict, they discovered the bodies of sixty Black men littering the ground.[28] Some others had been buried by family; still more had been tossed in the river. No one knows how many men died in the Colfax Massacre, but military witnesses indicated that it was almost certainly more than a hundred.[29] Those who could be located were buried in the defensive trench they themselves had dug, which readily converted to a shallow mass grave.

Federal troops, acting under the Ku Klux Klan Act and President Grant's direction, mobilized from New Orleans to bring the attackers to justice. US Attorney James Roswell Beckwith had obtained a grand jury indictment of 97 attackers,[30] but he knew he could not manage the logistics of charging them all. Nine white men were ultimately rounded up and charged on thirty-two counts under the 1870 Enforcement Act. The first 16 counts alleged that the defendants had conspired to deprive two of the Black defenders (one living and one dead) of their constitutional rights. Specifically, Beckwith accused the defendants of violating the Republicans' 1st Amendment right to free assembly, as well as the right to bear arms enshrined in the 2nd Amendment. The second 16 counts alleged that in carrying out the various elements of their conspiracy, the defendants had murdered Alexander Tillman, whose body had been identified after the fight.[31] During the trial, multiple Black men and women—including Benjamin Brim—stood in open court to testify against the white attackers.[32] After an acquittal for one defendant and a mistrial for the remaining eight, a majority-white jury convicted three of the defendants on Counts 1–16 in a second trial—but acquitted them on the murder charges. The defendants would escape with their lives, but they still faced 10 years in prison for conspiring to violate the Colfax defenders' 1st and 2nd Amendment rights.[33]

The verdicts stood for 18 days, until US Supreme Court Justice Joseph Bradley, as circuit justice for Louisiana, arrived in New Orleans and threw out the convictions.[34] Bradley's was not a foregone conclusion. With the Enforcement Act, Congress had empowered the Justice Department to prosecute individuals who sought to infringe on others' civil liberties. Moreover, Bradley could have read the 14th Amendment as a vehicle for ensuring that individuals' 1st and 2nd Amendment rights protected them against not just federal government actions but those by states, municipalities, or individuals as well.

Bradley was having none of this expansive interpretation of federal power, however. He held that, the 14th Amendment notwithstanding, the 1st and 2nd Amendments applied only to the federal government and limited neither state nor individual action. The intent of the Reconstruction Amendments, Bradley thought, was simple: to combat crimes motivated by race. A successful prosecution would therefore have to demonstrate a racial motivation. This presented a high bar for any prosecutor, and was not one that Beckwith had contemplated in his indictments. Bradley now used this opening to deem those indictments irrevocably faulty.[35]

The federal government appealed Bradley's ruling to the entire Supreme Court, but the justice had plenty of sympathetic ears in Washington. In a unanimous decision in *United States v. Cruikshank*, the full Court effectively echoed Bradley's original ruling.[36] Chief Justice Morrison Waite held not only that the 1st and 2nd Amendments would not apply to state actions but also that the 14th Amendment's due process and equal protection clauses applied *only* to states—not to individuals. Put differently, the *Cruikshank* decision held that the 14th Amendment barred only states from discriminating and was powerless against the actions of private citizens. And it was *individuals*, not the state, who had carried out the massacre. The message from *Cruikshank* was clear: Those seeking relief against the vast alliance of Democrats and vigilantes that was seeking to abridge Black voters' rights would have to find it in the states. The states, however, were unwilling to give it. With *Cruikshank*, the perpetrators of the Colfax Massacre were placed beyond the reach of federal prosecutors and would face no justice from the State of Louisiana.

The same year *Cruikshank* was decided, the disputed presidential election of 1876 resulted in a compromise that would end Reconstruction. The consequence-free violence enabled by *Cruikshank* contributed to the murder of hundreds of Republicans in South Carolina.[37] Voter intimidation and fraud utterly compromised the results there, in Florida, and unsurprisingly by now, in Louisiana. In each of these states, both parties declared victory and transmitted electoral votes to Washington, DC, fueling a constitutional crisis. Three days before the new president was to be inaugurated, the parties worked out a deal. Republican Rutherford B. Hayes would get the White House in exchange for backing Democratic governments in two Southern states and removing federal troops from the entire region. The states would control their own affairs once more.

The Southern states, now under total Democratic control, had no interest in offering Black citizens a remedy for violations of their civil rights. Instead, they adopted new "Black codes" and reconfigured their constitutions and voting laws to ensure that their Black citizens would never have a realistic chance of obtaining power again. For most of the following 90 years, Southern members of Congress would wield their influence to ensure that the federal government largely looked the other way while Black voters in the South were subjected to harassment, terrorism, and murder for attempting to exercise their constitutional rights.[38] In the Colfax cemetery, the surviving attackers erected a monument to the three white men who had died that Easter Sunday. It was dedicated "to the memory of the Heroes, Stephen Decatur Parish, James West Hadnot, and Sidney Harris, Who fell in the Colfax Riot fighting for White Supremacy."[39]

After *Cruikshank* and the Compromise of 1877, the prospects for Black Americans seeking full civil rights were bleak. The Supreme Court continued to winnow the Reconstruction Amendments and other civil rights laws that Congress had passed. The Court's targets included Congress's last-gasp effort to ensure equal public accommodations in the Civil Rights Act of 1875, which was intended to desegregate public accommodations and transportation and to ensure that Black Americans could serve on juries. The Court negated much of this law eight years later, following its own precedent in *Cruikshank* to declare that the 14th Amendment did not allow Congress to limit the power of private businesses to decide which customers to serve.[40]

Meanwhile, Congress in the late nineteenth century had little appetite to return to the muscular federal enforcement that characterized the Reconstruction years. The promise of multiracial democracy was gone; instead, the South was characterized by widespread disenfranchisement as the Southern states reconfigured their constitutions to lock Black citizens out of the system. Enacted after federal troops had departed the state, Mississippi's 1890 constitution provides a classic example of this approach. One section of the constitution was dedicated to setting the standards for who could register to vote in that state. It included some of the most notorious devices used to disenfranchise Black Americans throughout the South, including poll taxes, grandfather clauses, literacy tests, felony disenfranchisement, and others. All were typical features in Southern states, designed to frustrate Black citizens' efforts to participate and, indeed, to dissuade them from even trying.

Southern poll taxes usually required voters to pay one or two dollars before receiving a ballot. Some states, like Georgia, later made their poll taxes cumulative, so that a voter would have to pay all back taxes from any election in which they were eligible to vote before receiving a ballot. This policy effectively meant that missing one election's taxes would have a compounding effect that could permanently keep delinquent voters off the rolls. Likewise, Southern literacy tests were typically not a good-faith attempt to discern whether a voter could read; often, they required voters to interpret obscure sections of the state constitution and were administered unevenly between Black and white voters.[41] Indeed, depending on the state, voters could exempt themselves from the poll tax, the literacy test, or both by showing that their grandfather had been eligible to vote prior to the Reconstruction Amendments—a facially "race neutral" condition that only white voters could meet.

The South's "devices" therefore amounted to a maze that would ensnare any Black voter who attempted to register. Mississippi's constitution thus exemplifies a broader trend in the South: The widespread violence of the Reconstruction period had given way to a more bureaucratic form of disenfranchisement by law.[42] The poll tax was an especially nefarious tool of Black disenfranchisement, though literacy tests also worked to keep Black voters from the polls.[43] In total, modern analysis has found that Jim Crow's tests and devices were devastating for Black registration and voting rates.[44] In this period, historian Alexander Keyssar reports, "turnout levels of 60 to 85 percent fell to 50 percent for whites and single digits for Blacks."[45]

Decisions like *Cruikshank* and the negation of the Civil Rights Acts showed that the late-Nineteenth-century Supreme Court was in no mood to help Black voters out of the maze. Its treatment of the 1890 Mississippi constitution sent an even clearer signal that the federal judiciary was unwilling to wade into Southern states' elections—even in a literal life-and-death matter. Henry Williams, a Black resident of Mississippi, had been convicted of murder and sentenced to hang. Williams challenged the Mississippi constitution in federal court because, he argued, though ostensibly racially neutral, its application had all but ensured the outcome of his case. Williams contended that since juries were drawn from registered voters, disenfranchising Black voters in Mississippi meant that Black defendants would be judged by wholly white juries, as he had been. Williams's argument boiled down to a straightforward premise: While Mississippi's devices may pass constitutional muster on their face, the manner in which they were *applied* circumvented the 14th and 15th Amendments.

Williams's case made it to the US Supreme Court in 1898, which unanimously ruled in the state's favor. The Court held that "the constitution of Mississippi and its statutes do not *on their face* discriminate between the races" (emphasis added).[46] Williams's attempt to persuade the Court that the constitution's application flew in the face of the Reconstruction Amendments' intent had resoundingly failed. The message was clear: So long as the statues did not *explicitly* disenfranchise Black voters, they were not in violation of the federal Constitution—even if, as the Court opined in *Williams*, "evil was possible under them."

Only in the most clear-cut cases did the Supreme Court strike down state laws for violating the 15th Amendment. For instance, in a 1915 ruling in *Guinn v. United States*, the Court negated Oklahoma's grandfather clause.[47] Like other states, Oklahoma exempted voters from its literacy test if they could prove that they had been eligible to vote on or before January 1, 1866, or that they were a "lineal descendant of such person."[48] The grandfather clause was an obvious attempt to make an end run around the 15th Amendment and drew the ire of a unanimous Court. But the Court struck down the grandfather clause in *Guinn* only because the practice was so egregious that there was no possible justification for it other than racial disenfranchisement. By and large, as historian J. Morgan Kousser put it, the Court was in fact "potent in protecting white supremacy" following Reconstruction, interpreting the law narrowly and acting against racial disenfranchisement only when states left them no other choice.[49]

The saga of the so-called white primary in Texas offers a good example of the complex interplay between the Reconstruction Amendments, state law, and the Supreme Court. Republicans could certainly run a candidate for a Southern office, but the Democratic Party's post-Reconstruction Southern monopoly ensured that there was no hope for a Republican in a general election. The only elections that mattered in the South, then, were Democratic primaries.[50] But strictly speaking, American political parties are private organizations, a status that allowed Southern Democrats to claim that primary elections were merely a mechanism by which party members chose their nominees. Since primaries *technically* did not decide who would ultimately hold an office, it was not immediately clear whether voters in primaries were subject to the same constitutional protections as in general elections.

In 1921 the Supreme Court ruled in *Newberry v. United States* that federal limits on campaign spending could not apply to primaries, because the US Constitution authorized Congress to regulate only the election that resulted in the selection of an officeholder.[51] The Court held that the nomination process, as an internal party matter, was a private affair to be regulated not by Congress but by the states. The *Newberry* majority therefore declared the *general* election as the only one subject to congressional oversight.

In dissent, Chief Justice Edward Douglass White referred to this reasoning as "suicidal." Primaries, said White, could exist only because the constitution gave states the power to create them. To White, federal power to regulate primaries could not be denied. From a practical standpoint, White's premise also fed broader concerns: If the federal government would not assert authority over primaries, would that not create opportunities for the states to trample on citizens' federal rights?

It did not take long for Southern Democrats to grasp how this ruling could be used to further disenfranchise Black voters by manipulating primary rules. Texas was an early mover, passing a law in 1923 stating that "in no event shall a Negro be eligible to participate in a Democratic primary election."[52] The Texas law was a clear test of the principle in *Newberry*; if the federal government could not intervene in a purely state affair, Texas reasoned, a state could disenfranchise Black primary voters by statute. When the National Association for the Advancement of Colored People (NAACP) challenged the law in federal court, Texas argued that it was a nonjusticiable political question, beyond the reach of federal courts.[53] The case, *Nixon v. Herndon*, reached the Court in 1927. There, the Court distinguished between "political action" and "private damage," holding that the state cannot overtly discriminate merely by declaring primaries to be private, political events.[54] Texas's law was struck down on 14th Amendment grounds.

Texas Democrats soon showed that *Nixon v. Herndon* had not settled the question. The Court had ruled that the 14th Amendment prohibited *states* from locking citizens out of elections on account of their race. But what if the state looked the other way while parties, as "voluntary associations," did the same? Texas lawmakers quickly rewrote the statute to allow party officials to determine the qualifications for participation in their primaries.[55] This revision allowed the Democratic Party executive committee to change party rules so that Black Texans were barred from participating in primaries once again. In 1932, the Court overturned this action in *Nixon v. Condon*,[56] holding that the executive committee was given the power to determine qualifications under state law and therefore was bound by the previous holding in *Nixon v. Herndon*.[57]

Again, Texas Democrats were undeterred. In 1932, the party formally adopted the exclusion of Black voters during a convention. This time, it acted solely in its capacity as a private association; with the convention vote, party members determined who was eligible to participate in their association's elections. While the distinction between the first and now second attempts to circumvent *Nixon v. Herndon* is somewhat technical, it mattered to the Court. In its brief 1935 opinion in *Grovey v. Townsend*, the majority agreed with the Texas Supreme Court that parties are "voluntary associations for political action, and are not the creatures of the state."[58] Because they acted without state authority, the *Grovey* majority ruled that Texas Democrats could exclude voters of color—which they did for the remainder of the 1930s.

Nine years later, however, just two members of the *Grovey* Court remained. Most of the newly constituted court in the early 1940s had been appointed by Franklin D. Roosevelt, and its justices had a much different view of how the Constitution applied to federal election oversight. In 1941, the Supreme Court overturned its *Newberry* ruling, holding in *United States v. Classic* that the Constitution allowed for the regulation of primary elections.[59] And, in 1944, the Court voted 8–1 to strike down the white primary in *Smith v. Allwright*.[60] J. Morgan Kousser dates the Court's "liberal" era to this case, arguing that it was in *Smith* that "the Supreme Court began the protection of African-American voting rights."[61] For the first time in US history, the Court indicated that it might be willing to apply the 15th Amendment somewhat expansively. Later, it definitively struck down one more attempt by Texas Democrats to circumvent its ruling on the white primary.[62] While it had been slow to protect voting rights in the Democratic South, by the mid-1940s the Court was signaling that enough was enough. It would continue to play a central role in the protection of minority voting rights in the decades to come.

By the mid-1940s, the country was changing in other ways, too. More than a million Black veterans were returning from the blood-soaked fields of Europe and the Pacific where many of their brothers-in-arms had given their lives in the fight against fascism. Arriving back home, these veterans once again found themselves relegated to second-class citizenship in the South and throughout the nation. This juxtaposition between the patriotic fight for democracy and conditions in the Jim Crow South ultimately led many Black veterans to become key players in the Civil Rights Movement.[63] Others took a more immediate stand.

Like many other African Americans, Maceo Snipes served his county well in the Pacific theater and was honorably discharged following the war's end.[64] He returned home to Butler, Georgia, to a quiet life of farming.[65] Georgia's 1946 gubernatorial race—or, rather, the all-decisive Democratic primary—was the first to be conducted after the Supreme Court struck down the white primary.[66] Some 150,000 Black Georgians quickly registered to vote, eager to have their voices heard.[67]

Despite (or, more likely, because of) widespread Democratic registration by hopeful Black Georgians, the issue of the white primary played a central role in the gubernatorial election that year. Incumbent Eugene Talmadge campaigned on the issue directly, promising voters that he would reinstate the practice if elected. In his weekly political newspaper *The Statesman,* Talmadge went further, continuing to push for the total disenfranchisement of Black voters: "If the white citizens of the State of Georgia will wake up," he wrote, "they can disqualify and mark off the voters' list three-fourths of the Negro vote in this state."[68] Talmadge then went on to detail specific statutes governing voter registration rules, and the procedures under which a citizen's registration could be challenged. James V. Carmichael, meanwhile, ran in the primary as a relative racial progressive who would ultimately earn most of the Black vote.

Ignoring threats from the local chapter of the Ku Klux Klan, Maceo Snipes proudly cast his ballot on July 17. He was the only Black individual in Taylor County to take this risk, reasoning that anyone who had fought for their country should be able to vote for its leaders.[69] A day after the primary, four white men—rumored members of the Klan—caught up with Snipes at his grandfather's home. Snipes was shot in the back and, two days later, died from his wounds. No charges were ever brought after a coroner's jury accepted testimony from Snipes's white killer, who said he had acted in self-defense; Snipes, the killer said, had pulled a knife on him when he attempted to collect a ten-dollar debt. When the *Atlanta Constitution* covered the murder, its headline read, "Bullets, Vote Not Connected in Taylor Death," giving credence to the claim that Snipes's shooting was unrelated to his audacity to participate in the Democratic primary.[70]

After Maceo Snipes's murder, more warnings circulated among the Black community that people would suffer violence if they dared to attend his funeral. In 2014 Snipes's family members told the Georgia Civil Rights Cold Cases Project that they still do not know where his body is buried.[71] And yet his death came to play an extraordinary role in the civil rights battles to come. Snipes's murder (along with another horrific lynching a few days later) prompted a seventeen-year-old Black student at Morehouse College to write a letter to the editor of the *Atlanta Constitution*. "We want and are entitled to the basic rights and opportunities of American citizens," the student wrote. "The right to earn a living at work for which we are fitted by training and ability; equal opportunities in education, health, recreation, and similar public services; the right to vote; equality before the law; some of the same courtesy and good manners that we ourselves bring to all human relations."[72] The young author of that letter to the editor was Martin Luther King Jr. His father, Martin Luther King Sr., later pointed to this letter—prompted in part by Snipes's murder—as a major moment in his son's political awakening.[73]

A decade later, the political moment for civil rights had ripened further. The Civil Rights Movement was in full swing. Under the guidance of steadfast leaders who organized one of the most effective social movements in American history, a generation of Black men and women followed in the steps of Maceo Snipes, risking bodily harm to assert their claims to full citizenship. On behalf of the NAACP, Thurgood Marshall had successfully argued his first case before the Supreme Court, in *Brown v. Board of Education*, resulting in a federal order to desegregate public schools throughout the nation.[74] The cold-blooded murder of fourteen-year-old Emmett Till—and the subsequent acquittal of his murderers—had shocked the nation's and the world's conscience. Moreover, the Montgomery Bus Boycott and other collective actions had demonstrated the movement's economic power and organizational capabilities.

The Black community's increasingly organized resistance to Jim Crow was complemented by a political environment that all but demanded some action on the civil rights question. As the Soviet Union sought to increase its influence throughout the developing world, US racism was seen as a looming liability. In his book *An American Dilemma,* Gunnar Myrdal famously argued that fascism was based on a "racial superiority dogma," and that "in fighting fascism and nazism, America had to stand before the whole world in favor of racial tolerance and cooperation and of racial equality."[75] The Soviets consistently used America's treatment of Black Southerners in their campaigns to undermine the legitimacy of the United States,[76] making desegregation and other movements toward civil rights a Cold War "imperative" for American leaders.[77]

At home, the intraparty divisions on the civil rights question created political incentives for the Republican Party to compete for increasingly organized Black voters. Although Northern Black voters had been moving toward the Democratic Party since President Franklin D. Roosevelt's New Deal policies two decades earlier, their loyalty to Democrats was slipping by the mid-1950s. The presidential election returns from President Dwight D. Eisenhower's re-election in 1956 bore this out: According to George Gallup, a rising star in American polling at the time, no major demographic group shifted more from the Democrats to the Republicans that year than Black voters.[78]

Southern Democrats' stubborn intransigence on civil rights legislation was one major reason for this shift. A 1957 story in *The Atlantic* sums it up: "The Negro voter, and the white voter too, who feels strongly on the subject, sees only Mississippi's [Democratic] Senator Eastland blocking the door of his powerful Judiciary Committee and backed by Southern Democrats determined to filibuster any civil rights legislation."[79] The Senate had long been considered the "graveyard" of civil rights legislation, with the filibuster serving as the "grave digger."[80] By virtue of the one-party system they had constructed within their states, Southern Democrats usually occupied their seats as long as they wished, and therefore accrued considerable seniority and powerful positions. In a closely divided Senate, history suggested that they would be more likely to dig in their heels than heed the perils of intransigence.

By the late 1950s, Republicans recognized that by pushing for a civil rights bill, they could put Democrats on the defensive, giving Southern Democrats two bad strategic options. Democrats might once again filibuster a federal bill and own the negative press that would surely accompany it. Their other choice was to finally acquiesce, allowing the Republican administration to take credit for the legislation and demonstrate that the Grand Old Party could achieve real gains for Black Americans.[81] The moral incentives for a civil rights bill had existed all along, but they were beginning to align with the political ones for Republicans willing to work with Northern Democrats.

In 1957, President Eisenhower sent a proposed civil rights bill to Congress, which dutifully took up work on it. True to form, Senator Strom Thurmond (D-SC) did mount a filibuster in the form of a twenty-four hour, eighteen minute speech—a Senate record that would stand for sixty-eight years. Divided by the strategic uncertainty surrounding how to approach civil rights, the Southerners were not unified in their support for the effort, however, and the filibuster ultimately failed. Democratic majority leader Lyndon B. Johnson managed to shepherd what would become the Civil Rights Act of 1957 through the Senate and into law with bipartisan support. For the first time since 1875, Congress had acted to enforce civil rights.

The Civil Rights Act of 1957 authorized several new federal powers. For one, it increased the capacity of the Department of Justice (DOJ) by elevating its civil rights section to a full division, creating the position of an assistant attorney general tasked with ensuring 15th Amendment compliance. Under the 1957 act, the DOJ could also bring civil suits against individuals who had violated citizens' right to vote on account of their race. This provision was quickly challenged when the DOJ brought a civil suit against registrars in Terrell County, Georgia, for impeding the registration of Black citizens. The defendants moved to have the case dismissed because of its reliance on the new act, which they argued was unconstitutional—a position the Supreme Court ultimately rejected.[82]

This was a promising development for voting rights advocates, but other features of the 1957 Civil Rights Act were less ideal. The bill had been amended so that individuals accused of violating the 15th Amendment would be guaranteed the right to a trial by jury. Generally speaking, to that point, individuals who were sued to stop them from engaging in civil infractions were not entitled to jury trials in the United States. Southern senators knew, however, that the jury trial provision could take some of the teeth out of the new law. All-white Southern juries routinely found white defendants not guilty of even the most heinous crimes against Black Americans in the first half of the twentieth century. Southern Democrats reasoned then that all-white juries would be similarly unlikely to find white defendants guilty of violating Black voters' 15th Amendment rights. The inclusion of this provision led to much despair from civil rights supporters in the aftermath of the bill's passage, who understood that it would likely frustrate the new law's other goals. "It has been the advocates of segregation and white domination," said Senator Paul Douglas of Illinois about the jury trial provision, "who have won the major triumph."[83]

While not empowering the federal government to effectively *do* much about racial disenfranchisement, another feature of the law proved instrumental in other ways. Part 1 of the 1957 Civil Rights Act mandated the creation of the United States Commission on Civil Rights (USCCR). The USCCR was tasked with investigating allegations "that certain citizens of the United States are being deprived of their right to vote and have that vote counted by reason of their color, race, religion, or national origin."[84] To be sure, the creation of the USCCR could never have done much to change actual conditions for Black voters: It was, after all, little more than a study group. Nevertheless, the Commission's first report (published in 1959) served as a clarion call from the federal government about the rampant violations of Black Southerners' voting rights, arguing that the 1957 law was insufficient to address these problems:

> It has become apparent that legislation presently on the books is inadequate to assure that all our qualified citizens shall enjoy the right to vote. There exists here a striking gap between our principles and our everyday practices. This is a moral gap. It spills over into and vitiates other areas of our society. It runs counter to our traditional concepts of fair play. It is a partial repudiation of our faith in the democratic system. It undermines the moral suasion of our national stand in international affairs.[85]

The Commission also recommended a constitutional amendment to outlaw the typical means of Southern racial disenfranchisement, such as tests and devices affecting Black voters' ability to register. In doing so, the Commission pointed out that "most denials of the right to vote are in fact accomplished through the discriminatory application and administration of such State laws . . . when there is a will to discriminate, these [registration] tests provide the way."[86] The Commission's first report provided powerful commentary on the problems that Black Americans had been facing for generations, and suggested a way forward.

Two years later, the Commission released another report, again stuffed full of detailed evidence of race discrimination in voting. While reviewing the changes that had occurred since its previous report, the Commission noted, "In some 100 counties in eight Southern States there is reason to believe that Negro citizens are prevented—by outright discrimination or by fear of physical violence or economic reprisal—from exercising the right to vote. . . . There are many counties in the South where a substantial Negro population not only has no voice in government, but suffers extensive deprivation—legal, economic, educational, and social."[87] Two years after *that* report, the USCCR determined that it had been "overly conservative in finding denials in only these" 100 counties.[88] Filled with detailed statistics about registration and turnout, along with stories of individuals whose voting rights had been abridged due to their race, these USCCR reports demonstrated the need for a law with more power than the 1957 Act. They would also be widely relied on in congressional testimony in support of the eventual Voting Rights Act of 1965.

Congress passed a new civil rights bill in 1960, which sought to shore up the 1957 act in a number of ways. For instance, states were required to preserve their voting records for twenty-two months in case they were needed as evidence to prove discrimination later.[89] The 1960 Civil Rights Act also allowed federal judges to appoint federal registrars in areas where the court determined that a locality had blocked the registration of Black citizens "pursuant to a pattern or practice" in violation of the 15th Amendment.[90] Once a finding of a discriminatory practice had been established in a particular jurisdiction, judicially appointed federal registrars there could ensure that Black voters were added to the rolls.

In theory, this provision of the new law marked an important departure from previous attempts to ensure cooperation with the 15th Amendment. Prior to 1960, if a Black voter's registration was denied, the voter (or the Department of Justice) could bring a suit against the county or state that had abridged their rights. If this process resulted in a ruling that a particular practice was illegal, the court could order the practice stopped. The problem, of course, was that local judges were rarely sympathetic and, if necessary, local clerks could simply substitute a new, equally problematic procedure for the old one. To stop the new practice, litigation would have to begin again, in a process reminiscent of the multidecade fight over white primaries in Texas.

But Title VI of the Civil Rights Act of 1960 provided a route around recalcitrant registrars intent on discriminating against Black citizens. Instead of requiring voters to prove that the specific practice preventing them from registering to vote was illegal, the 1960 act allowed that *any* failure to register could be overcome in specific parts of the country *without* continuous litigation, provided that voters could establish proof that they were eligible to vote under state law—and that the county had a history of discrimination. Federal judges from the local circuit could presume that any denial of registration in these places was an illegal violation of the 15th Amendment and provide relief for voters *before* a particular practice had to be litigated.[91] While it did not eliminate the need for litigation, Title VI opened the door for increased federal involvement in the voter registration process in parts of the country that had previously engaged in racial discrimination with respect to voting—provided, that is, that Black citizens could convince the white, Southern federal judges to countenance such an intervention.

The new law also banned states from maintaining higher registration standards for Black voters relative to white voters. But the 1960 act was silent on whether one deceptively simple possibility would constitute a violation: a new registration requirement that applied equally to white and Black voters but that imposed substantial registration burdens on all. This was an obvious opportunity for Southern jurisdictions to continue hiding the ball on racial disenfranchisement. Since the vast majority of unregistered individuals in the South were Black, even though such a practice would appear to be racially neutral, it would actually freeze discrimination in place by locking new (mostly Black) voters out. Could such a policy stand? The responsibility for answering this question ultimately fell to the Supreme Court.

In *Louisiana v. United States*, the Court unanimously upheld a broad reading of the 1960 statute.[92] Louisiana had long employed the typical devices such as grandfather clauses and white primaries to keep Black voters from participating. After the Court struck down the white primary in *Smith v. Allwright*, however, the share of Black voters in Louisiana increased from less than 1% to as much as 15%. In response, the Louisiana legislature created a "segregation committee" that encouraged "wholesale purges of Negroes from the voting rolls" and a test requiring prospective voters to interpret a section of the state or federal constitution.[93] Because only local registrars judged whether an interpretation was correct, this test vested these officials with "a virtually uncontrolled discretion" over who would be registered.[94] The interpretation test soon became a powerful tool for registrars to keep Black Louisianans from the voting booth.[95]

After the new Civil Rights Act mandated that registration procedures must be race neutral, Louisiana introduced "a uniform, objective, standardized 'citizenship' test administered to all prospective voters alike."[96] In the new exam, all voters were presented with six random multiple choice questions; to pass, a prospective voter would be required to correctly answer four. This new test left far less room for registrars to judge Black voters' answers more harshly. In theory, it really *was* race neutral in this respect.

The Court took no position on whether Louisiana's citizenship test would be applied in a discriminatory fashion. Instead, it declared that disparities in registration rates at the time the new practice was adopted necessarily meant that the exam violated the Civil Rights Act of 1960. This claim rested on a commonsense assumption as to who would be subjected to it in the future given the realities of the past: "Most if not all . . . white voters," the justices reasoned, "had been permitted to register [before the new exam was implemented] on far less rigorous terms than [Black] applicants whose applications were rejected" prior to the new test.[97] Even though it might have been racially neutral in administration, the exam's burden would still fall disproportionately on Black voters. Recognizing this disparity, the Supreme Court held that if Louisiana wanted to require *all* voters to re-register under the new law—and, thus, subject all *white* voters to the new exam as well—it was welcome to do so (though the Court surely knew this suggestion would create chaos and be a nonstarter). But so long as most white voters had not been required to pass such a test, the Court held that the 1960 act prohibited the test for unregistered individuals in Louisiana going forward. This had the effect of "freezing" practices as they were when most white voters registered.

The Court's broad interpretation of the 1960 Civil Rights Act in *Louisiana v. United States* was consistent with a greater willingness in the federal judiciary by the mid-1960s to carve out some new legal space for voting rights. By 1965 the Supreme Court had held not only that some jurisdictions could be subject to stricter federal oversight of their elections if courts found evidence of a "pattern or practice" of discrimination, but also that lower courts had proven their capacity for supervising the minutia of day-to-day local election administration.[98] In a range of cases, the judiciary was displaying a newfound willingness to enforce the 15th Amendment.

Still, the 1960 Civil Rights Act largely failed to produce meaningful change on the ground. While the new powers assigned to the DOJ were a step forward, the new law did not give the federal government direct, proactive authority over states' election procedures.[99] The existence of persistent discrimination still had to be proven individually in each jurisdiction before federal registrars could be appointed, and this proved to be a slow process. Five years after the law's passage, only two registrars had been sent south.[100] The facts in *Louisiana v. United States* show that the states remained amply willing to contrive creative means of Black voter disenfranchisement. But in total, the federal government—encumbered by the realities of litigation—brought just seventy-one suits to enforce voting rights between 1957 and 1964. As the USCCR explained in its 1961 report,

> The Government, under present laws, must still proceed slowly—suit by suit, county by county. Each suit, moreover, is expensive and time consuming; and although the Civil Rights Division has been repeatedly increased in size and budget, and has concentrated its efforts in the voting field, it has not been able to prepare and file all the suits that appear warranted . . . While it can be truly said that present laws have proved to be effective tools to deal with discrimination in voting, the tools are limited in scope. There is no widespread remedy to meet what is still widespread discrimination.[101]

Hobbled by these realities, the 1960 Civil Rights Act did little to close racial gaps in registration and voting. In Mississippi, for instance, the Black registration rate was still below 7% by 1964, compared with a 70% registration rate for white residents.[102]

But, as previously noted, Congress's new civil rights laws were consequential in one respect: They had allowed for the collection of a tremendous amount of new data via the US Commission on Civil Rights. Its reports demonstrated incontrovertibly that even with expanded litigation powers, the federal government's case-by-case approach had not secured voting rights for Black Southerners. At mid-decade, then, the pieces for a new legislative approach were coming together, and the need for *real* federal oversight was clear. Even if it meant that Congress would need to take aggressive action, the Supreme Court was signaling a willingness to go along. The only missing ingredient was political will.

Given a push from the public, it seemed that Congress might finally stop Southern racial voter disenfranchisement in its tracks. As it turned out, that prod was about to come from an out-of-the-way locale that few Americans had thought much about: Dallas County, Alabama. The county had been a problem spot for years, so much so that it had attracted one of the two federal registrars who had been authorized to register voters under the 1960 Civil Rights Act. Dallas County's seat was a small town called Selma, and it was from there that the public support for the Voting Rights Act would soon come, purchased with blood on a bridge above the Alabama River.

Around 3:00 p.m. on March 7, 1965, John Lewis stood next to the Reverend Hosea Williams on the Edmund Pettus Bridge in Selma, Alabama. Named after a former Confederate brigadier general and grand dragon of the Alabama Ku Klux Klan, the bridge spanned the Alabama River, which in turn formed

Selma's Southern boundary. Earlier that day, Lewis and Williams had set out from the Brown Chapel AME Church in Selma with other leaders of the Dallas County Voters League (DCVL), the Student Nonviolent Coordinating Committee (SNCC), and the Southern Christian Leadership Conference (SCLC), at the head of about six hundred marchers. Their goal was to peacefully march the fifty-four miles to the state capital of Montgomery. The marchers wanted to have a dialogue with Governor George Wallace about the death of twenty-six-year-old civil rights activist Jimmie Lee Jackson, who had been shot on February 18 by Alabama state trooper James B. Fowler and had succumbed to his injuries eight days later.

The group's journey was cut short less than ten blocks after it began. As the flag-carrying protesters crested the bridge, they saw what Lewis would later remember as a "sea of blue," the color of Alabama's state trooper uniforms.[103] A line of troopers formed a wall, flanked by Sheriff Jim Clark and his deputized, mounted posse. A bull of a man, Clark was a staunch opponent of civil rights. He sometimes carried a cattle prod in addition to his nightstick and pistol, and often wore a button on his uniform emblazoned with the word "NEVER," which indicated his resistance to voting rights advocates who had focused their efforts on Selma.[104]

And focus on Selma they had. The county had a Black majority in both population and potential voters, but more than 96% of its registered voters were white. This disparity naturally drew the attention of civil rights leaders. Lewis, Williams, and others at the head of the marchers were seasoned veterans of the Civil Rights Movement with a keen understanding of how to stir the public mood, as they had shown before in efforts to fight segregation in Birmingham. Over a period of nearly three years leading up to March 7, organizers in Selma had worked with others like Bernard Lafayette and Martin Luther King Jr. to build the political consciousness of Selma's Black residents. SNCC had begun voter registration drives for Black citizens in 1963; the following year, Dr. King's SCLC increasingly focused its efforts on drawing attention to voting rights in Selma as well. The groups had harnessed the power of the press for years, and their leaders felt that shining a light on Selma could raise the profile of their struggle.

In this effort, they got plenty of help from Jim Clark. Indeed, civil rights organizers in Selma saw the prickly Clark not as an obstacle but as an asset who could be goaded into helping them accomplish their longer-term goals.[105] Clark had clashed with protesters in Selma for the better part of that three-year period, and they had provoked him into increasingly antagonistic actions.[106] In the first quarter of 1965, Clark and his deputies had aggressively dispersed protesters, arresting so many that he had to detain them in a repurposed "prison road camp" dubbed "Camp Selma."[107] By March, Clark was clearly having trouble suppressing his desire to deal with the protesters harshly. As he succinctly put it years later, "A lot of times I really wanted to get rough, but I didn't. Sometimes I didn't show restraint, though. I admit that."[108] Clark's efforts to quell protests were rooted in deep-seated resistance to civil and voting rights for nonwhite people, but his gradual escalation had the opposite effect, making him an unwitting touchstone for voting rights protests in Dallas County. As one civil rights worker explained to the press, "Every time it appears that the movement is dying out, Sheriff Clark comes to our rescue."[109]

Facing off with the protesters at the foot of the Edmund Pettus Bridge on March 7, Clark had already drawn attention to his opponents' cause on three separate occasions in 1965. In January the *New York Times* had printed pictures of Sheriff Clark's deputies pinning local Black resident Annie Lee Copper to the ground after she had struck Clark in response to his prodding her with his baton while she was waiting in line to register to vote.[110] Around the same time, Clark also had a violent encounter with C. T. Vivian; Clark punched him on the courthouse steps as Vivian led others in an effort to register. The beating was captured by television cameras and broadcast throughout America.[111] Finally, on February 18, Clark oversaw the attack on a night march in the nearby town of Marion that resulted in Jimmie Lee Jackson's death. This was the event that had ultimately triggered the planned March to Montgomery.[112]

No one truly knows what Sheriff Clark or the Alabama troopers were thinking as they sized up the protesters walking south toward their sea of blue. Clark was probably aware that escalation was likely to be counterproductive to his interests. But the troopers, Sheriff Clark, and his posse could not restrain themselves. Via a bullhorn, Trooper John Cloud announced to the protesters, "This is an unlawful assembly. You are ordered to disperse. Go home, or go to your church. This march will not continue." The marchers did not disperse. John Lewis instructed the marchers to kneel in prayer. He and his colleagues holding the front line stood in place, refusing Cloud's order to turn around.

The Alabama state troopers discharged tear gas and then advanced with their clubs. As they crashed into the protesters, the troopers gathered speed, forcing several people to the ground. Clark and his posse joined the fray, and many marchers came under attack by deputies wielding whips and clubs. Seventeen marchers would be hospitalized for their injuries, including Lewis, who suffered a fractured skull. Two days later, Reverend Jim Reeb—a white Unitarian minister from Boston who had come South to support the movement—was attacked by a mob in Selma and killed.[113] March 7, 1965, would become known as "Bloody Sunday."

That evening, nearly fifty million people tuned in to watch ABC's Sunday night movie, the television premiere of *Judgment at Nuremberg*. The film was a historical legal drama depicting the war crimes trial of Nazi officials after World War II. As viewers settled in to watch, ABC interrupted the programming to show footage from the Edmund Pettus Bridge. Just as organizers had hoped when they focused their efforts in Selma, the attack on the protesters put the treatment of peaceful civil rights protesters in the South on full display for all Americans to see. The juxtaposition of the film's Nazi war criminals against American officials clubbing peaceful protesters was especially jarring for the large, national audience. Many, confronted with such images for the first time, were outraged.

Before Selma, President Lyndon Johnson did not regard a voting bill as a top priority. The summer before, the Senate had passed the landmark Civil Rights Act of 1964, which held real power and promised to advance the fight against racial discrimination—but, like its predecessors of 1957 and 1960, promised to do little for voting rights specifically. It was only after a sixty-day filibuster mounted by Southern Democrats—the longest filibuster in the Senate's history—that cloture was reached on June 10 of that year. The bill eventually passed the Senate on June 19.[114] That fall, Johnson was rewarded with an overwhelming share of the Black vote: Although 69% of Black voters had cast their ballots for the Kennedy-Johnson ticket in 1960, *every single* Black voter in the 1964 Gallup presidential poll reported voting for the Johnson-Humphrey ticket, after the enactment of the Civil Rights Act.[115]

Still, Johnson recognized the need for even stronger action on voting. The president was willing to move on civil rights and throughout early 1965 was having ongoing conversations with Martin Luther King Jr. about a prospective voting rights act; King's lobbying efforts would prove crucial in the development of federal legislation. The president told King that a serious push on voting rights would require perfect political conditions. Simply, Johnson felt they needed a swell of public opinion on their side. As he put it to King in January 1965, "If you can find the worst condition that you run into in Alabama, Mississippi, or Louisiana, or South Carolina . . . and get it on, in the pulpits, get it in the meetings, get it everyplace you can, [the American public will] say, 'Well, that's not right. That's not fair.' "[116] In February, King met with President Johnson to discuss Selma's particular strategic importance; the president had agreed that while violence was possible in the upcoming actions there, a high-visibility campaign could provide a great deal of momentum for a voting rights bill.[117]

Without a groundswell of public opinion, the president worried that contesting a voting rights bill would burn up his political capital and diminish opportunities to pass other policy initiatives. As Dr. King recalled in his autobiography, the president had told King at the end of 1964 that he could not get a voting rights bill through that session of Congress "because I need the votes of the Southern bloc to get these other [Great Society programs] through. And if I present a voting rights bill, they will block the whole program."[118]

It seems, however, that the president's stance toward King overstated his reluctance to move forward on the voting question. Johnson was in fact making moves behind the scenes. Attorney General Nicholas Katzenbach later recalled that the very next day after the Civil Rights Act of 1964 was passed, Johnson demanded that Katzenbach write him "the goddamndest, toughest voting rights act that [the attorney general] could devise."[119] Even as Johnson was pushing King's expectations downward in December and January, Katzenbach and the Department of Justice were following the president's orders in drafting a powerful voting rights bill. And while Johnson did announce in early February that he would urge Congress to pass a voting bill that year,[120] his Great Society legislative ambitions meant that some initiatives would have to be put on the back burner—or so he thought.

President Johnson recognized that the events at Selma had given him exactly the kind of conditions he had described to King. The time was right to make the final push for voting rights, but he had to act fast. Thanks to Katzenbach, Johnson had the parameters of his bill in hand. He could unveil it to the public, and he knew that its chances would be improved if he could further galvanize public opinion in his favor. Johnson requested a televised address before a joint session of Congress on March 15, 1965—just eight days after Bloody Sunday. Before an audience of more than seventy million Americans, Johnson made a powerful case. His "American Promise" speech that evening is widely considered one of the most important American speeches of the 20th century.[121]

Its reputation is richly deserved. Johnson wasted no words in characterizing the nature of the struggle. He led with a straightforward declaration, describing Selma as a sea change akin to other crucial moments in the course of American democracy: "At times history and fate meet at a single time in a single place to shape a turning point in man's unending search for freedom. So it was at Lexington and Concord. So it was a century ago at Appomattox. So it was last week in Selma, Alabama."[122]

Later in the address, Johnson described the gravity of the issue. Aside from his declaration that he would not seek reelection in 1968, his appeal to Americans' sense of equality marks perhaps the best-remembered lines of his presidency:

> Rarely in any time does an issue lay bare the secret heart of America itself. Rarely are we met with a challenge, not to our growth or abundance, our welfare or our security, but rather to the values and the purposes and the meaning of our beloved nation.
>
> The issue of equal rights for American Negroes is such an issue. And should we defeat every enemy, should we double our wealth and conquer the stars, and still be unequal to this issue, then we will have failed as a people and as a nation.
>
> For with a country as with a person, 'What is a man profited, if he shall gain the whole world, and lose his own soul?'
>
> There is no Negro problem. There is no Southern problem. There is no Northern problem. There is only an American problem. And we are met here tonight as Americans—not as Democrats or Republicans—we are met here as Americans to solve that problem.[123]

Johnson had more than a description of the problem to offer; he had the bill ready to go. The middle section of the American Promise Speech was devoted to a clear declaration that Johnson intended to strike down barriers to registration and voting in all corners of the United States. Then, he made one more appeal to history. "It was more than 100 years ago," he said, "that Abraham Lincoln—a great President of another party—signed the Emancipation Proclamation. But emancipation is a proclamation and not a fact. A century has passed since the day of promise, and the promise is unkept. The time of justice has now come, and I tell you that I believe sincerely that no force can hold it back."[124] America would have its voting rights bill.

Midway through the speech, in his characteristic Texan accent with a stern look on his face, he assured the assembled members of Congress that the fight would be successful. Still, he warned them that, "even if we pass this bill, the battle will not be over. What happened in Selma is part of a far larger movement which reaches into every section and state of America." But, Johnson promised, "we shall overcome."[125] This invocation of one of the great anthems of the Civil Rights Movement, made by a white Southern president before Congress in front of a national audience, could be seen as the culmination of centuries of work, struggle, and sacrifice for full civil rights. It prompted the first tears that Martin Luther King Jr.'s colleagues and friends had ever seen the reverend cry.[126]

"The [19]65 Act was a piece of cake," recalled Nicholas Katzenbach during his oral history in 2005. "That was no problem."[127] While this characterization might have been an oversimplification—major fights over the poll tax, among other things, were looming—the Voting Rights Act of 1965 passed through Congress much more easily than the Civil Rights Acts of 1957, 1960, or 1964. In fact, the Southern Democrats never really mounted an attack on the bill at all. "Their heart wasn't in it," Katzenbach said. "That was partially because they lost the '64 Civil Rights Act, but I think it was partially because they really had a guilty conscience about the voting."[128] Absent strong opposition, Congress worked with astonishing efficiency. The nineteen-section bill, which would be one of the most consequential acts of Congress in American history, took only about four months to finish. After amassing an extraordinary legislative record in which the House testimony alone spanned more than twelve hundred pages,[129] the Voting Rights Act of 1965 (VRA) passed the House on August 2 and the Senate on August 4, 1965.[130]

The VRA marked a full assault on states' traditional means of suppressing voters on account of their race, and also contained language that would make it a powerful force against future efforts to disenfranchise minority voters. The VRA's power was divided between *general* and *special* provisions. The general provisions were permanent guidelines that affected every corner of the United States. For instance, Section 10 directed the US attorney general to challenge the constitutionality of poll taxes in federal court, wherever they were employed. Likewise, Section 4(e) outlawed English-literacy tests for voters in all states, asserting that literacy was established for voters who had completed the sixth grade, even in a school where the primary language of instruction was one other than English.

Foremost among the general provisions, however, was Section 2, which proscribed racially burdensome election practices everywhere: "No voting qualification or prerequisite to voting, or standard, practice, or procedure shall be imposed or applied by any State or political subdivision to deny or abridge the right of any citizen of the United States to vote on account of race or color." Section 2 is perhaps broadly worded, but its lack of specificity provides a deep well of potential power. For instance, the reference to "standard, practice, or procedure" casts a wide net that in theory empowers the federal government to intervene in a range of situations, as later chapters reveal.

The special provisions—which applied in jurisdictions that Congress determined had intentionally disenfranchised voters on account of their race—were contained in Sections 3–9.[131] The heart of the special provisions were Sections 4 and 5, which worked together to create unprecedented federal oversight over elections in geographies that Congress determined had violated the 14th and 15th Amendment prior to the law's passage. This designation was established by a "coverage formula" in Section 4(b), which defined criteria for determining whether jurisdictions would be covered by Section 5. Section 4(b) stated that coverage "shall apply in any State or in any political subdivision of a state which (1) the Attorney General determines maintained on November 1, 1964, any test or device, and with respect to which (2) the Director of the Census determines that less than 50 percentum of the persons of voting age residing therein were registered on November 1, 1964, or that less than 50 percentum of such persons voted in the presidential election of November 1964."[132] The formula covered all of Alabama, Alaska, Georgia, Louisiana, Mississippi, South Carolina, and Virginia, along with counties in North Carolina, Arizona, and one county each in Hawaii and Idaho.[133]

"Tests and devices" were defined in Section 4(c) as "any requirement that a person as a prerequisite for voting or registration for voting (1) demonstrate the ability to read, write, understand, or interpret any matter, (2) demonstrate any educational achievement or his knowledge of any particular subject, (3) possess good moral character, or (4) prove his qualifications by the voucher of registered voters or members of any other class." In short, if a jurisdiction maintained one of the common methods of disenfranchising Black voters in the election preceding the VRA's passage *and* demonstrated low rates of *either* voting *or* registration in that election, it was "covered" and therefore subject to several special provisions.[134]

There were direct throughlines from the Civil Rights Act of 1960 to the coverage formula. In the 1960 act, Congress had allowed for the federal government to act with a stronger hand in some places than in others. Namely, the law declared that federal registrars could add voters to the rolls under certain circumstances if they resided in a place where a federal court had found a "pattern or practice" of discrimination.[135] A three-judge panel in Louisiana had upheld the constitutionality of the 1960 act's use of this standard to determine which jurisdictions could be subject to federal intervention, which may have emboldened Congress to try another scheme (the coverage formula) that created distinct classes of states under the VRA.[136]

Here, the direct involvement of DOJ staff attorneys in the bill's drafting proved invaluable. The vast array of data compiled by the USCCR was crucial for justifying the preclearance formula's terms of coverage. Katzenbach's House testimony was replete with data on the abysmal turnout rate for Black Southerners, even after eight years of litigation under the earlier civil rights laws. This careful data collection provided powerful justification for the coverage formula. As the House Judiciary Committee report explained, in areas that would be covered by Section 5, "a statistical pattern emerges of a substantial nonwhite voting-age population, a high percentage of white registration, a low percentage of nonwhite registration and a low voter turnout in the presidential election in 1964."[137] While the eventual bill used *overall* registration rates due to a "lack of reliable racial statistics"[138] nationwide, the statistics compiled in the especially troublesome parts of the country provided enough proof of the correlation for Congress to move forward. The formula was clear: Racial participation gaps, a "substantial nonwhite voting-age population," and proven uses of tests or devices identified the jurisdictions where federal oversight was needed.

This data collection process was part of a larger trend: Throughout 1965 the VRA's primary drafters were not legislative aides on Capitol Hill but rather DOJ lawyers with a great deal of experience litigating the previous Civil Rights Acts.[139] These attorneys were intimately familiar not only with the limitations of the litigation-first approach pursued under the earlier laws but also with the vast proof of discrimination that the USCCR and courts had uncovered in the preceding decade. During his testimony before the House Judiciary Committee, Chairman Emanuel Celler (D-NY) asked Katzenbach for a justification of the formula. The attorney general responded, "Our experience in the areas that would be covered by this bill has been such as to indicate frequently on the part of State legislatures a desire in a sense to outguess the courts of the United States or even to outguess the Congress of the United States."[140]

The coverage formula put an end to the guesswork. Covered jurisdictions would no longer be allowed to employ tests or devices of any kind in the future.[141] But the more significant consequence of the coverage formula was

Section 5, which created a federal power that came to be known as *preclearance.* Section 5 expanded on the logic that was laid out in the 1960 act and that had been blessed by the Supreme Court in *Louisiana v. United States* just a few months earlier; namely, that even facially race-neutral registration policies would fall harder on Black voters, given their past disenfranchisement. Section 5 directed that jurisdictions covered by Section 4(b) would have their voting practices frozen exactly as they were on November 1, 1964—aside from the termination of their tests and devices, of course. From there, if a covered state or locality wanted to change any aspect of its election regulations or practices, the proposal had to be "pre-cleared" with the Department of Justice or the US District Court for the District of Columbia *before* it could go into effect. Moreover, the DOJ attorneys who reviewed the change would do so with the presupposition that it was intended to discriminate against minority voters, placing the burden of proof on the jurisdiction to show that minority voters would not be harmed. If the jurisdiction could not meet this burden, the DOJ would object to the change and it would not be implemented unless the jurisdiction could win over judges on the DC Circuit Court of Appeals. This reliance on federal judges in the nation's capital, and not where the offense occurred, was a strategic attempt to avoid falling prey to the reluctance of Southern judges to allow federal intervention that had hampered the 1960 act.

The VRA also offered a clear warning to jurisdictions not included in the original coverage formula: They could potentially find themselves "bailed in" to future preclearance under Section 3(c) if a judge determined that they had used a test or device to abridge minority voters' rights.[142] The preclearance process detailed under the bail-in process was different than that in Section 5. By and large, judicially determined preclearance was imposed for a discrete period of time, and bailed-in jurisdictions were required to submit proposed changes to only certain aspects of their election systems for preclearance. Between 1965 and 2025, Section 3(c) preclearance was imposed just twenty-two times.[143] Nonetheless, it provided an avenue for imposing proactive review of certain policies in jurisdictions that flagrantly violated voting rights—but that were not covered under Sections 4(b) and 5.

The special provisions of the VRA extended beyond a preemptive review of proposed changes to voting policies; they also opened jurisdictions covered by Section 4(b) for another form of disparate federal intervention (laid out originally in Sections 6 and 8). If the attorney general determined that it was warranted—either through their own judgment or because they received 20 written "meritorious" complaints from residents that their right to vote had been denied—they could authorize federal observers to set up camp in polling places on Election Day.[144] Tasked with "enforc[ing] the guarantees of the 15th Amendment,"[145] the observers were to be the federal government's boots on the ground. While the observers were not allowed to intervene in any elections while they were occurring, they were required to write reports for the DOJ on how Election Day played out in the local jurisdiction. Thus, if any discriminatory policies slipped past Section 5's preclearance powers, they might be caught by in-person federal observers.

Still, the VRA did not necessarily doom jurisdictions to the coverage list forever. Section 4(a) provided covered jurisdictions an option that subsequently became known as a "bail out," or a way they could remove themselves from the preclearance list. To do so, a jurisdiction would need to prove to a three-judge panel of the US District Court for the District of Columbia that no "test or device has been used during the five years preceding the filing of the action for the purpose or with the effect of denying or abridging the right to vote on account of race or color."[146] Considering that the use of such a device was a component of the rule that had landed them on the coverage list in the first place, the bail-out provision was a high bar in 1965.[147] Even so, Section 4(a) gave some hope to covered jurisdictions that their status would not be permanent. If they complied with the VRA for the duration of the special provisions' authorization—originally, until 1970—they had a chance of bailing out of preclearance since, by definition, they would not have employed any tests or devices during the requisite period.

The need to go county-by-county to determine the scope of preclearance spoke directly to a fairly unique aspect of election administration in the United States. While many countries have national systems for registering voters and administering elections, since its founding the United States has instead vested *local* jurisdictions such as counties and towns—and even smaller units such as utility districts—with a tremendous amount of discretion when it comes to these matters.[148] As previously mentioned, prior to the VRA this discretion was used unevenly, with many local officials using their power to perpetuate discriminatory practices. This was no accident of history; instead, members of Congress from the South had spent the previous century fighting to place the administration of key laws in the hands of local officials who would not upset the region's racial apartheid.[149] As scholars Kathleen Hale, Robert Montjoy, and Mitchell Brown put it, during this period "state and local election officials were functionally independent of federal authority."[150] The preclearance regime established by the VRA recognized the disjointed nature of election administration and worked within it. By allowing localities to continue to administer their elections as they best saw fit—provided they could demonstrate that their actions would not disproportionately burden nonwhite voters—the preclearance requirements in the VRA were faithful to the tradition of local control and the 15th Amendment alike.

Although the bill underwent major drafting changes over the course of 1965, it seems that preclearance was one of the central ideas from the outset: In his American Promise Speech to Congress, Lyndon Johnson had envisioned that the VRA would "eliminate tedious, unnecessary lawsuits which delay the right to vote."[151] Indeed, avoiding the onerous litigation process was one of preclearance's central goals. The process outlined in Section 5 flipped the order in which challenges to laws had always unfolded. In virtually every other context in the United States, government action operates under a presumption of legality. From the smallest municipality to the Congress, courts do not review actions before they go into effect unless a preemptive lawsuit is brought to challenge their legality.

The previous decade of litigation, however, had proved the futility of this approach with respect to voting rights. As Attorney General Katzenbach explained in his testimony before the House of Representatives, "The fact is that those who are determined to resist [allowing Black Americans to register and vote] are able, even after apparent defeat in the courts, to devise whole new methods of discrimination. And often that means beginning the whole weary process all over again."[152] Representative Claude Pepper of Florida expanded: "There have always been these ingenious devices which have been contrived by clever and capable hands; as soon as the courts would strike down one they would come up with another and if necessary, the Governor would call a special session of the legislature to put some more on the statute books."[153] The legislative testimony showed that at least with respect to voting rights, the Southern states covered by Section 4(b) had not earned the presumption of good faith.

Litigation was more than an annoying game of Whac-a-Mole, however; it was also both slow and costly. As Katzenbach explained in his House testimony, "It has become routine to spend as much as 6,000 man-hours only in analyzing the voting records in a single county—to say nothing of preparation for trial and the almost inevitable appeal."[154] It is worth stressing again just how directly the coverage formula flowed out of DOJ litigators' experience in prior voting rights cases. In 1965, Brian Landsberg argues, civil rights groups themselves "did not demand that states seek federal preclearance before implementing changes in voting laws and standards."[155] The idea underpinning Section 5 was, instead, a product of Solicitor General Archibald Cox working with Katzenbach's team.[156] This radical intervention, in other words, was not originally a *movement* demand but rather one from the government officials who were tasked with effectively ensuring that states followed the 15th Amendment.

Still, it was radical. The establishment of preclearance marked a dramatic shift in federal oversight of elections—traditionally the domain of states. In establishing preclearance, Congress relied on its ample constitutional authority over state administration of federal elections. The Elections Clause of the Constitution declares that Congress can assert control over federal election practices when it saw fit. Moreover, Section 2 of the 15th Amendment expressly gives Congress the power to guarantee voting rights for citizens of all races, for both state and federal contests. Section 5 of the 14th Amendment granted congressional authority to enforce that amendment as well, including its promise of equal protection of the law for all Americans.

Even so, it was not obvious to all that Congress had stayed within its powers while drafting the Voting Rights Act, given that the new law presented an important wrinkle in how the federal government exerted power over the states. With the coverage formula, the VRA created two classes of states—those that were subject either in whole or in part to preclearance, and those that were not. Although different treatment of certain states was not wholly without precedent when it came to civil rights, such an approach was and remained an ongoing source of legal conflict. This was no surprise to anyone at the time, but Congress recognized that the need for a tough law overruled concerns about treating some states differently than others—at least in the short term. Both to ensure that differential treatment would endure only as long as was necessary and to placate critics eager for a mechanism to challenge the law, the special provisions (including the coverage formula and preclearance) were enacted only for a five year period. Congress would assess the situation at the end of that term and decide whether to extend them. This reauthorization window also afforded Congress the opportunity to make important tweaks to the law, if needed.

The subsequent decades would prove that the VRA did indeed need amendments to keep up not only with an increasingly diverse nation but also with an evolving Supreme Court. But those fights were in the future. At the Capitol on August 6, 1965, the mood was celebratory as Lyndon Johnson prepared to sign the Voting Rights Act into law. Rosa Parks was there, as was John Lewis. Thurgood Marshall—who had recently been named the solicitor general of the United States—was also in attendance.[157]

The date of August 6 held importance in a number of respects. On that date in 1861, President Lincoln had signed the Confiscation Act, freeing enslaved individuals who were serving as soldiers in the fight against the Union. Johnson signed the bill in the President's Room at the Capitol—the same room in which Lincoln had signed the Confiscation Act. But the day might also have held private significance for Martin Luther King Jr., who stood immediately to Johnson's left. Exactly nineteen years earlier, in the early days of the fight for civil rights, King's letter to the editor of the *Atlanta Constitution* (prompted by the murder of Maceo Snipes) had been published. Surely the spirits of Benjamin Brim, Maceo Snipes, and countless others who fought and died in the fight for a true American democracy were also crowded in the President's Room that afternoon.

2

More Elaborate Measures

THE VRA ASCENDS

> The Voting Rights Act was aimed at the subtle, as well as the obvious, state regulations which have the effect of denying citizens their right to vote because of their race. Moreover, . . . the Act gives a broad interpretation to the right to vote, recognizing that voting includes "all action necessary to make a vote effective."
>
> —CHIEF JUSTICE EARL WARREN, WRITING FOR THE MAJORITY IN *ALLEN V. STATE BOARD OF ELECTIONS*[1]

THE DAY after Lyndon Johnson signed the Voting Rights Act—Saturday, August 7, 1965—the *New York Times* carried a banner head at the top of page 1: "Johnson Signs Voting Rights Bill, Orders Immediate Enforcement." This headline appeared over four distinct stories; only two, however, directly engaged the substance of the VRA and its passage. One of those articles provided details of the VRA and the conditions in which Johnson signed it, noting that (as chapter 1 points out), the President's Room in the Capitol was also where Abraham Lincoln had signed the bill freeing enslaved Black Southerners pressed into service in the Confederate military during the Civil War.[2] Another stressed Johnson's desire for speedy implementation, with 45 federal examiners ordered to train through the weekend so that, in Johnson's words, "by Tuesday morning, trained federal examiners will be at work registering eligible men and women in ten to fifteen counties."[3]

The other two stories under the banner head did not describe the mechanics of the law or its implementation at all. The first covered unfolding events in Americus, Georgia, which had been a hotbed of activity surrounding civil rights since at least 1963. Hundreds of people had come to the city that year for protests and voter registration drives, and Americus had shown a willingness to thwart them by force. Fifteen adolescent Black girls were arrested for attempting to enter a movie theater via the front door (reserved for white patrons) instead of the back. The girls were subsequently held in dismal conditions in the Leesburg Stockade for 45 days; they were not charged with a crime, and neither their location nor the conditions of their detention were disclosed to their parents.[4] The summer of 1963 also saw the arrest on insurrection charges (a capital offense in Georgia at the time) of four Northern organizers. These charges were subsequently dropped in November when a federal court blocked the prosecution, holding that it is unconstitutional to execute someone for protest speech.[5] In July 1965, four more people—all Black women—were arrested for standing in the "white only" voting line. Americus was, in short, just the sort of place that sprang to mind when one considered the need for a robust voting rights act.

The *New York Times* story about Americus on August 7 described how the town had responded to both the VRA and ongoing protests by suddenly appointing three Black deputy clerks on the day the law had been signed; these clerks promptly registered 97 Black voters that morning without employing literacy tests.[6] On its face, news of a town confronting its history of racial disenfranchisement was a positive development. An important detail lay buried in the story, however: In the middle of that first day of registration without literacy tests, registrars in Americus reimplemented the tests after learning that the VRA would take effect not on August 6 but sometime during the following week. Despite ongoing voting rights protests and the passage of a landmark bill, Americus signaled that it would remain committed to literacy tests until the bitter end. The next day, 700 Ku Klux Klan affiliates marched through the town in a show of force.[7]

The events in Americus showed that while the Voting Rights Act represented a major step forward in the fight to fully enforce the 15th Amendment, there were still forces in the South seeking any means to push back. These tactics might include simply ignoring the law, selectively enforcing it, or intimidating or otherwise dissuading Black voters. To anyone who had followed the long struggle for voting rights in Southern states, these possibilities were well understood, and the placement of the Americus story in *The New York Times*'s coverage of the VRA's passage that day might be seen as symbolic recognition that the fight did not end with the Voting Rights Act. The perceived likelihood of Southern resistance was precisely why President Johnson was pressing for federal examiners to head to the region immediately.

Another news story under the *Times*'s VRA banner also portended potential trouble for the new law, albeit of a less obvious kind. This one detailed a different tool of resistance—a lawsuit—originating in a location that many people might not have associated with racial disenfranchisement: New York City.[8] The suit was filed on behalf of a Brooklyn couple, John P. and Christine Morgan. The Morgans' suit alleged that by banning English-only literacy tests in Section 4(e) of the VRA, Congress had overstepped its authority over election administration. The crux of the Morgans' claim was a state constitutional amendment that a sizable majority of New York voters had approved in 1921, which mandated that, starting in 1922, "no person shall become entitled to vote . . . unless such person is also able, except for physical disability, to read and write English."[9] The New York assembly ultimately decided that voters could satisfy this requirement by obtaining a certificate of literacy, either by completing the eighth grade or passing a Regents literacy test demonstrating competence in English reading and writing.[10]

Supporters of New York's literacy test put forth civically minded arguments in its defense. As of the 1920 census, 6.4% of New Yorkers over 21 years old were illiterate.[11] By limiting civic participation to the literate, the test created particular incentives for illiterate citizens to learn how to read and write. While this is a laudable outcome, a deeper dive into the 1920 census reveals important insight into who was most likely to be literate: The illiteracy rate was just 0.7% for New Yorkers of native parentage, but it was 15.2% for New York adults classified as "foreign born white." This discrepancy made immigrants an easy target for a literacy test if the majority of New Yorkers wanted to keep them from voting. And it is important to note that the 1920s were a unique period in at least one respect: It was the final decade in a fifty-year period that saw more than 30 million immigrants settle in the United States, which also corresponded with a wave of nationalistic, xenophobic, and anti-immigrant backlash.[12]

The same year the amendment passed in New York, Congress enacted the Emergency Quota Act, which for the first time set annual ceilings on the number of immigrants from each country that the United States was willing to accept. These caps—initially set at 3% of the foreign-born population from a given country already in the United States—had the dual effect of slowing overall immigration and favoring immigrants from countries that had already sent a sizable number of people to American shores. This provision, of course, also kept immigrants from "less desirable" locations out. Between 1920 and 1924, the United States admitted 1.8 million European immigrants. This was a mere 40% of the European total between 1910 and 1914 but was about *eighteen times more* than the total from Asia. Only 3,917 Africans were admitted to the United States during that four-year period.[13] Given the realities in American culture and public policy during the early 1920s, it is difficult to accept that New Yorkers acted purely out of civic virtue when they cast a ballot for English literacy tests.

Requiring voters to be proficient in English created a barrier even for the most educated and civic-minded citizens who spoke some other language, which happened to describe a great many of the 600,000 Puerto Ricans who migrated to New York in just fifteen years after World War II.[14] As American citizens, Puerto Ricans enjoy not only the protection of both the 14th and 15th Amendments but also the ability to vote in whatever part of the country in which they reside. As of 1960, while 83% of Puerto Rican New Yorkers were literate, only about 38% could speak English.[15] Regardless of their reading proficiency, the literacy test barred these Spanish-speaking Puerto Rican New Yorkers from voting. Four years before Johnson signed the VRA, Bronx resident (and native Puerto Rican) Jose Camacho alleged in the US District Court for the Southern District of New York that the literacy test burdened Puerto Ricans more than other voters.[16] This burden—in tandem with his belief that the New York law was designed to prevent people of Spanish ancestry from voting—led Camacho to argue that the literacy test violated the new 1957 and 1960 Civil Rights Acts and amounted to a violation of Puerto Ricans' 14th and 15th Amendment rights.

A three-judge panel in the Southern District of New York dismissed Camacho's claim, citing a substantial body of case law that had long given states broad powers to determine the conditions in which people could vote. Chief among these was *Lassiter v. Northampton County Board of Elections*, a 1959 case in which the Supreme Court had held that literacy tests could stand unless plaintiffs proved that they were designed for the purpose of racial discrimination.[17] Writing for the majority, Judge Charles Metzner relied on the *Lassiter* precedent to brush aside Camacho's 15th Amendment claim, ruling that "[Camacho] is not being denied the right to vote because of race, creed or color, but because of his illiteracy in the English language." Metzner reasoned that the state had developed a literacy test that was fairly administered to all citizens—even if the test amounted to a much higher hurdle for some.

Moreover, the court posited that perhaps, on balance, the literacy test created positive incentives. As Metzner put it,

> The statute is not an unreasonable exercise of the powers of the state to provide requirements for exercising the elective franchise. It is not unreasonable to expect a voter not only to be conversant with the issues presented for determination in choosing between candidates for election, but also to understand the language used in connection with voting. For example, there are printed in English on the ballot synopses of proposed constitutional amendments, titles of the offices to be filled and directives as to the use of the paper ballot or voting machine. Finally, what is more proper than that the voter be literate in the language used to conduct the business of government in his state?

This story, of course, is consistent with countless others that unfolded during the first part of the twentieth century: States had enacted statutes that, while appearing neutral on their face, allowed election officials to exclude broad segments of the population who just happened to be nonwhite or non-English speaking. In other words, New York's literacy test was exactly the sort of device that the VRA was designed to combat, and Section 4(e) did just that. Banning the English literacy test paved the way for hundreds of thousands of Puerto Ricans and other non-English speakers to gain the franchise in the Empire State.

Rather than celebrate the expansion of voting rights, however, the Morgans—white English speakers from Brooklyn—sought to block it. The couple was represented by attorney Alfred Avins, a law professor at the University of Memphis and staunch critic of civil rights legislation who would later go on to write a number of controversial articles, including one in *The Catholic Lawyer* in which he argued that the Supreme Court had erred in applying the 14th Amendment to end school segregation and bans on interracial marriage.[18] In an interview with the *Times*, Avins acknowledged that the suit was funded by an unnamed "principal party" and that it sought to stop the DOJ from enforcing the VRA's ban on literacy tests—a section of the law he described as "Bobby Kennedy's personal contribution" due to the New York senator's cosponsorship of Section 4(e)(2).[19]

The Morgans' case was designed to get media attention and traction in the courts. It achieved both goals and ultimately became the first of a number of challenges to various aspects of the Voting Rights Act as the law's opponents shifted their tactics from blocking the legislation in Congress to seeking relief in the courts. In the months and then years following August 1965, scores of suits made their way through the federal courts, each designed to compel judges to provide states, counties, or subjurisdictions relief from some aspect of the VRA. And so it happened that, on the front page of the *New York Times* on the day after the VRA's passage, mixed in with all of the pomp and circumstance of the bill signing and analysis of how the law would affect Southern states, an esoteric story about an English literacy test in New York described the first shot fired in the legal war against the Voting Rights Act. The case was one of many such challenges that would ultimately be decided in the US Supreme Court.

The Morgans may have been the first to file a court challenge to an aspect of the Voting Rights Act, but theirs was not the first threat to the VRA that reached the Supreme Court. That distinction belongs to *South Carolina v. Katzenbach*.[20] South Carolina had long been in the vanguard of Southern "states' rights" arguments: It had been home to several prominent politicians—chief among them John C. Calhoun—in the years preceding the Civil War who argued that states maintained the right to nullify objectionable federal laws. The Palmetto State was also the first to secede in December 1860, and its militiamen fired the first shots of the Civil War shortly thereafter. Now it led the Southern states' response to what they said was an unconstitutional intrusion into the states' ability to regulate elections within their borders.

South Carolina brought the case directly to the Supreme Court, which exercised its original jurisdiction for only the fifteenth time in its history.[21] The state's claim was a direct challenge to the VRA provisions that most explicitly empowered the federal government to compel states to change their behavior. Specifically, South Carolina challenged Section 4(b), arguing that the coverage formula was unfair and arbitrary. The state also targeted Section 5, which required covered jurisdictions to obtain preclearance before making any changes to their voting laws or practices. South Carolina also objected to Section 6(b), which empowered the government to send federal observers to some covered jurisdictions.

South Carolina argued that these sections of the Voting Rights Act exceeded the regulatory authority granted to Congress in the 15th Amendment, infringed on the sovereign power of states granted in Articles 1 and 4 of the US Constitution, and created conditions in which some states were treated differently than others. The state also alleged that the Voting Rights Act amounted to a bill of attainder, which it defined as "a legislative act which inflicts punishment without a judicial trial."[22] In its petition to the Court, the state pointed out that such acts are banned in Article 1 of the Constitution, which South Carolina identified as clear evidence that Congress had exceeded its constitutional authority.

Against this backdrop, in his brief to the Supreme Court, South Carolina attorney general Daniel R. McLeod focused squarely on the offensive aspects of the VRA. South Carolina denied that there was any evidence that it had disenfranchised Black voters. Feigning innocence, the state asserted that of course no one agreed that minority voters should be disenfranchised on account of their race alone, as that would be an obvious violation of the 15th Amendment. South Carolina therefore claimed that it did not mean to challenge the VRA's core goal. Rather, McLeod wrote, the key issue was the manner in which Congress had sought to achieve a reduction in racial disenfranchisement.

McLeod asked the court to answer two major legal questions. First, in creating an uneven system that "punishes" states for alleged misdeeds and a belief that they will continue, did Congress exceed the authority over state elections granted by the 15th Amendment? Second, in treating some states differently than others, did the preclearance formula amount to an unconstitutional abridgment of state power? South Carolina hoped for an affirmative answer to both.

The state had plenty of help making its claim in the Supreme Court. Five other Southern states covered by the VRA's preclearance provisions—Alabama, Georgia, Louisiana, Mississippi, and Virginia—joined the suit and filed briefs in support of South Carolina's position. The Supreme Court heard arguments over two consecutive days in January 1966, over eight hours—an enormous amount of time by typical standards. On January 17, the states made their case in the first four hours.

South Carolina and its allies kept the coverage formula squarely in their cross hairs during the oral argument. The formula brought jurisdictions into "covered" status if the attorney general deemed them to have employed a "test or device" as a prerequisite for voting (or registering to vote) *and* fewer than 50% of their adult population had either registered or voted in the 1964 election. "Tests or devices" included not only those detailed in chapter 1 (such as literacy tests) but also others, such as requiring a demonstration of education or good character or having another voter vouch for them.

The states attacked both prongs of the coverage formula. Arguing for South Carolina, David W. Robinson II echoed the main points of the state's brief, clearly stating that South Carolina had no desire to disenfranchise its citizens on account of race. "We believe" he said, "that every man, white or black, who . . . possesses the reasonable qualifications prescribed by a State should be permitted to vote."[23] He further conceded that under the 15th Amendment, Congress was empowered to halt racial disenfranchisement wherever it was found. However, Robinson argued, Congress had overstepped with its approach to the "devices" standard in Section 4(b). South Carolina's literacy test required that the voter demonstrate an ability to read several sentences of the Constitution. The Court had upheld a similar literacy test in Virginia just seven years earlier in *Lassiter v. Northampton Board of Elections*. South Carolina claimed that its literacy test was well within the terms set forth in *Lassiter*. Arguing for Virginia, attorney R. D. McIlwaine III also noted that the legislative history of the 15th Amendment revealed its framers had explicitly rejected barring literacy tests on at least three occasions, which he said was evidence that they had no intention for the amendment to proscribe such tests.

South Carolina asserted that the tests advanced the state's interest in ensuring that only informed voters cast ballots, and objected to the VRA requiring it to register "both white and Negro illiterates." This compulsion, the state held, abridged its constitutional authority to determine voter qualifications. Here, its interest was not to suppress minority voters but to keep less educated voters from the polls. That is, the state wanted to bar illiterate voters of *all* races. Robinson argued that the provision in the preclearance formula characterizing literacy tests as an unlawful "device" was therefore not sufficient to demonstrate that South Carolina had discriminated: "We are told that the reason for these trigger sections is that literacy tests may be abused and a low vote indicates that they will be abused. . . . Any law administered by man is subject to abuse. The fact that these sections may be abused gives Congress no power to suspend [the literacy tests] under an enforcement power."[24]

This assertion provoked a question from Justice Potter Stewart. Stewart was skeptical of South Carolina's claim that it was an innocent party caught up in egregious federal oversight. Stewart had suspicions—shared by many in Congress—that the test allowed substantial discretion for local authorities to deny registration to Black voters. Stewart asked Robinson, "Isn't the theory that the combination of the literacy test and the low vote evidence not that they *may* be abused but that they *have* been abused?"[25] This compelled an important response from Robinson that illustrates South Carolina's views on the issue. After responding in the negative to Stewart's question, Robinson went on in some detail:

> I would ask you to compare the differences between the sections that we attacked and those that we don't attack. The sections that we don't attack are proper enforcement-type legislation. They've given the courts the tool to move in and correct these situations where they occur. The sections we attacked absolutely regulate. They suspend our literacy qualification. They paralyzed our legislature. We can pass no more laws in South Carolina dealing with elections, unless we come to Washington and get Washington's permission. This is regulation, and this power, Congress does not have. . . . Everybody [in South Carolina] has got to take the same test, everybody [has got to have] the same qualifications. This is proper.
>
> South Carolina's test is that its citizens be able to read and write only. We don't need to have an English requirement. . . . This test has been on these books for 70 years. We require re-registration every ten years, to make sure that if one guy slipped through ten years ago presumably, there would be new administrators in ten years, he'll have to take [the literacy test]. What more could you ask for? This is a simple test, all that we require.[26]

This was the crux of the states' position: They claimed that devices like South Carolina's literacy test were not in fact racially discriminatory at all, because they were given to all voters and therefore fell squarely within the state's authority to determine voter qualifications. Yes, the literacy test kept some people from voting, but it did so in a race-blind fashion that made them only *appear* to be discriminating: "20% of our adult population is illiterate," Robinson said, "and if you exclude 20% from the total [age 21 and older] vote then we are voting and registering—or we're certainly registering—right at the national average. . . . Any state that has a large percent of illiterates and a literacy test that keeps them from voting is always going to have a smaller percent of its population registered and a smaller percent that can vote than a state either which has no literacy test or which has a small percent of illiterates."[27]

Stewart was not the only justice who appeared skeptical of this claim, but he countered the states' assertion of race-blind literacy tests repeatedly. To R. D. McIlwaine of Virginia, Stewart asked, "If the former slave states had put in literacy tests at the time of the . . . ratification of the Fifteenth Amendment, . . . immediately thereafter, the very fairest kind of an application of such literacy test would probably have effectively disenfranchised something like 95% or 98% of the Negro potential voters, would it not?"[28] McIlwaine replied, "some said 50%, some said 99%. But if it was done, it would constitute no violation of either the letter or the spirit of the Fifteenth Amendment."[29]

South Carolina and its allies clearly echoed the claims that Louisiana had previously made in *Louisiana v. United States* (see chapter 1). The states argued that as long as a statute was worded in a race-neutral manner, it complied with the 15th Amendment, no matter how its application affected racial disparities in registration or voting rates. These disparities were precisely what the second prong of the coverage formula targeted: To be covered by the VRA, a state had to have a device in place *and* exhibit rates of voting or registration below 50%. This formula was designed to ensnare jurisdictions like South Carolina that had, contrary to Robinson's claims, used a facially neutral law to keep Black citizens from voting. It also explained why, to the consternation of Mr. Robinson, South Carolina was caught up in Section 5 but some other states with literacy tests, such as Massachusetts and California, were not.

While this fact allowed the Southern states to claim unfair treatment, it also afforded them the opportunity to mine data in support of their claim. For instance, on behalf of Georgia, E. Freeman Leverett argued that because his state's voting age was 18—lower than age 21, typical at the time—turnout in Georgia would naturally be lower than in other states.[30] This is similar to claims that Attorney General McLeod had made in his intial brief for South Carolina, in which he had asserted that low turnout alone was not proof that the state had suppressed Black citizens' votes: "The failure of 50% of South Carolinians over the voting age to vote in the 1964 election is due to economic and political factors without the scope of the Fifteenth Amendment."[31] In his oral argument, Robinson stressed this point too: "Our exhibits . . . show that South Carolina's population characteristics are the reasons she has a light vote. These are not dangerous grounds, these are grounds unrelated to race: low income, low education, more rural population, even the age of her population falls into non-voting groups. The religion of her population even falls into non-voting groups."[32]

While at times advocates from the various states conceded that in a few limited cases, voters had been discriminated against on account of their race, they brushed these instances aside as having been easily corrected. In this way, the states argued, they were being swept up in a wave of mob justice. After the public outrage of the Selma protest, calls had risen for the federal government to do *something*. But, as Leverett argued, in the view of the covered states, the VRA was an overly reactive law that pushed aside the sacred rights of the Southern states:

> We don't deny that discrimination has existed in some parts of the South. I don't deny that it has existed in some parts of Georgia. I'm not here to defend it. I'm ashamed of it and I join with the Court and everyone else in condemning it, but we would hope that simply because a state has erred in the past, it does not thereafter lose a right to claim the protection of the Constitution.
>
> The Voting Rights Act of 1965 was enacted in unusual circumstances. . . . All Americans know that the Congress was deliberating under the pressure and influence of people who were threatening revolution and rebellion in the streets, and I would hope that as long as this Court sits that Congress cannot, to appease a mob in the streets, invoke an unconstitutional means to achieve a constitutional end.

South Carolina and its fellow Southern states pleaded innocence, and claimed that they were a victim of an overzealous Congress that had created a reactionary policy in response to the mob mentality of the American public. Now it was the government's turn to make its case.

Attorney General Nicholas Katzenbach made his response in court on January 18, arguing in defense of the VRA for the United States. Katzenbach enjoyed a strong position. By our count, twenty states either filed or joined amicus briefs siding with the federal government.[33] This wide support from noncovered states was consistent with at least one point that the covered states had conceded in their argument: Katzenbach had public opinion on his side.

The cornerstone of broad public support for the VRA had been in place well before Selma. In May 1963—nearly two years prior to the events on the Edmund Pettus Bridge—a national survey conducted by the National Opinion Research Center asked which of the priorities of "Negro groups working for equal rights" Americans felt was *least* important to work on next. Only 2% of respondents selected voting rights.[34] In the same survey, 14% of Americans said voting rights should be the most important next step, far below the majority choice of equal job opportunities (61%), but still good enough for second place.

As the covered states had noted in their argument, after Bloody Sunday had been beamed into living rooms across the country and President Johnson delivered the American Promise Speech before a joint session of Congress, public opinion shifted substantially. Just three days after Johnson's speech, the

Gallup Organization fielded a survey that asked a simple question: Had Americans "heard or read about President Johnson's proposal to Congress on Negro voting rights?" An overwhelming majority of 78% said they had.[35] In the same poll, 76% of Americans said they supported sending federal observers into areas where people may have been disenfranchised, "to make sure Negroes and whites are given an equal opportunity to register and to vote." This of course ended up being a fair representation of one aspect of the VRA.

The polling firm Louis Harris and Associates regularly surveyed the public about voting rights and the VRA for the remainder of 1965. While the firm did not repeat questions throughout the year, the various aspects it did ask about provide important insight into the public mood as the VRA was debated, passed, and implemented. For instance, before passage in August, an April Harris poll found that 53% of the public supported federal observers, even after being reminded that "opponents of the bill feel [that sending observers] is an invasion of the rights of states to control their own elections."[36] In the same poll, 56% of Americans said they believed Black voters were not actually allowed to vote in Alabama, even after being told that Alabama governor George Wallace denied that claim.

In a May poll, Harris found that 48% of Americans said they sided more with civil rights groups "in the recent showdown in Selma Alabama over Negro voting rights," which was more than twice the number who sided more with the State of Alabama.[37] And in December, four months after passage and mere weeks before oral arguments in *South Carolina v. Katzenbach*, a staggering 95% told Harris pollsters that they approved of the Voting Rights Act.[38] As he rose to deliver his argument to the Supreme Court on the morning of January 18, 1965, then, there were strong winds at Katzenbach's back.

The attorney general came directly to the point:

> Mr. Chief Justice and may it please the Court: The position of the United States in this case can be very simply stated. Section 2 of the Fifteenth Amendment gives the Congress an express power to enforce the prohibition contained in Section 1 against the denial or abridgment of voting on account of race or color. We simply contend that the Voting Rights Act of 1965 is appropriate legislation. Viewed as a whole and in its operating context, it's well adapted. It operates fairly and reasonably to achieve an objective which is explicitly within the power of Congress to achieve and indeed the provision [Section 2 of the 15th Amendment] . . . puts a duty on the Congress to enforce that provision of Section 1.

> In developing this position, I want first to describe the actual problem of compliance as it was presented to Congress and as it exists in fact as Congress faced and understood it. The so-called triggers contained in Section 4 of the Act aren't mere mechanical abstractions pulled out of the air. They can't be fairly viewed or understood in isolation from their function, in relation to other provisions of the Act. For example, to the problem of enforcement of Section 1 of the Fifteenth Amendment as understood by Congress, these triggers are a temporary, automatic suspension of inherently dangerous tests and devices, and they're coupled with the provision in Section 4(d) which permits more detailed judicial inquiry at the request of any state or subdivision affected. In these two sections, Section 4 should be seen as a single integrated measure for solving problems revealed by experience and demonstrated to Congress by ample testimony.[39]

For the next several hours, Katzenbach deconstructed the history of discrimination in the South, stressed that Section 2 of the 15th Amendment gave Congress power to combat it, and defended the Voting Rights Act as a rational response to right historical wrongs. Characterizing the literacy and related tests as "engines of discrimination," he noted that litigation had not been capable of stopping them. The solution that Congress had crafted, Katzenbach argued, was the only realistic option for a country that had awakened to the rampant racial disenfranchisement within its own borders.

The opinion was released on March 7, 1966—the one-year anniversary of Bloody Sunday and exactly seven months after President Johnson signed the VRA. This pace exhibited the Court's commitment to lightning speed by typical standards, demonstrating an understanding that its decision had immediate consequences for American elections. In an 8–1 ruling, the Supreme Court sided with the federal government, upholding the entirety of challenged VRA provisions as a constitutional usage of 15th Amendment power. The majority brushed aside the states' claims about bills of attainders and 5th Amendment rights, and focused on the question at hand: Were states discriminating against minority voters in a manner that authorized Congress to exert the power afforded it under the 14th and 15th Amendments to oversee states' elections? Chief Justice Earl Warren's majority opinion not only was consistent with the broad strokes of Katzenbach's argument but also rested squarely on the legislative history and submitted evidence. Warren held that these revealed "unremitting and ingenious defiance in certain parts of the country of the 15th Amendment, which Congress concluded called for sterner and more elaborate measures than those previously used."[40] Citing the evidentiary record before the Court, Warren noted:

> Beginning in 1890, the States of Alabama, Georgia, Louisiana, Mississippi, North Carolina, South Carolina, and Virginia enacted tests still in use which were specifically designed to prevent Negroes from voting. Typically, they made the ability to read and write a registration qualification and also required completion of a registration form. These laws were based on the fact that, as of 1890, in each of the named States, more than two-thirds of the adult Negroes were illiterate, while less than one-quarter of the adult whites were unable to read or write. At the same time, alternate tests were prescribed in all of the named States to assure that white illiterates would not be deprived of the franchise. These included grandfather clauses, property qualifications, "good character" tests, and the requirement that registrants "understand" or "interpret" certain matter.[41]

The Court further held that the judicial record revealed that when subjected to scrutiny, a great many of these tests were clearly designed to keep Black voters from the polls. Like Katzenbach and a large majority of the American public, the justices simply did not believe that the devices employed in the South were race neutral. In fact, Warren concluded, the tests were "specifically designed to prevent Negroes from voting while permitting white persons to vote."[42] A so-called literacy test that was applied differently to Black and white voters—as had been done in most of the South—was a clear violation of the 15th Amendment even if race was not mentioned in the law authorizing the test. Therefore, in Warren's mind, arguments that suspending literacy tests somehow "diluted" votes from literate citizens could not stand against the fact that in actuality, states were permitting white illiterates to vote—and had done so for 70 years.

Furthermore, the Court held that "the coverage formula is rational as being aimed at areas where widespread discrimination has existed through misuse of tests or devices even though it excludes certain areas where there is voting discrimination through other means."[43] Because it used an ostensibly objective formula intended to identify jurisdictions that had employed a test or device specifically to disenfranchise some voters, Section 4 of the VRA seemed to the majority to be a proportional (and even restrained) response in that it did not scoop up jurisdictions that had proven to be less discriminatory.

Given its recognition of sustained, egregious disenfranchisement, the Court also held that the use of federal observers was a sensible exercise of congressional power via the 15th Amendment. As Warren put it, "In many of the political subdivisions covered by Section 4(b) of the Act, voting officials have persistently employed a variety of procedural tactics to deny Negroes the franchise, often in direct defiance or evasion of federal court decrees. Congress realized that merely to suspend voting rules which have been misused or are subject to misuse might leave this localized evil undisturbed."[44] It might be lamentable to put federal observers in roles the state had long enjoyed monopoly power over, but Warren and his colleagues thought that, in this instance at least, the states had brought this practice on themselves via their past actions. "After enduring nearly a century of systematic resistance to the Fifteenth Amendment," the chief justice wrote, "Congress might well decide to shift the advantage of time and inertia from the perpetrators of the evil to its victims."[45] While preclearance was certainly a "stringent remedy," it was nonetheless "a valid means for carrying out the commands of the Fifteenth Amendment," Warren wrote.[46] The Court also acknowledged that litigating each violation on a case-by-case basis had proven to be ineffective, which necessitated that Congress act to stop the widespread disenfranchisement of minority voters in the South. The Voting Rights Act thus survived its first major challenge. It was not going to be the last.

In *South Carolina v. Katzenbach*, the Supreme Court provided a definitive negative answer to the question of whether Congress's preclearance scheme exceeded its 15th Amendment power. There were still plenty of people prepared to argue that Congress had gone too far with aspects of the VRA that were unrelated to preclearance, however. In the next several years, a number of suits designed to narrow the law's scope worked their way through the judicial system. Shortly after ruling in *Katzenbach*, the Supreme Court turned its attention to the first such challenge, which had been filed on the very same day the VRA was signed: John and Christine Morgan's case from Brooklyn.

Section 4(e) of the VRA banned any literacy test that required voters to show English proficiency. The Morgans challenged only this section of law, arguing that the people of New York had offered a resounding endorsement of the English literacy test when they amended the state constitution in 1921, and that New Yorkers alone should determine who gets to vote in their state's elections. In zeroing in on Section 4(e), the Morgans' claim was not the broadside assault on the VRA that South Carolina had brought in the *Katzenbach* case. It did, however, blaze a trail that many VRA challenges would follow in the coming years: By focusing on a narrower aspect of the law, the Morgans' argument was designed to chip away at smaller pieces of the VRA's regulatory power, thereby returning some election authority to the states.

In Section 4(e), the Morgans argued, Congress had exceeded its authority by ordering New York to qualify non–English speakers as voters. The suit alleged that Spanish-speaking New Yorkers would not be sufficiently familiar with the issues of the day to cast informed votes. The VRA's forced addition of tens of thousands of new voters to the electorate, in the Morgans' mind, diluted the votes of New Yorkers who had been certified as English-literate. In mandating that these supposedly less informed citizens be allowed to vote, the Morgans argued that Section 4(e) violated their 5th Amendment due process rights because the power of votes cast by qualified English-literate voters such as themselves would be rendered less important. This claim was no doubt designed to confer on them standing to sue in federal court, ensuring that their case would gain traction. The major question presented to the Court, however, was quite similar to the one the majority had definitively answered in *Katzenbach*: Did Section 4(e) amount to an unconstitutional infringement on New York's election regulatory power?

The Morgans' suit was taken up by the US District Court for the District of Columbia in a matter of weeks. A three-judge panel released its opinion on November 15, 1965—barely three months after the VRA's passage.[47] Rendering its judgment before the Supreme Court had ruled on the South Carolina case, the 2–1 district court majority held that "the right of suffrage is not a privilege and immunity of a citizen of the United States as such, but is a right conferred by the States." For that reason, the court found, states held definitive power to exclude some citizens from the polls, as New York had done. The opinion noted that states had historically declared an ability to proscribe some people (such as women or nonwhite citizens) from voting. When Congress had wished to compel states to change these policies in the past, the district court majority held, it had done so by amending the federal constitution, not by enacting a statute. Overall, then, the two judges in the DC district court majority held that the ban on English literacy tests in Section 4(e) of the VRA was an unconstitutional infringement on states' power to regulate their own elections.

District courts do not have the final say, however, especially when the Supreme Court appears to have a much different view of appropriate congressional authority over elections. The Department of Justice appealed the district court's decision to the United States Supreme Court. The case, now known as *Katzenbach v. Morgan*,[48] waited its turn while the Court considered *South Carolina v. Katzenbach*. Once the Court ruled in the South Carolina case, Katzenbach and his team stood on solid ground to mount a defense of Section 4(e): If the comparatively obtrusive action of preclearance was constitutional, the attorney general reasoned, the Court would uphold congressional authority to restrict English literacy tests as well.

In a 7–2 decision, the Supreme Court did just that in *Katzenbach v. Morgan*, overruling the district court and declaring Section 4(e) to be well within congressional authority. Writing for the Supreme Court majority, Associate Justice William J. Brennan Jr. asserted that while states do have the right to establish qualifications for voting, "[they] have no power to grant or withhold the franchise on conditions that are forbidden by the Fourteenth Amendment, or any other provision of the Constitution. Such exercises of state power are no more immune to the limitations of the Fourteenth Amendment than any other state action. The Equal Protection Clause itself has been held to forbid some state laws that restrict the right to vote."[49]

The question, said Brennan, was not whether English-literacy tests were themselves constitutional but rather whether Congress had employed an appropriate remedy to what it saw as an equal protection violation; here, the disenfranchisement of Puerto Rican New Yorkers. Brennan noted "some evidence suggesting that prejudice played a prominent role in the enactment of the [English requirement],"[50] and underscored the majority's view in *Katzenbach v. South Carolina*: Congress had the ability to fight racial voting discrimination where it perceived that discrimination to exist. To do so, Brennan wrote, Congress may read the 14th Amendment broadly, because "Section 5 of the 14th Amendment is a positive grant of legislative power authorizing Congress to exercise its discretion in determining the need for and nature of legislation to secure Fourteenth Amendment guarantees."[51] In the *Morgan* decision, the Court therefore reiterated its logic in *Katzenbach* that Congress's efforts to combat racial disenfranchisement were within the confines of its power. Next, the Court would recognize the right of individuals to join the fight as well.

In the 1960 census, 42% of Mississippians were recorded as Black.[52] Yet, when the Mississippi state legislature convened in January 1966, every one of its 174 members was white.[53] The Voting Rights Act had the potential to change that profile, and the legislators knew it. Their state was fully covered by the VRA's preclearance provisions, but the members were determined to test the limits of the new law. Legislators introduced more than 30 bills that would have changed Mississippi election laws in 1966; 12 ultimately passed.[54] Together, the legislators hoped the new laws would maintain white Mississippians' power monopoly while avoiding federal preclearance.

One such bill drew new legislative and congressional districts, spreading Mississippi's Black voters across the state's five congressional districts in such a manner that they would have difficulty electing a Black candidate. Other bills authorized a switch from single member districts to at-large districts in elections for county supervisor and school board positions. These moves also diluted votes of Black residents; they may have been able to muster a majority in a district covering their majority-Black town, but rarely could they do so in the entire county. Another bill changed some education superintendents from elected to appointed positions.[55] Yet another abolished party primaries, mandating that candidates receive an outright general election majority before winning office—again, a clear attempt to thwart Mississippi's Black minority. It also became more difficult to qualify as an independent or school board candidate. And, in the ultimate fail-safe, the legislature authorized itself to combine Mississippi's counties into new ones with a two-thirds vote.[56]

Tactics like these became standard for covered jurisdictions throughout the country in the preclearance era—a point we return to later on. The new laws' sponsors also happened to come from areas with a sizable Black population where white citizens presumably had the most to lose under preclearance.[57] It is nearly impossible, then, to argue that these efforts were anything but a calculated effort to stop Black people from gaining political power in Mississippi.

Worse, Mississippi enacted the laws without subjecting them to preclearance. To justify this decision, Mississippi relied on a narrow reading of Section 5, which required preclearance in covered jurisdictions for "any voting qualification or prerequisite to voting, or standard, practice, or procedure with respect to voting." Mississippi's position was that because its new laws did not affect registration or the act of casting a ballot, they were not subject to preclearance at all. In a number of lawsuits, however (six in all), Mississippi residents challenged nearly all of the new provisions as mechanisms to dilute potential minority representation. Even if Mississippi's actions were not a violation of the letter of the law—which itself was in dispute—these citizens argued, the state certainly ran afoul of the VRA's spirit.

The Mississippi cases were consolidated with another from Virginia, which had a similar fact pattern. Virginia had changed its laws without subjecting them to preclearance, as well, requiring write-in votes to be recorded in the voter's handwriting—much to the detriment of illiterate citizens. That case, known as *Allen v. State Board of Elections,* lent its name to the next VRA-related question before the Supreme Court.[58]

Before ruling on the case, the justices first had to decide whether the citizens who had brought the suit could be there at all. The immediate question was whether citizens have a "private right of action" allowing them to sue when they believe states have infringed on their voting rights, or whether they instead have to wait for the federal government to intervene. Here, writing for the 7–2 majority, Chief Justice Earl Warren held that private individuals have the right to seek judicial enforcement of Section 5 of the Voting Rights Act "to insure the Act's guarantee that no person shall be denied the right to vote for failure to comply with an unapproved new enactment subject to that section."[59] This pathway, reasoned Warren, would likely result in more expeditious and vigorous enforcement, as people in various localities affected by some law that had not been submitted for preclearance would not need to wait for the government to notice before challenging it in court.

The second question the Court took on in *Allen* was how broad the reach of Section 5 preclearance actually was. Did it apply only to a narrow band of policies, as Mississippi argued, or was it more expansive? Again, Warren's majority sided with the citizens, holding that the changes to the election laws in both Mississippi and Virginia were indeed subject to Section 5 of the Voting Rights Act. Warren held that the legislative history of the VRA reveals a belief among its framers that "voting includes all action necessary to make a vote effective."[60] This belief, Warren wrote, "was aimed at the subtle, as well as the obvious, state regulations which have the effect of denying citizens their right to vote because of race."[61] The *Allen* majority ruled that the statutes in the two states would likely have the effect of either disenfranchising Black voters or diluting their political power.

To avoid similar under-the-radar policies from having the same effect in the future, Section 5 had to be interpreted as giving broad preclearance power to the federal government. Indeed, the majority in *Allen* held, in covered jurisdictions, *any* new law, no matter how minor, was subject to preclearance under Section 5 if it had the potential to affect voting rights. Mississippi and Virginia had picked a fight with the federal government and lost. The result was an even stronger VRA, with an expansive Section 5 and citizens empowered to fight for it in court. At the end of the 1960s, the Voting Rights Act had survived every legal challenge thrown its way. As a new decade dawned, it was about to get even stronger.

On its enactment in 1965, the preclearance formula in the VRA was good for only five years. This limitation was inserted to make the law more palatable to members of Congress who might otherwise have balked at new federal oversight in an area that had traditionally belonged to the states. The five-year period would give Black voters time to register, and offending jurisdictions a chance to get their house in order. If it wanted to return to the pre-VRA status quo, Congress did not need to take action. To extend preclearance, however, Congress would have to reauthorize the VRA before August 1970.

As the deadline neared, covered jurisdictions eyed the White House. It was now occupied by Richard Nixon, whose commitment to the "Southern Strategy," designed to bring white Southerners into the Republican fold, made him an ideal partner to weaken the VRA. Nixon's proposal for the VRA reauthorization was to terminate Section 5 and extend preclearance to the entire country for a three-year period, at the end of which proactive preclearance would end for covered jurisdictions.[62] With an ally in the president, covered jurisdictions could see a light at the end of the tunnel, so long as they could convince enough members of Congress that they had learned their lesson.

The timing of the Court's opinion in *Allen v. State Board of Elections* could not have been worse for the Southern states. The Court handed down its ruling on March 3, 1969, just as Congress was gearing up for the reauthorization debate. The ruling undercut covered states' argument that preclearance was no longer necessary. The Supreme Court had pointed to at least thirteen laws in two states that had attempted to dilute minority voters' power, all while attempting to elude preclearance. And the Court had warned that such laws were now the main likely conduit of future racial disenfranchisement, so much so that the *Allen* majority had endorsed an expansive view of Section 5's reach.

Mississippi's efforts had backfired tremendously.[63] Not only had the case resulted in stronger federal oversight but, on the eve of reauthorization, the *Allen* ruling seemed to suggest that vigorous preclearance was needed more than ever. Even so, after considering both Nixon's proposal and a "clean" reauthorization that would have simply extended the VRA for another five years, the House went with Nixon's bill in a surprisingly narrow vote. Clarence M.

Mitchell, a lobbyist for the NAACP, called the House's decision to end preclearance "a cataclysmic defeat" for voting rights advocates.[64] But the VRA still had allies in the Senate. Among them was Hugh Scott (R-PA), the Republican minority leader. Working with Senator Ted Kennedy (D-MA), Scott crafted a compromise bill with bipartisan support.[65]

The Senate bill extended preclearance for another five years, to 1975. However, in a nod to Southern Senators who thought that the original coverage formula had disproportionately captured Southern jurisdictions, the bill tweaked the coverage formula in Section 4(b), expanding the trigger to include the 1968 election, so that if registration or turnout was below 50% in 1964 *or* 1968, a jurisdiction would be covered. Under the new formula, any jurisdiction that had maintained a test or device and had seen the under-50% participation levels listed in the original version of the VRA would be brought into preclearance. The new formula covered several non-Southern jurisdictions, including three boroughs of New York City. Counties in Alaska, Arizona, California, Idaho, and Wyoming were also newly covered, as were towns in Connecticut, Maine, Massachusetts, and New Hampshire.[66] The bill also extended the bailout provision, mandating that jurisdictions show they had not used a test or device for ten years instead of the original five. This change kept the covered Southern jurisdictions squarely under preclearance as well.

While it kept Section 5 intact over Nixon's objections, the Senate bill did make a concession to the president: Bans on tests or devices were extended nationally. Thus, the 1970 bill spelled the end of literacy tests (whether to test for English proficiency, as the 1965 act had done, or otherwise), regardless of the level of voter participation in an area. As with the expanded coverage formula, this provision made the amended VRA less focused on the South.

The Senate bill also included wholly new provisions that were not present in the 1965 law. First, it standardized residency requirements for voters. The bill mandated that all states declare anyone who had lived in a jurisdiction for at least 30 days to be eligible to vote in presidential elections. It also required states to allow voters who moved to new jurisdictions within 30 days of an election to vote in their previous jurisdiction of residence. Finally, it mandated that states allow residents to cast absentee ballots in presidential elections if they requested one at least seven days before the election.[67] In tandem, these new regulations created a national 30-day residency period that would prevent states from imposing overly restrictive residency requirements that could disenfranchise voters—particularly those who had recently moved. It therefore foreclosed one of the paths by which states could use policies that did not ostensibly deal with voters' race to disenfranchise itinerant (i.e., younger and less white) populations.

Senator Kennedy added yet another new provision to the law. The previous year had seen a wave of political violence, including the assassination of Martin Luther King Jr. and Kennedy's brother Robert during his presidential campaign. Street violence surrounding the Vietnam Conflict had rocked the Democratic National Convention, and protest activity continued on college campuses. Kennedy reasoned that if the United States was sending eighteen-year-olds to Vietnam, they should be able to vote. Late in the legislative process, Kennedy placed language in the bill that guaranteed the right to vote for all Americans aged eighteen and over in state and federal elections.

The bipartisan bill sailed through the Senate and then the House, but Nixon was reluctant to sign it. The president believed strongly that Kennedy's amendment to lower the voting age was unconstitutional, and struggled to see how enacting it would help him in the South.[68] But the writing was on the wall; failing to sign it, his advisers argued, would unleash a powerful and unpredictable backlash. Nixon, realizing that the game was up, signed an even more powerful VRA into law.

The ink from Nixon's pen was barely dry when the 1970 reauthorization was challenged in federal court. Arizona, Idaho, Oregon, and Texas jointly lodged what was by now a familiar argument in VRA litigation: Congress had overstepped its authority in the 1970 law, infringing on rights that belonged exclusively to the states. The Court was tasked with deciding whether the three main additions to the VRA in the 1970 reauthorization—a national ban on literacy tests, a standard voter residency requirement, and the lower voting age—amounted to a constitutional exercise of congressional power.

The Supreme Court displayed substantially more fragmentation in *Oregon v. Mitchell* than it had in previous VRA cases, and each of the three areas of the law that the court considered received a different majority.[69] No majority opinion was given, but Justice Hugo Black delivered an opinion that offered his own view and that reflected a process of much discussion among the justices. The Court had considered each element of the 1970 VRA separately. First, as it had done several times before, the justices recognized that devices like literacy tests could be deployed as tools of racial disenfranchisement. The Court had previously held that banning them was therefore a legitimate exercise of Congress's 15th Amendment powers. By a 9–0 vote, the Supreme Court now ruled that extending these bans to the nation as a whole was fully within congressional authority under the 15th Amendment. The Court also, on an 8–1 vote, upheld the universal residency and absentee ballot requirements, ruling that they too were within Congress's constitutional powers.

However, with respect to the question of whether Congress could lower the voting age in state elections, Black and his colleagues in a slimmer, 5–4 majority turned to the 10th Amendment and Article 1 of the Constitution. As Black wrote, there was little evidence that the framers of the Constitution intended for Congress to set voter qualifications in state elections: "It is a plain fact of history that the Framers never imagined that the national Congress would set the qualifications for voters in every election from President to local constable or village alderman. It is obvious that the whole Constitution reserves to the States the power to set voter qualifications in state and local elections, except to the limited extent that the people, through constitutional amendments, have specifically narrowed the powers of the States."[70]

The Civil War amendments, according to Black, allow Congress to regulate state elections in order to fight racial discrimination, using "appropriate" remedies. But, he said, lowering the voting age did not further that goal. As Black put it, "In enacting the 18-year-old vote provisions of the Act now before the Court, Congress made no legislative findings that the 21-year-old vote requirement was used by the States to disenfranchise voters on account of race. I seriously doubt that such a finding, if made, could be supported by substantial evidence."[71] At the same time, Black affirmed that Congress had authority to regulate its own elections, as well as those for president. Thus, the five-justice majority struck down the mandated 18-year voting age in *state* and *local* elections but left it intact for *federal* ones. Three months later, Congress responded by passing the 26th Amendment to the Constitution. Subsequently ratified, the new amendment guaranteed the right to vote in every election to all citizens aged 18 and above.

The Court's ruling in *Oregon v. Mitchell* showed that the justices were not willing to read the Reconstruction Amendments as a free pass for Congress to regulate state elections in whatever way it saw fit. At the same time, however, it also underscored that the Court saw combating racial disenfranchisement as a worthy objective that Congress had power to reasonably pursue. By a large majority, the justices were willing to be partners in establishing a strong Voting Rights Act, so long as Congress did not stray too far from the clear mission of the post–Civil War amendments: ending racist voting practices. In five short years, the notion of a robust and far-reaching preclearance system had gone from a controversial exercise of Congress's 15th Amendment powers to settled law.

Lower federal courts applied the *Allen* precedent to compel covered jurisdictions to preclear changes to their election procedures, and when that process broke down, the Supreme Court was more than happy to maintain the strength of its previous affirmation—and sometimes to expand it. For instance, when officials in majority-Black Canton, Mississippi, failed to preclear new polling place locations, changes to city boundaries via annexation of outlying territory, and shifts to at-large elections instead of single-member wards in 1969, the Supreme Court held that per its ruling in *Allen*, the town should have gone through preclearance. In *Perkins v. Matthews*, the Court explicitly declared these actions as falling under Section 5—even though on the surface, an annexation may not seem on its face to be an election-related move. *Perkins* provided even clearer guidelines for just how far-reaching the Court viewed preclearance to be.[72]

The Court's consistent support for preclearance sent a strong message to the Department of Justice: Get ready for a lot more preclearance submissions. The DOJ had reorganized its Civil Rights Division in 1969, moving its staff away from a geographic focus and into subject-matter sections so that attorneys could specialize in specific areas of law. Accordingly, the VRA was now administered by the Voting Section.[73] Shortly thereafter, the DOJ established a working group of attorneys within the Voting Section who handled Section 5 cases exclusively; they watched preclearance requests rise steadily, from 110 in 1970 to 1,359 in 1972—and, as chapter 3 shows, the DOJ's objections rose in turn.[74] Active enforcement of Section 5 was the new normal in the early 1970s.

As the 1975 reauthorization neared, it became clear that Congress would not be weakening preclearance, either. Richard Nixon was no longer in the White House, and President Gerald Ford had a more progressive outlook on civil rights than his predecessor. As a member of the House, he had voted for the original VRA in 1965, and as president, he was looking to build bridges with Black voters. On January 15, 1975—Martin Luther King Jr.'s birthday—Ford signaled a willingness to sign a clean extension of the Voting Rights Act, saying, "Dr. King helped lead the way to passage of the Voting Rights Act of 1965. I supported the original act and its five-year extension in 1970. This law has helped to open our political processes to full citizen participation, and we must safeguard these gains through another five-year extension."[75]

With Ford's permissive posture, debate surrounding the 1975 reauthorization was much less contentious than it had been in 1969–70. By a vote of 346–56 in the House and 77–12 in the Senate, an extension of all of the 1970 VRA provisions sailed through, this time for seven (not five) years. As had happened in the prior reauthorization, though, rather than merely extending the previous protections of the VRA, Congress substantially strengthened the law. For example, the 1975 act made the nationwide ban on tests or devices permanent. But the new law also made important changes to the coverage formula, as well as to the definition of what a "test or device" was.

As it weighed the 1975 reauthorization, Congress heard testimony providing ample evidence that the VRA's protections should extend beyond areas where the primary minority comprised Black Americans.[76] A recent Supreme Court decision had found that a districting scheme in Texas diluted the power of Hispanic voters there.[77] Congress determined that in some parts of the country, Hispanic, Asian, and Native American populations were also facing substantial barriers to voting. The legislative record revealed that language often played an important role in erecting these hurdles. Congress therefore added several additional provisions to the VRA in the 1975 reauthorization. First among these was the expansion of Section 2 protections to language minorities. Although the original law disallowed abridging the right to vote "on account of race or color," the 1975 reauthorization expanded this ban to include discrimination against a voter "because he is a member of a language minority group."[78]

The amended VRA also expanded the scope of Section 5 along these same lines, changing the preclearance formula to include jurisdictions that had discriminated against a "single-language minority," defined as areas in which at least 5% of the population was composed of "persons who are American Indian, Asian American, Alaskan Natives, or of Spanish heritage."[79] In single-language minority jurisdictions, the 1975 amendments defined the provision of English-only ballots or voting materials as a test or device. At the same time, the coverage formula was amended to include the 1972 election. In tandem, these changes meant that if single-language minority jurisdictions had offered only English-language voting materials since 1965 *and* less than half of their population had voted in any of the presidential elections between 1964 and 1972, they were now subject to Section 5. This provision dramatically increased the breadth of preclearance: Alaska, Arizona, and Texas were now fully covered under Section 5, as were counties in California, Colorado, Florida, New Mexico, New York (including Brooklyn and the Bronx in New

York City), Oklahoma, and South Dakota, along with two townships in Michigan. Many of these jurisdictions would be bailed out of coverage in the decades to come—once they had successfully proved that they had curbed discriminatory practices—but for now they would submit their election policies to preclearance reviewers.[80]

Congress also added one last new protection: Section 203, which mandates the provision of election materials such as ballots and voter guides in languages other than English in some places. Like Section 4(b), Section 203 contains a formula for determining coverage. If a jurisdiction has a sizable single-language minority population,[81] and if the "illiteracy rate of the group is higher than the national illiteracy rate,"[82] election administrators are required to ensure that all materials made available in English are also available in the minority language(s) for which their jurisdiction is covered. In total, then, the language protections in the 1975 reauthorization dramatically expanded the VRA's reach, bringing language minority voters squarely under the protection of Sections 2, 5, and the new 203.

When the VRA was initially enacted in 1965, its opponents hoped that they could stanch its most objectionable aspects in the courts. If that strategy failed, they could take solace in the fact that the required reauthorizations would give them a chance to weaken the bill via the legislative process. Instead, Congress and the courts had proven themselves effective partners. Each branch recognized the scourge of racial disenfranchisement and Congress's constitutional authority to fight it. And, far from diminishing it over time, each reauthorization had only made the VRA stronger. As the 1976 election loomed, the VRA's preclearance formula applied to more jurisdictions than ever before. Literacy tests were banned nationally, and jurisdictions could no longer discriminate against language-minority voters.

It was a golden era for voting, and the broader gains from the robust Voting Rights Act were already becoming clear. Registration rates among Black voters had surged since the 1965 law's passage.[83] Mobilized by the threat that a unified bloc of Black voters presented, white Southerners also demonstrated a marked uptick in turnout.[84] Even so, Black candidates had a better chance of winning elections than at any point since Reconstruction and had begun claiming seats at all levels of government.[85] These gains translated to policy outcomes as well: Members of Congress who represented jurisdictions covered by Section 5 became substantially more supportive of civil rights legislation after the VRA's passage.[86] At the state level, the share of state funds flowing to counties with a larger percentage of Black voters also rose noticeably after the Voting Rights Act, with gains concentrated especially in counties that formerly employed tests or devices.[87]

Other positive outcomes would soon follow for Black Americans, presumably as a direct result of their enhanced political power. For instance, the wage gap between Black and white residents would decline more in covered counties than those not subject to preclearance.[88] Mortality rates for Black infants followed a similar pattern.[89] The news was not uniformly good for Black voters,[90] and storm clouds would soon gather on the horizon, threatening to weaken the 1975 Act. But in the meantime, the DOJ and federal courts would work together to create a vigorous preclearance system that would fiercely combat race-based vote disenfranchisement for two generations.

3

Vestiges of Discrimination

HOW WAS PRECLEARANCE UTILIZED?

> Although the VRA wrought dramatic changes in the realization of minority voting rights, the Act, to date, surely has not eliminated all vestiges of discrimination against the exercise of the franchise by minority citizens. Jurisdictions covered by the preclearance requirement continued to submit, in large numbers, proposed changes to voting laws that the Attorney General declined to approve, auguring that barriers to minority voting would quickly resurface were the preclearance remedy eliminated.
>
> —JUSTICE RUTH BADER GINSBURG, IN DISSENT, *SHELBY COUNTY V. HOLDER*[1]

AT THE stroke of midnight on December 31, 1969, revelers popped champagne corks and sang "Auld Lang Syne." There was good reason to celebrate. The fraught decade of the 1960s—characterized by political violence, an unpopular war, and the fight for civil and voting rights—was over. Many Americans looked ahead to the new decade in the hope that the country could heal old wounds and forge a new way forward. While the New Year's parties rolled on, though, a curious thing had happened when the clock struck twelve in Richmond, Virginia. The city had a slight majority of Black residents on the final day of 1969. On New Year's Day, however, the percentage of Black Richmonders appeared to have shrunk by 10 percentage points to 42%.[2] Richmond's Black majority was gone overnight.

Richmond had long stood out from most Southern cities with respect to Black political participation. Black civic leaders created an organization called the Crusade for Voters in 1956 that helped Black voters overcome the state poll tax; in the early 1960s—before the VRA—the Crusade registered more than 15,000 Black voters.[3] When the US Supreme Court struck down Virginia's poll tax in 1966,[4] the Crusade's efforts intensified. By the end of the 1960s, Black voters' political power rivaled that of whites; in 1968, three of the nine city council seats were held by Black officials.[5]

As was often the case in Southern cities experiencing a surge of Black voting and representation after the Voting Rights Act, white elites in Richmond were keen to maintain control. They kept a close eye on registration and voting figures and devised mechanisms to dilute the rising power of Black residents wherever possible. In 1966, white councilors devised a staggered-term scheme whereby the top four vote recipients in council elections would receive four-year terms, while the remaining five seats would be filled for two-year terms. As with many such moves throughout the South, this change was billed as a benign, racially blind reform: The idea was simply that mixing experienced councilors with neophytes would result in better government. However, given the racial makeup of Richmond's electorate, Black candidates were likely to be constantly relegated to the lower tier—with shorter terms.[6] The Crusade ultimately organized opposition to the staggered-term scheme when it was put to voters; after defeating that measure, the Crusade redoubled its organizational efforts and signaled that it would meet future dilution efforts with strength.[7]

White elites recognized that time was running out for them to maintain power in Richmond. In response, the city council turned its attention to neighboring Chesterfield County. If Richmond could annex a part of that county, white councilors knew they could add 47,000 new voters to the city—97% of whom would be white.[8] Richmond had initiated the annexation in 1962, well before the VRA and the Crusade's rise. But after a simultaneous failed annexation of part of Henrico County, the city's effort to acquire Chesterfield had gone dormant by the middle of the decade. Reactivating it presented a convenient path to diluting Black political power in Richmond while offering a plausible denial of intentionally doing so: After years of white flight to the suburbs following school integration orders, the city *did* need to increase its tax revenue.[9] A federal judge later described "a concern not only of the officials of the city and county, but of State officials as well, that the City of Richmond not become a city of the old, the poor and the Black."[10]

The Crusade conceded that Richmond had sound financial reasons for seeking greater tax assessments. Still, the Crusade understood well that the annexation would all but end proportional Black representation on the

Richmond City Council. With so many more white voters, the Crusade stood little chance of electing its candidates in at-large districts. One solution might have been simply moving to nine single-member council districts, which the Crusade did not rule out. However, as a compromise measure the Crusade advocated for a move to five single-member council districts with the remaining four elected at large. Such a shift would have more or less maintained the racial representation in place prior to the annexation,[11] but the Crusade lost this fight. In the 1970 at-large municipal elections, only one Black councilor was elected to the nine-seat body.[12]

In the context of everything we have presented to this point, the bare facts in Richmond seem like a familiar case of Southern whites acting in concert to weaken Black voters' political strength. After all, it is difficult to think of a clearer example of "vote dilution" than adding tens of thousands of overwhelmingly white voters to the city overnight. Given that Richmond was a covered jurisdiction, the annexation begs an obvious question: Why did Richmond fail to submit its annexation plan to the DOJ? The simple answer is that in 1969, the city did not believe it was obligated to preclear changes that were not explicitly linked to elections.

Of course, this belief offered a convenient excuse for municipalities looking to circumvent the VRA, and as we have shown, the Supreme Court in the early 1970s was onto that game. In 1971 the Court would rule in *Perkins v. Matthews* that not only did policies such as polling place locations and shifts from at-large to citywide municipal elections qualify as a "standard, practice, or procedure with respect to voting" under the VRA, but annexations did as well. The majority in *Perkins* reasoned that because changes to municipal boundaries "determin[e] who may vote in city elections through inclusion of certain voters," they hold the power to dilute minority votes. After *Perkins*, there was little doubt that the Court would scrutinize annexations like Richmond's—and would likely do so under the assumption that the city was attempting to circumvent the VRA.

Because *Perkins*—which was decided a year after Richmond's annexation—meant that the city should have precleared the move, Richmond submitted its plan to the Department of Justice retroactively. In May 1971, the DOJ issued an objection. David L. Norman, acting assistant attorney general for the Civil Rights Division, wrote that as long as the city maintained at-large elections, the annexation would have the effect of unlawful vote dilution. Norman encouraged Richmond to "consider means of accomplishing annexation which would avoid producing an impermissible adverse racial impact on voting."[13]

As was standard in all objection letters, Norman also advised Richmond that per the VRA, the city could seek relief in the US District Court for the District of Columbia. Meanwhile, two federal lawsuits challenged the annexation as a violation of the VRA, resulting in a district court blocking Richmond from holding future elections under the new rules. The city council elected in 1970 was frozen in place until the legal questions were settled.

The city availed itself of the opportunity to have its day in court but also continued negotiations with the DOJ. By the time the case reached the Supreme Court, a tentative plan was in place for nine single-member districts for the Richmond City Council: Four contained a large majority of Black voters, four a substantial majority of white voters, and the ninth district broke about 60–40 white. In *City of Richmond v. United States*, the Court found that while the city's initial annexation was an unlawful dilution of Black Richmonders' votes, the proposed move to single-member districts was an adequate remedy.[14] The Court held that the proportion of Black councilors would be approximately equivalent to the Black population within the *new* city boundaries; there was therefore no VRA violation.

The events in Richmond might be seen as an example of the VRA doing its job. The city was ultimately blocked from pursuing the totality of its original plan—which would have harmed Black voters—but was not thwarted from completing a necessary annexation. Still, the facts in *Richmond v. United States* also raised a warning. On its face, an annexation is a routine action of a local government with no direct linkage to elections or voting. But for communities looking to circumvent preclearance, the seeming detachment from elections was the point. What other kinds of moves were they willing to try?

So far, we have told the story of how the Voting Rights Act came into being. Chapter 4 describes how the Supreme Court ultimately struck down the preclearance coverage formula in Section 4(b) of the VRA—thereby also suspending the preclearance power in Section 5—and part II explores the effects of that decision. Before we can describe what happened in the formerly covered jurisdictions *after* the end of preclearance, however, we first focus on the actions that jurisdictions submitted for preclearance while Section 4(b) was in full effect. This chapter therefore leans heavily on data from the Department of Justice, which kept careful records of preclearance while Section 5 was still fully functional.

The DOJ maintains two distinct, publicly available electronic archives of Section 5–related actions. The first is a record of all attempted changes that covered jurisdictions submitted for review between April 1998 and the end of preclearance in June 2013. While this time frame does not reveal a full history of submissions over the entire run of preclearance from the VRA's 1965 passage to 2013, it does contain a complete record of all 70,098 proposals submitted by covered jurisdictions detailing the change(s) they sought to make to their election practices in the final years of preclearance—a period which, as we reveal, the Court weighted heavily in its decision to strike down the coverage formula.[15] Each record contains a unique submission number as well as information about the state, county (if applicable), and subjurisdiction (if applicable) from which the request originated. The records also include basic information about the nature of the requested change(s).[16]

The second archive is a complete record of all 1,084 "objection letters" sent by the Department of Justice over the entire period in which preclearance was in place (1965–2013). This archive contains most of the same information described above, including the requesting jurisdiction and a basic description of the proposed change(s) to which the DOJ objected in the letter. For each objection, the DOJ's archive also includes the letter it sent to the jurisdiction explaining its rationale for not allowing the proposed change.

We compiled the DOJ records in both archives into a database and then programmed a computer to read the requested policy changes and categorize them based on common keywords the DOJ used to describe each proposed change. This method allows the computer to locate all proposed policy changes, even when multiple requests were made in the same submission—and it was quite common for proposals to contain multiple requested policy changes. In the 70,098 proposals we scraped from the Department of Justice's submission archive (1998–2013), we identified at least 146,466 individual changes proposed by state governments, counties, or subcounty jurisdictions such as school or utility districts. Likewise, in the 1,084 objection letters, we identified at least 2,105 specific policies to which the DOJ objected.[17]

In tandem, therefore, these archives provide ample data on the nature of proposed changes to election laws requested by covered jurisdictions between 1998 and 2013, as well as a complete record of policies that the Department of Justice denied during the entire preclearance period. The data allow us to tell a comprehensive story about *when* preclearance requests were submitted, *where* they emerged (i.e., at the state, county, or subcounty level), and the *types* of policies that covered jurisdictions attempted to change. We can also detect differences between the nature of submitted proposals and those that were rejected.

As discussed in chapter 1, there were two distinct types of preclearance under the Voting Rights Act. The first, which is the principal focus of this book, is Section 5 preclearance, requiring that *every* change to a covered jurisdiction's election system be submitted for preclearance. Until the Court struck down the coverage formula in 2013, jurisdictions would remain covered unless they took steps to affirmatively "bail out" of coverage under Section 4(a). But Section 3(c) of the VRA also contains a preclearance condition, and was therefore left intact. If a federal judge finds that a jurisdiction has violated the 14th or 15th Amendment, the court can bail that jurisdiction into Section 3(c) preclearance.

Preclearance resulting from Section 3(c) action is typically more limited than it was for jurisdictions covered by Section 5. Judges tend to use Section 3(c) to mandate preclearance only for specific classes of voting policies in an offending jurisdiction—usually of the same type that had previously been found to violate the Constitution. Judges also typically impose Section 3(c) preclearance only for a limited period of time. Moreover, these powers are usually used sparingly; over the first 60 years of the VRA's life, Section 3(c) coverage has been imposed only 22 times. For the remainder of this chapter, we include proposals submitted for preclearance under both Section 3(c) and Section 5. However, the overwhelming majority of preclearance reviews were conducted under Section 5: Just 26 of the 70,098 preclearance submissions between 1998 and 2013 resulted from Section 3(c) actions, and the DOJ objected to only three of them.[18]

A holistic analysis of preclearance proposals also underscores the likelihood that a great deal of this kind of policy change failed to attract much attention. While major changes such as statewide redistricting or alterations to acceptable voting methods might attract public scrutiny, narrower concerns such as local districting or staggering local commissioner terms were less likely to receive scrutiny from journalists or advocates. A complete understanding of preclearance submissions can therefore provide a useful road map of where to look for jurisdictional actions in the current period that could create burdens on minority voters—much of which, we believe, is likely to fly under the radar.

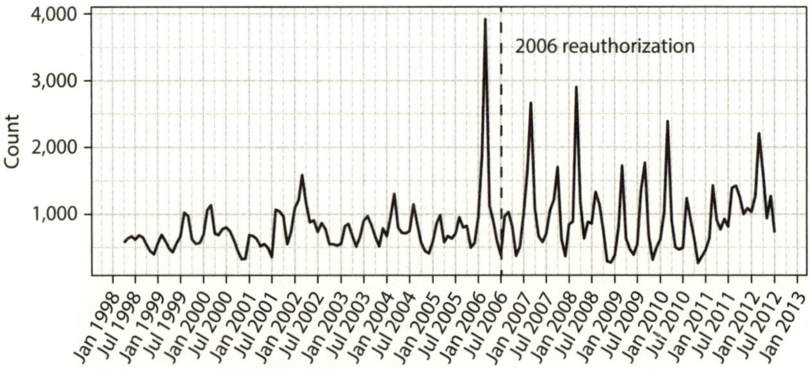

FIGURE 3.1. Election Changes Submitted by Section 4(b)–Covered Jurisdictions, 1998–2013, Binned by Month

We first examine trends in covered jurisdictions' preclearance *submissions* through time, using the data covering the period 1998–2013. Figure 3.1 shows the count of proposed policy changes we identified (irrespective of overall number of proposals) summed by month between October 1998 and the end of preclearance in 2013. The submission volume was cyclical, with clear spikes. It was not uncommon for some months to see a considerably higher number of submissions, with surges above 1,000 requests, especially later in the time series. These busy months typically occurred immediately following the November general election in even-numbered years as jurisdictions evidently sought to strategically maximize the time they had to navigate preclearance and then implement new policies. In comparison to these spikes, the volume of initial requests tends to be much lower earlier in even-numbered calendar years and during years in which there is no federal election.

Still, figure 3.1 reveals a considerable volume of preclearance submissions, even in "slow" months. On average across this time span, the Department of Justice received 407 submissions per month, containing an average of 851 proposed policy changes. This may seem like quite a lot, but there were, after all, *lots* of covered jurisdictions, and election administrators did not universally find the program to be especially onerous. As one North Carolina election administrator explained to the Senate in 2006, "From 'the trenches,' where the people deal on a day-to-day basis with preclearance . . . we do not consider Section 5 [a] burden,"[19] noting that "most submissions are routine matters that take only a few minutes to prepare."[20] In short, figure 3.1 therefore underscores the fact that the DOJ's preclearance attorneys were rarely lacking for work, as the submissions demanded a constant engagement with the minutiae of state, county, and local election laws supplied on a steady drip of mostly mundane changes to election laws.

Other patterns are worth noting in the time series as well. For one, the 2006 reauthorization—the only reauthorization that occurred in this time series—had a clear impact on the manner in which covered jurisdictions navigated preclearance. In the run-up to the July reauthorization (described in the following chapter), a flurry of submission activity occurred. There were 296 submissions in December of 2005, followed by 483, 1,040, and 1,808 in January, February, and March, respectively. This major spike then receded more or less to the baseline by the authorization vote that summer.

At first glance, this surge in preclearance submissions is curious: We might expect that jurisdictions would wait until *after* the reauthorization to submit their election changes. There was, after all, always a chance that Congress would decide to change the coverage formula or otherwise soften the VRA. There was even a chance, in the wishful eyes of election administrators in many covered jurisdictions, that Congress would simply refuse to reauthorize preclearance at all.

But, if election administrators were using history as a guide, they had little reason to believe that a weakened preclearance system would come to pass. To the contrary, as shown in chapter 2, in prior reauthorizations Congress had moved toward an ever *stronger* preclearance regime. Moreover, the three VRA reauthorizations prior to 2006 had shown that members of Congress could be quite resilient in extending the law, even against fierce political headwinds. For administrators who understood this history, the incentives therefore pointed to submitting their changes prior to the reauthorization instead of waiting it out. Better, they likely thought, to deal with "the devil you know." Regardless, figure 3.1 shows that administrators were clearly responsive to expected changes in the regulatory environment.

Another, more subtle shift in the time series occurred around the 2006 reauthorization as well. The overall trend in figure 3.1 offers no definitive evidence that the typical number of submissions changed after the reauthorization; that is, we do not see a clear upward trend in the line. This indicates that the volume of submissions that the DOJ handled was more or less consistent over time—at least in a typical month. That said, we do see some evidence that the typical post-November submission crush was more substantial later in the time series after the 2006 reauthorization. If anything, covered jurisdictions were making more efforts to change their election policies

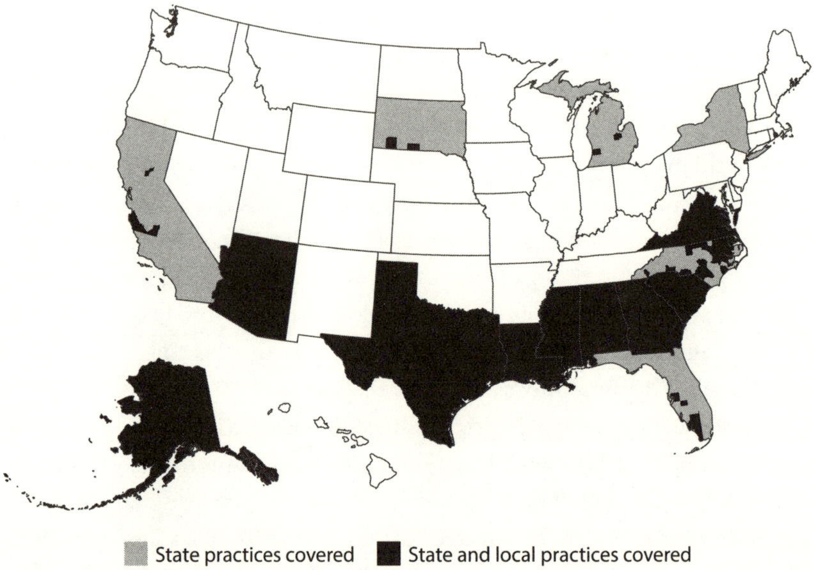

FIGURE 3.2. County Coverage Status as of June 25, 2013

immediately after each election in the late 2000s and early 2010s than in the decade before. In short, figure 3.1 suggests that the Justice Department was receiving as many preclearance proposals as ever at the time Section 5 was struck down.

Next, we look at where these submissions came from. Table 3.1 shows the number of requests initiated in each state, the state's coverage status (full or partial), and the percentage of requests originating at each level of government. Once again, we present the number of requested policy changes we identified, rather than a count of proposals. The state's coverage status is an important consideration because in fully covered states, *all* proposals that would have affected *any* election were subject to preclearance review. In partially covered states, only statewide policies or those in covered jurisdictions were sent to DOJ for preclearance. For clarity, in figure 3.2, we show the coverage status of regions around the nation as of 2013, the last moment when preclearance was operative.

With this distinction in mind, it is not surprising that Texas is the clear leader in terms of preclearance proposals submitted between 1998 and 2013, responsible for about half of the volume that the DOJ handled during this period. Not only is Texas the most populous Southern state, but it also has 254 counties and myriad sub-jurisdictions, all subject to preclearance due to

TABLE 3.1. Proposed Election Changes by Section 4(b)–Covered Jurisdictions, April 1998–June 2013, by State, with Percentage of Proposals Emerging from State, County, or Subcounty Level

State	Coverage Status	Proposal Count	% State	% County	% Subcounty
Texas	Full	73,993	1	13	86.1
Georgia	Full	18,150	2.3	35.2	62.5
Louisiana	Full	12,317	5.2	23.3	71.5
Arizona	Full	8,345	8.2	11.3	80.5
Alabama	Full	7,418	3.5	21.6	75
South Carolina	Full	6,603	2.4	24.2	73.4
Mississippi	Full	4,515	8.1	33.8	58.1
Virginia	Full	4,373	14.2	51.2	34.5
North Carolina	Partial	4,340	6.9	31.2	62
Alaska	Full	2,149	15.7	21.8	62.4
California	Partial	2,139	25.1	15.5	59.4
Florida	Partial	966	16.8	18.5	64.7
New York	Partial	532	24.8	66.7	8.5
New Hampshire*	Partial	323	96.3	3.7	0
South Dakota	Partial	148	57.4	42.6	0
Michigan	Partial	137	41.6	10.9	47.4
New Mexico*	Full	14	7.1	92.9	0
Arkansas*	Full	4	100	0	0
Total	Partial	146,466	4	20.2	75.9

*Not impacted by *Shelby County v. Holder*. Ten New Hampshire towns were covered by Sections 4(b) and 5 following the 1970 reauthorization, but were bailed out under Section 4(a) in early 2013. New Mexico was bailed into Section 3(c) preclearance in 1990, and bailed out in 2000; five New Mexico counties were also bailed into Section 3(c) preclearance during the 1980s and 1990s. Arkansas was bailed into Section 3(c) preclearance in 1991, though only for "laws, standards, or practices designed to enforce or enhance a majority-vote requirement."

Texas's fully covered status. It therefore makes sense that fully covered states occupy the top next seven ranks as well—and nine of the top ten spots.

Table 3.1 also shows the percentage of requests that were tied to either a county or a sub-jurisdiction below the county level. Examples of sub-jurisdictions include municipalities, school districts, utility districts, and other similar entities with oversight over some aspect of elections. Table 3.1 reveals the often hyper-local nature of preclearance requests, especially in fully covered states. For instance, in Texas, only 1% of requests emerged from the state itself. Another 13% of proposals came from county governments, which

TABLE 3.2. Proposed Election Changes by Section 4(b)–Covered Jurisdictions, April 1998–June 2013

Proposed Change	Count	Percent
Administration	95,577	65.3
Districting/Boundaries	36,804	25.1
Method of Election	6,918	4.7
Terms of Office	3,105	2.1
Voter Registration/Roll	2,190	1.5
Candidate Qualifications	1,193	0.8
Other	679	0.5
Total	146,466	100

Note: There were 70,098 submissions containing 146,597 distinct policy changes during this time period. We collect the requested changes into seven distinct categories, which reduces the total number of requests to 85,881. For instance, if a jurisdiction requested to change compensation *and* term length for an office on the same proposal, here that counts only as a single effort to change terms of office. The Justice Department preempted 84 of the 70,098 submissions (0.1%).

especially in Texas may themselves be quite small and/or heavily rural. The vast majority of proposals in Texas and most other states, however, originate from jurisdictions *below* the county level. In total, our analysis of the submission data shows that most proposed election law changes emerge in places that, due to their small size and lack of dedicated constituency, may not attract attention from media or other observers.

Finally, we examine the content of the proposals. In table 3.2, we show counts of the types of policy proposals requested by covered jurisdictions between 1998 and 2013, gathered into six broad categories that emerged from the DOJ's classification system. Changes that can be categorized as "administrative" compose a majority of the policies that covered jurisdictions sought. These proposals include those that refer to changes in "election procedures" or to the timing or manner of specific types of elections, such as primaries, special elections, or referenda. The next most frequently requested policy type was geographical in nature, relating to districts (legislative, judicial, municipal council, and the like), the boundaries of towns (via annexations or deannexations), or the shape of electoral precincts. Together, administrative and geographical requests amount to about 90% of all proposed policy changes.

While they constitute a smaller percentage of policy proposals than those in the two leading categories, a number of other policy types are still well represented in absolute terms, with more than 1,000 attempted changes taking place between 1998 and 2013. For instance, changes to the method of election—such as moving from a plurality to majority system—account for nearly 5% of proposal requests. Changes to the terms of office, like implementing staggered terms for city councilors or the length of term a school board member serves, account for 2.1% of requests. Alterations to voter registration, voter lists, and related items (such as removing voters from the rolls) make up a similar proportion of overall requests. And, finally, proposed adjustments to candidate qualifications, such as residency or age requirements, compose about 0.8% of the total volume. Overall, table 3.2 indicates that, while most proposals can be categorized as relating primarily to broad administrative or geographical concerns, covered jurisdictions sought a fairly wide range of policy changes.

The picture we obtain from the submission data is one of constant changes to election policies in covered jurisdictions. This is not inherently a problem; after all, election administration is a complicated and ever-evolving task. However, the sheer volume of this activity makes clear the potential for racial discrimination (intentional or otherwise) to go unnoticed unless someone is paying close attention. We also show that these policies are most often enacted at the municipal level and frequently occupy arcane areas of election administration. They are, in other words, just the sort of changes that could disenfranchise minority voters without attracting a great deal of attention and are reminiscent of the facts that fueled a number of the court cases we have described so far. Preclearance was designed to stop policies that infringed on voters' 15th Amendment rights, no matter how small the jurisdiction that implements the problematic policy. Next, we analyze the submissions that the DOJ *blocked* to see whether similar patterns emerge.

Important features of the objection data affect how we present them here. For instance, given the smaller number of objections (compared to submissions), figure 3.3 shows objection counts for every year (instead of month) that preclearance was in effect. In addition, unlike the proposal data, the objection records also refer not only to the policy content of the rejected proposal but, often, also to the *number* of such policies in the rejected proposal. A town's planned annexation of 47 distinct outlying tracts would be designated as a single "annexation" in the proposal record. If it objected to some aspect of the

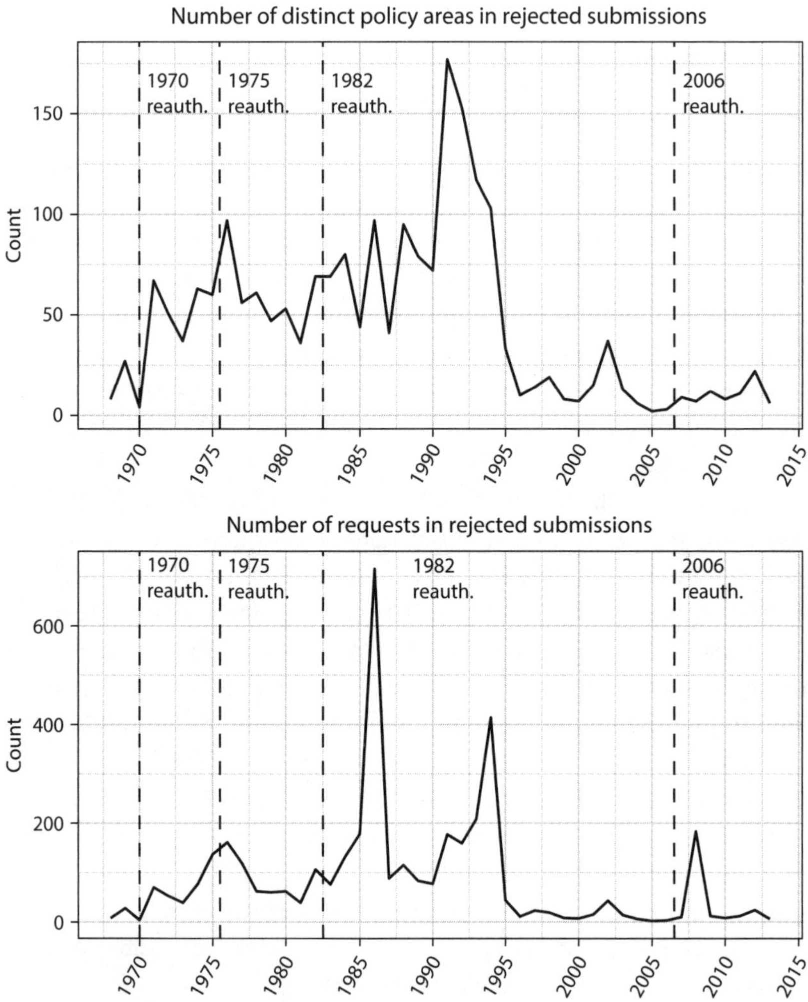

FIGURE 3.3. Election Changes Submitted by Section 4(b)–Covered Jurisdictions Blocked by the Department of Justice, 1965–2013, by Year

annexation however, the DOJ would typically view each tract as a separate annexation; sometimes reviewers would log an objection to all of them, and other times just a few. In describing rejection trends, we might therefore show counts of each policy *area* (as we do with proposals above), or the *number* of policies that the DOJ cited in its objection.

Figure 3.3 depicts both metrics. The figure's top pane shows the trend in the number of policy *areas* that DOJ reviewers referred to in their objection, regardless of how many individual changes were objected to. The bottom pane shows the number of distinct requests rejected in each proposal. To be clear, if the DOJ objected to 10 tracts in an annexation plan proposing the annexation of 47 tracts, this would be counted as a single annexation in the top pane and 10 blocked annexations in the pane below. Similarly, an objection to a request to annex two tracts and redistrict both city council and school board districts would be counted as one annexation request and one redistricting request in the top pane, and two of each in the bottom pane. These examples should make clear that with either metric, it is common for a single objection letter to count as more than one rejection in our data, because in that letter the DOJ might express misgivings about a number of policy proposals. Finally, given that the two panes of Figure 3.3 reflect different quantities of interest, readers should also note the disparate ranges of the two y-axes.

The bottom pane of figure 3.3 reveals that, with some notable exceptions, the raw number of rejected proposals was fairly consistent over time. The most obvious of these exceptions is an objection to the city of Summerville, South Carolina's request that the DOJ retroactively approve 649 annexations it had completed between 1964 and 1985; the DOJ objected to 572 (by our estimate) of these annexations in 1986.[21] Similarly, by our count, the DOJ blocked approximately 414 policies in 1994; the vast majority of these came from one objection to a similar retroactive annexation request from Shreveport, Louisiana. In the Shreveport objection, the DOJ did not log the exact number of requested annexations, instead describing "hundreds" of annexations as objectionable.[22] We have therefore estimated the number of blocked annexations at 300. These cases are the only two in which we had to guess as to the number of requests the DOJ found objectionable.[23] Overall, then, in the case of both Summerville and Shreveport, the jurisdictions' failure to obtain preclearance for the entirety of their annexations explains the large spikes. Ignoring those spikes, we see that the number of rejected proposed changes in the late 1990s settling in at a slightly lower level than the period prior to the 1982 reauthorization—a point we return to below.

Of the two metrics shown in figure 3.3, the number of policy areas noted in each objection (depicted in the top pane) is more directly comparable to the patterns in submissions we describe above. Examining that trend line, we see that the number of proposals blocked in a given year was *always* quite low compared to the number of proposals we reported earlier, indicating a very low rejection rate in the preclearance process. We cannot calculate the objection rate for the entire time series due to lack of data availability for policy proposals prior to 1998. However, we can say that comparing the number of submissions against the number of rejection letters—regardless of how many policy proposals were contained therein—between 1998 and 2013, the DOJ objected to some aspect of only 0.12% of preclearance proposals.[24] As we describe below, this latter period saw the smallest number of objections observable in the time series, so the rejection rate we are able to calculate probably reflects a historic low point. Yet, even in the earlier period of the time series, it was rare for a single year to see 100 rejections, leading us to conclude that the rejection rate was likely never substantial.

The relatively low rejection rate notwithstanding, we can observe several apparent structural breaks in the time series, suggesting distinct epochs in the way the DOJ approached preclearance. For instance, we see that relatively few proposals were blocked in the immediate aftermath of the VRA's passage; until 1970, no year saw more than 30 objections. That year coincided with both the expansion of Section 5's purview thanks to *Allen* and the 1970 reauthorization, which covered more jurisdictions under Section 4(b). It also marks a break in the time series, with the number of annual objections gradually rising through the next reauthorization in 1975, which expanded the coverage list. Then, objections gradually declined before spiking again in advance of the 1982 reauthorization.

For the remainder of the 1980s, we see a period of relative stasis before another spike in the early 1990s. Notably, this spike coincided with the 1992 Voting Rights Language Assistance Act, which extended the language protections codified in Section 203 of the VRA until 2006. It also reflects the submission of new district maps in the aftermath of the 1990 census. After a peak of 177 policies drawing objections in 1991, we again observe a decline into the previously mentioned period of relative stasis from the late 1990s to 2013—with the exception of a brief flurry of activity coinciding with the 2002 redistricting cycle.

In total, then, the top pane of figure 3.3 shows that, especially early on, preclearance activity moved in response to reauthorization activity. This may be taken as providing evidence either that the various reauthorizations affected how the DOJ approached its preclearance work, or that jurisdictions submitted more problematic regulations in the run-up to anticipated congressional action. Regardless, the reauthorizations clearly played a role in shaping objection patterns.

Finally, as alluded to above—and as we also found when we examined the count of distinct policies—figure 3.3 also indicates that the DOJ objected to fewer policies in the later years of preclearance (after the mid-1990s) than it had in earlier decades. We cannot fully account for this disparity. It could be that covered jurisdictions learned the boundaries of preclearance in the VRA's early years and were less likely to push them later on. Alternatively, maybe the DOJ simply grew more complacent in issuing rejections. Or perhaps some combination of these or other forces were at work.

Additional data might shed at least some light on the underlying dynamics here. The formal power of Section 5 was most obvious in the policies that were blocked following an objection from the Department of Justice or the DC circuit court. However, preclearance reviewers also exercised what we might call soft power, as well, in that they could do more than just object to a policy: Reviewers could also request more information from the submitting jurisdiction before they made a decision. Jurisdictions understood that receiving an "additional information request" indicated that in the DOJ's view, the original submission had not included enough detail to prove that the proposal would not disproportionately harm voters of color.

Often, jurisdictions would respond by providing this information, allowing preclearance reviewers to assess the implications and complete their review. But, other times, jurisdictions would react by changing, withdrawing, or abandoning their proposals altogether—likely in the belief that the information request signaled that the policy would ultimately not pass muster with the reviewers.[25] In such cases, there is a bit of a gray area when it comes to identifying policies to which the DOJ "objected." While no formal objection would exist for such cases in our data, it can be argued that the jurisdiction ultimately did not implement a policy it had sought as a direct result of DOJ action—and that the requested policies would have been implemented in the absence of preclearance.

To understand the role of these additional information requests, we requested and received data from the Department of Justice about every policy for which preclearance reviewers ever requested more information.[26] Importantly, these data allow us to see what happened *after* the DOJ made the request. Most of the time (in about 78% of cases), the jurisdiction submitted the information and the DOJ did not object to the policy. However, the objection rate was considerably higher for policies that the DOJ requested more information for than for others. Although, as noted above, the DOJ objected to considerably fewer than 1% of *all* proposals in the final years of preclearance, the objection rate exceeded 7% for the policies for which reviewers requested and received more information.

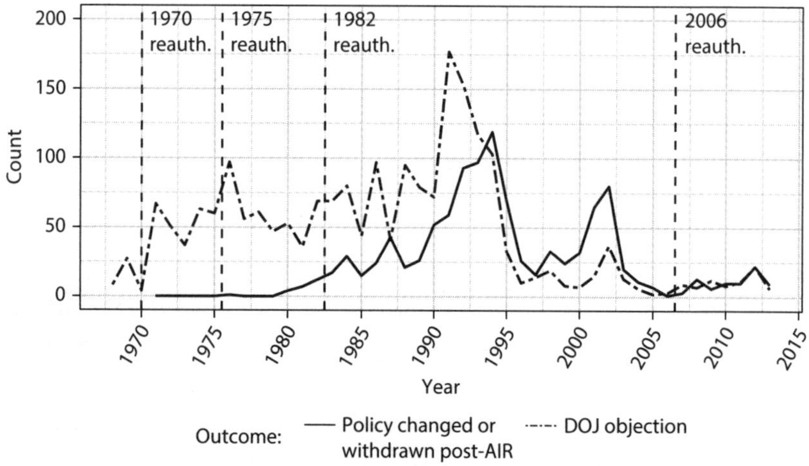

FIGURE 3.4. Formal Objections and Additional Information Request (AIR)–Induced Policy Changes, 1965–2013, by Year
Note: "Year" refers either to the year of the objection letter or that of the last action taken for a given submission for which additional information was requested.

That said, the number of policies that were *changed* or *withdrawn* following a request for more information was even higher. In figure 3.4, we replot the number of distinct policies to which the DOJ formally objected, along with those that were informally stopped by preclearance review, that is, those that were amended or withdrawn following an additional information request. The figure makes clear that in the early years, the number of policies to which the DOJ formally objected was much larger than the number of those altered in response to an information request. In the 1980s and 1990s, however, the number of policies informally altered after information requests rose considerably. And in the last two decades before *Shelby County* was decided, nearly 50% more policies were stopped through this informal process than were formally blocked (673 versus 462). In total, jurisdictions changed, withdrew, or abandoned more than 1,000 proposed policies after the Department of Justice requested more information from them. Some of the withdrawals appear in DOJ objection records, but most do not. Thus, any analysis of formal objections alone (including ours) likely understates the true impact of VRA preclearance: The number of policies stopped by the preclearance review is considerably higher than what the number of formal DOJ objections would imply.

TABLE 3.3. Election Changes Submitted by Section 4(b)–Covered Jurisdictions Blocked by the Department of Justice, 1965–2013, by State, with Percentage of Proposals Tied to Counties and/or Subcounty Jurisdictions

State	Objection Count	% State	% County	% Subcounty
Texas	394	9.6	23.6	68.3
Georgia	386	10.4	27.7	61.9
Louisiana	324	31.5	37.7	30.9
Mississippi	278	14	55.8	30.2
South Carolina	221	10.9	31.7	57.5
Alabama	196	15.3	44.9	42.3
North Carolina	147	15.6	26.5	57.8
Virginia	55	18.2	43.6	38.2
Arizona	45	17.8	33.3	48.9
Florida	18	38.9	61.1	0
New York	17	29.4	5.9	64.7
California	13	0	76.9	23.1
South Dakota	6	0	100	0
Michigan	2	0	0	100
New Mexico*	2	100	0	0
Alaska	1	100	0	0
Total	2,105	15.6	35.2	49.7

*Not impacted by *Shelby County v. Holder*. New Mexico was bailed into Section 3(c) preclearance in 1990, and bailed out in 2000; five New Mexico counties were also bailed into Section 3(c) preclearance during the 1980s and 1990s.

This fact notwithstanding, still other important information can be gleaned from the objection records. In table 3.3, we show the political geography of these objections, just as we did for submissions above. Here, however, we show only a count of the distinct policy areas receiving rejections (the same metric shown in the top pane of figure 3.3), rather than the number of such policies in the submission. Again, several interesting results emerge. First, as was true in our submissions data, Texas, Georgia, and Louisiana occupy the first through third ranks, respectively, in the number of objections. This finding might be expected; the more submissions a state initiates, the more objections we should probably expect. Despite being in seventh place in our late-term submissions data, however, Mississippi comes in *fourth* for the number of objections. This may indicate that Mississippi was submitting more problematic policies and therefore climbed the rejection rankings despite a relatively modest number of proposed changes.

Of course, this pattern may also indicate that Mississippi proposed more policy changes prior to the period in which we can observe that quantity (which begins in 1998) and slowed its submission rate thereafter. The fact that the rankings for states other than Mississippi in the submission data (1998–2013) and the objections data (1965–2013) align fairly closely, however, leads us to suspect that jurisdictions in Mississippi were significantly more likely to have a policy blocked than those in other states. And, indeed, when we limit the objection data only to the period that overlaps with the submissions data we have (1998–2013), Mississippi remains in third place. We therefore conclude that, compared to other covered states, Mississippi and its subordinate jurisdictions were disproportionately more likely to submit proposals that the DOJ ultimately blocked.

Table 3.3 also indicates that in all but two cases (Alaska and New Mexico), a large majority of objections were directed at policies submitted by jurisdictions below the state level. Taking the example of Texas once more, more than 90% of objections were to substate jurisdictions' proposals. For only one state in the top six is this figure less than 80%, and aside from the two states mentioned above, it is higher than 60% in all others. Thus, once again, we see that a great deal of the action with respect to Section 4(b) occurred around policies that may have escaped close media scrutiny: The smaller the jurisdiction, the more proposals blocked.

Finally, we consider the blocked policies themselves. Table 3.4 shows the frequency of objections, using the same policy classification scheme described above. There are some key differences apparent in table 3.4 relative to the pattern we observed for overall proposals in table 3.2, however. For instance, whereas administrative changes constituted a majority of *submissions* between 1998 and 2013, when we examine the entire objection time series, we see that proposals falling into that category account for only 12.2% of objections. Instead, proposals related to some aspect of political geography—such as apportionment, districting, or annexations—amount to more than half of all objections. Changes in the method of election are the second most rejected category but lag boundary changes by more than 40 points. Changes to terms of office compose a percentage of the rejection pool slightly lower than that of administrative changes, while shifts in candidate

TABLE 3.4. Election Changes Submitted by Section 4(b)–Covered Jurisdictions Blocked by the Department of Justice, 1965–2013

Proposed Change	Count	Percent
Districting/Boundaries	1,174	55.8
Method of Election	292	13.9
Administration	257	12.2
Terms of Office	217	10.3
Candidate Qualifications	82	3.9
Voter Registration/Roll	73	3.5
Other	10	0.5
Total	2,105	100

Our efforts to code objections located 1,084 distinct objections issued by the Department of Justice during the period in which Section 4b of the Voting Rights Act was in effect, spanning nearly 1,400 unique submission IDs. These rejections include requests from states, counties, and subcounty jurisdictions and cover at least 3,978 distinct policy proposals, using the broadest possible classification criteria. Here we bin the requested changes into seven distinct categories. Before we do so, we first count only the granular *type* of policy in each rejected submission (as defined by the DOJ), *regardless of how many policy changes in each category were requested.* This step reduces the total number of rejected policy "types" to 2,105. For instance, if a town requested 16 separate annexations *and* new city council and school board districts, here that counts only as a single annexation effort and a single districting request, adding two to the count in the "Districting/Boundaries" category.

qualifications or voter registration procedures each comprise less than 4% of objections.

On the whole, our analysis sheds light on the massive scale of preclearance occurring under Section 5 of the Voting Rights Act. Understanding both what jurisdictions attempted to do and what they were prohibited from doing yields important information about where to look if we are to gain a holistic picture of how policy changes at all levels of government have affected American elections. This is true not only for the period covering the peak of the VRA's power but also for the time since preclearance ended.

The sheer number of policies being proposed at the county or local level makes clear just how diffuse electoral policy making is in the United States. While scholars have recognized the importance of the 50 different *state*-level regimes for democratic access in recent years,[27] an overwhelming majority of proposed electoral changes in the covered states between 1998 and 2013 came from one of many thousands of counties, towns, or school boards. This highly distributed system makes the importance of federal oversight clear, especially in an era of declining local news media.[28] Preclearance balanced this system in areas with known histories of discrimination by allowing local administrators to run their elections as they saw fit so long as they could demonstrate that their decisions would not harm minority voters. Absent federal oversight, these administrators are now free to do whatever they wish, with only subsequent litigation to decide the legality of their actions.

The results we report in this chapter also shed light on the type of policies that jurisdictions submitted for preclearance, as well as those that were blocked. We find that geography-related changes such as districting or apportionment account for a majority of the objections, despite constituting only about one-quarter of submissions (at least in the latter preclearance period for which we have data). We also find that hundreds of objections were issued for more mundane changes, such as implementing staggered terms or changing the terms of a county office. Especially since they tend to originate from county or local governments, in contrast to the splashy statewide voting laws that have garnered significant media attention in recent years, these policies may escape significant scrutiny. Broad changes to statewide policies are likely to draw criticism and court challenges that could result in a reduction of their deleterious effects. Changes to the election procedures in a rural school district, however, may attract less (or even no) such attention. As such, with preclearance removed, these policies may be more likely to be enacted—even if they burden minority voters in a way that would not have passed preclearance with the DOJ.

Our results also make clear that the prophylactic nature of Section 5 review extended well beyond the policies to which the Department of Justice formally interposed an objection. We also examine the number of policies that were changed, withdrawn, or abandoned after the DOJ signaled that it would take a closer look at the proposal. In the final years of preclearance, the number of policies that were "informally" stopped via these information requests was considerably higher than the number of policies formally blocked from going into effect. All told, we estimate that the preclearance review processes stopped thousands of illegal policies during the decades during which it operated.

The data we present in this chapter, however, probably represent only the lower bound of the VRA's impact. As mentioned in chapter 1, coverage under Section 4(b) also opened jurisdictions to additional potential federal oversight of their elections, found under Sections 6 and 8 of the act.[29] If a jurisdiction was covered under Section 4(b) *and* the attorney General determined it was necessary, the Office of Personnel Management would send "federal observers" authorized to enter the jurisdiction's polling places.[30] While they were prohibited from interfering with the election in any fashion,[31] the observers were required to file a report with the DOJ afterward detailing what they saw. In these reports the observers were required to describe conditions such as the race of and languages spoken by poll workers, the configuration of the polling place, and the hours during which the polling place was functionally open.[32] During the 2006 reauthorization, Congress recognized the important supplementary role the observer program played in preclearance, noting that observer reports would "often become the foundation of Department of Justice enforcement efforts" and were "instrumental in enabling Federal prosecutors to proceed against county officials for discriminatory conduct against African Americans in polling locations."[33]

Although these federal observers did not stop discriminatory practices in the same way as Section 5, administrators' knowledge that they would be observed might nevertheless have constrained them from carrying out discriminatory election procedures. This would obviously not be reflected in the administrative records that we analyze in this chapter, even if the observers substantially reduced illegal election administration. With the invalidation of the coverage formula, however, the federal observers were no longer authorized.

By removing both the prophylactic effect of preclearance and the federal observer program, the effects of *Shelby County* extend beyond formally stopping policies under Section 5. Now, freed from preclearance and the possibility of observers, we might expect jurisdictions to pursue a faster pace of changes that could disproportionately impact minority voters, potentially escaping the attention of even the most engaged watchdogs. We return to this point in part II. But first, we must describe how preclearance—which we show to have been a vigorous means of federal oversight of election practices—ultimately met its demise.

4

Chops on the Log

THE END OF PRECLEARANCE

> Things have changed in the South. Voter turnout and registration rates now approach parity. Blatantly discriminatory evasions of federal decrees are rare. And minority candidates hold office at unprecedented levels. These improvements are no doubt due in significant part to the Voting Rights Act itself, and stand as a monument to its success. Past success alone, however, is not adequate justification to retain the preclearance requirements.
>
> —CHIEF JUSTICE JOHN ROBERTS, *NORTHWEST AUSTIN MUNICIPAL UTILITY DISTRICT NUMBER ONE V. HOLDER*[1]

THE PORT city of Mobile was booming in the first decade of the twentieth century, growing more than 33% over those ten years and solidifying its position as Alabama's second largest municipality, with just over 50,000 residents.[2] Yet this growth belied stark racial divisions in the community that were reflected in its political organization. The city's population was about one-third Black, and its neighborhoods were heavily segregated. Mobile had implemented ward elections during Reconstruction that allowed voters from the various sections of the city to elect representatives; this system resulted in the election of several Black councilors who represented areas of the city with a majority-Black population.

Backlash soon followed. Conservative Republicans allied with Democrats as early as 1870 to advance policies that would diminish Black residents' power in Mobile. In some cases it was at least possible to argue—if disingenuously—that the motivation for the new policies was something other than what it was. Mobile's shift away from neighborhood wards to at-large elections in which all councilors were elected from the city's majority-white population could be spun as a move toward more efficient municipal government, even as it foreclosed the possibility for Black residents to elect Black candidates. The true purpose of Mobile's overhaul, however, was more clearly illustrated in its implementation of the nation's first "white primary," in which only white residents were allowed to participate.[3]

The new rules did their job, allowing white residents of Mobile to consolidate control of their city government. This shift was broadly consistent with contemporary actions in other communities throughout Alabama. In 1901 Alabama Democrats convened to author a new constitution for the state. Attorney John B. Knox was elected as the convention's president, and his opening remarks left little doubt as to the meeting's objectives:

> In my judgment, the people of Alabama have been called upon to face no more important situation than now confronts us, unless it be when they, in 1861, stirred by the momentous issues of impending conflict between the North and the South, were forced to decide whether they would remain in or withdraw from the Union. Then, as now, the negro was the prominent factor in the issue. The Southern people, with this grave problem of the races to deal with, are face-to-face with a new epoch in Constitution-making, the difficulties of which are great, but which, if solved wisely, may bring rest and peace and happiness. If otherwise, it may leave us and our posterity continuously involved in race conflicts, or, what may be worse, subjected permanently to the baneful influences of the political conditions now prevailing in the State.
>
> So long as the negro remains an insignificant minority, and votes the Republican ticket, our friends in the North tolerate him with complacency, but there is not a Northern State, and I might go further and say there is not an intelligent white man in the North, not gangrened by sectional prejudice and hatred of the South, who would consent for a single day to submit to negro rule. . . . One has studied the history of recent events to very little purpose who has failed to discover that race prejudice exists at the North in as pronounced a form as at the South, and that the question of negro domination, when brought home, will arouse the same opposition in either direction.
>
> And what is it that we want to do? Why, it is, within the limits imposed by the Federal Constitution, to establish white supremacy in this State.[4]

True to this mission, the convention produced a new Alabama constitution that guaranteed segregated public schools, outlawed interracial marriage, and implemented several tests and devices intended to disenfranchise Black voters, including a poll tax, literacy tests, and a grandfather clause. A statewide white primary soon followed. By 1909 these devices had done their appointed work: All but 4,000 Black voters had been purged from Alabama's voter rolls; 193 of those who remained lived in Mobile.[5] Perhaps emboldened by this success, in 1907 the Alabama legislature reorganized municipal government, requiring single-member-district election of aldermen. Mobile was forced to return to ward elections.

Although few Black voters remained on the rolls, race continued to play a prominent role in the 1908 Mobile elections, as incumbent mayor Pat Lyons faced accusations of having attempted to curry favor among the Black voters who had maintained eligibility. His opponents rushed to defend white-only primaries. In a May 15, 1908, letter to the editor of the *Mobile Register,* a resident lauded the white primary as an effective mechanism to keep Black voters from participating, which in turn would tamp down any ambition they had for elected office themselves: "The Negro, if not ambitious, is as mimetic as his Darwinian prototype. Admitted to the full Democratic communion table in Mobile, what assures against his claim to sit at [its] head: what forbids in the law of logic his demand to be put upon its tickets, or even to head them?"[6] Lyons's critics' suspicions seemed to be confirmed when the mayor was reelected in 1908, with one of his principal allies winning election from a majority-Black ward. To them, the experiment with ward elections had supposedly proved that even the small remaining Black vote was enough to influence elections in Mobile.

Frederick Bromberg was a prominent Mobile citizen. He represented the city in Congress in the 1870s and had recently completed a term as president of the Alabama Bar Association. Bromberg opposed ward elections and advocated for a return to an at-large council system as a means to keep Black voters' power at bay. On July 25, 1909, Bromberg went further, authoring an open letter to the Alabama legislature that plainly communicated views shared by many white voters in Mobile. His central desire was to amend "the state constitution so as to exclude negroes from holding elective offices in this state." As John Knox had done at the 1901 constitutional convention, Bromberg exhibited a great deal of candor: "We have always, as you know, falsely pretended that our main purpose was to exclude the ignorant vote, when, in fact, we were trying to exclude not the ignorant vote, but the negro vote."[7] Bromberg's letter admitted that seemingly race-blind policies often cloaked deeper, racist motivations.

Mobile wanted the freedom to devise a municipal government that would permanently sideline Black political power. Until 1911 Alabama law limited most cities to a mayor-council form of government in which an elected mayor wields executive power and a city council maintains legislative authority. That year, however, the Alabama legislature bowed to pressure from cities like Mobile by relaxing the mayor-council requirement. Large municipalities would be able to shift to a commission form wherein commissioners elected at large would share executive and legislative duties over certain areas of the city's affairs. Mobile promptly made this change, implementing a three-person commission. Each of the three commissioners would be responsible for one key municipal department (Public Works, Public Safety, or Finance). Because their responsibilities now affected the entire city instead of a smaller part of it, Mobile's commissioners would be elected not from neighborhood wards but from the city at large. Proponents of the shift characterized it as a move toward more efficient, transparent government, but Frederick Bromberg and John Knox had let the mask slip. No Black candidate would be elected in Mobile for the following seventy years.

Into the early 1970s, as previous chapters show, the Supreme Court was an able partner as Congress wielded regulatory authority over covered states' elections not only in the original 1965 act but also in two subsequent reauthorizations. As the new decade set in, this trend seemed poised to continue. In its 1973 decision in *White v. Regester*, the Court found that multimember districts drawn in two Texas counties diluted minority voters' power by making the path to election more difficult for candidates of color.[8] In that ruling, the majority relied on an examination of the "totality of circumstances" in a community—its history of racial disenfranchisement, the extent to which segregation lingered, and similar factors—to rule that the multimember districts were conceived as a vehicle for minority vote dilution. Considering these circumstances allowed the Court to make a reasonable inference that the districts were designed with discriminatory intent, even if no evidence of such intent was readily available. In short, if questionable election practices were implemented in areas with a long history of discrimination, the *Regester* ruling meant that a court might conclude that if its election practices resulted

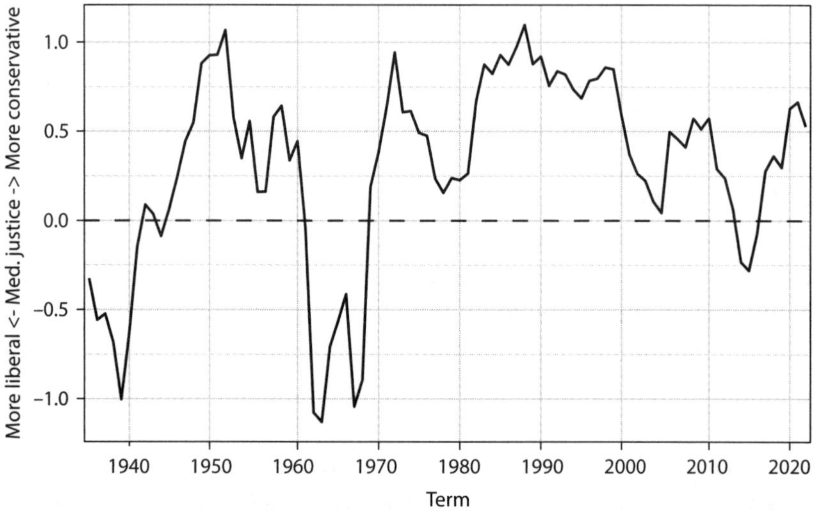

FIGURE 4.1. Median Supreme Court Justice's Ideal Point, by Term, 1937–2022. Martin-Quinn scores taken from the 2022 court data. See Martin and Quinn (2002).

in diminished power for minority voters, it was probably not by accident.[9] This was another win for a vigorous VRA, but to the keen observer, there was reason to believe that the Court's permissive stance toward congressional authority over state election practices might wane as the 1970s progressed.

Researchers Andrew D. Martin and Kevin M. Quinn have developed methods to use Supreme Court justices' behavior on the bench to derive an ideological score that positions them in a single-dimensional space.[10] These "ideal points" can be interpreted as a justice's preferred location on a liberal-conservative scale in each term: More negative scores indicate more liberal justices, and more positive ones are consistent with more conservative preferences. In figure 4.1, we use Martin and Quinn's data to depict the median justice's ideal point for each Supreme Court term from 1937 to 2022. That is, in a given term, half of the justices would be to the median justice's left, and the other half on that justice's right. Examining the location of the median justice can therefore yield insight into the ideological leanings of the Court as a whole.

Figure 4.1 yields an important insight: The Supreme Court of the 1960s, led by Chief Justice Earl Warren, was a historically liberal institution, with a median ideal point comparable only to the post–New Deal era in the time series for which we have data. It should therefore come as no surprise that throughout the 1960s, the Supreme Court took an expansive view of permissible congressional powers in state elections. The 1970s brought new faces onto the Court, however. Republican presidents Nixon and Ford jointly appointed four justices between 1970 and 1975 to backfill departures from the Warren Court. Harry Blackmun ended up shifting to the left during his time on the Court, but Martin and Quinn's data indicate that Blackmun began his tenure as a reliable conservative. When he took the judicial oath in 1970, Blackmun replaced Abe Fortas, a well-known liberal whose nomination as chief justice had failed four years earlier due to a combination of anti-Semitism and objections among some US senators to Fortas's left-leaning views. Likewise, the conservative Lewis Powell replaced center-left justice Hugo Black in 1972, moving that position on the court to the right as well.[11]

The same day Powell took his seat, an arguably even more consequential change occurred when Nixon replaced the retiring Associate Justice John Marshall Harlan II with William H. Rehnquist. Although both justices were conservative, Martin and Quinn's data indicate that Rehnquist was much more so in his first term than Harlan had been in his last. Indeed, Rehnquist found himself to the right of most justices on most matters. On his arrival at the Supreme Court, Rehnquist was nicknamed the "Lone Ranger" because his positions often attracted few allies. As a young clerk to Justice Robert Jackson in the 1950s, Rehnquist had argued that the "separate but equal" standard allowing segregation in *Plessy v. Ferguson* was good law,[12] and also wrote a memo to Jackson in favor of white primaries in which he laid out a view of civil rights that would almost certainly have been too extreme for the outgoing Harlan: "It is about time the Court faced the fact that the white people of the South do not like the colored people. The Constitution restrains them from effecting this dislike through state action but it most assuredly did not appoint the Court as a sociological watchdog to rear up every time private discrimination raises its admittedly ugly head."[13]

After clerking for Jackson, Rehnquist moved to Arizona, where he gained notoriety for opposing equal access to public accommodations and other civil rights laws on the grounds that they interfered with property rights.[14] Rehnquist was also involved with Republican politics in Arizona during this time. One of his projects was overseeing an effort designed to challenge minority voters in Democratic precincts in Maricopa County. Rehnquist was alleged to have approached minority voters with a card in 1962, asking them to publicly read it as a literacy test—which ultimately dissuaded many Black voters from attempting to vote. In 1964, the effort went statewide as "Project Eagle Eye," with Rehnquist as a key principal.[15] There was, in short, no reason to expect that Justice Rehnquist would champion the Voting Rights Act.

The arrival of Rehnquist and his other new colleagues helps to explain the sudden movement we see in figure 4.1 around 1970, which depicts a large rightward shift of the median justice's ideal point. Even aside from Rehnquist's known feelings about civil rights at the outset of his tenure as a justice, the profound ideological shift on the Supreme Court had important implications for the Voting Rights Act in the 1970s and later. Justices Black, Douglas, and Fortas been been reliable votes in favor of Sections 4 and 5. Replacing them even with moderate justices could chip away at the large majorities the government had been able to win while defending the VRA before the Supreme Court. But Rehnquist was no moderate on voting rights. He had already shown what might be charitably called "a skepticism" toward some of the VRA's goals. In combination with the other new justices, his presence meant that defending the VRA before the nation's highest court would no longer be a slam dunk.

In 1976 the city of New Orleans brought a new VRA case to the Supreme Court. Two decades earlier, the city had adopted a mayor-council government comprised of five councilors elected from single-member districts each representing part of the city, and two elected at large. Redistricting was to occur following each census to ensure that the districts represented approximately the same number of New Orleanians.[16] After the 1960 census, the city drew just one district in which Black residents were the majority, though the Black voters in that district found themselves about even with white voters in terms of voter registration—an arguably more important metric. In the remaining four districts (and the two at-large ones), Black residents were a clear minority. During the decade when these districts were employed, no Black candidate was elected to the council.

When it came time to redistrict for the 1970s, there was a key difference: New Orleans was now a covered jurisdiction, and its districting plan would need to gain DOJ approval prior to implementation. The city again drew five districts while preserving the two long-standing at-large council positions. This time, *two* of the districts had a majority of Black residents. However, due to disparities in registration rates (and in an echo of the 1960s map), in neither district did the Black share of *registered voters* exceed 45.2%. This districting plan failed to receive preclearance. The DOJ determined not only that the plan spread Black voters across districts in a way that diluted their power, but also that the at-large positions exacerbated the problem. If white voters in New Orleans voted along racial lines, Black candidates had little hope of getting their preferred candidates elected.

The core issue was relatively simple. With the exception of the heavily Black easternmost section of New Orleans, in general fewer Black residents lived in the city's northern neighborhoods. Black residents congregated nearer to the Mississippi River as it snaked through the city's southern boundary, so that a relatively unbroken line of majority-Black neighborhoods ran from west to east in south New Orleans. But the city was drawing districts that ran from north to south, which effectively guaranteed a Black majority in at most the easternmost district. This pattern formed the basis of the DOJ's objection.

Undaunted, New Orleans tried again. It still drew north-south districts, but this time, one district had a slim majority of Black registered voters. After the DOJ objected to this map as well, the city brought the matter into federal court, asking the US District Court for the District of Columbia to approve its districts. The court sided with the federal government, noting that Black residents made up 34.6% of the electorate and 45% of the population (of course, this gulf between the Black share of the population and registered electorate was evidence of past discrimination in the registration process). Applying straight arithmetic, a representative district plan, in the mind of the DC circuit court majority (to which the district court's ruling was appealed) would have resulted in at least two districts in which Black voters could reasonably expect to see their candidates elected.[17]

New Orleans was not allowed to hold elections under the new districts, so it held no elections at all. The councilors who were in office in 1971 simply held their positions until the city could have its day at the Supreme Court. Five years later, in *Beer v. United States*, the Court and its new conservative members hewed close to their interpretation of the VRA's intent.[18] Writing for the majority, Justice Potter Stewart (joined by Justices Burger, Blackmun, Powell, and Rehnquist) held that "the purpose of Section 5 has always been to insure that no voting procedure changes would be made that would lead to a retrogression in the position of racial minorities with respect to their effective exercise of the electoral franchise."

This reading of the law was not controversial given where the Supreme Court had been before, but the conclusion that stemmed from it broke slightly from one the Court may have made a decade earlier. According to Stewart, the VRA empowered the judiciary to consider only the effects of *changes* to election laws; regulations in place prior to the VRA's passage were beyond Section 5 review. Thus, the Court ruled that the VRA did not empower the Justice Department to consider the racial representation likely to result from New Orleans's at-large districts, because they had existed unchanged since 1954.

Moreover, when it considered changes, the Court signaled that it would apply a new standard: Regardless of whether it would fall short of delivering descriptive representation, was the change going to harm minority voters relative to the old policy, or not? The majority in *Beer* held that if the 1960s districts had resulted in no Black councilors and the 1970s districts would likely result in the election of one and possibly in two, then it could not be said that New Orleans's districting plan amounted to a "retrogression." Far from diluting the power of Black residents with a districting map that would underrepresent them, the Court accepted New Orleans's premise that the city was *enhancing* Black voters' power relative to the system in place before.

The new retrogression standard from *Beer* still allowed the federal government to block policies that truly did make things worse for minority voters, as the Court subsequently reaffirmed.[19] But the decision also signaled that the Court's new justices would not give the DOJ free reign in its preclearance actions. Moreover, if the Court was going to view Section 5 as allowing federal oversight of only *changes* to election rules, then those who wanted to challenge policies that were in effect prior to 1965 would have to ground their claims in the 14th Amendment and Section 2 of the VRA.

The first such challenge came from Mobile in 1980, brought by a group of Black citizens who argued that the city's commissioner government and corresponding at-large elections were designed to dilute their votes. Because the system had been in place since 1911, the citizens asked for relief under Section 2 and both the 14th and 15th Amendments. Mobile's long history of racial discrimination factored heavily into initial court rulings on the case. In the Southern Alabama US District Court, Judge Virgil Pittman heard testimony from scores of witnesses and toured the city of Mobile, where he found ongoing segregation, a stark difference in quality and services in the white and Black sections of town, and a severe under-representation of Black municipal workers.[20] The totality of circumstances led Pittman to conclude that Mobile's commissioner form of government served to dilute the voices of Black residents—and had done so for more than a century. Judge Pittman sided with the plaintiffs in finding that regardless of the city's intent, the commissioner system in Mobile was racially discriminatory in practice. The 5th Circuit Court of Appeals affirmed Pittman's ruling, and the city appealed to the Supreme Court.

With *Beer,* the newly composed Court had found an opportunity to limit Section 5. Now it had a Section 2 case to consider. In *City of Mobile v. Bolden,* the Court had to craft a standard by which to view Mobile's form of government against the law and the Constitution.[21] During oral argument, Charles S. Rhyne asserted for the City of Mobile that "no Black [person] has ever lost an election in Mobile because of polarized voting." Elections in Mobile, Rhyne said, were free and fair. There was nothing stopping anyone from registering and nothing to impede any resident from voting. The fact that no Black candidate had won election in Mobile for decades had more to do with demographics and voting behavior than its form of government, Rhyne said.

Crucially, Rhyne argued that the *intent* of the law was racially neutral, and forcing Mobile to create a majority Black district cut against equal protection for other residents. "The ultimate issue in this case," said Rhyne, "is whether the only way to satisfy the Constitutional requirement of equal participation in the voting processes of a government is by electing a Black [person] to the Mobile governing body." Mobile's position was that it had not intended to discriminate, and as such it could not be ordered to require that the racial demographics of its council reflected those of its population.

The Supreme Court sided with Mobile. Writing for a divided court, Justice Stewart in his opinion brushed aside Section 2 as a vehicle to decide the case. Stewart held that "Section 2 makes clear that it was intended to have an effect no different from that of the Fifteenth Amendment itself." As Section 2 was merely a restatement of the principles in the 15th Amendment, Stewart considered the case on constitutional grounds. On that front, Stewart wrote, "Our decisions . . . have made clear that action by a State that is racially neutral on its face violates the Fifteenth Amendment only if motivated by a discriminatory purpose." Stewart's opinion emphasized that evidence of a discriminatory *result,* without proof of discriminatory *intent,* was insufficient to invalidate an election system under the 14th and 15th Amendments. To win a Section 2 case, plaintiffs would have to show that jurisdictions had intentionally established discriminatory procedures. Proving such intent would no doubt be very difficult to do, and the Court's intent standard therefore threatened to substantially weaken the VRA. In a scalding dissent, Justice Thurgood Marshall (now a member of the Court) described the ruling as meaning that "in the absence of proof of intentional discrimination by the State, the right to vote provides the politically powerless with nothing more than the right to cast meaningless ballots."

The Supreme Court sent the case back to Judge Pittman in the district court for further consideration under its intent standard: Absent evidence of intentional discrimination, Mobile's council structure would stand. On reargument in 1982, the plaintiffs surfaced several new pieces of evidence from 1911 and before, including a number of letters to the editor in local newspapers and other correspondence.[22] Among these letters was the one from Frederick Bromberg we shared earlier, which had not been part of the evidentiary record that went to the Supreme Court. Bromberg's missive was printed as an open letter to the Alabama legislature in the *Mobile Register* on July 25, 1909, in which the author alluded to the fact that everyone has "falsely pretended" that seemingly race-neutral policies were not designed to discriminate. Judge Pittman concluded that the letter was a "smoking gun" that proved discriminatory intent, and struck down Mobile's councilor government once and for all.

Nevertheless, the chilling effect of *City of Mobile*'s intent standard on efforts to reign in discriminatory election practices was immediate and stark. Before Pittman could rule in the remanded case, Mobile's school board dismissed its two Black members (elected from single-member districts); more broadly, in the first part of 1980, federal suits alleging election discrimination shrank to one-sixth of their volume from the prior year.[23] The message of *City of Mobile* was clear: Absent the smoking gun proving that a law was crafted for a discriminatory purpose, further vote dilution claims were almost certain to fail.

Two years later, Congress struck back. In October 1981, the House passed a ten-year VRA reauthorization by an overwhelming vote of 389–24. The House bill amended Section 2 to undo the *City of Mobile* decision. If the Senate passed the House bill, the VRA would now include a results test, clarifying that a policy's alleged discriminatory effects could be weighed regardless of a jurisdiction's intent. Foreseeing the shape the debate would take in the Senate, the House bill also included an important disclaimer: "The fact that members of a minority group have not been elected in numbers equal to the group's proportion of the population shall not, in and of itself, constitute a violation."[24] This language represented a compromise of sorts: Discriminatory intent need not be present for a violation to occur, but demonstrating underrepresentation *alone* would also not suffice as evidence of discriminatory results.

Still, this caveat was not likely to guarantee passage in the Senate, where the House's attempt to push back against *City of Mobile* faced uncertain prospects. For the first time, Republicans controlled the Senate during a VRA reauthorization, and no one expected newly elected President Ronald Reagan to champion voting rights. In somewhat of a surprise, however, in August 1981 Reagan publicly announced his support for racially equitable voting, claiming that he had shifted from his former Nixonian position that Section 5 of the VRA apply to all states instead of just Southern ones. A national preclearance system, Reagan said he had learned, would "make [the VRA] so cumbersome as to not be effectively workable."[25] Reagan's support for the VRA was not absolute, however, and as of that summer, he still shared the view of many senators looking to codify *City of Mobile*'s intent standard over the House's preference for a results standard, even if that was the only concession Republicans could extract. Before the Senate took up the bill, Reagan reiterated his opposition to the results test, presumably well aware of how difficult it is to prove discriminatory intent.[26]

Debate in the Senate centered on the intent-versus-results question, and early indications were that the winds were blowing the Republicans' way. In testimony before the Senate Judiciary Committee's Subcommittee on the Constitution, William Bradford Reynolds, Reagan's assistant attorney general for civil rights, blasted the House bill. Disclaimers about underrepresentation aside, Reynolds said that the "logical terminal point" of a results-based test was something akin to "proportional representation" or "quotas."[27] This latter word especially carried loaded meaning during Reagan's presidency; the president had campaigned against racial quotas in employment and housing, and would maintain a steadfast opposition to "affirmative action" policies for the duration of his tenure. The VRA's opponents in the Senate knew that comparing the House bill to other racial quotas might be an effective way to kill it altogether.

Into this moment of uncertainty stepped Senator Robert Dole (R-KS). Dole worked out a bipartisan compromise bill that extended the VRA by 25 years instead of 10. It also retained the House's results standard and explicitly noted that proof of discriminatory intent was not required to halt an election policy, contravening the *City of Mobile* precedent. At the same time, Dole's bill borrowed from *White v. Regester* and its consideration of the "totality of circumstances" in a community alleged to have been discriminated against. To quell fears of quotas, Dole's bill clearly stated that there would be no requirement that minority groups have representation equivalent to their percentage of the population; the VRA would remain focused on whether election policies impeded equal participation or prevented minority populations from electing their preferred candidates. The number of minority elected officials in a jurisdiction would therefore not be a benchmark, but rather one of many factors that judges could weigh when considering the totality of circumstances.[28]

A Senate report accompanying the bill mined evidence from previous dilution cases to lay out the major factors that could be used to show discriminatory effects when a judge considered the totality of circumstances in examining the electoral environment resulting from a challenged policy:

1. The extent of any history of official discrimination in the state or political subdivision that touched the right of the members of the minority group to register, to vote, or otherwise to participate in the democratic process.
2. The extent to which voting in the elections of the state or political subdivision is racially polarized.
3. The extent to which the state or political subdivision has used unusually large election districts, majority vote requirements, anti-single shot provisions, or other voting practices or procedures that may enhance the opportunity for discrimination against the minority group.
4. If there is a candidate slating process, whether the members of the minority group have been denied access to that process.
5. The extent to which members of the minority group in the state or political subdivision bear the effects of discrimination in such areas as education, employment and health, which hinder their ability to participate effectively in the political process.
6. Whether political campaigns have been characterized by overt or subtle racial appeals.
7. The extent to which members of the minority group have been elected to public office in the jurisdiction.[29]

The report also identified two additional factors that "have had probative value as part of plaintiffs' evidence to establish a violation": Whether elected officials have been unresponsive to the minority group's concerns, and whether the justification that a jurisdiction offers for its policy is "tenuous."[30] The Senate report made clear that courts did not have to find that more than one of these factors exist, and also that judges could craft their own additional criteria. Thus, the bill provided judges with considerable grounds to find in favor of minority plaintiffs alleging discriminatory election practices. It was truly a stark break from *City of Mobile*.

At the same time, Dole's bill made it somewhat easier for covered jurisdictions to bail out of preclearance and remove themselves from the coverage list. Substate jurisdictions would now be able to bail out independently of those higher up; in theory, a county could bail out even if a state was covered. Moreover, under Dole's bill, jurisdictions would be able to bail out if they could convince a three-judge panel of the US District Court for the District of Columbia that they and all of their subdivisions had complied with the VRA for ten years preceding the request; that is, that they had employed no test or device to discriminate, that they had no negative preclearance judgments or pending actions, that no federal observers had been assigned in their borders, that they had consistently submitted all required changes for preclearance, and that they and all subdivisions had "taken affirmative steps to protect voting rights."[31] Dole's bill overcame a filibuster and passed the Senate 85–8. After it cleared the House as well, Ronald Reagan signed it into law. Two days later, the Supreme Court acquiesced, reversing its *City of Mobile* ruling.[32]

To conservatives in the Senate and DOJ, far from being a compromise, the new law must have felt like a giveaway to the left; in their mind, the enhanced bailout provisions were not enough to justify losing the intent test. President Reagan's Department of Justice had marshaled all hands in an effort to keep the intent standard from *City of Mobile* intact, but one young DOJ attorney must have been particularly disappointed to see its demise. He had just started in his position as special assistant to the attorney general, fresh from a clerkship with Justice Rehnquist that overlapped with the *City of Mobile* decision. With voting rights as a major component of his new responsibilities at DOJ, he had been in the vanguard of the administration's efforts to steer the Senate back toward the *City of Mobile* precedent, and many DOJ officials' public statements during the reauthorization fight had actually originated from his pen.

During the 1982 reauthorization, the new DOJ attorney had become a vociferous firebrand. He had written more than two dozen memos before and during the legislative battle, offering legal analysis and talking points intended to dissuade Congress from adopting a results test.[33] At the same time, he prepared administration witnesses for congressional testimony, attended strategy sessions, and personally lobbied senators against the results test in a campaign that journalist Ari Berman has since described as an "obsession."[34] In a series of memos to Attorney General William French Smith, the attorney had explained how the DOJ could convince senators that a results test would chart a dangerous course. Early on, in November 1981, he wrote, "[A results test] would make challenges to a broad range of voting practices much easier, and give courts far broader license to interfere with voting practices across the country. In particular, such widely accepted practices as at-large voting would be subject to attack, since it is fairly easy to demonstrate that such practices have the effect of diluting Black voting strength."[35]

In December, he went further, sending another memo, titled "Why Section 2 of the Voting Rights Act Should be Retained Unchanged." In it, he argued that a jurisdiction's intent to discriminate was not nearly so difficult to prove as the results test's proponents were arguing. "A so-called smoking gun" he wrote, "is simply not necessary. Plaintiffs can rely on the historical background of official actions, departures from normal practice, and other indirect evidence in proving intent."[36] And, at any rate, he continued,

> violations of Section 2 should not be made too easy to prove, since they provide a basis for the most intrusive interference imaginable by federal courts into state and local processes. The district court judge in the *Mobile* case, for example, acting solely on the basis of perceived discriminatory "effects," struck down the city's three-member, at large commission system of government, which had existed in Mobile for 70 years. In its place the federal judge ordered a mayoral system with a nine-member council elected from single-member districts. It would be difficult to conceive of a more drastic alteration of local governmental affairs, and under our federal system such an intrusion should not be too readily permitted.[37]

The results test, the author argued, simply created too much risk of aggressive federal interference in state and local matters. It was far better, he believed, to tack more closely to the reasonable standard that the Supreme Court had established in *City of Mobile*, avoiding the potential adverse effects that the results test invited. By January, he had formulated key talking points for Reagan administration officials that, as previously discussed, featured prominently in the public debate. For instance (and consistent with his extant memos), he advised administration officials to assert that the VRA was a highly effective law that the president simply wanted reauthorized without changes—at least as the Court had interpreted it.[38] Reagan himself articulated this view.

Furthermore, because under a results test "any election law or practice which produced results which did not mirror the population make-up of a community could be struck down," the author advised equating the results test to "a quota system for electoral politics."[39] Tying the results test to a loaded term used to combat other civil rights policies (such as affirmative action), he hoped, would make the results test unpalatable for enough congressional Republicans to kill it. Despite efforts by Assistant Attorney General Reynolds and others to deploy this strategy, it was ultimately unsuccessful. The DOJ lawyer had lost the fight for the Supreme Court's conservative intent standard, but he had certainly made a name for himself as an advocate for a restrictive view of the Voting Rights Act. That name was John Glover Roberts.

Until the 1960s the Supreme Court had been reluctant to impose "fairness" in legislative districting schemes, even when states allowed vast inequality across district populations.[40] The inherently political nature of districting allowed the justices to sidestep the question out of deference to the legislatures whose job it was to draw the lines. As Justice Felix Frankfurter declared in his 1946 majority opinion in *Colegrove v. Green*, in which the Court refused to provide relief to Illinois voters concerned about decades-old districts that had developed significant population inequality due to internal migration throughout the state: "Courts ought not to enter this political thicket."[41] To do so, the Court reasoned, risked permanent entanglement that would harm the Court's stature by giving it the sheen of a political body.

But even before the 1965 Voting Rights Act, the Warren Court had shown an increased willingness to wade into this thicket when states produced (or failed to change) maps that featured wide disparities between the most and least populous districts. In its 1962 ruling in *Baker v. Carr*—a case from Tennessee with essentially the same facts as *Colegrove*—the Court asserted that when states create unequal districts, voters in populous districts receive less representation than voters in less populated ones. The resulting 14th Amendment equal protection issue presented a harm sufficient to compel the Court to mandate equally sized districts even when state legislatures would not.[42] Two years later, the Court subsequently (and more famously) stated the principle of "one person, one vote" in *Reynolds v. Sims*, declaring that it would police 14th Amendment violations in districting schemes when states fostered population disparities in their maps.[43] The Court largely adhered to this doctrine in the following decades,[44] which saw significantly reduced inequality in public spending where district population had previously been unequal—an apparent vindication of the Court's view that unequal district sizes erode the quality of representation.[45]

The new results test in the 1982 reauthorization invited districting litigation of a slightly different sort. Now, plaintiffs could assert that regardless of legislative intent, districting schemes that *resulted* in diluted political power for minority communities violated Section 2 of the VRA. The first major case to reach the Supreme Court after the 1982 reauthorization, *Thornburg v. Gingles*, originated in North Carolina.[46] *Gingles* centered on North Carolina's state legislative redistricting plan following the 1980 census. Minority voters challenged seven of the new legislative districts, six of which were multimember districts in which more than one legislator would be elected. The voters alleged that these new districts spread minority voters' power too thin and would make it very difficult for them to elect legislators of their choice. This sort of challenge fell squarely within Section 2 of the VRA, which forbids election practices that dilute the political power of minority communities. Following the 1982 reauthorization, however, the district court was able to assess the *results* of North Carolina's districting plan in light of the "totality of circumstances"—both standards in the new law. After doing so, the district court ruled that North Carolina had unlawfully diluted Black residents' votes in the districts.

North Carolina appealed directly to the Supreme Court. Charles Fried, President Reagan's solicitor general, joined the case on North Carolina's side—arguing for reversal of the district court decision. Fried's involvement leaves little doubt as to how Reagan's DOJ viewed the new standards in the 1982 law. In *Gingles*, the Court upheld the district court's findings regarding the multimember districts at issue, citing the Senate report in finding that North Carolina had achieved "vote dilution through submergence" with the multimember districts since, as Justice Brennan put it in his majority opinion, "where minority and majority voters consistently prefer different candidates, the majority, by virtue of its numerical superiority, will regularly defeat the choices of minority voters."

At the same time, the Court recognized that the assumption of racial-bloc voting may not always hold. To consider vote dilution claims, it was therefore necessary to examine not only the criteria set forth in the Senate report but also the racial and political characteristics of the community in question. The Court therefore established the *Gingles* test, holding that three criteria must be met for a claim of vote dilution to succeed:

1. The minority group must be able to demonstrate that it is sufficiently large and geographically compact to constitute a majority in a single-member district.
2. The minority group must be able to show that it is politically cohesive.
3. The minority must be able to demonstrate that the white majority votes sufficiently as a bloc to enable it—in the absence of special circumstances, such as the minority candidate running unopposed—usually to defeat the minority's preferred candidate.

If a dilution claim failed on one of the prongs, then, under *Gingles*, it could not succeed. If a minority group could establish a claim that meets the *Gingles* test, however, Brennan wrote, "the minority group demonstrates that submergence in a white multi-member district impedes its ability to elect its chosen representatives." Once the test is met, courts can apply the totality of circumstances using the guidelines from the Senate report to determine whether a policy in question reduces minority voters' ability to elect a candidate of their choice.[47]

Gingles marked a substantial shift in the scope of VRA application, opening the door for large, politically cohesive minority groups to bring Section 2 challenges alleging vote dilution. In a report accompanying the 1975 reauthorization, Congress had clearly communicated that "citizens must have the opportunity to recover what it costs them to vindicate these rights in court."[48] The threat of paying six-figure (or higher) plaintiff's legal bills on top of their own defense costs convinced many jurisdictions to preemptively move away from at-large districts.[49] Even so, the post-*Gingles* period saw a marked increase in cases alleging discriminatory districting practices from all parts of the country—and from a number of minority groups.[50] These cases usually centered on allegations of unfair districting practices such as racial gerrymanders or the by-now-familiar use of at-large or multimember districts.

When they challenged districting plans, plaintiffs generally argued that existing districts would result in insufficient minority representation. Beginning with the redistricting cycle after the 1990 census, the DOJ incorporated Section 2 considerations (including the results standard) into preclearance reviews of proposed districting plans, blocking those that reviewers believed would not survive a Section 2 challenge in court. Including Section 2 in this way shifted redistricting reviews away from preventing retrogression to a more active footing, allowing the DOJ to order states to create minority districts where possible. Ultimately, the Section 2 inclusion led to early-1990s majority-minority districts in at least five states.[51]

The shift to active, Section 2–style review of districting plans led to a series of cases in which the Supreme Court tried to create standards for permissible ways to incorporate race into districting considerations. Like *Gingles*, *Shaw v. Reno* came from North Carolina.[52] After submitting its congressional districts for preclearance following the 1990 census, North Carolina was ordered to create a second majority-minority district (it had included one in its initial plan). In response, the state drew a snake-like 12th District that stretched for 160 miles, following Interstate 85 to link Black communities—sometimes, just neighborhoods—throughout the state. At points, the district encompassed only the highway itself.

Five white North Carolinians challenged the plan, alleging that the contorted shape of the districts flew in the face of commonsense districting: compact districts that tracked municipal or other geographical boundaries. The districts in question, they argued, could have been drawn only to put Black voters together; apart from their race, the Black voters of District 12's far-flung neighborhoods had no community ties or other obvious traits in common. The plaintiffs alleged that this practice resembled segregation and resulted in substandard representation not just for white voters but for *all* voters: Because distinct communities sometimes hundreds of miles apart had been pulled together into one district, it was more difficult to effectively represent anyone in District 12, denying all involved the equal protection guaranteed under the 14th Amendment.

The majority in *Shaw* agreed with the plaintiffs. In her opinion, Justice Sandra Day O'Connor held that "what appellants object to is redistricting legislation that is so extremely irregular on its face that it rationally can be viewed only as an effort to segregate the races for purposes of voting, without regard for traditional districting principles and without sufficiently compelling justification." The Court was convinced that the plaintiffs had a legitimate 14th Amendment equal protection claim, holding that only race could explain District 12's shape—and race alone could not determine district boundaries. The Supreme Court sent the case back to the district court, ordering that strict scrutiny be applied in its assessment of the facts. This is the highest standard of review, which makes it difficult for policies that might infringe on equal protection to survive judicial scrutiny. For the 12th District to stand, North Carolina would have to prove it had a compelling government interest in creating it and would also have to show that the district was narrowly tailored and amounted to the least obtrusive remedy to meet that need. Ultimately, the state was unable to meet this standard, and the 12th District was disallowed.[53]

Four dissenting opinions were filed in *Shaw*, revealing stark division among the justices. The dissents noted that the Court had previously held that states could use race as a factor in drawing districts—even if the districting plan preestablished a certain number of majority-minority districts.[54] Nevertheless, the Court leaned on *Shaw* in two subsequent cases that put 1990s redistricting to the test.

The first was *Miller v. Johnson*, a case from Georgia with a fact pattern extremely similar to that in *Shaw*.[55] In *Miller*, the Court held that strict scrutiny must be applied whenever race is "the overriding, predominant force" in drawing district lines. These principles were also upheld in *Bush v. Vera*, which originated in Texas.[56] Race could be considered in drawing equitable districts, the Court decided, but not when they clearly deviated from well-established traditional practices of compactness and contiguity. Quoting her own opinion from *Shaw* two years earlier, Justice O'Connor, writing for the majority in *Bush*, reiterated that the Court would be highly suspicious of a redistricting plan that was "extremely irregular on its face."

The story of the 1990s racial redistricting cases is one of the judiciary clawing back power that the executive branch had asserted. If the DOJ was going to order states to draw majority-minority districts while preclearing districting plans, those districts would have to survive strict scrutiny if they resembled twisting monstrosities. The Court had left some daylight in its prior rulings, however. If, for example, a state could draw a majority-Black district that adhered to traditional districting methods, preserved communities of interest, and passed the "eye test," the Court would likely not stand in its way—at least given what it had signaled in its opinions. In theory, then, even in the late 1990s the DOJ was still empowered to demand race-proportionate districting plans as part of the preclearance process.

That door was soon slammed. As the next round of decennial districting loomed, in *Reno v. Bossier Parish School Board*, the Court held that Section 5 exists *only* for the purpose of preventing retrogression.[57] This ruling meant that districting plans could be evaluated in preclearance only by the standard of whether they made things *worse* for minority voters. In *Georgia v. Ashcroft*, the Court ruled that a lower court's finding of Section 5 retrogression in Georgia's districting plan was erroneous because, while retrogression was possible in some districts, the plan resulted in gains for minority voters in others; thus, it was not clear whether retrogression had occurred overall.[58] These decisions substantially limited the DOJ's ability to take proactive steps to make districts more equal. In tandem, these actions put the final nail in the coffin for the DOJ to apply Section 2 standards to assess districting plans during Section 5 preclearance. They also once again put the Supreme Court on a collision course with Congress.

When William Rehnquist died in office on September 3, 2005, the Supreme Court was a very different institution than the one he had joined during the Nixon administration. All vestiges of the distinctly liberal Warren Court were gone. Ronald Reagan had elevated Rehnquist to chief justice in 1985; he assumed that role on the same day Antonin Scalia took Rehnquist's old position as associate justice. With Clarence Thomas, who had replaced staunch voting rights supporter Thurgood Marshall in 1992, the trio comprised a reliable conservative bloc that, together with moderate conservatives Sandra Day O'Connor and Anthony Kennedy, had shifted the balance of power on the Court even further to the right.

President George W. Bush maintained this balance with the selection of John Roberts as the new chief justice. Given his prior clerkship and close relationship with Rehnquist—combined with his lobbying efforts against the results test in the 1982 reauthorization while at the Justice Department—there was little reason to expect Roberts to view the VRA much differently than his predecessor had. In 2006, when Bush replaced Justice O'Connor with reliable conservative Samuel Alito, the Court gained a fourth member of its staunch conservative bloc, with Kennedy serving as a swing vote. In the history of the VRA, the political dispositions of the justices on the Court had never been more uniformly hostile to certain aspects of the law. Section 5 seemed most vulnerable, though the redistricting cases from the 1990s suggested there were certainly votes on the Court now that might imperil Section 2 as well, even if these did not yet constitute a majority.

These dynamics at the Court were largely in the background as the expiration of the 1982 reauthorization's 25-year extension neared. On the surface at least, the legislative atmosphere this time was devoid of much of the significant opposition that had emerged at various points in prior reauthorizations. Work on the reauthorization began a year early so that Republicans could take credit for positive action on minority voting rights. Members of Congress from both parties praised the VRA as a paragon of effective law and an ongoing bulwark against racial disenfranchisement. By wide margins in both houses, Congress reauthorized Section 5 and the language minority protections in Section 203 for an additional 25 years.

The 2006 reauthorization also rolled back the Supreme Court's decisions in *Reno v. Bossier Parish School Board* and *Georgia v. Ashcroft*, clarifying that a change may fail preclearance if it was discriminatory, regardless of whether it was retrogressive. The new law explicitly stated that a policy should *not* be precleared if it abridged minority voters' ability to elect a candidate of their choice. These changes restored the positive power in the preclearance process for DOJ regulators looking to craft districting maps that increased the number of minority representatives. Once again, Congress had responded to the Supreme Court's narrowing of the law by codifying new elements in a reauthorized VRA—and with considerably less contention than previous reauthorizations had seen.

The reauthorization moved especially efficiently in the Senate, which adopted the House version of the bill without amendment and passed it unanimously. This sheen of bipartisan consensus in the Senate belied turmoil beneath the surface, however. In their excellent history of Congress's work on the reauthorization, Bullock, Gaddie, and Wert describe a palpable feeling among some members and expert witnesses that the preclearance formula was in danger of being declared an unconstitutional infringement on state power.[59] In *South Carolina v. Katzenbach*, a substantially more voting rights–friendly Court had allowed different treatments of covered states because their offenses were so severe. Extensions of five or seven years in initial reauthorizations had allowed Congress to declare an ongoing need for preclearance. But with the 25-year extension in 1982, by the time 2006 came around, Congress was proposing to extend the coverage formula forward to 66 years beyond the VRA's initial enactment, begging a question: Considering that it had already recognized it as a "stringent" remedy in *Katzenbach*, how much longer would the Supreme Court tolerate Section 4(b)'s coverage formula?

This question was of central concern to legal experts Richard Hasen and Samuel Issacharoff, who offered testimony before the Senate Judiciary Committee. Both scholars pointed out that the Supreme Court was unlikely to have infinite patience with an unaltered, decades-old formula that exercised exceptional regulatory oversight of state power; a shorter reauthorization period might therefore be safer to ensure the law survived judicial scrutiny.[60] The experts also noted that in justifying the reauthorization, Congress had established little evidence of racial discrimination outside redistricting practices, and Hasen in particular noted that picking a fight with the Supreme Court over *Bossier Parish School Board* and *Ashcroft* could be inviting interbranch conflict. Hasen also suggested that perhaps Congress should amend the formula in some way to reflect more contemporary concerns. Finally, both witnesses stated that making it easier for covered areas to bail out—perhaps by offering an off-ramp to jurisdictions with perfect records—would help the law survive a court challenge.[61]

Hasen's and Issacharoff's ideas made it into several proposed amendments in the House, all of which were offered by representatives from covered areas. Congressman Charlie Norwood (R-GA) took the view shared by several members representing covered states that the formula was ripe for an update. Modernizing the coverage criteria, these members reasoned, might free their states from preclearance. Norwood offered an amendment that would have created a moving trigger, so that any jurisdiction that had seen turnout below 50% of the voting age population in any of the last three presidential elections would be covered. The amendment attracted support from members representing covered states, but failed after Representative Jim Sensenbrenner (R-WI) described it as "a farce," pointing out that the only fully covered state in Norwood's plan would be Hawaii.[62] Amendments to reduce the extension to ten years, to strike the minority language provisions from Section 203, and to provide expedited bailout procedures also all failed.[63]

There is evidence that some of the legislators fighting over the 2006 reauthorization knew that even if they failed to soften the VRA in the legislative process, they could lay the groundwork for future efforts to advance their objectives.[64] Describing the proposed House amendments later, Representative Lynn Westmoreland (R-GA) explained this strategy: "We knew we didn't have a chance to change [the coverage formula]. . . . But we wanted to point all these things out, and create a record if it was ever taken to the high court. I knew that if we got to the high court, we would win."[65] A similar approach was evident in the Senate as well, where Republicans invited Hasen and Issacharoff to testify about issues with the coverage formula. With their concerns on the record, Senate Republicans could be assured that future litigation would find issues articulated not by partisans but by avowed supporters of the VRA. This testimony allowed Republicans to avoid the political costs of opposing the VRA while sowing the seeds for its future demise in federal courts. Comments made by Senator Jeff Sessions (R-AL) prior to the floor vote put this strategy on full display: Although he spoke in favor of the reauthorization in the Senate, Sessions also noted, "The witnesses we have heard in the Judiciary Committee over the past couple of months have had many different ideas, and after hearing from them, I am concerned that we should have listened more carefully to the recommendations."[66]

Senators John Cornyn (R-TX) and Tom Coburn (R-OK)—among the most conservative members of the Senate Judiciary Committee—used the committee report to further advance this argument. Among the report's notable aspects was that it was not released until six days after the reauthorization had passed the Senate.[67] Despite unified Republican control of both the House and the Senate, Cornyn and Coburn used the report as a vehicle to describe progress in the South on voting rights since the original 1965 VRA. They also complained about the rushed process, lamenting that "it would have been advisable for the committee or the Senate as a whole to consider an updated coverage formula to ensure that the appropriate jurisdictions were covered *according to constitutional requirements*. That kind of deliberative process simply was not allowed to occur" (emphasis added).[68] Thus, even as the Senate unanimously passed the 2006 reauthorization into law, the Senate Judiciary Committee report cast doubts on its very constitutionality. Only half of the committee's 18 members endorsed the report; 9 of 10 Judiciary Republicans—all of whom had voted for the bill on the floor—signed on, while all 8 Democrats on the committee objected to its content.[69] The report therefore underscores the complex dynamics at work: Sensitive to the political costs they would have incurred by attacking the VRA head-on, senators looking to weaken the law instead created a record that provided ammunition for the Supreme Court to use in doing what its opponents in Congress could (or would) not.

But this was a future concern. For now, few people asked a question that would prove crucial: Why did two expert witnesses—both of whom were pro-VRA and deeply knowledgeable about the Supreme Court's thinking on voting rights—seem to agree with Southern representatives about the need to change the coverage formula? Perhaps the many members who supported the lightning-fast reauthorization had grown complacent, since the Supreme Court had not heard a serious challenge to Section 5 for decades. But to keen observers like Hasen and Issacharoff, explicitly rolling back the Court's decisions while extending a 40-year-old coverage formula for two more decades invited a response from the Supreme Court and its new chief justice, who had started his career as a DOJ lawyer fighting the 1982 VRA reauthorization. As Hasen and Issacharoff feared, Congress had poked a sleeping bear. Future challenges to the coverage formula would be heard in Chief Justice John Roberts's Court.

There are more than 1,000 municipal utility districts (MUDs) in Texas. They provide services that typically fall under the purview of a municipality—such as water and sewer or the construction of roads and parks—in unincorporated areas or where an existing city wants a new development to bear the costs of necessary infrastructure. These MUDs are hyperlocal political subdivisions. The people who live in the MUD elect members to a board that works with consultants to set water rates and decide which potholes to fix. In many ways, the MUD acts as a town government where no town exists.

In 2009, Northwest Austin Municipal Utility District Number One (NAMUDNO) provided water, trash collection, and park maintenance for several developments north of Austin, Texas. The MUD was not responsible for registering voters or maintaining voter rolls, but it did have elections for its board. These were very small affairs, but residents still had to be registered Texas voters to participate. No one had ever alleged that NAMUDNO discriminated against minority voters in elections to its five-member board. But when the board wanted to move a polling place from a resident's garage to a local school in 2002, it discovered that because it was in Texas—a fully covered state—the MUD was subject to preclearance just like every other Texas substate jurisdiction.[70]

In 2002, jurisdictions would have to bail out under the rules set forth in the 1982 reauthorization, which required them to prove they had been in full VRA compliance for ten years. When the 2006 reauthorization brought no easier bailout standard, NAMUDNO brought suit in an attempt to escape the preclearance list. The MUD argued that it met the statutory requirement of a clean record for ten years. In theory, NAMUDNO was in a good position to ask for a bailout. Its narrow scope meant that there were no sub-jurisdictions within the MUD to worry about, and all it had to do was show in district court that it met the requirements of the 1982 bailout provisions. If the court did not allow it to escape preclearance, NAMUDNO was prepared to argue that Section 5 of the VRA was unconstitutional.

A three-judge panel of the US District Court for the District of Columbia ruled against NAMUDNO. The court upheld the constitutionality of Section 5 and maintained that NAMUDNO was ineligible for bailout. It reasoned that because the MUD was not responsible for registering voters, it is unlike the typical substate jurisdiction (like a county or town) that Congress had in mind when it established the bailout procedures. NAMUDNO subsequently appealed to the Supreme Court, arguing that the VRA's bailout provisions are not conditional on whether a jurisdiction maintains voter rolls, and reiterating its conditional Section 5 challenge.

In his majority opinion, Chief Justice Roberts provided a concise summation of the issue in *NAMUDNO v. Holder:* "The plaintiff in this case is a small utility district raising a big question—the constitutionality of Section 5 of the Voting Rights Act."[71] Yet that was just one question that the Court *could* answer. The other was whether NAMUDNO, as a small utility district that did not register voters, was eligible to seek a bailout from the preclearance requirements of Section 5. The 8–1 majority resolved the case here. In a sidestep of the constitutional claim, Roberts wrote, "Our usual practice is to avoid the unnecessary resolution of constitutional questions. We agree that the district is eligible under the [VRA] to seek bailout. We therefore reverse [the district court] and do not reach the constitutionality of Section 5." Having determined that it *could* be bailed out, the Supreme Court sent the case back to the district court to decide whether it *should* be.

In *NAMUDNO*, the Supreme Court had decided to interpret the bailout provisions more broadly than the district court had, finding that "all political subdivisions . . . are eligible to file a bailout suit." The MUD might not register voters, but it conducted political activities, and that was enough to fall under the VRA's definition of a political subdivision. Deciding the case on statutory instead of constitutional grounds avoided the worst fears of pro-VRA advocates, who had worried that the Court might happily take up the MUD's invitation to strike down Section 5 altogether. The MUD had explicitly stated that it merely wanted to be bailed out. Roberts' opinion afforded this relief, resting on the principle of "constitutional avoidance." As it had done in prior voting rights cases, the Court held that if it had other grounds on which to decide a case, it need not adjudicate constitutionality.[72]

But the Court's ruling in *NAMUDNO* also contained ample warning signs that with different facts, it might be perfectly willing to take on the question of whether Section 5 could survive constitutional scrutiny. Roberts noted the "federalism costs" of imposing preclearance on only some jurisdictions. As Roberts put it, "The evil that Section 5 is meant to address may no longer be concentrated in the jurisdictions singled out for preclearance." The federalism costs that Roberts identified could render Section 5 unconstitutional if they exceeded the protective benefits for minority voters nearly 50 years after the coverage formula was derived, a point Roberts spoke to directly:

> The historic accomplishments of the Voting Rights Act are undeniable, but the Act now raises serious constitutional concerns. The preclearance requirement represents an intrusion into areas of state and local responsibility that is otherwise unfamiliar to our federal system. Some of the conditions that the Court relied upon in upholding this statutory scheme in *South Carolina v. Katzenbach* and *City of Rome v. United States* have unquestionably improved. Those improvements are no doubt due in significant part to the Voting Rights Act itself, and stand as a monument to its success, but the Act imposes current burdens and must be justified by current needs. The Act also differentiates between the States in ways that may no longer be justified.

In a dissenting opinion, Justice Clarence Thomas went even further. Thomas argued that the Court had not provided full relief to NAMUDNO (because it had not granted bailout), and therefore should have taken up the constitutional question. "I would," Thomas wrote, "decide the constitutional issue presented and hold that Section 5 exceeds Congress' power to enforce the Fifteenth Amendment." While Thomas's colleagues did not share his willingness to strike down Section 5 in *NAMUDNO*, there were clear signals that with a different case, at least several of the justices could be convinced to reexamine whether preclearance remained a constitutional exercise of congressional power. Across the South, jurisdictions that had long been subject to preclearance saw a potential light at the end of the tunnel. One of them was a small town just over 50 miles from the Edmund Pettus Bridge.

In some ways the demise of VRA preclearance began with a quixotic 1992 congressional campaign in Houston. Stockbroker Ed Blum had moved to the downtown area two years before. When he voted in the 1990 midterm election, he realized that his Congressman, Craig Washington (D-TX), was running unopposed. A political novice with little understanding of the dynamics of the majority-Black 18th District, Blum filed to run as a Republican in the next cycle. Blum figured that no matter his chances, voters should have a choice, and he designed a shoe-leather campaign that leaned heavily on personal interactions with voters at their front doors. As he and his wife, Lark Blum, went door-to-door in Houston, Blum confronted firsthand the contorted nature of the district, which snaked throughout Texas. The Blums recounted the experience years later:

ED BLUM: I would take the even side of Oak Street, and my wife would take the odd-numbered side of Oak Street, and we would start to walk.

LARK BLUM: It was peculiar because we had maps that we had to follow and it was very odd the way that some streets were in the district and some weren't. It took a while for it all to really sink in as to how this could really happen.

ED BLUM: After I guess about a week of this, we realized that neighbors had been separated, almost house by house because of their race.[73]

In a separate interview, Ed Blum elaborated on how this experience shaped his views of equitable districting in the campaign he eventually lost by more than 55,000 votes out of 172,000 cast:[74]

> When you looked at the shape of the 18th Congressional District, it ran from many dozens of miles in one direction and many dozens of miles in a different direction, with the goal of harvesting African-Americans out of multi-racial, multi-ethnic neighborhoods, in order to create safe majority minority districts. . . . What bothered me about losing . . . wasn't the electoral outcome; it was the fact that these neighborhoods that were multiracial and multiethnic were split apart to create a racial outcome. When I went door to door, neighbors were concerned about their neighborhood, their local schools, the issues of crime, whether businesses were coming and going. . . . They weren't interested in the fact that, "well, my little neighborhood is connected to another African-American neighborhood 75 miles due east of here, and our representative is Black."[75]

Blum decided to sue Texas over the 18th District, and recruited plaintiffs from other areas of the state to challenge other districts he felt had been drawn primarily on the basis of race. Blum's case ultimately reached the Supreme Court as *Bush v. Vera* (described earlier in this chapter), in which the Court struck down Texas's majority-minority districts because race was the overriding factor in their creation. The victory was not the end for Blum, however. He decided to find test plaintiffs who could bring additional suits in other states, which he also won. As Blum put it, "The day that we won [the *Bush v. Vera*] lawsuit, I was hooked forever. It became a passion."[76]

Blum had stumbled upon a winning formula for combating what he saw as policies that fostered racial inequality under the guise of remedying racial injustice: Find plaintiffs who could bring a compelling claim to the federal court system, raise enough money to cover their expenses, and use the cases as battering rams. Blum's early work on districting took him to the Supreme Court for the first time. By the mid-2000s he had put Sections 4 and 5 of the VRA squarely in his crosshairs, and got before the High Court again.

Blum's group, the Project for Fair Representation, had bankrolled NAMUDNO, which he saw as a solid test case to strike down both sections altogether. Blum had wanted to go big in *NAMUDNO*. "I thought we should go immediately for striking down Section 4 and Section 5," he said, "whereas counsel . . . said, 'Let's put a chop on the log first. Let's give the Court the opportunity to broaden this a little bit.' . . . So that's how that case was framed, . . . over my objection actually, but as it turned out *Northwest Austin* was the first chop on the log."[77]

Blum's attack on Section 5 failed in *NAMUDNO*, but the broadside had left its mark. It seemed that conditions had never been more favorable for jurisdictions chafing under preclearance to finally convince the Court to strike down the "temporary" provisions that had, to them, apparently become permanent. Blum just needed another jurisdiction to take the ride with him. He found a willing partner in Shelby County, a rural jurisdiction of a few more than 200,000 residents in north-central Alabama.

The trouble began in the town of Calera, whose population had more than tripled between 2000 and 2006, growing to well more than 10,000.[78] One of the core drivers of this growth was the annexation of new developments cropping up on the town's outskirts as people sought small-town living in close proximity to Birmingham. New geography meant not only new municipal boundaries but also a new districting plan for town government. In 2007 Calera submitted to the DOJ for preclearance a plan for 177 annexations and new municipal districts.

The DOJ objected to Calera's plans. Under the map in place since 1990, the town had one district with a majority of Black voters; a Black councilor had represented this district over the entirety of that time. In the proposed plan, the majority-Black district was gone. Moreover, the DOJ noted, the town had supplied no verifiable population data in its submission, and the annexations were not new. The 177 annexations in Calera's submission had occurred over thirteen years, and the city had not submitted them for preclearance review. Absent reliable data about how the annexations affected Calera's racial demography—and especially considering the elimination of the majority-Black district—the DOJ would not allow Calera's plans to go ahead.[79]

By 2008, the playbook for local officials following an objection was fairly straightforward: Gather data that the DOJ requested, compile a new plan, and resubmit. Challenging preclearance in court would mean spending potentially hundreds of thousands of dollars of taxpayer money with an uncertain outcome. But where officials in Shelby County saw annoyance, Ed Blum saw opportunity. Unlike NAMUDNO, subjurisdictions in Shelby County had received four other preclearance objections over the VRA's history, with the most recent in 2000.[80] Therefore, under the 1982 reauthorization, there was no option for bailing out—and no statutory off-ramp in a legal challenge. If Shelby County brought a case challenging Sections 4(b) and 5 that made it to the Supreme Court, the justices would have to adjudicate it on constitutional grounds. Blum saw that there would be no more "chops"; the Court would have to cut down the whole tree.

In a 2012 interview with Charles L. Bullock III, Blum described how it came together.[81] He approached Shelby County attorney Frank "Butch" Ellis, who was no fan of preclearance but a big fan of Blum's financial backing. Ellis understood that striking down Section 5 would free Shelby County and other jurisdictions covered under the preclearance formula from future federal oversight. And if Blum could raise the money to pay for the legal fees, there was much less downside to trying. Ellis, fresh off the objection in Calera, was receptive. He convinced the county board to initiate a direct challenge to Sections 4(b) and 5, and Blum got his case.

Shelby County v. Holder was argued before the US Supreme Court on February 27, 2013.[82] The county mounted a direct challenge to Section 4(b) (the coverage formula) and Section 5 (preclearance), arguing that in failing to update the coverage formula in 2006, Congress had exceeded its 14th and 15th Amendment authority. Shelby County wanted the Court to weigh Congress's intrusion on states' regulatory power against the 10th Amendment and Article 4 of the Constitution. These arguments had twice lost in lower courts,[83] but the Supreme Court had signaled an openness to reconsidering the questions that the county was asking.

For Shelby County, Burt W. Rein made clear that he thought that *NAMUDNO* had opened the door to a constitutional challenge and that the basis for this challenge was the contention that the old discrimination that had justified preclearance—as the Court had upheld in *Katzenbach*—had faded away. In the new South, jurisdictions were no longer looking to disenfranchise minority voters, and the old formula, said Rein, simply could not continue to stand.

Rein's first point alluded directly to *NAMUDNO*: "Almost four years ago, eight Justices of the Court agreed the 2005 [*sic*] 25-year extension of Voting

Rights Act Section 5's preclearance obligation, uniquely applicable to jurisdictions reached by Section 4(b)'s antiquated coverage formula, raised a serious constitutional question. Those Justices recognized that the record before the Congress in 2005 [*sic*] made it unmistakable that the South had changed. They questioned whether current remedial needs justified the extraordinary federalism and cost burdens of preclearance."

This was as far as Rein got with his prepared argument. His claim of a changed South was immediately engaged by Associate Justice Sonia Sotomayor, one of the Court's bloc of liberal justices, who was an active thorn in Rein's side for the duration of his time. Sotomayor asked, "Assuming I accept your premise, and there's some question . . . that some portions of the South have changed, your county pretty much hasn't. In the period we're talking about, 240 discriminatory voting laws were blocked by Section 5 objections; there were numerous remedied by Section 2 litigation. You may be the wrong party bringing this. Why would we vote in favor of a county whose record is the epitome of what caused the passage of this law to start with?"

Justice Ruth Bader Ginsburg took this point up as well, noting that even though a dissenting judge in the DC Circuit Court of Appeals (who had wanted to rule in Shelby County's favor) had objected to the outdated coverage formula, the judge still admitted that Section 5 might lawfully apply to "Mississippi, Louisiana, and Alabama," given their records. This fact, to Sotomayor, was important. She argued that in *Katzenbach*, the Court had eschewed concerns about whether the South at large was actively disenfranchising minority voters, and had focused instead on South Carolina's problematic record. To this point, Rein replied:

> We're not here to parse the jurisdictions. We are here to challenge this formula because in and of itself it speaks to old data, it isn't probative with respect to the kinds of discrimination that Congress was focusing on and it is an inappropriate vehicle to sort out the sovereignty of individual States. I could tell you that in Alabama the number of legislators in the Alabama legislature are proportionate to the number of Black voters. There's a very high registration and turnout of Black voters in Alabama. But I don't think that that really addresses the issue of the rationality in theory and practice of the formula. If Congress wants to write another statute, . . . that would present a different case. But we're here facing a county, a State, that are swept in by a formula that is neither rational in theory nor in practice. That's the hub of the case.

In one important respect, Rein was correct: The formula did rely on old data. Congress had disregarded experts who had advised it to modernize the coverage formula, because it had feared that doing so would lead to just the sort of argument Rein now made at the Supreme Court. How could Congress justify the preclearance condition based on forty-year-old turnout figures, when turnout between white and Black voters had approached parity in recent years? One obvious response was that it was the effectiveness of the VRA itself that led to the *appearance* that the problem had gone away. Justice Stephen Breyer suggested as much in a hypothetical:

> The closest analogy I could think of is, imagine a state has a plant disease and in 1965 you can recognize the presence of that disease, which is hard to find, by a certain kind of surface movement or plant growing up. Now, it's evolved. So by now, when we use that same formula, all we're doing is picking out that state. But we know one thing: The disease is still there in the state. Because this is a question of renewing a statute that in fact has worked. And so the question I guess is, is it rational to pick out at least some of those States?

Justice Elena Kagan, meanwhile, did not appear swayed by the registration and turnout numbers. While these showed undeniable progress, the coverage formula continued to pick out *other* current problems. As she noted, while "covered jurisdictions [had] less than 25 percent of the nation's total population, they account[ed] for 56 percent of all successful published Section 2 lawsuits." Although Section 5 had forestalled many of the most egregious practices in the covered jurisdictions, those jurisdictions *still* committed far more than their share of Section 2 violations. In this respect, the old data proved remarkably adept at identifying where modern violations would arise.

And so it went. Oral arguments in *Shelby County* can be characterized as a debate among four liberal justices (Ginsburg, Breyer, Kagan, and Sotomayor) and four conservative ones (Alito, Roberts, Scalia, and Thomas), signaling their preferences via their questions, helping their allies, and arguing against the other side. The conservatives were clearly sympathetic to Rein's argument: The coverage formula had gone too long without adjustment, and now the differential treatment based on these old data amounted to a constitutional overreach. The liberal justices were skeptical that the old forces that had made the Voting Rights Act necessary in 1965 had simply faded away. Indeed, they believed that the VRA itself was responsible for the appearance of less racism in Southern elections.

With this dynamic, astute observers turned to Justice Anthony Kennedy. As he had done so many times in the previous decade, Kennedy was poised to break the tie between his more liberal and conservative colleagues. Kennedy's questions were consistent with this positioning; rather than joining a clear side, he probed for facts. But Kennedy did appear skeptical. At one point, he asked Solicitor General Donald B. Verrilli Jr. whether preclearance could effectively be extended to the nation as a whole. Near the end of Rein's time, the justice asked whether simply bailing in jurisdictions that offend in the future would be an effective stand-in for preclearance. Later, in another exchange with Verrilli, he wondered whether Section 2 litigation had become a substitute for preclearance, which may have signaled that he was envisioning a world without Section 5.

Perhaps the strongest signal of Kennedy's thinking came during the government's argument, when Verrilli said: "Congress in 2006 was not writing on a clean slate. . . . Congress did have before it very significant evidence about disproportionate results in Section 2 litigation in covered jurisdictions, and that, we submit, is a substantial basis for Congress to have made the judgment that the coverage formula should be kept in place, particularly given that it does have a bail-in mechanism and it does have a bail-out mechanism which allows for tailoring over time."

To this, Kennedy replied, "This reverse engineering that you seem so proud of, it seems to me that that obscures the real purpose of the statute. And if Congress is going to single out separate states by name, it should do it by name. If not, it should use criteria that are relevant to the existing [time]. And Congress just didn't have the time or the energy to do this; it just reenacted it." In response to this ominous signal of how Kennedy might vote, Verrilli said, "I think the formula was rational and effective in 1965. The Court upheld it then, [and] it upheld it three more times after that." Kennedy's response was a death knell to any hope among observers who thought he might side with continued preclearance: "Well, the Marshall Plan was very good, too, the Morrill Act, the Northwest Ordinance, but times change."

Four months later, in an opinion authored by Chief Justice John Roberts following a 5–4 decision, the Supreme Court invalidated Section 4(b) of the Voting Rights Act. The coverage formula was no more. Roberts held that the VRA's preclearance requirements sharply departed from the "fundamental principle of equal sovereignty among the states." As Justice Roberts put it, "While one state waits months or years and expends funds to implement a validly enacted law, its neighbor can typically put the same law into effect immediately, through the normal legislative process." In *Katzenbach*, the Court had held that the desperate struggle of the 1960s warranted exceptional measures. "At the time," Roberts wrote, "the coverage formula—the means of linking the exercise of the unprecedented authority with the problem that warranted it—made sense." But, Roberts continued,

> nearly 50 years later, things have changed dramatically. Shelby County contends that the preclearance requirement, even without regard to its disparate coverage, is now unconstitutional. Its arguments have a good deal of force. In the covered jurisdictions, "voter turnout and registration rates now approach parity. Blatantly discriminatory evasions of federal decrees are rare. And minority candidates hold office at unprecedented levels." The tests and devices that blocked access to the ballot have been forbidden nationwide for over 40 years. Those conclusions are not ours alone. Congress said the same when it reauthorized the Act in 2006, writing that "Significant progress has been made in eliminating first generation barriers experienced by minority voters, including increased numbers of registered minority voters, minority voter turnout, and minority representation in Congress, State legislatures, and local elected offices." The House Report elaborated that "the number of African-Americans who are registered and who turn out to cast ballots has increased significantly over the last 40 years, particularly since 1982," and noted that "in some circumstances, minorities register to vote and cast ballots at levels that surpass those of white voters." That Report also explained that there have been "significant increases in the number of African-Americans serving in elected offices"; more specifically, there has been approximately a 1,000% increase since 1965 in the number of African-American elected officials in the six States originally covered by the Voting Rights Act.

Roberts conceded that many of these improvements were no doubt the result of the VRA itself, but lamented that "the Act has not eased the restrictions in Section 5 or narrowed the scope of the coverage formula in Section 4(b) along the way. Those extraordinary and unprecedented features were reauthorized—as if nothing had changed. In fact, the Act's unusual remedies have grown even stronger." At the same time, he wrote, "history did not end in 1965." Roberts and his colleagues in the majority could not justify continued differential treatment of covered jurisdictions in the absence of a coverage formula reflecting evidence of recent racial disenfranchisement.

In the 2006 reauthorization, expert witnesses had warned Congress that a failure to modernize the coverage formula would invite judicial criticism. Their stomachs must have turned in response to Roberts's sharp rebuke of Congress, which was centered on these very grounds. "Congress did not use the record it compiled to shape a coverage formula grounded in current conditions," Roberts wrote. "It instead reenacted a formula based on 40-year-old facts having no logical relation to the present day." Preventing racial disenfranchisement was a worthy goal, but if it wanted to subject states to different regulatory regimes, the justices demanded either more recent evidence of widespread illegal activity or a new coverage formula that reflected contemporary events.

Although Justice Clarence Thomas wrote in a concurring opinion that Section 5, too, should be struck down, the majority left it intact. Without the coverage formula to identify which jurisdictions required preclearance, Section 5 could not be enforced, so there was little need to judge its constitutionality. While the Court's decision in *Shelby County* therefore left the door open to a revised coverage formula (or, as several justices suggested, national coverage) in the future, preclearance as it had existed for half a century was gone. Ed Blum had won. "When *Shelby County* came down," he said, "I burst into tears."[84]

Justice Ruth Bader Ginsburg was known for a good dissenting opinion, and she delivered one in *Shelby County*, joined by the three other liberal justices. Ginsburg's dissent reflects the long tension between Congress—tasked with enforcing the 15th Amendment—and the Court. "The question this case presents," she wrote, "is who decides whether, as currently operative, Section 5 remains justifiable: this Court, or a Congress charged with the obligation to enforce the post–Civil War Amendments 'by appropriate legislation.' " Ginsburg believed that extension of preclearance was well within congressional authority, both to continue moving away from election policies that disproportionately burden minority voters and to "*guard against backsliding*" (emphasis added). To Ginsburg and her colleagues in the minority, it was obvious that while they may be diminished, underground, or more subtle, the forces that mandated the VRA's initial passage were still present in the covered regions and therefore still warranted ongoing enforcement via Section 4(b)'s coverage list. In one of the most quoted lines of her storied career, Ginsburg asserted that "throwing out preclearance when it has worked and is continuing to work to stop discriminatory changes is like throwing away your umbrella in a rainstorm because you are not getting wet."

While Ginsburg's is perhaps the best known criticism of the *Shelby County* opinion, it is not the only one. When the opinion was announced, a number of scholars questioned whether the principle of equal state sovereignty was actually as "fundamental" as the Court held it out to be, or whether it was merely a convenient rationale to strike down the coverage formula. Some observers characterized the equal sovereignty principle as having been "seemingly pulled . . . out of thin air" in *NAMUDNO* just four years earlier.[85] Notably, these criticisms did not come exclusively from the political left. Law professor Edward Cantu later noted that "even conservative scholars were incredulous" at the invocation of equal sovereignty in *Shelby County,* with one former George W. Bush–appointed federal judge calling it "made up."[86] Most prominently of all, Richard Posner, a highly regarded conservative legal scholar then on the federal bench, also critiqued this aspect of the *Shelby County* decision. "There is no doctrine of equal sovereignty," Posner wrote at the time. "The opinion rests on air."[87]

The evidence cited in the *Shelby County* opinion is also considerably narrower than it could be. In his opinion, Chief Justice Roberts pointed only to the relative increase in turnout rates among Black voters (relative to white voters) during the VRA's life as evidence that the coverage formula no longer properly identified the worst actors. However, the glaring disparities in Section 2 violations committed by covered jurisdictions are not mentioned in the opinion. Ironically, the majority opinion criticizing the coverage formula for relying on old metrics also had an outdated view of Section 4(b) itself. In arguing that the preclearance condition was no longer justified, the Court looked only at turnout patterns among white and Black voters in the six states *originally* covered under the 1965 version of Section 4(b). It ignored Congress's subsequent recognition that other groups—like Native Americans and Latinos—were discriminated against using language devices, tactics that led to states such as Texas being wholly covered by preclearance. Our analysis in chapter 3 shows that the DOJ objected to more submissions from Texas than any other state; the Court's failure to consider evidence from it and other states covered by the formula it was striking down is therefore a somewhat odd omission.

Factoring a broader range of evidence into the opinion could have led to different conclusions about whether preclearance was a constitutional exercise of Congress's 15th Amendment powers in 2013. Indeed, such a consideration *did* lead two lower courts to uphold Sections 4 and 5. Regardless, absent the ongoing protections that preclearance afforded to minority voters, the liberal justices worried that the very gains celebrated in Roberts's opinion would soon erode. They fretted that in ways overt and subtle, future policies would come to once again disadvantage minority voters in the formerly covered jurisdictions. The so-called "first generation" methods of disenfranchising voters via denying registration, so common in the Jim Crow Era, might be obsolete. But "the evolution of voting discrimination into more subtle second-generation barriers," Ginsburg warned in her dissent, "is powerful evidence that a remedy as effective as preclearance remains vital to protect minority voting rights and prevent backsliding." In the immediate wake of the *Shelby County* ruling, it was too soon to tell whether these concerns were well founded. More than a decade later, we can answer that question.

PART II

Voting Rights Since *Shelby County*

5

Similar Maneuvers

THE TURNOUT GAP

> Congress knew that some of the States covered by Section 4(b) of the Act had resorted to the extraordinary stratagem of contriving new rules of various kinds for the sole purpose of perpetuating voting discrimination in the face of adverse federal court decrees. Congress had reason to suppose that these States might try similar maneuvers in the future in order to evade the remedies for voting discrimination contained in the Act itself.
>
> —CHIEF JUSTICE EARL WARREN, *SOUTH CAROLINA V. KATZENBACH*.[1]

IT WAS August 16, 2018, and the only things hotter than the south Georgia summer were tempers in Cuthbert, the seat of Randolph County. A week earlier, the county board of elections had published notice of a public meeting at which plans to consolidate voting precincts would be discussed. Despite the bland language, the proposal was radical: The board intended to vote on whether to reduce the number of polling places in majority-Black Randolph County from nine to two, and one of the precincts marked for closure was 97% Black. The proposed polling place consolidation would require many rural Black voters to travel up to 30 miles round trip to cast their ballot, presenting a major problem in a county where nearly one in four households lacked access to a personal vehicle (compared to one-in-fourteen statewide) and where nearly one in three residents fell below the federal poverty line.[2]

The county's proposed action quickly drew attention. The same day the notice was published in the *Southern Tribune* (August 4), the ACLU (American Civil Liberties Union) of Georgia sent a public records request to the county's Board of Elections and Registration seeking all emails and internal communications about the proposed changes. After the county failed to respond to the Georgia ACLU's request within the legal time frame, the group sent another letter, on August 14, arguing that "these polling place closures will virtually gurantee lower voter turnout in a Black Belt county that is predominantly African-American."[3] The ACLU's letter characterized the proposed closures as a Section 2 violation and demanded that the board reject the proposal or face litigation. The ACLU released its claims to the public, and the controversy went national overnight. The next day, the Associated Press covered the proposed precinct closures in a story that also ran in the *New York Times*.[4] Suddenly, considerable attention was focused on a small county of just 7,000 residents, all due to a seemingly run-of-the-mill change to election administration.

On Thursday, August 16, dozens of Randolph County residents descended on the courtroom in the low-slung Randolph County Government Building. The tension was especially notable in the broader context of an acrimonious 2018 campaign. As presiding secretary of state (and therefore, the top election official in Georgia), Republican gubernatorial nominee Brian Kemp was overseeing the administration of his own bid for the governor's office. Kemp had already been on the receiving end of multiple allegations of intentional voter suppression. Meanwhile, his opponent Stacey Abrams was the first Black woman to be a major party's gubernatorial candidate in American history. Georgia's fraught past in terms of ensuring racial equality lent a steady subtext to the campaign for governor that year.

The particulars in Randolph County only stirred this pot further. Much of the meeting at the County Government Building focused on Mike Malone, the consultant who had proposed the polling place consolidation. A well-known associate of Kemp, Malone had already successfully recommended that polling places be closed in some ten other counties around the state—all of which had large Black populations.[5] During the meeting, Malone tried to justify his recommendation to close the polling places. The closures were not, Malone argued, an attempt to impose burdens on certain communities but were instead part of an effort to comply with the public access requirements of the Americans with Disabilities Act (ADA). Malone claimed that closing the precinct locations that did not afford access to disabled voters would actually *increase* the convenience of voting for them.

But, to many, this argument rang hollow. According to the ACLU, the county had known about potential ADA compliance issues in its polling places since at least 2012.[6] And, when asked by a member of the public whether he had looked for potential nearby locations that might be ADA compliant, Malone stated simply that he was "not hired to find alternatives." Malone's claims seemed even more dubious because the polling places in question had been in use through the 2018 primary season that spring. The Kemp-aligned consultant encouraged the county to close them only as the general election campaign got under way, and in the case of the gubernatorial election, most analysts anticipated that every vote would count. Making it more difficult for a few likely Democrats to vote here and there might have seemed a viable way to increase the odds of Kemp's victory, especially if no one paid attention to boring precinct changes in rural counties. But those Democratic voters were overwhelmingly Black in Randolph County, and the Section 2 implications were apparent to observers beyond just the ACLU of Georgia. Now squarely in the spotlight, ADA compliance was the best explanation Malone could muster. Sean Young of the ACLU later described the ADA argument as "a total sham."[7]

Over the next week, local and national actors alike weighed in on the issue before the scheduled August 24 vote. On August 22 residents gathered at the Stonehouse Restaurant to rally against the vote; that same day, the county fired Mike Malone.[8] On the 23rd, the Congressional Black Caucus (CBC) sent a letter to the Randolph elections board, urging board members to reject the proposal. The CBC also took the opportunity to remind Randolph County administrators that *Shelby County* had facilitated the enactment of new policies that, while cloaked in race-neutral appearances, held the potential to disenfranchise minority voters in large numbers. While the formerly covered states "are no longer conducting literacy tests," the CBC members wrote, "the effects of their new policies are nearly as precise and effective."[9] On August 24, both members of the Randolph County Board of Elections and Registration voted against the proposal, and all nine polling places remained open that November.

The tale of Randolph County is instructive not because ultimately nothing happened but because of what almost *did* happen. It is not difficult to imagine a different ending to this story. Prior to the uproar, one local resident described coming across the announcement of the vote on the polling place closures while "scanning the local newspaper's legal section with his magnifying glass."[10] What if fewer people in Randolph County had been so diligent? The vote could have come and gone with little notice, with voters unaware until it was too late.

Without the preclearance protection of the VRA's Section 5, minority voters must rely on Section 2 litigation instead. But to challenge discriminatory laws, people with the means to do so must be aware of them. Given trends in American media, voters in Randolph County might count themselves lucky to have any local newspaper at all. Unfortunately, the reach of local media has declined precipitously throughout the nation,[11] and in no place more so than in rural America. Recent research makes clear that the decline in local media reporting reduces the ability of citizens to hold their elected leaders accountable[12]—and makes governments less transparent about their actions.[13] Given this trend, the likelihood of catching potential Section 2 violations in rural localities is shrinking. *Shelby County* thus tipped the federal balance of power over electoral practices back toward the local level at a moment when local governments were less accountable to the public than they had been in decades.

This danger was foreseen by many, including the partially covered states of New York, California, and North Carolina, as well as fully covered Mississippi. In their amicus brief supporting the continuation of preclearance prior to the *Shelby County* argument, these states jointly claimed, "Absent Section 5, it would be difficult or in some cases impossible for interested parties to obtain the information needed to determine whether and where to bring a Section 2 lawsuit, or even to learn that a voting change is contemplated. This is particularly true in the case of smaller governmental entities that may attract less scrutiny."[14] That these covered states themselves recognized the difficulty involved in tracking and assessing administrative changes within their own borders absent DOJ oversight underscores the potential for formerly covered counties, towns, and other substate jurisdictions to enact discriminatory policies without attracting much attention.

The events in Randolph County exemplify this problem. Prior to *Shelby County*, Randolph County administrators would have been required to submit their precinct closure proposal to the Department of Justice for preclearance review, just as every other covered jurisdiction—no matter how small or out of the way—would have been required to do. In Randolph's case, the DOJ would almost certainly have deemed the changes likely to create discriminatory results for voters. The preclearance reviewers thus served as a bulwark against racial disenfranchisement in jurisdictions great and small, and as shown in chapter 3, they processed a considerable volume of paperwork. Recall that the DOJ was processing about 200 proposed policy changes every week in the formerly covered jurisdictions prior to preclearance's demise. At the oral argument in *Shelby County,* Justice Sonia Sotomayor noted that volume can intersect with ingenuity to frustrate efforts to tamp down discriminatory election practices. As Justice Sotomayor put it, "The reason Section 5 was created was because states were moving faster than litigation permitted to catch the new forms of discriminatory practices that were being developed. As the courts struck down one form, the states would find another."

Absent the scrutiny of preclearance reviewers—and in many cases with no local reporters asking questions—there is a clear potential for a large number of formerly covered communities to enact election rules with discriminatory effects. These policies may even be well intended, if poorly considered. In Randolph County, the precinct closure proposal was subjected to scrutiny and was ultimately abandoned as a result. We may never know how many other potentially discriminatory policies were implemented in formerly covered jurisdictions in 2018 (and every other year) since *Shelby County* without attracting any controversy. But, as it turns out, we *can* assess how these changes unleashed by *Shelby County* have shaped minority voters' access to the ballot box. That is the focus of this chapter.

The majority opinion in *Shelby County* rested on a crucial belief: The justices were not convinced that in the absence of preclearance, covered jurisdictions would return to the racial disenfranchisement and vote dilution that had characterized their election practices prior to the VRA. Indeed, in his opinion Chief Justice Roberts expressed the belief that "things have changed dramatically [since 1965]." A careful examination of available data can allow us to determine whether, more than a decade later, the *Shelby County* majority's assumptions still hold. In the remainder of this book, we examine events and important data sources to do just that. In this and the chapters that follow, there is a single guiding question: Is there reason to believe that voting practices have slid backward since *Shelby County* in jurisdictions formerly subject to preclearance? We bring a wide range of data to bear on answering it in the context of various policies that are in the news from time to time. But first, we have to acknowledge that while the cases we describe later on are informative, there is simply no way we can closely examine every policy that formerly covered jurisdictions have implemented since 2013.

In chapter 3, we describe the huge volume and wide range of requests that jurisdictions made under the preclearance system. There is no reason to believe that the pace or breadth of change slowed after the demise of preclearance. Indeed, we might even expect that the frequency of election changes accelerated after *Shelby County* as formerly covered jurisdictions released some pent-up energy. The immediate trend after *Shelby County* seems consistent with this—at least at the state level. Of the 15 states where statewide election changes were subject to preclearance, 11 had enacted more restrictive election policies by the 10-year anniversary of the decision.[15] While not all of these policies would necessarily have been blocked under Section 5, at least a few almost surely would have been: The Voting Section of the U.S. Department of Justice has brought or joined ten lawsuits against formerly covered jurisdictions for violating other provisions of the Voting Rights Act or the 1964 Civil Rights Act since *Shelby County* was decided (including five in Texas).[16] Other statutes were struck down following federal court challenges waged by private parties in several states—including (but not limited to) Alabama[17] and North Carolina.[18] Still other local changes surely went into effect without attracting any legal challenge.

Did the new wave of state reforms impede turnout among minority voters? In academic research, a common way to approach questions like this is to examine how a given policy affects turnout of voters with certain racial identities. Some scholars have argued that restrictive voting laws in the post–*Shelby County* era, in the aggregate, perhaps have not affected minority voters all that much more than white voters.[19] Other work has found, however, that changes to election laws in formerly covered states disproportionately burdened minority voters.[20] At the state level, then, there is reason to believe that outcomes for minority voters may have been different in the formerly covered states than they would have been without the *Shelby County* decision—perhaps to the point of reducing their turnout relative to white voters.

When states pursue major election changes that are alleged to harm minority voters, the story is typically covered not only in local outlets but also in national media. These changes therefore tend to attract attention from academic researchers looking to assess their effects. But we have already shown that a clear majority of both preclearance requests and objections originated not at the state or even county level but in covered municipalities, school districts, conservation zones, and the like. This makes sense. In the United States, election administration is largely a local affair. State and federal law—or directives from state election officials—may provide guidelines to local election officials (LEOs) or county election boards (following convention among political scientists, we refer to all local election administration apparatuses as

LEOs). In most of the country, however, LEOs have wide latitude to conduct elections as they see fit: Routine decisions like the siting of polling places, the hours available for early voting, or the advertisement of voting requirements are regularly left to county- or municipal-level actors.

The importance of local practices in shaping Americans' electoral experiences is well understood.[21] Much academic work on this topic has considered the potential for LEOs' discretion to foster uneven or discriminatory election practices—intentionally or otherwise. Several previous studies have raised concerns about how LEOs' attitudinal or partisan traits might shape outcomes like provisional ballot counting, election infrastructure spending, and polling place location.[22] While some of this work has found little evidence that partisan election officials aid candidates of their own party,[23] other results demonstrate that LEOs, acting as "street level bureaucrats," sometimes exercise their discretion in a discriminatory manner.[24]

The most comprehensive study of local actions in the aftermath of *Shelby County* is a report from the Leadership Conference on Civil and Human Rights,[25] documenting widespread polling place consolidation in formerly covered counties well beyond Randolph County—though the report did not compare these trends to what was happening elsewhere in the country. In a followup study, McInerney and colleagues focus on Alabama and how new election laws affected turnout there;[26] ultimately, they changed the focus of their project to instead document the "challenges that arose throughout the process and their implications for voters' access to public polling information." McInerney and colleagues' study shows just how difficult it is to obtain local data on election practices. For instance, they were able to contact fewer than half of the LEOs in Alabama; of those that responded, just 80% provided data on polling place closures. Other researchers have found that even data as "simple" as precinct-level election results are often unavailable.[27] Gathering data on how all American localities changed their practices in the aftermath of *Shelby County* would require collecting information from thousands of covered and noncovered jurisdictions over a period of more than fifteen years. This is a functionally impossible task—and a major negative outcome from *Shelby County*.

Thus, while there is ample reason to expect that local election officials might have responded to *Shelby County* in different ways, low-visibility local actions present something of a problem for researchers. Even though local laws may attract less attention than other, higher-profile ones, they can still have substantial effects on aggregate voter participation in a formerly covered state. What's more, the coverage formula also allowed for the DOJ to send federal observers into polling places in covered jurisdictions to look for racially discriminatory practices that might not ever have been submitted for preclearance; this program, too, was brought to a halt by *Shelby County*. Our goal in this chapter is therefore not to assess the impact of a policy (or set of policies) in a single town or county. Rather than going micro, we deal with the problem of unknown changes in small jurisdictions by going *big* in our focus. We consider the electorate as a whole in each formerly covered jurisdiction. We want to determine whether the totality of post–*Shelby County* legal and administrative changes in formerly covered jurisdictions—including seemingly mundane, local decisions that attract little notice—has impacted minority voters in a manner that the Voting Rights Act was designed to prevent.

It is reasonable at this point to ask just how we plan to observe the voting behavior of the entire electorate. The answer is in voter file data from all American states. Federal law requires states to keep publicly available lists of all registered voters.[28] These voter file data do not indicate which candidate someone voted for, but they do provide an unambiguous administrative record indicating whether a registered voter turned out in a given election. If we have this information for all voters in a jurisdiction, we can easily calculate turnout among registered voters—or even among subgroups of voters. For our purposes, using information from the voter file is a dramatic improvement over other methods we might use to build a historical record of individual voting behavior. If, for instance, we asked people in surveys about whether they voted in a prior election, there is a good chance that many will say they turned out even if they stayed home, because voting is a socially desirable action and people want to appear civically engaged. This tendency has obvious implications for accurately measuring turnout.[29] In creating an unambiguous record, the voter files allow us to avoid this problem altogether.

To ensure that our estimates are as close as possible to the "true" electorate, we rely on snapshots collected by data vendors shortly after each federal election from 2008 to 2022.[30] In total, we analyze the records of nearly one billion votes cast in these elections. Because some voters are deregistered before the files reflecting turnout are made available, voter file snapshots are never perfect. However, we estimate that we have the individual-level records for more than 97% of all ballots cast in these years.[31] With such a long time period, we can observe turnout in three federal elections before the *Shelby County* decision, and five after. This is a crucial first step in determining how the end of preclearance may have impacted turnout.

We need to go even further, however. The main objective of the VRA was to narrow what political scientists often refer to as the *racial turnout gap*, or the difference in turnout between white and minority voters.[32] If the racial turnout gap is high, it means that a higher percentage of white voters than minority voters have turned out to vote. This was definitely the case throughout the South in 1964, when widespread racial disenfranchisement kept Black voters from the polls. In *Shelby County*, the Court noted that the VRA had worked as intended and that the racial turnout gap had narrowed in the five decades since the law's implementation. To the majority's justices, this suggested that racial disenfranchisement was a thing of the past, rendering the preclearance process unjustified. If that reasoning was correct, suspending federal preclearance should not have affected the racial turnout gap.

The voter files allow us to determine whether discrimination has in fact ended in elections that have occurred since the Court's ruling. The data include a variety of individual-level characteristics, such as the voter's name and address, and sometimes other attributes like party affiliation, age, and gender. Because we are interested in calculating turnout separately for white and minority voters, we also obviously need data on voters' race. In some formerly covered states, this information is straightforward, as the election authorities there have long collected voters' self-identified race or ethnicity.[33] We use the racial identities that voters reported to these states whenever possible. In the states that do not collect it during their registration process, we use a statistical procedure to estimate each voter's race, using a combination of their last name and known demographic traits of their neighborhood. Social scientists commonly use this method to predict Americans' races.[34] We provide more detail about how we do this in the Methodological Appendix.

The core outcome (or dependent variable) in our analysis is the racial turnout gap; that is, the turnout of a given minority group subtracted from turnout among white voters.[35] At various times, we focus on the *white-Black* and the *white-nonwhite* gaps,[36] though we generally center the *overall white-nonwhite*

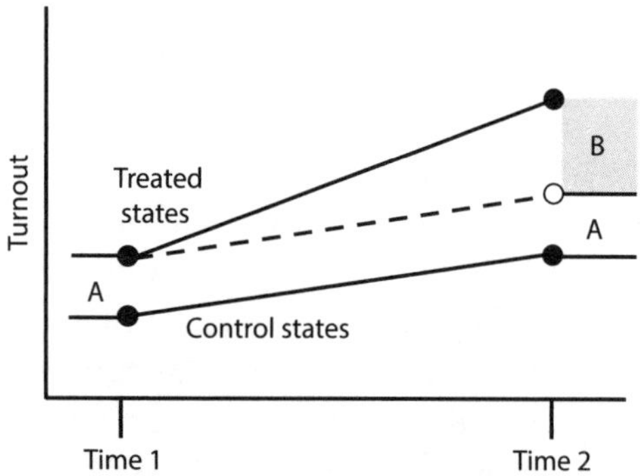

FIGURE 5.1. Hypothetical Example: Difference in Differences

turnout gap in our results. We do so because the Voting Rights Act did not distinguish between minority groups; it could be triggered if *any* racial or language minority group was systemically disenfranchised. However, we also examine the *white-Black* turnout gap, for three reasons. First, that metric featured prominently in the Supreme Court's opinion in *Shelby County*; for that reason, it is worth looking for any notable trends there. Second, Black voters make up a much larger share of the nonwhite population in formerly covered states than in the rest of the country (approximately half, compared to about 25% elsewhere; see Methodological Appendix). Third, even though the VRA targets all racial voting discrimination, Congress enacted it in direct response to discrimination against Black voters.

The more technical details of our empirical approach can be found in the Methodological Appendix, but the core idea that underpins the analysis we present in this chapter and in the remainder of the book is fairly simple. To illustrate how, we pause here to describe a simplified example that might help readers who do not spend their days steeped in social science. In figure 5.1, we show how we might approach a similar, albeit hypothetical research question. Here, at a point between Time 1 and Time 2, suppose Congress made grant money available to states for voter education before an election that occurred at Time 2, but not all states accepted the funds. To answer questions such as how the grant money affected turnout in the states that accepted it, social scientists often borrow from the language of experiments. We would consider states that took grant money to be "treated" in much the same way that, say, someone who participated in a drug trial and received a dose of a medication (as opposed to individuals in the "control group" who received a placebo or no drug) is described as having received a treatment. The states that did not receive funds in this example are therefore referred to as "control states."

Our example reveals why it is not sufficient to simply look at average turnout in the two groups at Time 2—after the money was dispersed—to judge the program's effect on turnout: The treated states already exhibited higher turnout *prior* to receiving the treatment; the magnitude of that initial difference is denoted as *A* in figure 5.1. This initial difference makes sense. We would not expect the two groups to start at exactly the same point anyway, but here it tracks that the states that already had a high-turnout culture were especially likely to seek optional civic education funds. Regardless, merely calculating the difference between the two groups at Time 2 would overstate the grant's effect in our example, because doing so ignores the higher turnout level that treated states had already shown prior to the grant program.

To solve this problem, we need an estimate of the *counterfactual* for the treatment group, or an indication of what would have happened in the treatment states had they not taken grant money. To estimate the counterfactual, we observe the trend in the control states from Time 1 to Time 2. In figure 5.1, we see that turnout went up in those control states, even though they did not take any of the grant money. Perhaps campaigns were more effective in Time 2, or economic conditions were such that voters were more motivated, even though there was no new civic education program in their state. For our purposes, finding the reason for the growth among control states is less important than knowing that it occurred. If turnout trended upward in states that opted out of the grant money, it stands to reason that it would have gone up in the treated states too had they declined the extra funds, and if we do the analysis correctly, we can assume that it would likely have gone up by about the same amount.[37]

If we want to estimate where turnout would have ended up in treated states had they not taken grant money, we therefore simply apply the slope of the control states' line to the treatment states, beginning at the initial treatment state turnout estimate at Time 1. This counterfactual trend is represented by the dashed line in figure 5.1, culminating in the open circle at Time 2. From here, it is straightforward to estimate the effect of the grant program: We simply subtract the counterfactual level of turnout from the one we observe in the treatment group at Time 2. That quantity, represented by the shaded region *B* in figure 5.1, gives us the "treatment effect," which in this example is the bump in state-level turnout that we attribute to accepting the grants. Astute readers will see that we have taken the *difference* between the groups in the *differences* they exhibit at Time 2 relative to Time 1.

This "difference in differences" setup, common in the social sciences, is useful because, if done right, it supports conclusions about how events *caused* changes in affected units. Because in the social sciences we are always concerned about how other factors might bias our results if we fail to account for them, we ultimately employ much more sophisticated methods than simple arithmetic to calculate the differences; we refer interested readers to the Methodological Appendix for more detail on our approach. Still, the underlying intuition is the same, and the basic logic we have just shown guides much of our analysis for the remainder of this book.

We can use this approach in our county-level analysis because just as in the example above, not all American counties were covered by the VRA's preclearance requirement prior to *Shelby County*. The counties in our treatment group were subject to preclearance. For the noncovered counties, however, the world continued in much the same way after 2013 as before; *Shelby County* could not have directly affected the turnout gap in these counties because preclearance never applied to them at all.[38] These counties compose our control group. As in the hypothetical example just described, we lean on the control counties to provide the counterfactual.

This approach has the significant benefit of incorporating *all* changes in the aftermath of *Shelby County*, regardless of the level of government at which they occurred. It does not require us to identify every polling place that was moved or every limitation on early voting from the past decade. If the turnout gap widened more in formerly covered jurisdictions after *Shelby County* than it did in places that were not subject to preclearance, our analysis provides evidence that a crucial assumption made by the justices in that case—that because the turnout gap had shrunk in the formerly covered states, preclearance was no longer necessary—may have been wrong.

Our first expectation is that after *Shelby County*, the racial turnout gap widened more in jurisdictions that had previously been subject to preclearance than it did in the control counties. This expectation is based on simple logic: One goal of the VRA was to narrow the racial turnout gap in areas where it had previously been massive. Absent the law, we might expect the turnout gap to return. Just as we showed in the hypothetical example in figure 5.1, we trace the racial turnout gap in the control and treatment groups across time. *Shelby County* was decided in 2013, an "off year," with no federal election. The

Court's decision represents an important threshold, then, as it allows us to look at the average difference in the racial turnout gap in both treated and control counties, before and after the decision was handed down.

Before we look at the county-level data, we first preprocess them with a matching algorithm that ensures the treated and control counties used in our analysis were similar on a range of factors prior to the *Shelby County* decision.[39] In plain English, we pair each treated county to a control county that matches up well with it on factors such as population and the typical age and race of their residents in 2012. We jettison control counties that do not pair well with any treated counties from the data, and weight the matched control counties so that they provide a well-balanced comparison to the treatment group. This process results in a dataset that is highly similar on relevant "pretreatment" factors, reducing the chances that key dissimilarities between the two groups of counties would somehow bias our results. In the Methodological Appendix, we show the socioeconomic characteristics of the formerly covered counties, the non-formerly-covered counties, and the characteristics of the matched controls.

In the left panel of figure 5.2, we depict the white-nonwhite turnout gap from 2008 to 2022; in the right panel, we show the white-Black turnout gap. In both panels, we see the two groups moving in parallel before the *Shelby County* ruling. Although the average turnout gap in covered counties was higher even before *Shelby County*, the fact that they move up and down together prior to "treatment" increases our confidence that any divergence thereafter is attributable to the Court's ruling. And we do observe divergence after *Shelby County*. When we examine the white-nonwhite turnout gap, we see that the covered and noncovered counties continued to move in similar fashion, rising steadily until about 2016. At that point, the turnout gap *declines* in the formerly noncovered counties before resuming a less steep incline relative to formerly covered ones.

By the 2022 election, the white-nonwhite turnout gap is about five points higher in the formerly covered counties—more than double its widest point prior to the *Shelby County* decision. The disparity between the two groups is even clearer in the white-Black turnout gap (figure 5.2, bottom panel). There, we see a widening beginning almost immediately following *Shelby County*, with a consistently higher turnout gap in the formerly covered counties for

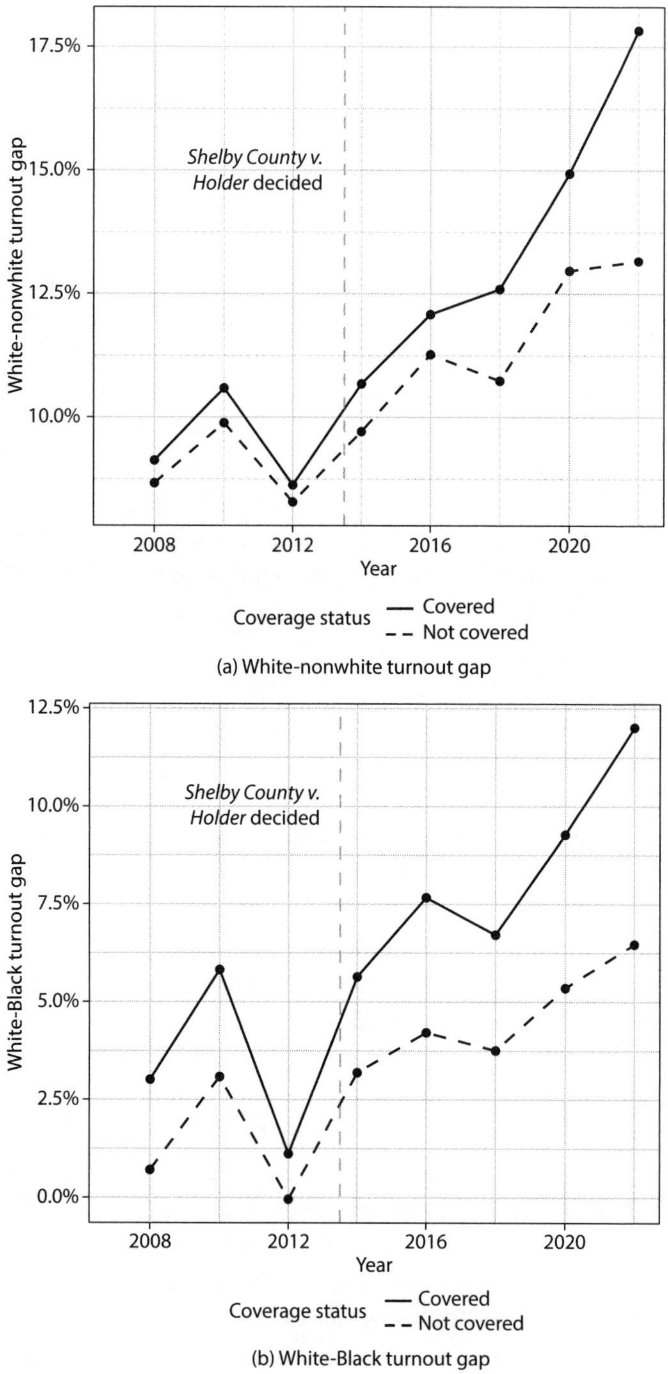

FIGURE 5.2. Turnout Gap Time Series

the next eight years. By 2022, the white-Black turnout gap in formerly covered counties was approximately twice that in the noncovered ones.

In figure 5.3, we show the results from statistical models constructed from the matched data, which are a more technical (but methodologically correct) way to calculate "treatment effects" akin to the one in figure 5.1, Region *B* (see Methodological Appendix).[40] The treatment effect from these models tells us how much the *Shelby County* ruling affected the covered counties relative to the noncovered ones.[41] The models also give us a confidence bound—represented by the vertical lines—around the treatment effect so we can tell with 95% confidence whether the difference is greater than zero. When the vertical line does not cross zero, that means that a measured effect is "statistically significant"; put differently, it means that we can rule out that the relationships we find are caused by random chance. That is, we are 95% confident that there really was an effect of *Shelby County*.

We find compelling statistical evidence that the *Shelby County* ruling led to a greater increase in the turnout gap in formerly covered counties relative to ones that were not subject to preclearance. Figure 5.3 is quite consistent with the time series trend described above. With respect to the white-nonwhite turnout gap, figure 5.3 shows that the gap grows steadily in the elections following *Shelby County*. The white-nonwhite turnout gap becomes significantly greater in treated counties than in control counties in 2018 and remains so thereafter. By 2022, the model indicates, the *Shelby County* ruling caused an increase of more than 4 percentage points in the white-nonwhite gap in the treated counties, relative to controls. In the right pane of figure 5.3, we see a similar pattern in the white-Black turnout gap: Immediately following the *Shelby County* decision, the treatment effect is positive and soon becomes statistically significant.

But the data allow for even deeper exploration, and common sense provides a good guide for what we might expect to find. One of the most obvious factors that merits more consideration is that preclearance treatment is not always a simple, either-or condition. As it turns out, some jurisdictions were impacted more by preclearance requirements than others. We explain in chapter 3 that there were really *three* main categories of counties with respect to the preclearance condition. First, we had covered counties. For them, both proposed county actions *and* state actions were subject to preclearance, because state law also affected the covered counties.[42] On the other end of the spectrum were noncovered counties in states that were themselves noncovered. These jurisdictions never experienced preclearance of any kind during our

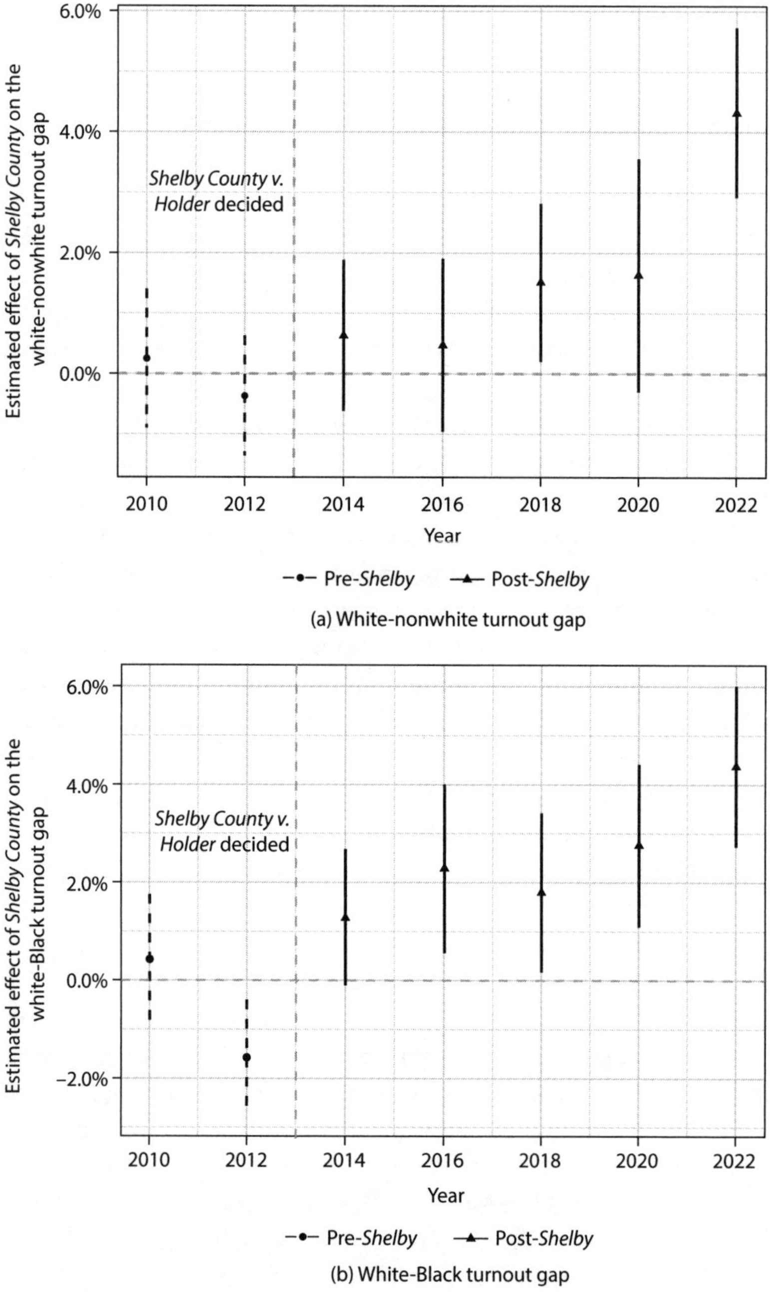

(a) White-nonwhite turnout gap

(b) White-Black turnout gap

FIGURE 5.3. Statistical Effects of *Shelby County* on the Turnout Gap

study period. As noted above, they therefore serve as our controls, because *Shelby County* did not affect their election administration in any way.

In a handful of other "partially covered" states, only a subset of local jurisdictions were subject to preclearance of local election policies.[43] In these states, however, it turns out that even noncovered jurisdictions were subject to *some* preclearance. Because a proposed change to state policies would affect noncovered and covered counties alike, any potential changes to statewide election policies in partially covered states were also subject to federal preclearance.[44] Take North Carolina, for instance, which has 100 counties in total. There, the 60 noncovered counties were free to make whatever local changes they desired. But preclearance applied to proposed changes not only in North Carolina's 40 covered counties but also those proposed by the state itself.[45] Thus, even noncovered counties in North Carolina were subject to some DOJ review of potential regulatory changes, via review of state laws.

This kind of variation is not a problem to be overcome but instead a feature that we can exploit to learn even more about how the removal of preclearance affected the racial turnout gap. For instance, we might expect that because *Shelby County* altered only how *some* changes were implemented in an uncovered county in a partially covered state, these counties might constitute a middle category with respect to how the Court's ruling affected their racial turnout gap. That is, we should expect that if the racial turnout gap in noncovered counties located in partially covered states grew relative to control after the *Shelby County* decision, it did so less than in covered counties.

To look at how county-level variation like this affects the manner in which *Shelby County* impacted the turnout gap, we switch up our modeling approach somewhat. We continue using a similar statistical model, with all the covered counties and the same set of matched, uncovered counties. But now we are interested in whether or not we can explain variation in the growth of the turnout gap *within* the set of formerly covered counties. Changing to a new modeling setup allows us to examine whether county factors such as coverage status matter (see the Methodological Appendix for more information on this change).[46]

The first question these models can answer is the one posed immediately above: Did counties subject to preclearance of both county and state election laws experience greater changes in their racial turnout gap after *Shelby County* than those that were subject to state-level preclearance alone? To answer this question, we sort all counties into one of the three groups described above: uncovered in a state with no covered counties (where neither statewide nor local

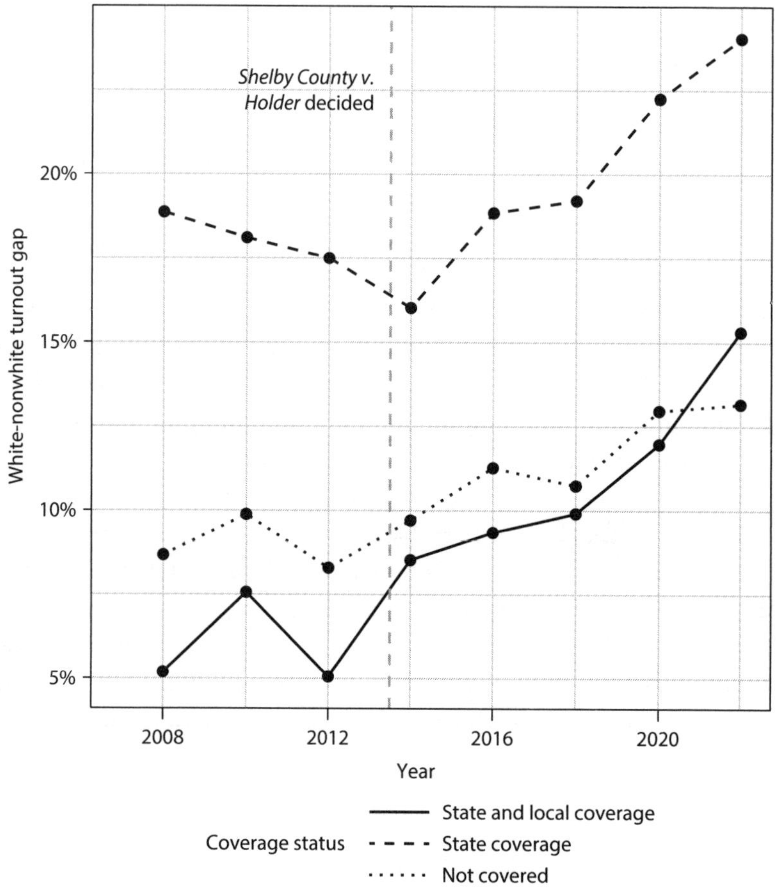

FIGURE 5.4. Evolution of the White-Nonwhite Turnout Gap by Coverage Status

policies were constrained by preclearance), uncovered counties in a state with at least one covered county (where *statewide* practices were constrained but local ones were not), and covered counties (where local *and* statewide policies were subject to preclearance). We present the statistical results from our models in the Appendix, but visually show the data here. Figures 5.4 and 5.5 indicate that in uncovered counties in partially covered states, the white-nonwhite and white-Black turnout gaps grew at about the same rate as they did in uncovered counties. But both the white-nonwhite and white-Black gaps grew considerably more quickly in the counties where Section 5 previously constrained state and local practices alike (as we show in the Methodological Appendix, these results are statistically significant). This is exactly the result we would expect if

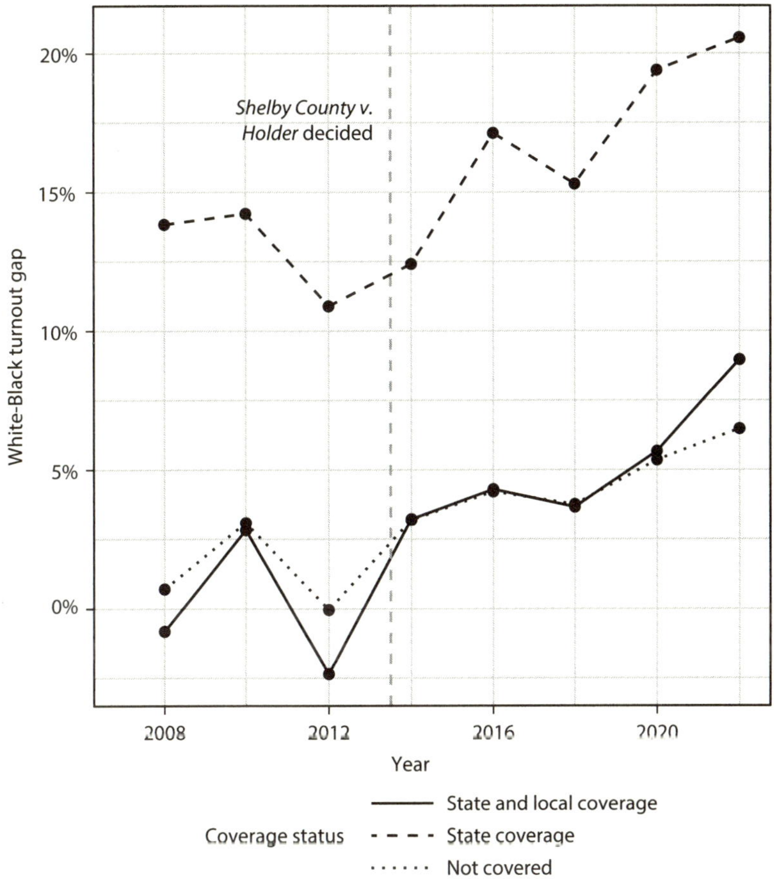

FIGURE 5.5. Evolution of the White-Black Turnout Gap by Coverage Status

preclearance was holding fully covered jurisdictions back from implementing policies that would have fueled the turnout gap prior to Section 4(b)'s demise.

Beyond coverage, there are other important factors that should shape how jurisdictions responded to the *Shelby County* opinion. Chapter 3 shows that the bulk of the DOJ's Section 5 objection letters blocked not state laws but proposed county- or local-level practices. These objection letters provide us with a set of counties that prior to 2013 attempted to enact practices that the federal government deemed likely to be racially discriminatory. Since preclearance assessed the likely *results* of a policy, rather than requiring evidence of intentional discrimination, we cannot say whether the counties that received objection letters intentionally sought to enact discriminatory voting policies.

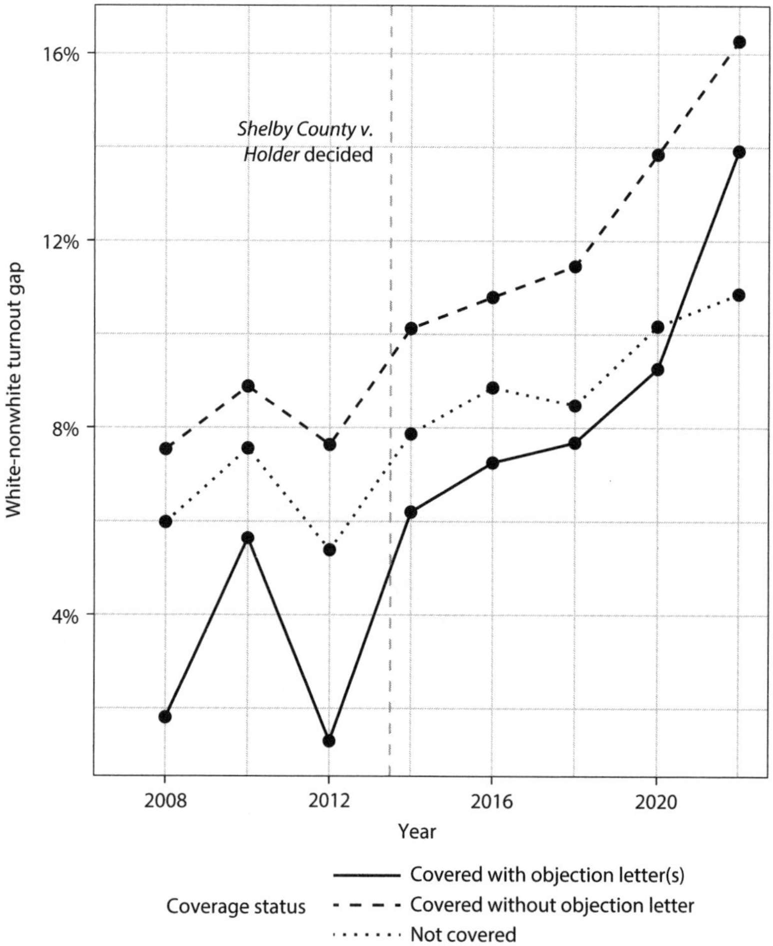

FIGURE 5.6. Evolution of the White-Nonwhite Turnout Gap by Objection Letter

Nevertheless, these objection letters identify the counties that would have implemented a change to their voting regime that, according to the Justice Department, disadvantaged minority voters. It is therefore conceivable that potentially discriminatory policies in the post-preclearance era would be concentrated in these same places—and, thus, that the turnout gap would grow most quickly in these jurisdictions after *Shelby County*.

Figures 5.6 and 5.7 indicate that the effects of *Shelby County* were largest in the places that sought to implement a racially discriminatory election policy or practice prior to the ruling. In these counties, the turnout gap grew by 2

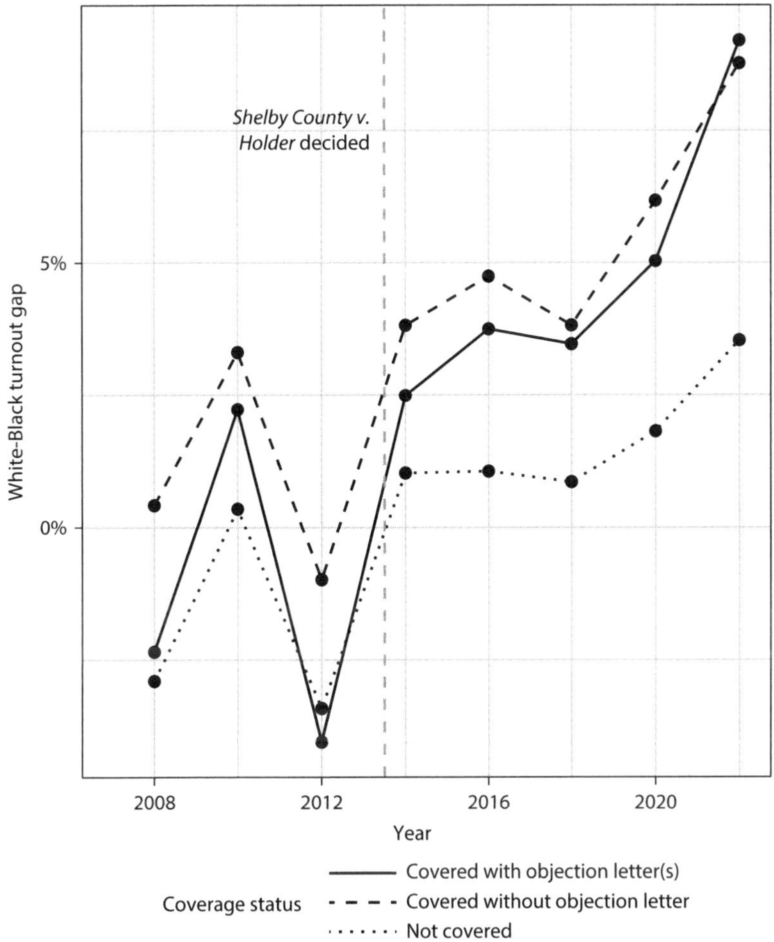

FIGURE 5.7. Evolution of the White-Black Turnout Gap by Objection Letter

to 3 points more than in the counties that were never covered, and a point or 2 more quickly than in the covered counties that never tried to implement a policy that was blocked by the DOJ. This analysis raises the possibility that some counties exercised their newfound latitude in the aftermath of *Shelby County* to implement policies similar to those they sought to enact prior to 2013—some of which the DOJ had objected to.[47]

Finally, we test whether the effect of *Shelby County* varied according to the partisan composition of the locality. It at least seems possible that if conservative state legislators pushed to make voting more difficult after 2013, such moves might have been contested at the local level in areas where more

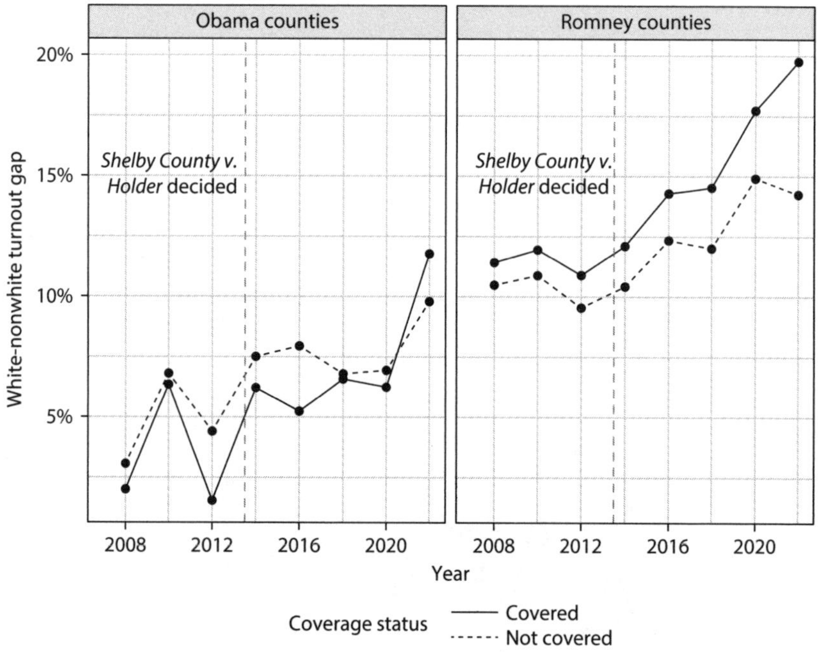

FIGURE 5.8. Evolution of the White-Nonwhite Turnout Gap by 2012 Presidential Winner

Democrats have power. Similarly, local election officials in more Democratic areas might be less likely to institute racially regressive policies in the absence of preclearance. That would lead to a smaller effect of *Shelby County* on the turnout gap in counties where Barack Obama received a larger share of votes cast in 2012—the last federal election before the Court's decision. Figures 5.8 and 5.9 indicate that this was in fact the case: We find strong evidence that the growth in the gap was concentrated in counties won by Mitt Romney, the Republican presidential candidate in the final pre–*Shelby County* presidential election. In the Methodological Appendix, we include statistical models for all of these split-sample plots we show here.

The larger post–*Shelby County* turnout gaps we observe in the Romney counties are a reminder that local politics can play an important role in blunting (or exacerbating) the effects of *Shelby County*—potentially along the lines we outline above. We therefore close our analysis by discussing important caveats to our findings—and why they differ from some of those of scholars who have approached this question in recent years. Although our use of voter file data sets us apart from some previous academic research into how

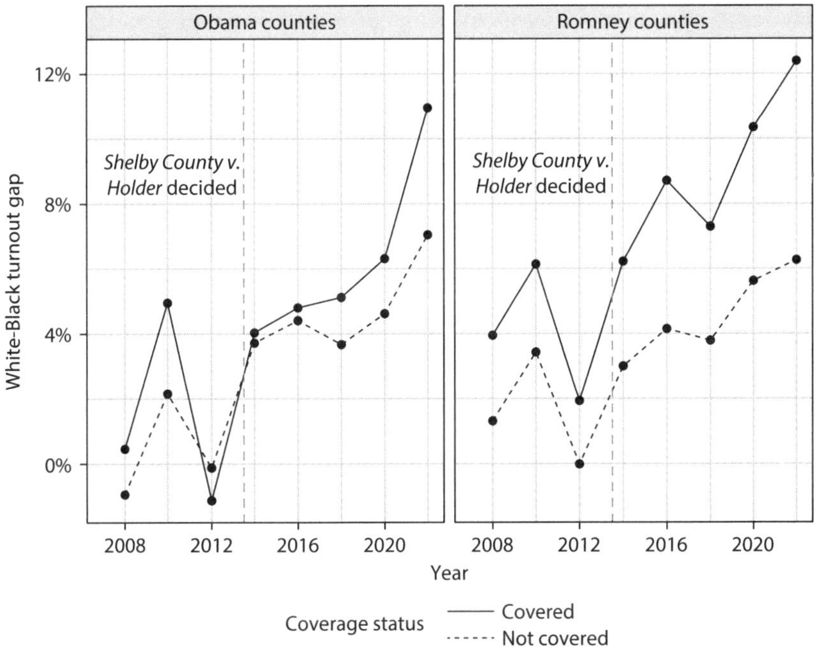

FIGURE 5.9. Evolution of the White-Black Turnout Gap by 2012 Presidential Winner

Shelby County affected the racial turnout gap,[48] two serious studies have been published in recent years exploring the effects of the decision using similar data to ours. Like this book, a 2024 paper by Billings and colleagues finds that the *Shelby County* ruling increased the turnout gap between Black and white voters in formerly covered counties, with less clear evidence of a gap between Anglo and Latino voters.[49] Billings and coauthors do not attempt to estimate voters' race; instead, they rely on estimates of the racial composition of the census blocks in which voters live, identifying areas with high and low shares of Black, Latino, and white voters. While this is an important study, the paper relies on a single snapshot of the voter file and can assess the effects of *Shelby County* only on voters who were registered in 2012 and remained so nearly a decade later. It must by definition exclude all new registrants over the time period (including all Americans who turned 18 or moved into the state), as well as anyone who died or moved across state lines (and were therefore removed from the rolls).

Like Billings and colleagues, Komisarchik and White[50] rely on data from voter files to test the effects of *Shelby County* on turnout gaps. In an approach similar to ours, they use voter file data collected shortly after each election. The voter file data they received from the vendor Catalist were aggregated to the county level, using the Catalist racial prediction algorithms. Although Komisarchik and White conclude that *Shelby County* did *not* increase the racial turnout gap, the reason for our seemingly different conclusions is that their research question differed slightly from ours—and the differences between our approach and theirs highlight an interesting wrinkle about the effects of *Shelby County* that results of our examining counties' party balance may foreshadow.

In their study, Komisarchik and White weight each county by its Black population. This means that larger counties contribute more to their estimates of the turnout gap—and that *individuals* are counted equally in their analysis. This perfectly valid research design indicates that *most Black voters* in formerly covered counties did not live in an area where the racial turnout gap grew in response to *Shelby County*. But, in the analysis we presented above, we have asked a slightly different question: We want to know whether the end of preclearance led to worse outcomes in the *average election jurisdiction*. For that reason, we count each county equally, regardless of its population. If we were interested in the behavior of US senators, we would not weight the actions of each senator by the population they represent. Likewise, because we are interested in the actions of local election officials, we allow each jurisdiction to carry the same weight in our analysis, obtaining quite different results from Komisarchik and White's.

The differences between our studies can shed important light on how *Shelby County* operated: If we find no effects of *Shelby County* on the turnout gap when we weight by population (as Komisarchik and White did) but more sizable effects in formerly covered jurisdictions when we weight each county equally (as our analysis indicates), that might imply that voters in the very largest counties were somehow protected from the negative effects of preclearance's demise. That is precisely the state of play when our results are considered in light of those reported in Komisarchik and White. Moreover, when we remove the largest 5% of covered counties from our data, weight by population, and rerun the analysis we present in this chapter, our core conclusions remain unchanged: The turnout gap increased more in the formerly covered jurisdictions. This gives even more credence to the possibility that something different may have been happening in the larger jurisdictions.

The case of Harris County, Texas, may provide some insight into what that difference might be. Harris is a racially diverse county with more than 5 million residents. That is a *really large* county—only two American counties are more populous—so when we weight our analysis by population, Harris counts as much as the smallest 393 formerly covered counties *combined*. But Harris County (and other large counties under Democratic control) may not be representative of the election administration that the post-*Shelby* years brought to formerly covered jurisdictions. During that period, Democratic officials in Harris County increased the number of polling places by a factor of three and the county election budget by a factor of more than *eight*—from $4 million to $33 million—in an effort to make voting easier for residents.[51] These moves proved controversial in the Republican-controlled state capital, however. In 2023 the state passed several laws curtailing the autonomy of Harris County (and only Harris County) to administer its own elections, prompting the county to sue the state.[52] Not all large, Democratically controlled urban counties went this far, but many have taken steps of their own to mitigate the impact of restrictive state voting policies on their residents.

As we show above, the effects of *Shelby County* on the turnout gap were smaller in Democratic-leaning areas, and these also tend to be larger counties. Barack Obama carried four-fifths of the covered counties with at least a half million voting-age citizens in 2012 but just 22% of the rest of the covered counties. Election administrators in large counties are therefore considerably more likely to be Democrats, elected by Democratic voters, or appointed by Democratic officials. Separate from the policies preferred and implemented by the LEOs themselves, larger counties are also considerably more likely to have local news sources;[53] if officials are concerned about scrutiny of their plans, they may be less likely to make discriminatory changes. In this way, local media might perform a function similar to the DOJ preclearance reviewers themselves.

Other factors might also allow for greater countermobilization in larger counties. Democratic gubernatorial candidates—who are generally preferred by minority voters—are more likely to campaign in urban counties,[54] perhaps offering a countervailing force. Community groups might similarly be able to activate voters to overcome the new costs imposed by any discriminatory voting regimes that officials have attempted to erect in these large, formerly covered counties. In total, then, there are multiple actors, forces, and resources in more populous counties that could push against discriminatory voting practices more effectively than in smaller locales.

The fact that *Shelby County* might not have had a very large effect in the biggest of counties, however, does not mean that it did not distort representation in the South. To test the on-the-ground effects of a larger turnout gap

TABLE 5.1. Effect of *Shelby County* on Majority-Minority Lower-Chamber Districts in 2022 (as Share of Participants)

	No. of Nonwhite-Majority Districts			No. of Black-Majority Districts		
State	Actual	Counter-factual	Net Change	Actual	Counter-factual	Net Change
AK	4	4	0	0	0	0
AL	19	23	4	17	21	4
AZ	1	1	0	0	0	0
GA	51	55	4	41	44	3
LA	19	23	4	16	20	4
MS	44	44	0	44	44	0
SC	11	13	2	11	13	2
TX	53	54	1	2	2	0
VA	12	12	0	9	10	1
Total	214	229	15	140	154	14

attributable to *Shelby County,* we estimated the number of lower-chamber state legislative districts in which minority voters (overall, or just Black voters) made up a majority of those who cast a ballot in the 2022 election. We then estimated how many more ballots would have been cast by voters of color in each district if preclearance were still in effect, using models sensitive to the fact that the end of preclearance had a smaller effect in larger counties. In fact, the models assume that *Shelby County* had no effect at all on Black turnout in 13 of the 15 covered counties with the largest Black population, and no effect on nonwhite turnout in each of the 15 counties with the largest nonwhite populations. The results of this exercise can be seen in table 5.1. Across the nine fully covered states, we estimate that nonwhite voters in the 2022 election would have made up a majority of participants in 15 more legislative districts than they actually did if preclearance were still in effect. Black voters would also have made up an outright majority in 14 more districts (these are not necessarily the same districts, as some were already majority-nonwhite without being majority-Black). For more on this analysis, interested readers can see the Methodological Appendix.

To be sure, we do not know whether the outcomes of any elections would have been changed in the districts where racial and ethnic minorities would have made up a majority of voters if preclearance were still in effect. But this analysis makes clear that the turnout effects of *Shelby County* may have hampered the ability of minority voters to elect candidates of their choosing. Given that the effects of *Shelby County* seem to be growing with time, this is particularly concerning.

A central premise underpinning the majority's decision in *Shelby County v. Holder* was that, absent evidence of continued racial disenfranchisement in covered jurisdictions, the geographic preclearance requirements could not be further justified. The majority posited that while racial disenfranchisement was once a scourge of Southern politics, by 2013 "things [had] changed dramatically."[55] Writing for the majority, Chief Justice John Roberts pointed specifically to the white-Black turnout gap. During the time that Section 5 was operable, he wrote, "largely because of the Voting Rights Act, voting tests were abolished, disparities in voter registration and *turnout due to race* were erased, and African-Americans attained political office in record numbers." Elsewhere the Court noted that in 2012, "African-American voter turnout exceeded white voter turnout in five of the six States originally covered by Section 5, with a gap in the sixth State of less than one half of one percent."

In 2012, there was some truth to what the Court said: The white-Black turnout gap in covered jurisdictions was relatively small and in line with the rest of the country. But things did not remain that way. Of course, the data the Court relied on did not tell the whole story. The justices considered only the white-Black turnout gap, not the full white-nonwhite one. The Court also looked only at the states *originally* covered under Section 5, ignoring places like Texas that were added to the preclearance list later. Finally, they focused on the 2008 and 2012 elections, when Barack Obama's candidacy likely led to more minority voters participating. But, as we show, the end of preclearance has led to a dramatic expansion of the racial turnout gap in formerly covered jurisdictions. We estimate that, absent *Shelby County*, the white-Black turnout gap would have grown by about 4 or 5 percentage points in those counties by 2022; instead, it grew by 9 points. In real terms, this means *Shelby County* led to hundreds of thousands fewer ballots being cast by Americans of color in the 2020 and 2022 elections. While the effects were muted in the very largest counties, they nonetheless reduce the number of legislative districts in which voters of color make up a majority of voters.

Our research design does not demand that we individually identify the policies that each county enacted; instead, we measure the effect of the totality of the changes on the racial turnout gap. Moreover, in addition to identifying the effect of *Shelby County* across formerly covered jurisdictions as a whole, we present evidence that the decision's effects were concentrated in the counties we would theoretically expect: where local practices were constrained by preclearance in addition to state policies, where counties tried to implement a racially discriminatory policy prior to 2013, and where we would expect fewer Democrats in power. The especially rapid growth in jurisdictions formerly covered by Section 5 of the Voting Rights Act points to continued discrimination in these areas.

These results also lay bare another troubling finding. Although the turnout gap is growing considerably more quickly in formerly covered areas in the wake of *Shelby County*, it is also increasing in the rest of the country as well. Another look at figure 5.2 reveals that since 2008 the white-nonwhite turnout gap has grown from about 8 percentage points to 13 percentage points in noncovered counties (at least, the ones that our matching procedure identified as being similar to the counties that were covered). The white-Black turnout gap, meanwhile, was below 1% in those areas in 2008 and virtually disappeared in 2012; today, it stands above 6%. So, while *Shelby County* has undoubtedly had a negative effect on the increasing racial turnout gap in the United States, it does not bear full responsibility. Instead, the decision has poured gasoline on the fire of declining relative minority political participation. This effect is likely due in part to Obama leaving public life, but the restrictive policies going into effect in places not formerly covered by Section 5 have likely played a role, too: In the decade following the *Shelby County* ruling, 18 states that were not subject to Section 5 passed restrictive voting laws.[56]

This chapter provides important insight into how the Supreme Court's ruling in *Shelby County* affected racial turnout patterns. But as we have seen, Section 5 not only blocked attempts to make voting more difficult but, since *Allen v. State Board of Elections* all the way back in 1969, also thwarted attempts to dilute minority voters' power through racial gerrymandering and other techniques. If the votes that *were* still cast were less likely to translate into real political power for minority communities, looking at the impact of *Shelby County* on turnout rates alone will not tell the whole story. We must also take on the question of whether the Court's decision made it easier for jurisdictions to dilute their minority citizens' votes. We now turn to that task.

6

Unlawful Dilution

DISTRICTING

> Try as we might, we cannot understand the 2023 [redistricting] plan as anything other than an intentional effort to dilute Black Alabamians' voting strength and evade the unambiguous requirements of court orders standing in the way.
>
> —US DISTRICT COURT FOR THE NORTHERN DISTRICT OF ALABAMA (PER CURIAM), *SINGLETON V. ALLEN* AND *MILLIGAN V. ALLEN*[1]

THE US Constitution requires the federal government to conduct a census every ten years for the purpose of assigning states their share of representatives in the US House. States may gain or lose seats in the House following this count, which obviously necessitates new congressional district lines. However, since the Supreme Court signaled in the mid-1960s that it would view a state's failure to maintain districts of equal population size as a 14th Amendment violation, states have typically engaged in regular decennial redistricting of both their congressional and state legislative districts.[2] As the population changes *within* a state, districts are supposed to be drawn to ensure relatively equal representation of each person who resides within them.

The Voting Rights Act and its subsequent reauthorizations expanded the scope of what "equal representation" meant for minority groups. Congress declared in the 1982 reauthorization that a law's result (and not the jurisdiction's intent) was the relevant standard by which to judge a vote dilution claim. When the Supreme Court subsequently ruled that it would intervene only if changes resulted in *worse* outcomes for minority voters, Congress clarified that discrimination was enough to constitute a violation of the VRA, regardless of whether "retrogression" had occurred. In both preclearance and Section 2 litigation, jurisdictions therefore had to show that they had taken steps to ensure adequate representation for politically cohesive minority groups.

Of course, assessing potentially problematic districting plans was a quite different exercise when done during preclearance, compared to the time and money that is typically devoted to litigation. The controversy surrounding Alabama's efforts to draw congressional district lines following the 2020 census provides a good example of what the latter path looks like. Like most states, Alabama relies on its state legislature to set district boundaries. In its first round of redistricting after *Shelby County,* the legislature produced a congressional district map that contained one district (out of seven) in which Black voters could reasonably hope to elect their preferred candidate; such districts are often referred to as *opportunity districts,* or *majority-minority districts* if they contain a majority of nonwhite voters.

This single opportunity district was not a new addition to Alabama's map; the state's 7th Congressional District had since 1992 occupied the western part of the state's "Black Belt." Originally named for the color of its fertile soil, this section of Alabama—which spanned the state's entire width like a belt around its midsection—became home to tens of thousands of freedmen after the Civil War. They endured the same violent oppression that many other freed Black voters experienced during Reconstruction, including the so-called "Election Massacre of 1874," in which dozens of Black voters were killed and up to 1,000 were driven away from the polls in majority-Black Barbour County, in the eastern Black Belt.[3] Many of those same voters' descendants still reside in Barbour County and the rest of the Black Belt, which includes cities like Selma. Today, the region's majority-Black population gives its name a second meaning.

The large, geographically contiguous concentration of Black (and heavily Democratic) voters in the Black Belt is more or less the definition of a "community of interest" whose ability to secure representation is protected under the VRA. Moreover, the 2020 census found that Alabama's overall population was 25.8% Black. There was thus no realistic possibility that members of the legislature could get away with "cracking" Black voters, spreading them out over multiple districts so that they would have insufficient numbers in any single one to elect a Black representative. If the new districts were unlikely to result in the election of *any* Black representatives, the Republican-controlled Alabama legislature recognized that it would certainly lose a Section 2 challenge in court.

To the contrary, the Republican majority's incentive was actually to pursue a "packing" strategy by grouping as many Black voters as possible into a single district—just as they had done in District 7 since the 1990s. By this method the legislators would concede that one Black Democrat would be elected from Alabama's seven seats, but if they were careful in how they drew the other districts, Republican legislators could likely guarantee not only that no other Black representative would be part of the state's congressional delegation but that no other *Democrat* would be elected—regardless of their race. In other words, a great many Democrats would be packed into the 7th, and the rest would be cracked across the other districts in numbers insufficient to elect another representative. This is exactly the strategy that the Alabama legislature put forward in its 2021 districting plan.

Almost immediately after the new plan was presented, a number of Black Alabamians and affiliated groups challenged the new districts in federal court in three separate cases that eventually became entwined. The plaintiffs argued that the map amounted to a textbook case of vote dilution, considering that there were enough Black voters in the Black Belt to warrant a second opportunity district. While one such district might have sufficed in the past, the plaintiffs asserted that the legislature had ignored a key demographic shift: The white share of Alabama's population had declined by 1.7 points since the 2010 census, but the proportion of Black residents in the state had actually *increased* by 3.6 points over the same period. According to the plaintiffs, this swing of more than 5 points merited a closer look at whether Alabama's traditional districting practice allowed its Black citizens a reasonable chance of electing their preferred candidates at rates commensurate with their share of the electorate. The 26% of the population that Black voters composed, the plaintiffs argued, was large enough to require a second opportunity district. If they could elect a second Black representative from that district, Black voters would have 28% of the state's seats in the House. In the plaintiffs' view, cutting this proportion in half was indefensible in light of Section 2 of the VRA.

The case began in the Northern District of Alabama, in two separate trials. After weighing Alabama's political demographics, the district court found that the state's congressional map likely violated Section 2. The court directed Alabama to redraw its congressional map to ensure that it included "two districts in which Black voters either comprise a voting-age majority or something quite close to it."[4] Predictably, the state appealed this ruling to the Supreme Court, which leaned on something called the *Purcell* Principle.[5] In a nutshell, *Purcell* directs federal courts not to change state election rules close to the date of an election if it can be helped, to avoid causing disruptions that could affect the outcome. Federal courts tend to take this directive seriously. Courts might even strike down illegal state election rules for future elections but use the *Purcell* Principle to leave the problematic policies in place for an impending one, especially if overturning the policy would change the election's strategic dynamics or competitive environment. In the Alabama case—which ultimately became known as *Allen v. Milligan*—the Supreme Court therefore put the district court's ruling on hold until it could hear arguments.[6] That move meant that the original map with one opportunity district—which the district court had declared likely illegal—would be used in the 2022 election. When the votes were counted, seven white Republicans and one Black Democrat won House seats in Alabama.

The Supreme Court heard arguments in *Allen v. Milligan* in October, just before the elections. In June 2023, the Court issued its ruling affirming the district court's opinion that a Section 2 violation had likely occurred. The Supreme Court lifted its previous stay and ordered Alabama to follow the district court's instructions to create a map that featured a second district with a majority-Black voting-age population.

Given the stories we have shared so far, the sequence of events in *Allen v. Milligan* is a familiar one by now: A state made an election-related policy, was sued for allegedly violating the VRA, and was ordered to change course. But what sets this case apart from the many others we have described to this point is that the Alabama legislature decided to test what the district court meant when it ordered that a second district have "close to" a majority of Black voters. Roughly a month after the Supreme Court's decision, the state enacted a new congressional district map. This one retained the 7th District as a majority-Black district and increased the share of the Black population in the 2nd District—but only nominally, to 39.9%.

The 2nd District was the most obvious choice for a second opportunity district; it contained a solid chunk of the majority-Black eastern Black Belt (including Barbour County, site of the 1874 Election Massacre). Adjusting the Black population of the district to a mere 40%, therefore, seemed to meet neither the spirit nor the letter of the court's order. The Alabama legislature's own analysis found that Black-preferred candidates in the revised district would have lost every projected election in the data it examined.[7] Most observers (and, presumably, most state legislators) recognized that a voting population that was only 40% Black was not sufficient to give Black residents of the new district a meaningful opportunity for congressional representation.

It was up to the district court to decide whether Alabama had complied with its order, and the state made its case before that court on August 14. During oral arguments, the lawyers defending Alabama's new map came under intense fire from the judges. Alabama solicitor general Edmund LaCour argued that the Black Belt was a contiguous community of interest and therefore should be kept intact as much as possible in the 7th District alone. For this to happen, LaCour claimed, the maximum feasible proportion of Black voters in the 2nd District was "probably right around 40%."[8] Going further, said LaCour, would necessitate using race as a predominant factor in the district boundaries and would fracture the Black Belt's community of interest—potentially running afoul of the Supreme Court's directive in *Bush v. Vera* (which we describe in chapter 4).

During the oral argument, Judge Terry F. Moorer effectively accused the solicitor general of ignoring the court's clear directive to draw a *majority*-Black district. Moorer seemed to believe that LaCour was arguing that the state's actions were self-justifying. "Isn't what you are essentially arguing," Moorer asked, "is whatever the state does, we can just say they shot a bullet, and we have now drawn a bull's eye where the bullet hit, and so it's good? It's just some veneer to justify whatever the state wanted to do that was short of [complying with] the VRA."[9] Later, Judge Moorer was even more pointed with LaCour: "What I hear you saying is that the State of Alabama deliberately chose to disregard our instructions to draw two majority-Black districts . . . Did they disregard it or not?"[10]

Again, LaCour reiterated the position that to comply with the Supreme Court's prior directives to keep communities of interest together as much as possible, the state had placed as many Black voters as was feasible in District 2. The district court judges found the state's arguments unconvincing. Writing a few weeks later, the judges said they were "deeply troubled that the state enacted a map that the state readily admits does not provide the remedy" they had demanded, and accused Alabama of "not even nurtur[ing] the ambition to provide the required remedy." The judges' incredulity is palpable in their order. "We are struck by the extraordinary circumstance we face," they wrote. "We are not aware of any other case in which a state legislature—faced with a federal court order declaring that its electoral plan unlawfully dilutes minority votes and requiring a plan that provides an additional opportunity district—responded with a plan that the state concedes does not provide that district."[11] Finding no reason to trust that the legislature would enact fair districts if given yet a third opportunity to do so, the district court ordered a Special Master to draw a new map, which the court approved on October 5, 2023. The new map increased the percentage of Black voters in the 2nd District to almost 49%. In the 2024 election, voters there elected Democrat Shomari Figures, a young Black man born and raised in Mobile.

The courts got their way in the end, but there is good reason to suspect that had preclearance still been operative, Alabama's map would have been blocked before it was ever implemented, and the 2nd District's voters would not have had to wait until 2024 for the chance to elect the representative of their choice. The 2006 reauthorization of the Voting Rights Act invested the DOJ with the authority to block any "standard, practice, or procedure with respect to voting that has the purpose of or will have the effect of diminishing the ability of any citizens of the United States on account of race or color . . . to elect their preferred candidates of choice." This change clarified that DOJ preclearance reviewers did not have to prove that an election policy would make things *worse* for them; perpetuating ongoing vote dilution also violated the law. After the 2006 reauthorization, Section 5 was restored to the powerful tool it had been during the 1990 redistricting cycle, and it turns out that in that cycle, the DOJ had objected to Alabama's maps.[12]

A close examination of that rejection reveals that history was repeating itself with Alabama's 2021 redistricting efforts. John Dunne, assistant attorney general for civil rights during the 1991 redistricting cycle, authored a letter objecting to Alabama's plan that year. The 1991 map was the first in which District 7 (or any district) comprised a majority of Black voters in Alabama, but it also dispersed the remaining Black Belt voters across several others. In his objection, Dunne employed language in 1991 that sounds remarkably similar to the points that federal judges subsequently made three decades later. Despite creating a long-overdue majority-Black district, Dunne was concerned that Alabama could have done even more. "An underlying principle of the congressional redistricting" in Alabama that year, Dunne wrote, "was a predisposition on the part of the state political leadership to limit Black voting potential to a single district."

Dunne continued, "Our analysis further indicates that the fragmentation of Black population concentrations outside of the one district with a Black voting age population majority was unnecessary. Indeed, it is clear that at least the outlines of alternative plans that avoided such fragmentation were available . . . and that such alternatives would provide for two congressional districts with Black voting age population majorities."[13] Ultimately, the state achieved preclearance of a revised districting plan that did not add an additional majority-Black district, but Dunne made it clear that the DOJ would heavily scrutinize future cracking in the Black Belt. To be sure, it is impossible to know whether the 2021 plan would have been cleared under Section 5. What we do know beyond a shadow of a doubt is that the Department of Justice would have looked very closely at Alabama's post-2020 census districts *before* they went into effect if *Shelby County* had never been handed down.

Alabama was not the only formerly covered state to draw legal challenges following post–*Shelby County* redistricting plans; federal courts took action against discriminatory maps in other states as well. In the first such case, voters in Georgia sued in December 2021 to stop their state's new map from taking effect. The plaintiffs argued that the proposed districts in Georgia reduced Black voters' political power in a number of parts of the state. They prevailed three months later, when the US District Court for the Northern District of Georgia found that Georgia's new maps diluted minority representation in a manner that probably constituted a Section 2 violation.[14] As in the Alabama case, however, even though the district court was convinced that Georgia's districts were illegal, it followed the *Purcell* Principle and opted to leave the new maps in place for the approaching 2022 election. Consistent with its desire not to interfere with an ongoing election, the court held off until October 2023, when it finally ordered new districts in the state.[15] Georgia complied with the district court's order to create new maps, implementing them prior to the 2024 election. At the same time, the state appealed to the 11th Circuit Court of Appeals. At the time of this writing, this litigation is ongoing and it remains to be seen whether the 11th Circuit will allow Georgia to return to the 2021 maps.

The story of Louisiana's districting process following the 2020 census is also quite similar to Alabama's. Voters sued the state in April 2022, arguing that Section 2 required map drawers to create a second opportunity district for Black voters instead of the single majority-Black district the state had included in its new map. In June, the Middle Louisiana District Court agreed that the maps were likely illegal and blocked Louisiana from using them in that fall's election.[16] The district court ordered the state to come up with a new plan in just two weeks. Instead of complying, Louisiana appealed to the Fifth Circuit Court of Appeals and also to the US Supreme Court.

Justice Samuel Alito stayed the district court's order for new maps until the Supreme Court could address the Alabama redistricting case in *Allen v. Milligan*, which presented the Court with essentially the same legal question as the one coming from Louisiana.[17] This stay may have been sensible given the related considerations before the Supreme Court, but it meant that Louisiana's maps were in effect for the 2022 midterms. That year, Louisiana sent five white Republicans to Congress, in addition to one Black Democrat, Troy Carter, who represented the majority-Black 2nd District. In November 2023—after the Supreme Court ruled in *Allen v. Milligan*—the Fifth Circuit informed Louisiana that it would restart the litigation process if it failed to enact new districts by the end of January.[18] The state responded with a new map that featured a second opportunity district for Black Louisianans, which took effect prior to the 2024 congressional elections.[19] That year, for the first time ever, Louisiana sent two Black members to the US House of Representatives.

But the districting fight in the Pelican State is not yet over. After the new congressional maps were approved in April 2024, a separate group of "non-African Americans" sued Louisiana in federal court, arguing that the creation of a second opportunity district for minority voters amounted to an impermissible racial gerrymander.[20] The plaintiffs' position echoed the one that Alabama had made when it had defended its own districts: When Louisiana drew the new map, the plaintiffs alleged, it had relied on voters' race to ensure that sufficient numbers of minority voters resided in the opportunity districts. In doing so, the state had divided other existing communities of interest, which diminished the quality of their representation. The plaintiffs therefore argued that the new map was illegal, even though in this case the district in question was drawn to *increase* the number of Black legislators representing Louisiana.

A three-judge panel in the Western Louisiana District agreed with plaintiffs that because Louisiana had made race a predominant factor in its considerations for new district boundaries, the state had violated the 14th Amendment equal protection rights of non-Black voters.[21] The district court ordered Louisiana to draw new maps without centering voters' race in its process. Pending its review of the case, the US Supreme Court stayed this order (which allowed the map with two opportunity districts to be used in the 2024 election). In November 2024, the Supreme Court agreed to consider the case. Oral arguments in *Louisiana v. Callais* were heard on March 24, 2025. In August the Court asked the parties to return for a reargument in October. The Court widened the scope of the litigation to consider the constitutionality of Section 2 in redistricting cases. On April 29, 2026, the Supreme Court handed down its decision, which undermined Section 2's ability to invalidate districting practices that discriminate against minority voters. As such, *Callais* could prove to be an instrument as destructive to Section 2's protections against vote dilution as *Shelby County* was to Section 5.

Finally, there is Texas. Shortly after Texas completed its 2021 redistricting process, the DOJ joined private citizens to allege that the state's congressional and state legislative districts diluted minority representation in a manner that violated Section 2 of the VRA.[22] This lawsuit marked a departure from the manner in which postdistricting challenges unfolded in Alabama, Georgia, and Louisiana, where voters had initiated complaints. Here, the federal government was the plaintiff. In its complaint, the DOJ noted Texas's problematic districting history during the preclearance era. "After each decennial census during the period when Texas was required to obtain preclearance of redistricting plans under Section 5 of the Voting Rights Act," DOJ attorneys wrote, ". . . the State enacted redistricting plans for the Texas House that violated Section 5." The DOJ's brief strongly signals that the Texas map would not have withstood preclearance and therefore never would have taken effect prior to *Shelby County*. Because it must now be adjudicated via protracted litigation instead, the process of judging Texas's maps has slowed to a snail's pace. The challenged maps were in use for both the 2022 and 2024 elections as the action worked its way through court. In early 2025, the Trump administration's Department of Justice dropped the claims that the maps violated Section 2 of the VRA, though the case continues at this writing with private plaintiffs.[23]

Together, these cases paint a dim prospect for redistricting in the aftermath of *Shelby County v. Holder*. In each case, credible contentions of racial dilution were made, and in total, millions of voters were affected. Unlike the period preceding *Shelby County*, however, no immediate remedy was available to minority voters. It is a simple fact that in this post-preclearance world, cases move slower and judges are often unwilling to make dramatic changes to election rules, leaving enforcement of the VRA substantially less efficient than it once was. Indeed, the recently decided *Louisiana v. Callais* poses an existential threat to Section 2's power to protect minority voters against dilution, but even if this power had survived, contemporaneous conditions were hardly ideal for its efficient enforcement. Way back in 1966, Chief Justice Earl Warren's *Katzenbach* opinion had recognized that in the absence of preclearance, a litigation-first approach would confer "the advantage of time and inertia" on jurisdictions whose actions would impede minority voters' ballot access or otherwise dilute their political power.[24]

The first redistricting cycle without Section 5 has borne that prediction out. In Alabama, Georgia, and Louisiana, lawsuits were brought the very same day the maps were signed into law. These actions represented the most expeditious remedies available to plaintiffs. And, although federal courts found that maps in the three states likely violated Black Americans' rights *before* the 2022 midterms, each map was nevertheless used that November thanks to *Purcell* and the glacial pace of the American legal system. In total, these cases provide examples of precisely the kinds of inefficiencies stemming from litigation that Section 5 was designed to ameliorate.

The litigation in Texas at least yields another important reminder that problematic districting practices are not limited to state actions. In its suit against Texas, the DOJ raised a key point about the scope of its concern: "During the 38 years that Texas was covered by Section 5 of the Voting Rights Act, the Attorney General issued . . . 50 objection letters regarding local districting or redistricting plans [in Texas]."[25] Districts for town councils, county commissions, or school boards are just as consequential for American voters' representation. Yet districting procedures for these offices are substantially less likely to draw attention from media, interest groups, or attorneys looking to shed light on changes that might make things worse for minority voters. Prior to *Shelby County*, preclearance served as a proactive mechanism to keep local jurisdictions in good standing with the VRA. Now that no one is looking over their shoulder, it is worth wondering whether new districts in counties and municipalities are diluting their minority residents' power. Put another way, are the illegal congressional maps in the post–*Shelby County* era merely the tip of the iceberg?

The structure of local government varies wildly from state to state. In Texas, elected county commissioners are typically responsible for day-to-day county business; they manage road construction and maintenance and oversee public safety, among other things. The county commissions (known formally as "county commission courts" in Texas) are led by a county judge, who, in addition to presiding over the county court, is the county's chief executive and highest elected official. Together, the county judge and commissioners oversee the unglamorous but necessary grunt work that keeps the county running. This process plays out across all of Texas's 254 counties.

Following each census, however, the county government has an additional responsibility: Each county judge leads the commissioners through a districting process whereby they draw districts for their own offices as well as those for other county officials (county districts are typically known as "precincts"). Among these other offices are constables and justices of the peace who adjudicate local matters within the precincts (which we refer to as "constable precincts" for simplicity), each comprising part of the county. While districts for county offices are less visible and typically affect a small segment of a state's population, the VRA applies to county districting in Texas and all other states just the same: Commissioners may not lawfully create maps that dilute minority voters' political power in even the smallest corner of the tiniest county. But in Galveston County, Texas, where a sizable proportion of the population is nonwhite, precinct maps for constables and commissioners have repeatedly landed on the wrong side of the VRA.

The Port of Galveston was a major point of entry in the nineteenth-century international slave trade, and the city housed the largest western slave market during the antebellum period. Indeed, slavery survived longer in Galveston (and the rest of Texas) than anywhere else in the Confederacy. On June 19, 1865, Union forces took command of Galveston Island and posted a simple order to finally fully enforce the nearly three-year-old Emancipation Proclamation. It read in part, "The people of Texas are informed that, in accordance with a proclamation from the Executive of the United States, all slaves are free."[26] The event is now commemorated as the Juneteenth federal holiday.

Galveston County was a covered jurisdiction while preclearance was still in effect, so its maps were subject to review by DOJ examiners. Following the 1991 redistricting process, Galveston County submitted its constable precincts for preclearance. The map caught the eye of skeptical reviewers in Washington, namely, John Dunne—the same DOJ attorney who objected to Alabama's statewide maps that year. Dunne's interest was piqued by a 1988 ruling from the 5th Circuit Court of Appeals in another local districting case from Texas known as *Campos v. City of Baytown*.[27] That case originated in the city of Baytown, which spanned two counties that bordered Galveston. There, the appeals court had considered whether the sizable Black and Latino minorities in Baytown could be grouped together and considered as a single minority bloc. Neither community was large enough to warrant its own majority-minority district. However, Black and Latino voters tended to vote "cohesively"—jointly backing either Black or Latino candidates—while the city's white voters generally acted in concert to vote against them. Given these long-standing behaviors, the 5th Circuit ruled that the Voting Rights Act protected Baytown's sizable *coalition* of minority voters. In Baytown, that meant that the combined representation of Black and Latino voters could not be lawfully diluted in local election procedures.[28]

Dunne applied that logic to Galveston County less than four years later, noting that although 31.4% of the county's residents were either Black or Latino in 1990, none of the eight proposed constable precincts held a mixed Black-Latino majority.[29] Dunne further commented on the history of the proposed districts, stressing that Black and Latino residents had worked together to advocate for a majority-minority district. These efforts were spurred by the election of the first Black Galveston county commissioner, in 1988, following a hard-fought election in which voting largely followed racial lines.[30] Instead of heeding the concerns of Black and Latino residents, "at the request of an Anglo justice of the peace and constable," the county cracked Black and Latino voters, spreading them across the precincts so that they could reasonably expect white voters to elect (presumably white) candidates in each.[31] To comply with the VRA, Dunne informed Galveston County that it would have to craft at least one majority-minority constable precinct. Subsequent negotiation (and litigation) ultimately resulted in two constable precincts comprising a majority of combined Black and Latino residents, as well as another in which Black and Latino candidates could still wage a competitive campaign, even if their respective racial groups did not form an outright majority of the population.[32]

Preclearance reviewers objected to Galveston County's proposed districts again following the 2010 census. Now twenty years after Dunne's objection, the county was even less white. The combined Black and Latino population of Galveston County had risen to 36.2%, but the county's districting plan again diluted minority voters' power. Thomas Perez, now the assistant attorney general in charge of preclearance, took issue with several aspects of the county's maps. For starters, Perez raised questions about the procedures that Galveston County had followed in drawing new commissioner districts. Perez found that some county commissioners had been solicited for feedback about the new districts—but not Commissioner Stephen Holmes, who had represented Precinct 3 (the single majority-minority district) since 1999. Not coincidentally in Perez's mind, the new map impacted Precinct 3 quite a bit. By adding a heavily white area to it, the county court had diluted the percentage of Black and Latino voters to the point that they would lose "the ability . . . to elect a [county commissioner court] candidate of choice to office in Precinct 3."[33] In response to Perez's objection, the county would subsequently increase the Black population of District 3, thereby maintaining its status as a majority-minority district for county commissioner elections.[34] Holmes was ultimately reelected.

But this was not Perez's sole objection. The assistant attorney general also questioned Galveston County's proposed constable precincts—the same ones that had been at issue in 1991. There, rather than merely redraw district lines, the county proposed reducing the number of districts from eight to five. While the county's desire to pare down the districts was ostensibly motivated by a desire to save money, Perez noted that it had conducted no financial analysis of the new districting plan. Even more problematically in Perez's view, the centerpiece of Galveston County's district reduction strategy was the proposed collapse of the two majority-minority precincts—as well as the other opportunity precinct with a relatively high percentage of Black and Latino voters—into just one precinct. This change would have reduced the percentage of constable precincts in which Black and Latino voters could reasonably expect to elect a candidate of their choice from 37.5% to 20%. Perez halted this change, as well, because of its clearly retrogressive character.[35] As it was designed to do, the preclearance process had blocked Galveston County's proposed districts *before* they were implemented, just as it had done twenty years before.

With the end of preclearance, however, Galveston County no longer had to worry about DOJ reviewers thwarting its districting plans. Just two months after the *Shelby County* ruling, the county changed its constable precincts without any federal oversight. In its 2013 map, Galveston County reduced the number of constable precincts not to five (as it had proposed unsuccessfully in 2011) but to *four*, cutting the number of minority opportunity districts from three to one in the process.[36] In a trick of math, however, by packing Black and Latino voters into a single precinct, Galveston County argued that *more* voters now actually resided in a majority-minority constable precinct, which would result in more effective representation. While this argument is controversial in light of established Section 2 law, Galveston County prevailed in a Section 2 suit challenging the 2013 constable map.[37] It is worth noting here that this map was more or less the same one it had tried to implement just two years before, and to which the DOJ had objected. Without the prospect of skeptical preclearance reviewers, the county felt it was worth rolling the dice on litigation, which proved to be a safe bet.

Having successfully reduced the number of majority-minority constable precincts, when it came time to draw new county commissioner districts following the 2020 census, the county once again eyed the majority–Black and Latino Precinct 3. That precinct was still represented by Commissioner Holmes—at the time, the county's only Black commissioner.[38] As was typical, the responsibility for mapmaking fell to the commissioners themselves, led by County Judge Mark Henry, a Republican elected in 2010. Henry requested that the county hire attorney Dale Oldham to consult on the precinct lines. Having performed the same role for the county in the past, Oldham had considerable expertise with Galveston County's population dynamics. Indeed, he had designed the 2011 maps to which the DOJ had objected.

Henry wasted little time in communicating his goals. Even before the release of the census data in November 2020, he asked Oldham whether the county was still required to maintain a majority-minority district; Oldham replied that it would depend on what the census data ultimately looked like.[39] With the data in hand the following August, Oldham was able to study where Black and Latino voters resided in the county, and noted that while Galveston County's Black population remained heavily concentrated in Precinct 3, the Latino population had grown in many parts of the county. In theory, this shift could allow Galveston County to argue that the Latino community was too far-flung to encircle in any one district. There was at least some rationale, then, for attempting a map that reduced their presence in Precinct 3, if that was the county's goal.

Oldham's first map reflected "minimum changes" in that it eroded the minority population of Precinct 3 somewhat but still preserved it as a majority–Black and Latino district. But Oldham oversaw the production of another map as well, which followed a clear directive he had received from Judge Henry: The second map should look "like the one [Oldham] conceived in 2011," which the DOJ had blocked. Oldham obliged, providing "very specific instructions" to a demographer about "where to place the lines." The resulting map spread Black and (to a greater extent) Latino voters across Galveston's precincts. In 2020, Galveston County was 25.3% Latino and 13.3% Black. Despite composing 38.6% of the county's residents in 2020—an even larger percentage than ten years earlier—with the second map, Black and Latino voters would have no real expectation of electing a candidate of their choice in any of the proposed county commission precincts. Much as with the prior districting schemes that the DOJ had thwarted, under Galveston's 2021 plan, none of the four districts had a combined Black and Latino population larger than

35%. At 28% (down from its pre-2020 benchmark of 58.3%), Precinct 3—the historically majority-minority district—would have the *lowest* population of Black and Latino voters from 2021 onward.

In another echo of past events in Galveston County, Judge Henry did not consult with Commissioner Holmes of Precinct 3, whose district would be substantially altered by the proposed map. Henry also held just a single public hearing about the proposed districts, on November 12, 2021—the day before the new map was to take effect. Moreover, Henry moved that hearing away from the county courthouse, the typical venue for "serious, non-run-of-the-mill county business." Instead, the hearing was held in a smaller annex, 27 miles away. The annex was far too small to accommodate the large numbers of minority voters who wished to speak against the proposed map, which may have been the point. This choice was not a one-off; relocating meetings to this smaller, less accessible venue had become common practice in Galveston County whenever "topics involving race [were] to be taken up." The resulting proceedings were chaotic: When residents in the crowd—consisting largely of Black, Latino, and older residents—complained to Henry that it was difficult to hear, he replied, "I'm going to speak at this tone. That's all I can do. I'm not going to scream. I don't have a microphone. . . . I will clear you out. If you make a noise, I will clear you out of here. I've got constables here." After showing what the federal district court later held to be a "disregard for public input from the minority communities," the hearing ended and the map was implemented.

In short, Galveston County's 2021 districting process followed the same playbook the county had utilized in the past: Minority voters were thinly spread across the four commissioner precincts while their own commissioner was shut out of the process and the county threw up procedural hurdles that impeded their input. It was no accident that Galveston County pursued such an aggressive overhaul of its districts in 2021. Oldham subsequently testified in district court proceedings that "the elimination of preclearance facilitated the dismantling of the majority-minority precinct in the 2021 process." Just as it had done with the constable precincts, Galveston County had seized on the end of preclearance to act as it had long wished.

With preclearance no longer in the picture, litigation was the DOJ's only option to contest the districts. It did just that, claiming in federal court that by fracturing a majority-minority district that the federal government had mandated for three decades, the new county commission maps amounted to a clear Section 2 violation. The DOJ's challenge was merged with two others from area residents and the NAACP, and the case was slated for trial in the US District Court for the Southern District of Texas. But the litigation surrounding Galveston County's maps moved much slower than preclearance would have. The trial did not begin until August 2023, meaning that, like the contested state districting plans following the 2020 census described above, the 2022 election for Galveston County commission districts was conducted with the new map. This did not affect the composition of the entire county commission court, though; due to staggered terms, Commissioner Holmes was not up for reelection until 2024. Still, his political future—and the ongoing representation of Black and Latino voters in Galveston County—hinged on the outcome of the case.

During the ten-day trial that would become known as *Petteway v. Galveston County*, the county's main contention was that its map was simply an effort to create a district that hugged the Gulf Coast, preserving voters there as a community of interest. It also raised questions about whether Black and Latino voters should be considered a single coalition to be afforded VRA protection. Ultimately, these arguments did not move Judge Jeffrey V. Brown of the Southern District of Texas. He swiftly set aside the county's expert testimony questioning the cohesiveness of Galveston County's minority voters. Brown also ruled that the DOJ's claims easily cleared the *Gingles* test we describe in chapter 4. Taken together, he found that Black and Latino voters constituted a "large and geographically compact" population. Judge Brown also heavily weighed the plaintiffs' expert testimony, finding strong evidence of racially polarized voting in Galveston County: Statistical analysis had consistently shown that Black and Latino voters tended to vote cohesively, while Anglo voters generally acted together to defeat Black and/or Latino candidates. In total, these circumstances meant that a majority-minority district in Galveston County was certainly appropriate.

The record surfaced plenty of evidence that Galveston County had placed race squarely at the center of its considerations in drawing the new judicial precincts—and not to foster minority representation but to dilute it. The trial revealed several maps drawn by experts, as well as Oldham's first proposed map, that preserved a majority-minority precinct while also meeting Galveston County's other stated concerns. Judge Brown found that with the new maps, Galveston County's Black and Latino voters would typically fail to elect a candidate of their choice. Brown also noted that the rationale that key players gave for the new maps often shifted with the context in which it was offered. In light of what the judge characterized as "ongoing discrimination" in Galveston

County "touching on participation in voting," Judge Brown ruled that Galveston County had violated Section 2 of the VRA. Its actions flew in the face of 30 years of proactive efforts from the DOJ to preserve opportunity districts for Black and Latino residents in Galveston County, and the proposed county commission districts could not stand. Judge Brown ordered the county to draw new maps within the week.[40]

But this order was not the end of the story. Within four days of Judge Brown's ruling on October 13, Galveston County appealed to the Fifth Circuit Court of Appeals. Throughout the district court trial, lawyers for Galveston County had been arguing that interracial coalitions were not protected by the Voting Rights Act—a position that, as noted above, Judge Brown had found wholly unpersuasive.[41] It was true, the county had argued, that Black and Latino voters combined to make up more than a third of the population. And even though Black and Latino voters showed political cohesion while Anglo voters had worked together to defeat their preferred candidates over a decades-long period, the county's attorneys argued that this pattern was not enough to trigger a VRA violation. Galveston County's position was that only *individual* racial groups were entitled to districts that would allow them to elect candidates of their choice. If voters of color were made up of two different racial groups rather than a single one, Galveston County asserted, the VRA was powerless to protect them from vote dilution. This position was in clear conflict with *Campos,* which is precisely why Judge Brown had rejected it.

The county raised this issue again on appeal, where the possibilities of success were somewhat different. Unlike the district court—which is obligated to follow 5th Circuit precedent—the 5th Circuit Court of Appeals may reconsider its own prior decisions. So, while the three-judge panel at the 5th Circuit might have simply taken on the question of whether Galveston County's districts constituted a Section 2 violation under *Campos* (which was the only question available to the district court), it could also decide to assess whether *Campos* should still be the guiding principle when making district maps in counties like Galveston. Ultimately, the panel decided to do both. The judges agreed that Judge Brown had interpreted the *Campos* precedent correctly as allowing for the protection of a Black-Latino political coalition, but they also made explicit their desire to revisit the *Campos* decision itself. Accordingly, the panel asked for the case to be reconsidered by *all* the judges of the 5th Circuit. The *Campos* precedent factored heavily into proceedings, and it was clear that the 5th Circuit judges were focused on the question of whether minority coalitions like those in Galveston and Baytown jointly merited VRA protections.

The full court issued its ruling in August 2024. *Campos* was overturned. The majority opinion characterized *Campos* as "erroneous," holding that "Section 2 does not require political subdivisions to draw precinct lines for the electoral benefit of distinct minority groups that share political preferences but lack the cementing force of race or ethnicity."[42] The 5th Circuit's opinion in *Petteway v. Galveston County* snuffed out any hope for Black and Latino residents in Galveston County of maintaining their political power. If they had to be counted separately, there simply were not enough of either to warrant a majority-minority precinct.

The *Petteway* decision raises several practical questions that the dissenting judges were more than happy to point out. For instance, Judge Dana Douglas wondered how the decision might be applied in the context of the likely "absurdities and judicial complicity in impossible racial classifications" that would accompany any attempt to police the boundaries between cohesive minority groups.[43] To drive this point home, Judge Douglas quoted at length from Judge Damon Keith's dissent in a similar case from the 6th Circuit, *Nixon v. Kent County*,[44] in which that court had also held that coalition districts were not protected under the VRA. The *Nixon* decision marked the 6th as the only other circuit court, besides—now—the 5th, to rule in this manner. "If we are to make these distinctions, where will they end?" wondered Judge Keith in his dissent. Keith continued,

> Must a community that would be considered racially both Black and Hispanic be segregated from other Blacks who are not Hispanic? Should the dwindling numbers of Native Americans be further decimated by a parsing of Navaho from Apache? Must Puerto-Ricans and Dominicans in the same neighborhood be separated based on their separate cultural and historical backgrounds? Perhaps we will return to a time of classifying African-Americans as quadroons and octoroons for the purposes of racial classification.[45]

It remains to be seen whether the Supreme Court will be asked to weigh in on the question of whether minority voter coalitions can receive Section 2 protections. In the meantime, on November 5, 2024, Galveston County held elections using the maps for which its leadership had spent decades fighting. The old Precinct 3 was gone. Commissioner Holmes, who had served it for more than two decades, lost by more than 37 points.

Galveston County is far from the only substate jurisdiction that has used some form of districting to dilute minority voters' power. Chapter 4 describes how the city of Mobile's shift from ward elections to at-large ones—another common tactic—frustrated Black residents' efforts to elect a city councilor of their choice. These sorts of districting anecdotes are not difficult to uncover among hundreds of preclearance records and trial transcripts over the years. Indeed, we could have used scores of other stories to make the same point. The same conclusion emerges from a more holistic analysis: Drilling down into the data we describe in chapter 3 reveals that a whopping 99% of proposed districting plans we identified as submitted to the DOJ for preclearance review between 1998 and 2013 came not from states but from counties or municipal governments; 83% of the redistricting-related policies *blocked* under preclearance originated at the county or local level. The City of Galveston—seat of Galveston County—drew Section 5 objections from the DOJ for vote dilution schemes in 1992,[46] 1998,[47] and 2011.[48] These actions did not stop with *Shelby County*: Section 2 suits have ended multiple vote dilution schemes in formerly covered counties, cities, and school boards since 2013.[49] We have abundant evidence, then, that districting practices at all levels of government might have been problematic since *Shelby County*. A deeper investigation into the depths of the problem is certainly warranted.

The central problem we face in this effort, though, is that identifying all changes to all maps is probably impossible. Our analysis of raw counts in the preclearance submission data we describe in chapter 3 reveals that between April 1998 and June 2013, the DOJ was asked to approve more than 100 county and city districting plans *every month* on average. Volume alone is a significant obstacle to comprehensive municipal districting analysis, but data availability further compounds the practical problems confronting researchers (including us). Take, for instance, a recent effort by Diana Da In Lee and Yamil Ricardo Velez to understand how well minority interests are represented by American city councils.[50] As part of this work, these scholars set out to collect the electronic data on city council districting plans for 200 of the largest cities in the nation, but only 166 of them had publicly accessible district plans.

These cities represent less than one-third of the municipalities that a different team of scholars identified as having local elections occurring within districts.[51] But even de Benedictis-Kessner and colleagues' work—which relies on a major data collection effort that they claim (and we agree) amounts to "the most comprehensive publicly-available source of information on local elections across the country"—includes election information about just 663 municipalities in the United States.[52] That pales in comparison to the more than 18,000 American municipalities identified in US Census Bureau data.[53] These statistics should by no means be read as a criticism of the major contributions of both Lee and Velez and de Benedictis-Kessner and colleagues. Rather, the fact that their enormous data collection efforts barely scratched the surface of municipal districting plans indicates just how difficult it is to collect systematic data on how local governments draw district lines. As with so many of the issues we describe throughout this book, without the DOJ actively reviewing proposals from governments subject to preclearance, a holistic analysis of these policies is virtually impossible.

Nevertheless, it is important that we take up the question of how *Shelby County* affected not just ballot access for minority voters but also their representation in government. Put differently, chapter 5 focuses on the cumulative *vote denial* effects of *Shelby County*—practices and policies that make casting a ballot more difficult—but questions about *vote dilution* are also important. Previous chapters show that questions about the racial fairness of legislative maps were central not only to the jurisprudential development of Section 5 and the preclearance process but also to the interplay between Congress and the federal courts that shaped the VRA's historical development. As such, while we are conscious that districting data can be hard to come by, this difficulty does not let us off the hook in terms of exploring the potential effects of *Shelby County v. Holder* on vote dilution at the local level.

Because the data limitations surrounding district boundaries mean we cannot look at the evolution of all local district plans since 2013, we take a different approach to the question. "Packing" and "cracking" voters of color are common tactics when mapmakers have an entire state or county to work with, but they are not the only two avenues through which vote dilution has historically occurred in local government. One reason for broader potential dilution tactics at the local level is that states cannot change their borders, but cities can. It is true that municipalities draw council or school board district lines just like states and counties, but in most cases cities can also annex outlying areas to literally change the city's boundaries—and with them, the share of the voting population that belongs to a given racial or ethnic group.

This was not a rare maneuver during the roughly 25-year period for which we have submission data (described in detail in chapter 3), when more than

16,500 annexations were proposed to the Department of Justice by covered areas for preclearance.[54] Moreover, the DOJ objected to at least 87 proposals containing approximately 1,800 individual tracts between 1965 and 2013, presumably because they would have changed the city in a way that diluted minority residents' power. This is exactly what the city of Richmond did in the case we describe in chapter 3, which led to *City of Richmond v. United States*. Perhaps even more notably, it is also what the DOJ attempted to block the City of Calera from doing, leading to the case that ultimately became *Shelby County v. Holder*. In short, we know that some formerly covered states and counties tried to enact illegal legislative maps in the aftermath of *Shelby County*, but we also know that prior to that decision, there is ample evidence that then-covered local governments attempted to dilute minority representation in their towns using the annexation process. What have these municipalities done since?

When the *Shelby County* decision was handed down in 2013, more than one-third of Americans lived in areas that were outside formal, incorporated municipalities. Unincorporated communities may be extremely rural or barely outside the edge of a city. Regardless, instead of relying on town governments, unincorporated residents typically receive the bulk of their local services (such as trash collection and police protection) from either private providers or county offices. As existing incorporated communities grow, they often expand their boundaries (and tax base) by annexing nearby unincorporated territory.

This can be a piecemeal process, however. Residents of outlying areas that towns seek to annex may resist it—though their ability to do so is subject to state laws. At other times, unincorporated communities that would appear to naturally fit inside an incorporated town or city are never annexed at all, because the town government does not attempt to do so. This process of "underbounding" municipalities can be fueled by judgments about how adding an incorporated area will ultimately affect their demography, tax base, or political dynamics: Especially in the South, underbounding has often left racial and ethnic minorities beyond cities' borders—even when preclearance was in operation.[55] For example, there is some evidence that even when Section 5 was functioning, it did not prevent minority vote dilution via underbounding in the Houston metro area in the 1990s.[56]

In another recent study, one with broader scope, researcher Noah Durst found that when residents of cities covered by Section 5 of the VRA were given the opportunity to vote on annexations, they were less likely to incorporate areas with heavier Black populations.[57] Moreover, Durst's analysis reveals "little evidence that such patterns of underbounding are driven by economic or fiscal considerations."[58] Instead, race appears to have motivated these decisions to leave Black neighborhoods beyond city borders. Given everything we have found in this book so far, the clearly racialized nature of the annexation process throughout the broader South warrants a close examination of annexation practices in the post–*Shelby County* era. Preclearance may not have stopped all racially motivated underbounding, but now that cities know that DOJ examiners are not looking over their shoulder, things may be even worse.

We are not the first to raise this question. In recent years, two other research projects have explored the relationship between *Shelby County* and the annexation process. The first of these, also by Durst, uses a difference-in-differences design to test whether neighborhoods that were annexed into communities within formerly covered counties after *Shelby County* were less likely to have a sizable Black population.[59] Durst's analysis is limited to neighborhoods annexed into the 276 cities that incorporated land both before and after *Shelby County*. This is a sensible choice, but it is worth noting that this approach might exclude the worst actors. If the DOJ objected to a given municipality's attempt to annex land before the end of preclearance (or if the municipality anticipated that a desired annexation would be blocked), the municipality might not have annexed any land until 2014—and would thus be dropped from Durst's analysis. Even though this decision means that Durst's conclusions are likely to be conservative, his work yields evidence that after *Shelby County*, formerly covered municipalities were indeed less likely to annex unincorporated areas with large Black populations.

A second recent paper, from Iris H. Zhang,takes the municipalities as its object of study to ask whether formerly covered municipalities increased the rate at which they annexed outlying areas and, separately, the rate at which they annexed areas that were whiter than the overall city (the annexation rate is defined as the share of municipalities that annex any land or residents over a given time period).[60] Zhang finds no evidence that *Shelby County* influenced the annexation rate. Thus, prior work has yielded mixed conclusions about the effect of *Shelby County* on municipalities' annexation activities.

In the remainder of this chapter, we take up several questions that are informed by this previous work. We start by identifying every census block group that was incorporated into a municipality between 2010 and 2023. While a longer timeline would be ideal, we are limited to this fourteen-year period because the Census Bureau started an annual release of municipalities' geographical boundaries only in 2009. We define a census block group as annexed in a given year if its geographic center fell inside of an incorporated municipality in that year but was not part of any municipality in the previous one. We continue this process for all census block groups, for each year in the time period. Tying these acquisitions to the municipality that annexed them allows us to understand how each community across the country changed as a result of annexations in a given year. This is an obviously more inclusive approach than attempting a partial analysis of the districting actions we might uncover even with an exhaustive search. In total, about 88 municipalities annexed a populated block group in any given year. The average number of annexed block groups each year was about 115, collectively home to around 200,000 residents. Between 2010 and 2023 a total of just over 3 million residents were brought into municipalities via annexations that fit our definition.

We analyze annexations before and after *Shelby County* using the difference-in-differences approach we deployed in the previous chapter, which allows us to account for meaningful differences in annexation trends between the jurisdictions that were and were not subject to preclearance. If *Shelby County* had no effect on annexations, we should see that the difference between formerly covered municipalities and the rest of the country is of similar magnitude in the post–*Shelby County* era as it was when preclearance was in effect. If, however, patterns in annexations *do* shift in distinct ways in formerly covered places in the aftermath of the ruling, we can attribute that change to the suspension of preclearance. Annexations are tremendously complicated, and the rules governing them vary significantly from state to state. But, by analyzing patterns in annexations in both the pre- and post-*Shelby* eras, we can incorporate this variation into our baseline expectations. (As always, interested readers can refer to the Methodological Appendix for more information on our approach.)

Like Zhang, we ask whether formerly covered municipalities—once freed from the constraints of preclearance—took advantage of the lack of federal oversight to annex outlying territory at a higher rate than they did before. Even if municipalities did not increase the *rate* at which they annexed new residents, however, the character of the annexations they *did* pursue might have changed. For that reason, we also consider whether the size of the typical annexed population shifted after 2013. Finally—and of central concern given the focus of

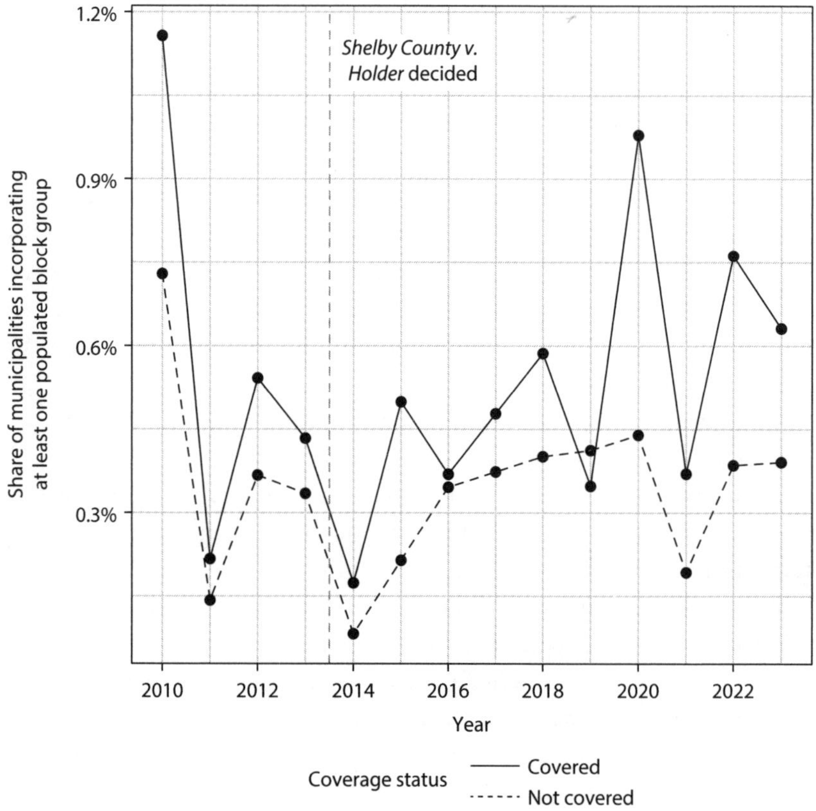

FIGURE 6.1. Annexation Rates Among Covered and Not Covered Municipalities

this book—we ask whether *Shelby County* influenced the racial composition of neighborhoods that were annexed. Freed from preclearance, formerly covered municipalities may have sought to shift their racial demographics by passing over heavily Black unincorporated areas or annexing predominantly white neighborhoods and, in so doing, to reduce the share of the electorate that is not white.

Our first task is to examine patterns in annexation rates, conditional on municipalities' former coverage status. Figure 6.1 plots an annual time series of the share of municipalities in covered and noncovered locations that annexed any new population each year from 2010 to 2023. Generally speaking, figure 6.1 shows that annexations were not common; in a typical year, only around 0.5% of municipalities annexed new residents. Moreover, over the entire time series, formerly covered municipalities annexed more land than municipalities in the rest of the country. This said, while the time series in figure 6.1 is a bit noisy, there is no real indication that the annexation rate in formerly covered municipalities changed much in the years after *Shelby County* relative to the rest of the nation. Although the annexation rate in formerly covered municipalities did spike in 2020 and 2022, perhaps in anticipation of redrawing district lines in the aftermath of the decennial census, the annexation trends we observe among formerly covered municipalities remain fairly in line with the rest of the nation in the post *Shelby County* period.

As we did in chapter 5, we further interrogate these visual trends using a statistical model that also accounts for other differences between the municipalities. Specifically, we account for differences in their population size and racial characteristics, along with their residents' average education levels, income, and age. The results of these procedures are presented in figure 6.2, which provides two pieces of information. First, the point in the center of each vertical line represents our best estimate of the effect of *Shelby County* on the annexation rate in that year. The vertical line represents the range that we can, statistically, be about 95% sure covers the "true" effect. As in other analysis we have presented so far, when these lines do not cross zero, we say that there was a statistically significant effect; that is, with 95% confidence we can rule out that random chance has led to the appearance of an effect that is not actually real.

In the years prior to *Shelby County*, of course, the decision could not have affected the annexation rate. However, the results prior to 2013 *can* help us to understand whether the covered and noncovered sets of municipalities were moving in parallel *before* the suspension of Section 5. The fact that the dashed confidence lines in figure 6.2 overlap zero in each of the three pre–*Shelby County* years suggests that they were; the overlap indicates that the difference in annexation rates between the two groups is effectively zero during this time period. If *Shelby County* affected annexation rates in some way, this pattern should diverge, with confidence bars no longer overlapping zero after the Supreme Court's decision (indicating the emergence of a difference between the two groups). But this is not what we observe in figure 6.2. In the post–*Shelby County* era, once we account for all of these differences and test the relationships statistically, the overlap remains; there is still no difference between the formerly covered and noncovered jurisdictions. This lack of difference indicates that the annexation rate did not change in any meaningful way in the formerly covered places following *Shelby County*, relative to similar municipalities that were

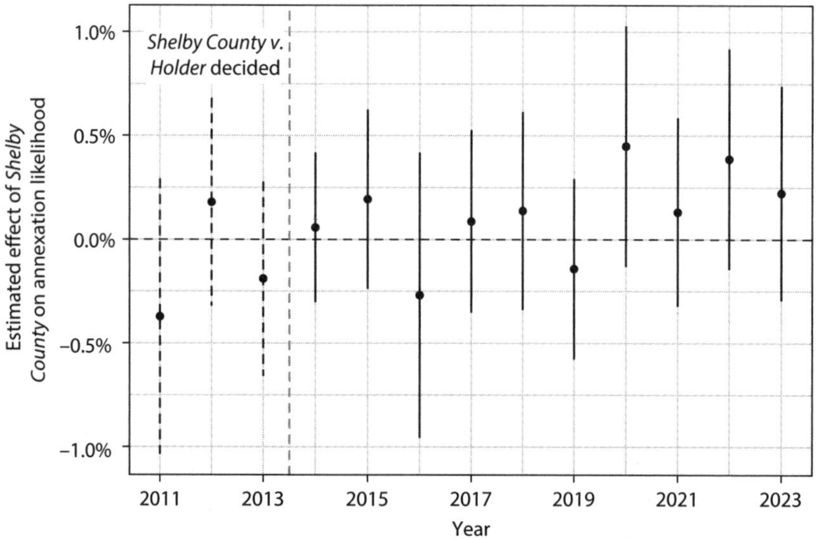

FIGURE 6.2. Estimated Effect of *Shelby County* on the Annexation Rate

never covered under Section 5. Our analysis therefore reveals no meaningful effect of *Shelby County* on the annexation rate in formerly covered municipalities.

Next we ask whether the annexations that did occur have changed in size as a result of *Shelby County*. Larger annexations, of course, have a greater potential to shift the city's demographics. Even if formerly covered municipalities are not annexing outlying areas more often, they might become more aggressive when they do, pulling in more new residents. Figure 6.3 plots the average size of annexations occurring each year in the formerly covered and noncovered regions. Although figure 6.1 showed that the *rate* of annexations was little different in formerly covered municipalities relative to other areas following *Shelby County*, figure 6.3 indicates that the size of annexations did increase in formerly covered areas. Prior to *Shelby County*, the average annexation in formerly covered municipalities was smaller than in the rest of the nation, bringing in around 2,500 new residents on average. Between 2015 and 2018, however, the average annexation size increased dramatically, to nearly 4,000 new residents. The average annexation in non-formerly-covered municipalities, meanwhile, has largely trended downward over time. In recent years, the average size of annexations in formerly covered municipalities has come back down, but only after a period in which the cities that opted to annex new

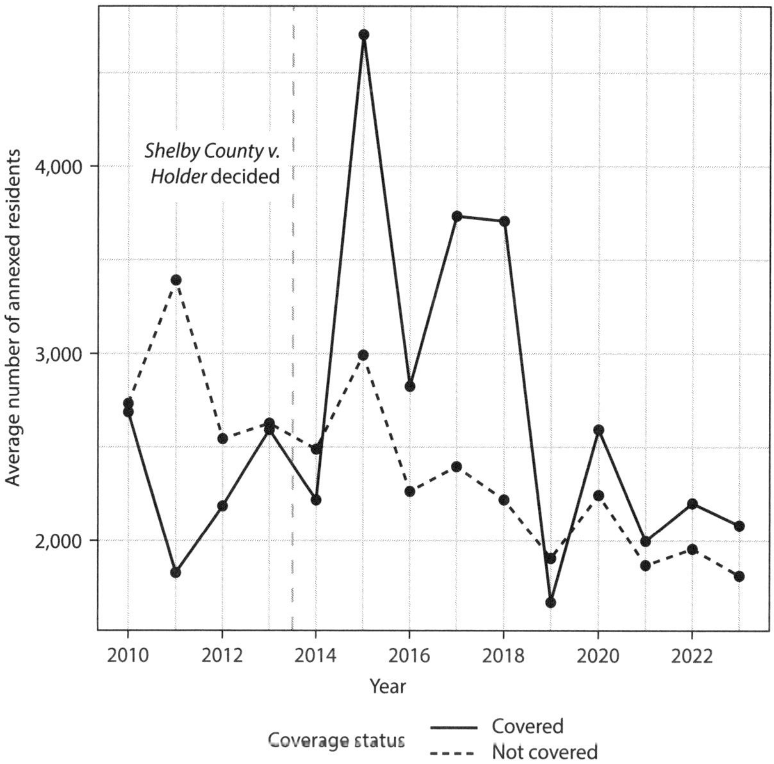

FIGURE 6.3. Size of Annexations in Covered and Not Covered Municipalities

residents did so aggressively. We also can plainly see that most of the increase was done prior to the 2020 decennial census, after which many municipalities would redraw their districts.

Figure 6.4 provides evidence that these trends are statistically significant (note that, for a number of years following *Shelby County,* the ranges are positive and do not cross zero). Although these estimates are "noisier"—that is, they move around more than most of the other ones we show elsewhere in this book—they nevertheless corroborate the visual evidence from the time series plotted in figure 6.3, namely, that there was a period in the mid-2010s when formerly covered municipalities dramatically increased the populations they annexed when they brought in new residents. *Shelby County* may not have have led to an increase in the annexation *rate,* but it does seem to have had an effect on the *size* of the typical annexation.

Finally, we move away from using municipalities to consider the composition of the annexed neighborhoods themselves. Our approach here is

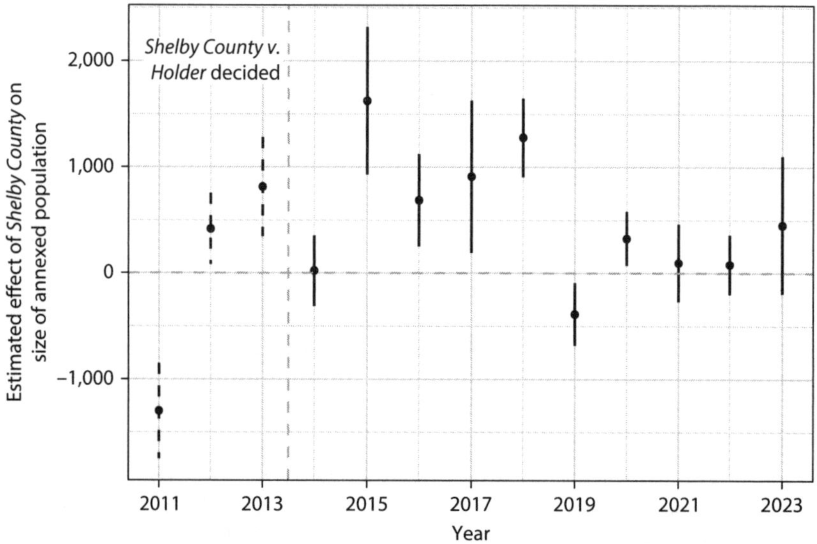

FIGURE 6.4. Estimated Effect of *Shelby County* on the Population Size of Annexations

relatively straightforward. Examining all annexations that occurred in our entire set of municipalities, we consider the preannexation characteristics of the block groups *and* the municipalities into which they were annexed. In other words, for block groups that were annexed in 2010, we ask how their 2009 characteristics differed from the 2009 characteristics of their new town: Did the annexed block group contain a larger percentage of white voters than the town that annexed it? To answer this question, we simply divide the non-Hispanic white share of the block group by the non-Hispanic white share of the municipality. If this measure for a given block group is, say, 1.1, the block group was 10% whiter than the city into which it was incorporated—and, thus, the annexation diluted the nonwhite share of the city's population.

In figure 6.5, we plot the evolution of the racial characteristics of annexed neighborhoods over time separately for the formerly covered and noncovered municipalities.[61] Figure 6.5 reveals that there has been a good amount of variation in the relative demographics of the block groups that have been annexed throughout the country. Nationally, in both formerly covered and noncovered municipalities, relatively nonwhite neighborhoods were incorporated in 2012; the opposite was true in 2014, when the national trend was toward the incorporation of whiter areas into less white cities.

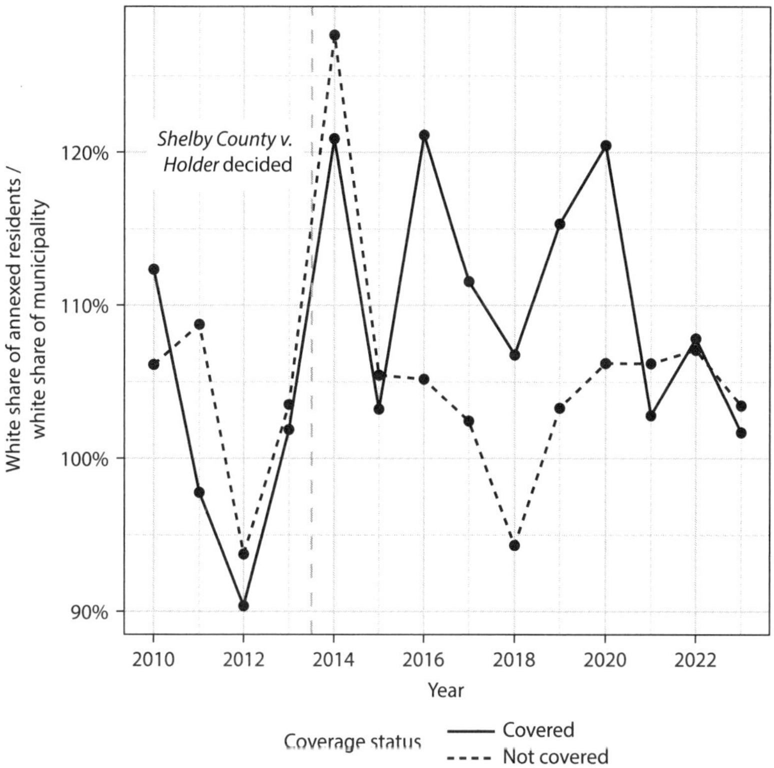

FIGURE 6.5. Relative Demographics of Block Groups Annexed into Covered and Not Covered Municipalities

The most important takeaway from figure 6.5 is that between 2010 and 2015, the neighborhoods that were annexed into formerly covered and noncovered municipalities generally moved in parallel with each other. That relationship changed, however, between 2016 and 2020. During this five-year period, the geographies annexed into formerly covered municipalities suddenly became substantially whiter than the cities into which they were being annexed.

Again, we show the results of models allowing us to test for statistical significance.[62] These results are shown in figure 6.6. Because the estimates in the post–*Shelby County* era are, for a few years, positive numbers without confidence bands that cross zero, we conclude that *Shelby County* did lead to a statistically significant increase in the relative percentage of white residents in the block groups that were annexed in the 2010s. The estimates in figure 6.6 indicate that block groups incorporated into formerly covered municipalities

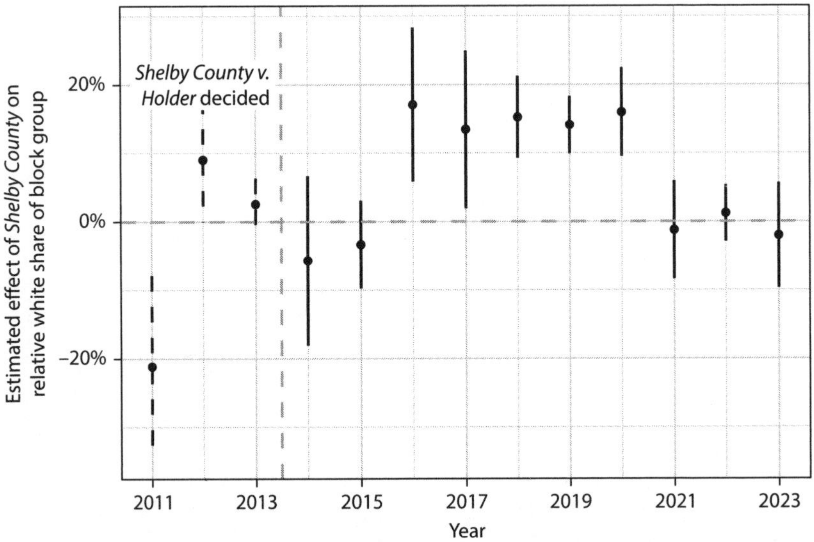

FIGURE 6.6. Estimated Effect of *Shelby County* on the Relative Demographics of Annexed Census Block Groups

were frequently more than 15 percentage points whiter than the towns that annexed them, compared to what we would expect based on trends in the rest of the country. This is particularly true between 2016 and 2020.

Taken as a whole, these results indicate that vote dilution attributable to *Shelby County* has very likely occurred in municipalities that were once required to preclear these changes with the federal government. While the number of annexations taking place in any given year might not have been larger, the character of the annexations that have occurred changed markedly in the years since *Shelby County*: In the run-up to the 2020 census, these municipalities incorporated more new residents, and these residents were considerably whiter than they probably would have been if Section 5 of the Voting Rights Act were still in effect. This is precisely what we would expect to see if these municipalities were seeking to dilute the nonwhite share of the population by adding white voters into the mix. Alternatively, the pattern could indicate that these municipalities were systematically underincorporating—or underbounding[63]—nearby racially diverse areas that would otherwise be good candidates for incorporation.

More broadly, the pattern we see in annexations is consistent with considerable anecdotal evidence of ongoing vote dilution efforts in states, counties, and municipalities. Cities have the option of changing their boundaries via annexations, but district lines also have profound implications for the quality of representation at all three levels of government. There are myriad examples of new districts that "pack" minority voters into a single majority-minority district when their composition in the population warrants more than one. This tactic is often coupled with a "crack" that spreads the remaining minority voters thinly over the remaining districts, so that one representative in total is all they can hope to elect. We saw this in the state-level redistricting cases after the 2020 census, as well as in the long saga of Galveston County (and in other stories we share elsewhere, such as the discussion of *Beer v. United States* in chapter 4). At the municipal level, it is also common for majority-white cities to move away from single-member districts—which can result in the election of minority council members from wards with substantial non-white populations—to an at-large system where white voters act in concert to elect a universally white council. This was the City of Mobile's strategy in its effort to check the power of Black residents there (which we describe in our discussion of *City of Mobile v. Bolden* in chapter 4).

The fact that we can readily point to decades-old examples of these actions indicates that they have been in use since well before the *Shelby County* decision. The long story of districting in Galveston County illustrates preclearance's potential to thwart vote dilution in every corner of covered jurisdictions. Section 5 was not perfect in this respect, but it served as a powerful deterrent against bad actors. Moreover, for jurisdictions that did choose to engage in questionable districting or annexation practices, the DOJ could bar the changes from taking effect while litigation proceeded.

Things are very different in the wake of *Shelby County*. With the DOJ no longer empowered to stop vote dilution schemes before they take effect, the only remedy available to minority voters is in the courtroom. Many federal judges have shown themselves willing to enforce Section 2 if districting schemes result in inadequate representation for minority voters, but getting to that point can take years. While they wait for their cases to unfold, plaintiffs might have to endure one or more elections in districts that illegally dilute their political power, as well as the ensuing legislative sessions in which they are denied the effective representation to which they are entitled by law. More than a decade after *Shelby County*, there is little evidence that the pace of vote dilution schemes has slowed. But there is growing concern that justice for affected voters is not so swiftly delivered as it once was.

7

First-Generation Barriers

VOTER LIST MAINTENANCE

> In assessing the overall effects of the VRA in 2006, Congress found that "significant progress has been made in eliminating first generation barriers experienced by minority voters, including increased numbers of registered minority voters, minority voter turnout, and minority representation in Congress, state legislatures, and local elected offices. This progress is the direct result of the Voting Rights Act of 1965." On that matter of cause and effects there can be no genuine doubt.
>
> —RUTH BADER GINSBURG, DISSENTING OPINION IN *SHELBY COUNTY V. HOLDER*.[1]

IT WAS March 13, 2018, a brisk Tuesday in Kansas City, and Kris Kobach was already having a bad week. The second-term Kansas secretary of state was running for governor of that state in what would ultimately be an unsuccessful bid, but Kobach's difficulties that spring had little to do with campaign politics. Kobach was in a federal district courtroom, personally defending part of an election law that Kansas had passed in 2011. It was not going well. The Secure and Fair Elections Act (SAFE Act) had several components, including a voter ID requirement. But the bench trial in which Kobach was leading the state's litigation team—known as *Fish v. Kobach* at the time but later as *Fish v. Schwab*, after Kobach's term expired—was focused squarely on how the SAFE Act affected voter registration.[2]

The new law required voters registering in Kansas to provide proof of their citizenship by producing a passport, birth certificate, naturalization papers, or some other document indicating that they were eligible to register. If they could not do so, the prospective voter's registration would be suspended and then canceled if they did not submit evidence of citizenship within 90 days. This provision was clearly intended to curb what the law's framers believed to be a raft of ballots being cast by noncitizens, but it had also ensnared quite a few otherwise-eligible citizens as well. Indeed, within about four years after the SAFE Act's implementation, plaintiffs' expert witness Michael McDonald testified, more than 23,000 potential voters had been prohibited from registering for failing to prove their citizenship, and younger voters and those who were unaffiliated with a political party were disproportionately affected.[3] Almost all of them were, in fact, citizens. US District Court chief judge Julie Robinson now had to decide whether the alleged state interest in preventing fraud could overcome the collateral damage that the proof of citizenship requirements had caused.

The case was brought by Kansas residents, all of whom were United States citizens who were eligible to vote in that state when they attempted to register in 2014. For various reasons, however, these voters did not furnish evidence of citizenship and had therefore been removed from Kansas's voter roll. Plaintiff Wayne Fish had been born on an Air Force base in Illinois and did not know how to obtain his birth certificate. Donna Bucci could not afford the $20 fee that her native Maryland required to obtain her birth certificate. Two other plaintiffs brought their birth certificates to the Department of Motor Vehicles, but were not asked to show them during the registration process. Thinking they were duly registered, the voters arrived at their polling place to vote in 2014 but were turned away. The League of Women Voters also sued the state, arguing that voter registration drives (a central part of the League's mission) were all but impossible because almost no one walks around with their birth certificate on their person.

Together, the plaintiffs argued that the SAFE Act was not consistent with the 1993 National Voter Registration Act (NVRA; more commonly known as the Motor Voter Act). The NVRA had streamlined voter registration, requiring states to offer people the opportunity to register when they otherwise interact with the state government, such as at a state department of motor vehicles. The NVRA also imposed uniform federal regulations on voter registration, requiring states to use a federal form when adding voters to the rolls. This form includes a requirement that registrants affirmatively declare that they are a citizen. By imposing additional layers to registering in the way of documentary *evidence* of citizenship, Kansas was moving beyond the NVRA's mandate—and was therefore potentially in violation of federal law.

In part for this reason, before the bench trial, the 10th Circuit Court of Appeals had determined that for the citizenship requirement to survive, Kobach had to prove that noncitizen voting posed a substantial threat to election integrity in Kansas. This was no small task, though, because it simply was not the case. Up to that point, Kobach had been able to identify only 43 noncitizens who had registered in Kansas since 2000 (a rate of fewer than three per year), and only eleven of those ever voted.[4] At the trial itself, Kobach and his team struggled with rules of evidence and procedure, earning several rebukes from the judge. More problematic, Kobach's witnesses had failed to provide anything close to compelling evidence of noncitizen voting in Kansas or anywhere else.

Kobach's defense of the law now rested squarely on the shoulders of his final expert witness, political scientist Jesse Richman. To that point, Richman was best known for a paper he coauthored in 2014 entitled "Do Non-Citizens Vote in U.S. Elections?"[5] In that paper, Richman and his colleagues used data from the Cooperative Congressional Election Study, a biannual survey of a gigantic sample of voters.[6] In addition to its sample size, the CCES also featured a "voter validation" whereby the researchers who conducted the survey checked with voter files to determine whether each survey respondent had actually voted. Recall from chapter 5 that one benefit of the voter file is the unambiguous administrative record that an individual actually cast a ballot. Thus, the voter validation approach greatly reduces measurement error because survey respondents might not remember whether they actually voted, or could even lie to researchers about having voted. The voter validation in the CCES data reduced the potential for this kind of error.

Unfortunately for Richman and colleagues, however, measurement error was *not* eliminated in the key independent variable in their analysis: respondent citizenship. Richman and his colleagues executed a relatively simple research design: They isolated the CCES sample to respondents who reported being noncitizens, and then used the vote validation measure to see whether the self-identified noncitizens had voted. Using the CCES in this way, they determined that the turnout rate among noncitizens was likely more than 3 percent—but could have been as high as 14.7%. Applying some back-of-the-envelope calculations to their estimate of 19.4 million noncitizen adults, Richman and coauthors concluded that in the 2008 election, "the number of non-citizen voters . . . could range from just over 38,000 at the very minimum to nearly 2.8 million at the maximum." Moreover, they found that the vote choice of the supposed noncitizen voters was overwhelmingly Democratic.

Unsurprisingly, the findings from this paper were like catnip to Republican politicians looking to cast doubt on election integrity after the contentious 2016 election. Donald Trump was chief among them. Despite his unambiguous victory in the Electoral College, Trump frequently (and falsely) claimed that he had actually won the popular vote as well. In so doing, President Trump often cited the upper bound of noncitizen turnout reported by Richman and colleagues to make his case: "I won the popular vote," he falsely tweeted on November 27, 2016, "if you deduct the millions of people who voted illegally."[7] The only source that underpinned this claim was Richman and colleagues' paper, and even Richman himself told the *New York Times* in a comment that foreshadowed things to come, "The high-end estimates are likely incorrect."[8]

But Trump did not stop with misleading tweets. On May 11, 2017, he issued Executive Order 13799, which established the Presidential Advisory Commission on Election Integrity.[9] The commission's primary objective was to find evidence supporting Trump's repeated assertions that the 2016 election had been tainted by widespread voter fraud. The commission met twice (but only once in public) and sent two requests to states to turn over their voter files, ostensibly to find evidence that ineligible persons—including noncitizens—had voted. In its request of Texas, the commission specifically asked for data on voters with Hispanic surnames.[10] Texas never delivered the data, as the commission's request was caught up in a flurry of lawsuits. The same was true of requests in several other states, and many others simply ignored the commission's request altogether.

A mere eight months later, the Commission on Election Integrity was quietly disbanded without finding any evidence of voter fraud in the 2016 election.[11] During its fruitless search for fraud, Vice President Mike Pence chaired the commission. Hans von Spakovsky, a former Republican commissioner of the Federal Election Commission and well-known supporter of voting restrictions, was a member. The vice chair—and to many, the man supplying the commission with most of its vigor—was Kris Kobach.

Just a few months after the commission's demise, Kobach got the band back together in Kansas City. In line with their goals for the trial, the plaintiffs' experts had stressed not only the lack of evidence for rampant noncitizen voting in Kansas but also the thousands of citizens who had not been allowed to register because they could not produce necessary documents. To prove that noncitizen voting did exist at levels necessary to justify the burden on citizens, Kobach had to rely on expert witnesses.

Hans von Spakovsky was up first. His testimony centered on cases of noncitizen voting from other states and also on a report—supplied to him by Kobach—of about 30 noncitizens who had been improperly registered in Sedgwick County. Thirty voters in one county may not be many in the grand scheme of things, but to von Spakovsky, "anytime a non-citizen registers . . . they are defrauding legitimate citizens from a fair election."[12] Von Spakovsky also believed that the 30 noncitizen voters strongly suggested that a larger problem was lurking just out of sight. In his expert report, von Spakovsky characterized these voters as "the tip of the iceberg" in that they likely represented only a fraction of the noncitizens registered in Kansas.

Von Spakovsky was ably cross-examined by Dale Ho, lead attorney for the plaintiffs. Ho went after von Spakovsky's credibility, prompting his witness to admit not only that he was not fully aware of the voter traits stored in the Kansas voter file but also that he had little expertise with voter file matching. Moreover, Ho had von Spakovsky admit that at least two of the cases of noncitizen voting he had previously cited from jurisdictions other than Kansas ultimately ended up being much less serious than he had initially reported—and that von Spakovsky had never issued corrections.

There were similar problems with von Spakovsky's characterization of the 30 voters in Sedgwick County, where a number of the noncitizen registrants had themselves pointed out to election authorities that they had never intended to register and had been placed on the rolls by mistake. To Ho, this was consistent with a characterization by plaintiffs' expert Lorraine Minnite that for "fraud" to occur, there must be bad intent by someone to purposefully circumvent the law.[13] Administrative error was something different, and Ho's cross-examination made that clear for anyone in the room. By the time Ho was done, von Spakovsky's testimony looked like a slanted and selective version of events.

Judge Robinson's skepticism during von Spakovsky's testimony was plain. It is not uncommon for federal judges to question witnesses themselves during bench trials if they feel that a relevant point has not been fully explored. Before Ho's cross examination, Robinson focused on von Spakovsky's characterization of these rare events as fraud. She asked, "When there are thousands of otherwise qualified United States citizens over the age 18 [with] no disqualifying status, [who] are denied the right to register, much less vote, would that not also be defrauding the electoral process?"[14] Robinson's question revealed that she viewed von Spakovsky's testimony with some skepticism.

On March 18, several days after von Spakovsky's testimony, Kobach must have known he was in trouble. He had just completed his direct examination of Jesse Richman, the expert witness he truly needed to show that noncitizen voting was in fact rampant. Richman's approach largely mirrored the one he had taken in his 2014 paper. Using the 2008 CCES (the same data he had used in that paper), Richman testified that 19.8% of self-reported noncitizens "either had a voter file match or said they were registered to vote."[15] Almost immediately, he qualified that claim however, citing a more conservative estimate of 3.3%—a figure that he expressed high confidence in.[16]

After that, the wheels fell off for Kobach and Richman. In an effort to estimate the number of noncitizens registered in Kansas, Richman multiplied the 3.3% by the number of noncitizens in Kansas, which he had obtained from the census. This operation was problematic because it did not appear in his report, differed from other figures that *did* appear in his report, and methodologically, applied a national estimate of the noncitizen registration rate to a single state—facts that Ho was happy to point out. This was also not the only time Richman presented figures that did not appear in his submitted reports. Ultimately, the testimony devolved into cross talk as the parties attempted to sort through the dueling figures, culminating in Judge Robinson silencing Richman with a curt "I'm done."[17] All of this was *before* he was subjected to cross-examination by Ho.

That Richman would have difficulty making his case should have been foreseeable, because almost from the moment of its publication four years prior, political scientists had rejected his paper's findings. Indeed, the principal investigators responsible for the data source Richman and colleagues had used—Stephen Ansolabehere, Samantha Luks, and Brian F. Schaffner—wrote a rebuttal whose title, "The Perils of Cherry Picking Low Frequency Events in Large Sample Surveys," captured the heart of the problem.[18] Ansolabehere and his colleagues explained that measurement error likely fueled Richman's conclusions. If even a tiny percentage of survey respondents accidentally claim to be noncitizens by erroneously selecting the wrong survey option, and if the overall survey sample is large (as it was in the CCES), the measurement error can result in a wild distortion of the true percentage of noncitizen voters.

To demonstrate how, the CCES investigators tracked the way the same people responded to the citizenship question in 2010 and 2012, finding that a large percentage of them said they were citizens in the former year but not the latter—a highly implausible scenario which suggests they simply made a mistake in responding to the 2010 citizenship question. Importantly, the authors found that none of the people who claimed to be noncitizens in both years voted, which fueled the central claim that Luk and Schaffner made: "The likely percent of non-citizen voters in recent US elections is 0." By 2018 Ansolabehere, Luks, and Schaffner's conclusions had been widely accepted as a cautionary tale for researchers hoping to examine small subgroups within large populations, and Richman, Chattha, and Earnest's paper had been pretty well debunked.

This exchange had been published for more than two years when Richman took the stand, and his utilization of the same dubious methods provided plenty of ammunition for any attorney looking to cross-examine him. But, to make matters worse, after hearing that Richman would testify, more than 200 political scientists had signed an open letter reiterating the methodological issues with Richman's approach and concluding: "The scholarly political science community has generally rejected the findings in the Richman et al. study and we believe it should not be cited or used in any debate over fraudulent voting."[19]

Dale Ho pounced on all of this scholarship, and also thoroughly critiqued other elements of Richman's report—most notably, his conclusion about the citizenship status of people on the suspended-registration list. Richman had surveyed voters on that list and asked about their citizenship status, finding only seven of 1,380 respondents (0.5%) who claimed to be noncitizens in the raw survey data. Ho also asked about the 2.2% of self-identified citizens on the suspended list whom Richman had found to lack immediate access to proof of citizenship. Ho wanted to know about the method that Richman had used to weight the data on one particular variable: "foreign name." He asked Richman, "In determining whether someone had a name foreign to you, you primarily looked whether their name, in your view, looked sort of anglophone; correct?"

Richman responded, "That was part of the process, but we had a variety of other criteria as well. . . . We looked at other things, for example, the match between the names. So if somebody had one name that we might have otherwise coded as foreign that was from—that was culturally Indian and another name that was culturally Russian, we wouldn't necessarily code that as a foreign name because of the lack of a match."

"What do you mean by 'appears to you to be foreign?'" Ho asked.

Richman replied, "Well, that was a very subjective coding. So—it was an aspect of whether the name looked like a sort of anglophone name or not primarily, but I'm sure we made many mistakes in this specific coding. The goal here was to get some sense of whether we had unequal response rates across different groups of respondents."

The subjective nature of Richman's coding was the point Ho was trying to make. He was about to call his own experts, including Stephen Ansolabehere, to deconstruct Richman's methods. But first, Ho had Richman admit that of the five people with the surname Lopez in his data, two were coded as having a foreign name, and three as nonforeign. No objective coding scheme should have grouped people with the same name into different groups. It was sloppy work and could not provide a reasonable basis for conclusions about the extent of noncitizen voting rates in Kansas. Now Ho went in for the kill. "Just hypothetically, Dr. Richman," he asked, "if you came across the name Carlos Murguia, would you code that as foreign or nonforeign?"

Richman asked Ho to spell the name, and then replied, "Probably."

"Probably what?"

"[We] probably would code it as foreign."

"Okay," Ho said. "Are you aware that Carlos Murguia is a United States District Court Judge who sits in this courthouse?"

Richman's answer provided every reporter in the courtroom with their story for the day: "I am not."

Three months later, in a scathing opinion that characterized von Spakovsky's testimony as "misleading and unsupported" and Richman's analysis as "not statistically valid," Judge Robinson threw out the SAFE Act's proof-of-citizenship requirements. In the judge's view, Kobach had not come close to meeting the burden of proof that rampant noncitizen voting threatened the integrity of Kansas elections; indeed, she found he had barely provided evidence of any noncitizen voting at all. Robinson also imposed sanctions on Kobach, whose struggles with the rules of evidence had been an ongoing source of consternation at trial. Kobach had struck out in his quest to demonstrate rampant noncitizen voting, both at trial and on the Election Integrity Commission. The SAFE Act was dead.

Kansas's push to require proof of citizenship was not new, nor was the federal government's concern that such requirements would likely disenfranchise minority voters. The Department of Justice had monitored this possibility for decades during the preclearance era. In 1995, Texas sought to empower local election officials to "make determinations of an individual's eligibility to register based on citizenship information contained in the [election] agency's file."[20] In practice, registrars would compare potential registrants' information against a database of "known" noncitizens. If, say, the registrant's name matched a name in a database of noncitizens, that individual's registration would not be processed. The DOJ recognized, however, that "with the rapid rate at which minority persons are becoming citizens, there is a strong likelihood that some of the citizenship information contained in agency files may be outdated or incorrect."[21] In denying preclearance for the proposed Texas policy, the DOJ concluded: "We are concerned that persons who have become citizens since they last filled out forms at a particular agency will not be offered registration."[22]

A decade later, in 2009, Georgia sought to implement a process similar to the Kansas SAFE Act—comparing registration applications against other databases that included information about citizenship. Flagged registrations would then be passed to local registrars, who could follow up in more depth to verify the matches. But the data were extraordinarily bad, which the DOJ noted while denying preclearance to the Georgia law as well: "Our analysis shows that the state's process does not produce accurate and reliable information and that thousands of citizens who are in fact eligible to vote under Georgia law have been flagged."[23] Indeed, in its preclearance denial the DOJ informed Georgia that it had determined that *more than half* of the individuals identified as potential noncitizens were, in fact, eligible Americans. Black, Latino, and Asian voters were all more likely to be flagged for additional scrutiny. The DOJ concluded, then, that the threats stemming from the proposed Georgia policy "are real, are substantial, and are retrogressive for minority voters."[24] Kansas had never been subject to VRA preclearance, but the Kansas trial, it turns out, was a rerun of tactics that preclearance had blocked prior to *Shelby County*. It was also a preview of things to come.

Maintaining voter rolls is an extraordinarily complicated process in the United States.[25] Local officials must keep close tabs on voters in their jurisdiction, adding all registrants who are eligible and removing any who move away, die, or become ineligible for other reasons (such as felony convictions). This task generally falls to officials in the thousands of local election offices around the country, who often work independently without much centralized oversight. It is important work if for no other reason than the fact that accurate voter lists play a key role in preventing fraud. Resource allocation and cost efficiency are also important concerns, however. For instance, many states require a certain number of polling places and voting machines per registered voter to ensure that elections run smoothly. Similarly, sending election materials (and, in vote-by-mail states, ballots) to ineligible voters is an unnecessary cost that county governments would rather avoid.

Despite the clear importance of well-maintained registration lists, keeping the rolls "clean" is no simple task. The United States has no readily accessible national database containing records of where all citizens live. This means that election administrators often find themselves working with imperfect information and must therefore be both resourceful and proactive when it comes to rooting out registrations of people who are no longer eligible to vote in their jurisdiction. Since 2018, administrators have increasingly relied on sending a postcard to individuals who have not voted in recent years. The Supreme Court has held that if voters fail to respond to the postcard and then go another four years without voting, they can then be removed from the rolls.[26]

But postcards are not the only method of identifying voters who have moved. Many (but by no means all) Americans fill out change-of-address forms with the US Post Office when they move; local election administrators can use this information to identify voters who have left their area and are no longer eligible to vote there. Similarly, administrators might also look through other data sources, such as death records, obituaries, or incarceration records to identify ineligible voters. Because election administrators often rely on data sources that were not originally designed for election administration purposes, the process can be messy. In many cases, administrators have to "link" these records using limited information like a voter's first name, last name, and date of birth. At first glance, this process might sound relatively straightforward. After all, how many possible people could be out there with the same name and birthday?

In practice, however, merging disparate data sources can present real headaches for election administrators, whose decisions can have major consequences. One reason why is embodied in a phenomenon that may be well known to readers who have taken a college statistics course: the so-called Birthday Problem.[27] College instructors love the Birthday Problem because it illustrates just how unintuitive probability can be and it can usually be demonstrated to great effect in a midsized lecture hall. Imagine you are in such a hall with, say, 60 other students and the instructor asks you to look around and calculate the probability that two people in the room share the same birthday (excluding the year). You might guess that the probability is quite small; after all, there are only 61 students in the room, and 366 potential birth dates.[28] We spare readers the math, but it turns out that it takes just 23 people for the probability of a match to exceed 50%, and with just 61 students, the probability of a match would be above 99%! This is far higher than most people would have expected.

Extending the thought experiment a bit further, if we imagine that all students in the class have the same name, we can easily see why name-birthday matches can cause serious problems in election administration. Voters with common names are highly likely to share a birthday with at least one other person who has the same first and last name, and as the pool of common-named voters grows larger, we are likely to see a year match in addition to the month and day. For instance, consider how an election administrator might handle the case of a Texas voter named José Martinez. In the state of Texas as of this writing there are more than 3,000 registered voters with that name, and four of them were born on the same day in February 1976. If a citizen named José Martinez were to register in Harris County tomorrow while listing that same birth date, the local election officials would have to look at all the available data and make their best guess as to whether this was a *new* José Martinez or one of the *previously registered* ones leaving his old address and moving into Harris County.

If the former case is true, the officials could simply add the new José to the roll. But if the latter, they would register him in Harris County and simultaneously begin the process of canceling his now-outdated registration in the jurisdiction where he formerly resided. Now, suppose officials get this wrong, believing they have an already-registered José when they actually have a new José, who just happens to have the same birthday as the others. That means that one of four existing Josés would likely find himself "purged" from the voter roll—even though he had not moved, and even if he had voted regularly until the new José came to Texas. This voter might not even learn that he was wrongfully purged until arriving on Election Day to vote, by which point it would be too late for him to reregister.

This example reminds us that the stakes here are quite high for all involved, and we know that the chances of a mistake are not trivial. Across Texas alone, our analysis indicates that more than 50,000 voters have the exact same first name, last name, and birth date as at least one other registered voter, and the likelihood of a mistaken match is not race-neutral. White Texas voters (who compose a plurality of the voter file) make up just 27% of those who share a first name, last name, and birth date with another voter. In contrast, despite making up less than a third of the electorate, 57% of voters who share information with another voter are Latino. Black voters are also more than 50% more likely to share a name and birth date with another voter compared to white voters in Texas. The practical problems with cross-database matches are thorny for all voters, but minority voters seem to be especially vulnerable to matching problems.

Regrettably, honest mistakes in list maintenance are not the sole worry for minority voters. Nothing was more central to the Voting Rights Act than concerns about voter registration. Prior to the VRA's passage, Southern jurisdictions wielded registration procedures as their primary means of voter disenfranchisement, employing numerous tests and devices to stop Black voters from ever placing their name on the voter roll. The VRA authorized federal registrars to register Southern voters. To protect registration over the long term, Congress crafted the coverage formula in Section 4(b), placing jurisdictions on the preclearance list if they had failed to register at least half of their voting-age citizens in 1964 (or jurisdictions in which fewer than half of voting-age persons voted in that election). The message was clear: The voter roll would no longer offer a viable means of race-based voter suppression.

The VRA so successfully ensured that minority voters had equal opportunity to register that by the early twenty-first century, few observers thought that covered jurisdictions were maintaining their voter lists in an unfair manner. Indeed, many simply took it for granted that monitoring registration procedures was no longer a central concern. During the oral argument in *Shelby County*, Justice Ruth Bader Ginsburg's questioning of the advocates exhibited this way of thinking about registration. Addressing Bert W. Rein, who was arguing on behalf of Shelby County, Ginsburg said, "Mr. Rein, you keep emphasizing over and over again in your brief . . . [that] Congress was well aware that registration was no longer the problem [when it reauthorized the VRA in 2006]. This legislative record is replete with what they call second generation devices. Congress said up front: We know that the registration is fine. That is no longer the problem. But the discrimination continues in other forms." In Justice Ginsburg's theory of the case, the "first generation" of voter disenfranchisement via list maintenance was over, even if there was acute need to continue monitoring for less overt methods of diluting minority representation. To Ginsburg and many others at the time, concerns about registration were primarily historical, serving modern analysis mainly as a predictive factor for where "second generation devices" might be especially likely to emerge. Of course, as her own question indicated, Ginsburg's was not the only view as to the meaning of voter registration being "no longer the problem." Rein's position—which was ultimately joined by the majority of justices—was that the absence of obvious racial disparities in voter registration indicated that the coverage formula had served its purpose and was no longer needed at all.

We show throughout part II of this book that the liberal justices had good reason to worry about what would happen in the absence of preclearance, and much of the retrogression we identify does indeed stem from the "second generation devices" that Ginsburg referenced during the *Shelby County* argument. Justice Ginsburg was wrong on another front, though: Registration was *not* fine. The VRA had blocked covered jurisdictions from managing their voter rolls in a discriminatory fashion. Given the devastating historical effectiveness of list maintenance in disenfranchising voters—and especially those of color—anyone concerned with maintaining the VRA's efficacy ignored voter registration at their own peril. While the truly first-generation registration barriers like literacy tests and grandfather clauses have not returned, the procedures for *de*-registering voters have gotten considerably more aggressive in recent years—especially in areas with a history of racial discrimination.

Before either the Kansas trial or Donald Trump's election commission, Kris Kobach oversaw the dramatic expansion of a multistate program called the Interstate Voter Registration Crosscheck. Crosscheck, as it was commonly called, was launched by Ron Thornburgh, Kobach's predecessor as Kansas secretary of state, in 2005 as a joint effort with Missouri, Iowa, and Nebraska, and was intended to help election administrators identify individuals who were registered to vote in multiple states. As discussed earlier, this is a common problem for election administrators. Following an interstate move, many people will find it easy to register at their new address, perhaps while obtaining a new driver's license or vehicle registration. Few people cancel their registration at their old address, however, which may mean that they end up being registered to vote in two states at once. Crosscheck built a common database from participating states' voter files, thereby promising a way to identify duplicate names of voters possibly registered in more than one place. The program expanded from the original 4 states to 13 in 2010. On Kobach's watch, this count more than doubled, reaching 29 states in 2014.

Matching voters can be difficult in just about any context. In theory, then, the Crosscheck program promised a solution to one of the most common and vexing issues that complicates election administration in the United States.

As it turned out, however, Crosscheck was extremely ineffective at what it purported to do. According to guidance it provided to member states in 2014,[29] Crosscheck considered voter registrations from two different states to be potential matches so long as they had the same value on three attributes: first name, last name, and date of birth. In such cases, states could flag the registrations, move the voters to an "inactive" status, and even begin the cancelation process. They could do so even if the middle names on the registrations were different or missing, if the last four digits of the voters' social security numbers were different or missing, or if the signatures associated with the registrations were different.

Our discussion above of both the Birthday Problem and the match patterns we found in the Texas voter file offer a cautionary tale for this approach. It should go without saying, however, that to potentially "match" voters *even when they display nonmatching information* is deeply problematic. To put the three-variable matching procedure into appropriate context, let's revisit the example we describe above: A Crosscheck-style match we conducted on the Texas voter file flags more than 50,000 registrations in that state *alone*, and that number would be far larger if we were to compare Texas voters to the entire set of registered voters anywhere in the country. Some of these duplicates are no doubt people who have moved within Texas and never canceled their old registrations, but a great many are also false positives. In 2014 the Crosscheck program flagged more than 7 million potential duplicates,[30] but a subsequent study found that more than 99% of these "matches" were in fact distinct voters.[31] The Crosscheck approach, the authors of that study estimated, would "impede approximately 300 legitimate votes for each double vote prevented."[32]

Academics were not the only ones who noted that Crosscheck's inaccuracies created real problems around the country. Virginia joined the Crosscheck consortium in December 2012.[33] Just months after *Shelby County* was decided, the Virginia Department of Elections sent Crosscheck matches to election administrators without first confirming their accuracy. Local election officials were also not provided any guidance about the data or sufficient time to conduct a thorough review. Some eligible voters were wrongly flagged as having moved from Virginia *to* another state when they had in fact moved *from* another state to Virginia.[34] These errors were not identified until after local election officials had already started removing some voters. A 2017 report by the commonwealth's Department of Elections determined that only about 10% of the Crosscheck data was "usable" for list maintenance purposes.[35]

Given that (as shown above) the DOJ objected to a Georgia proposal to use similarly faulty data to flag "noncitizens," it is plausible that preclearance might have preempted these problems.

Worse, Virginia was not the only formerly covered state relying on Crosscheck for list maintenance following the *Shelby County* decision. By the end of 2014, 11 of the 15 states where at least one substate jurisdiction had been subject to preclearance participated in Crosscheck, and several of them went down the same path Virginia did.[36] In Florida, where a handful of covered counties meant statewide practices were covered by preclearance, the 11th Circuit found that the state violated federal law with a 2014 purge of its own.[37] In 2016 a judge in the formerly partially covered state of North Carolina found that local boards of election similarly likely violated the National Voter Registration Act,[38] calling one removal practice "insane."[39] And, as discussed in greater detail below, New York City (which was also on the preclearance list) engaged in a massive, illegal purge following *Shelby County*.

In 2018 the ACLU sued Kris Kobach and the Crosscheck program for illegally exposing voters' sensitive information;[40] according to an investigation by ProPublica, Crosscheck's security protocols were woefully lacking.[41] Kobach's successor as Kansas secretary of state, Scott Schwab, settled with the ACLU and issued an apology for the program. Crosscheck has been dormant ever since, but the dramatic role it played in list maintenance—and, in many cases, *illegal* list maintenance—in the years following *Shelby County* demonstrates how quickly states and localities were able to shift their practices once federal preclearance was removed.

Even before Crosscheck's demise, many states had begun moving to an alternative offered by the Electronic Registration Information Center (ERIC). The intuition behind ERIC is similar to that undergirding Crosscheck in that it offers states the opportunity to pool data and check for duplicates. However, for a number of reasons, ERIC is a more effective option than Crosscheck. For one, in addition to voter rolls, ERIC incorporates data from member states' motor vehicle departments, as well as death records from the Social Security Administration.[42] ERIC also employs sophisticated matching algorithms that go far beyond using just the person's name and date of birth; its methods lead to false positive rates far lower than Crosscheck's rate. In short, with a broader base of data and more careful matching procedures, ERIC accomplishes many of the goals that Crosscheck originally set out to achieve—with far fewer errors.

In the program's history, 34 states and the District of Columbia have been members of ERIC at some point; membership peaked in 2022, when 31 states and DC were active members. Over the life of the program, ERIC has helped election officials identify more than 13 million cross-state movers, as well as more than 28 million voters who did not move across state lines but whose registrations still required updating. Election officials of both parties heaped praise on the program; indeed, ERIC enjoyed strong support from Republican election officials. Frank LaRose (the Republican secretary of state of Ohio) called ERIC "one of the best fraud-fighting tools that we have when it comes to actually catching people that try to vote in multiple states."[43] When Florida joined ERIC in 2020, Secretary of State Laurel Lee (also a Republican) boasted, "Joining ERIC keeps Florida at the forefront of election security and will help us ensure a fair and accurate election in 2020 and beyond."[44] And Brad Raffensperger, the Republican secretary of state of Georgia, said, "States that prioritize best practices and actual election integrity over politics are going to stay in ERIC."[45]

But not all of those states stayed in ERIC. Since 2022, nine Republican-controlled states have left the program amid concerted efforts from right-wing activists to discredit it.[46] These efforts started with a January 2022 article appearing on *Gateway Pundit*, one of the top websites spreading misinformation about the 2020 election.[47] The *Gateway Pundit* article falsely claimed that ERIC was "originally funded by the Soros Open Society," calling it "essentially a left wing voter registration drive disguised as voter roll clean up."[48] Despite its dubious claims, the article stirred a reaction. Just one week after its publication, Louisiana secretary of state Kyle Ardoin announced that his state would be leaving the program. Ardoin subsequently said that the *Gateway Pundit* report had nothing to do with the decision, but his office refused to say what *did* lead to Louisiana's departure.[49]

Why did election officials in nine states abandon a program that other Republicans—indeed, that some of the nine—had roundly praised? A partial answer may lie in the requirements that ERIC imposes on member states. To be sure, ERIC is used largely to help election administrators identify and update duplicate voter registrations; in fact, member states must do this list maintenance to remain in good standing. But that's not all: ERIC *also* requires member states to use their data to affirmatively contact individuals who are unregistered but otherwise eligible to vote. Prior to the 2020 election, ERIC identified 17 million eligible but unregistered Americans.[50] The *Gateway Pundit* piece noted this requirement and inferred from it that ERIC was a nefarious tool to register left-leaning constituencies—an allegation later repeated elsewhere in the election denialism movement.[51] This framing gathered steam despite the fact that there is actually no evidence that new voters uniformly help Democrats: In Louisiana (the first state to leave ERIC), 38% of the voters who cast their first ballot in 2020 were registered Republicans; just 32% were Democrats.[52] This disparity underscores the fact that voter list maintenance, like many other areas of election administration these days, is simultaneously susceptible to partisan forces and misinformation.

ERIC is still functional. As of early 2025, 24 states remain as ERIC members, along with Washington, DC. But the withdrawals have undermined the program's ability to identify both duplicate registrations and unregistered Americans. In 2024, ERIC flagged only about 20% as many cross-state movers as it had at its peak. Its capacity to find unregistered but voting-eligible citizens is even worse: In 2024, just 7% as many were identified as in 2020.[53] A weakened ERIC is simultaneously bad for everyone who wants secure voting lists *and* everyone who wants to maximize voter registration, but leaving ERIC is a near guarantee that states will miss improperly registered voters on their rolls. States formerly subject to preclearance were much more likely to be "leavers": 50% of ERIC member states that were formerly subject to preclearance have abandoned ERIC, compared to just 14% of noncovered states. This said, while states once covered under Section 5 were sued for their misuse of Crosscheck and have been more likely to leave ERIC, it is still not clear whether voters' ability to stay on the rolls has worsened since *Shelby County* in places once subject to the preclearance condition. It is now time to turn to that question.

On April 19, 2016, voters in New York City went to the polls to cast their ballots in the first presidential primary since *Shelby County* removed the city from the preclearance list. Less than a week before, Hillary Clinton and Bernie Sanders had debated in Brooklyn, the city's most populous borough. On the Republican side, the field had been winnowed to just Donald Trump, Ted Cruz, and John Kasich. In a city unaccustomed to playing a pivotal role in presidential politics, enthusiasm ran high. There was one catch, however: In violation of federal law, more than 100,000 Brooklynites had unwittingly been removed from the voter rolls. Many of them were perfectly eligible to vote and discovered the city's error only when they arrived at their polling place that day. According to the New York State Attorney General's Office, in excess of 1,000 complaints were made regarding registrations in Brooklyn on April 19—more than six times as many as had been made in the 2012 primary.[54]

On the eve of the primary election, National Public Radio affiliate WNYC published a story noting that some 60,000 New Yorkers had been removed from the voter rolls since November of the year prior.[55] As it turned out, this was just the start. After WNYC's initial reporting, city and state officials began digging into what exactly had happened. The numbers reported by WNYC were striking in their own right—representing some 7% of all registered Democrats in the borough—but the investigations uncovered more improper voter removals that had occurred even earlier. The city's Board of Elections had illegally removed more than 120,000 voters in two purges on June 15 and July 5, 2015. A team at WNYC dug into the records from individuals who had been removed, and what it found was troubling:[56] The removals were concentrated in Brooklyn neighborhoods with large Latino populations. What's more, some 15% of individuals with Latino surnames were removed from the rolls, compared with 9.5% of the rest of the electorate. This whopping 58% differential would have raised the eyebrows of any preclearance administrator at the Justice Department. But even that was not the whole story; a further investigation showed that the true number of illegally removed voters exceeded 200,000.[57]

By the end of 2017, the Board of Elections of the City of New York had settled in court and admitted that it had violated federal law.[58] The issue was the board's decision to remove voters who had neither voted in an election nor updated their information since 2008. This move came in flagrant violation of the National Voter Registration Act's requirement that voter list maintenance "shall not result in the removal of the name of any person from the official list of voters registered to vote in an election for Federal office by reason of the person's failure to vote."[59] Had New York City submitted the proposed removal criteria for Section 5 review, preclearance might have stopped the illegal purge; the DOJ had objected to similar proposed criteria for removing voters based on a failure to vote in Georgia and South Dakota because of the likelihood of disproportionately harming voters of color.[60] But preclearance was defunct in 2015, and although improperly purged voters were eventually added back to the rolls, the problem was not fixed until after those voters had been prevented from casting a ballot in that 2016 primary. No court-ordered remedy or settlement could undo their exclusion from that contest.

And yet, though they were disenfranchised in the 2016 primary, the Brooklyn voters were relatively lucky. If not for robust local media scrutiny in New York City, the problems with the city's list maintenance might never have been widely discussed, much less rectified. Sometimes, as with the SAFE Act in Kansas, state legislatures guide restrictive voter registration practices. But the case of New York raises an important point: When it comes to list maintenance, no legislative act is usually required. The decision of whether to remove voters from the rolls generally falls to the discretion of local administrators. And, as this chapter demonstrates, it is relatively easy for even statewide election officials to fall prey to misinformation or their own predilections when it comes to decisions affecting potentially thousands of voters. This fact begs an important question: What's happening to voter rolls in places where there is no local media to dig into election administration and, especially, where historically there has been a pattern of discrimination?

A central premise of the *Shelby County* decision is that the old, first-generation method of disenfranchising minority voters via registration practices was a thing of the past. However, we have explored abundant anecdotal evidence from the years since *Shelby County* that illustrates the potential for list maintenance to disenfranchise voters—with a particular threat to voters of color. This is true in jurisdictions that were formerly subject to preclearance as well as in some that were not. It is important, then, to more fully consider whether jurisdictions formerly covered by the VRA's preclearance provisions have removed voters more aggressively than noncovered jurisdictions since the *Shelby County* ruling.[61]

To measure the number of voters removed from the rolls in counties nationwide, we turn to data collected by the US Election Assistance Commission (EAC). Since the 2006 election, the EAC has administered a national survey to local election officials called the Election Administration and Voting Survey (EAVS).[62] The EAVS captures a wealth of information about the experience of running elections in each county, from statistics about registration, to the number of voting machines used on Election Day, to how difficult poll worker recruitment is. Here, we focus on the number of voters that election officials reported removing from their rolls during the preceding two-year federal election cycle. For instance, following the 2022 election, election administrators reported the total number of voters whose registrations were canceled between November 3, 2020, and November 8, 2022. Because most officials reported this information for each of the eight election cycles between 2008 and 2022, we can observe how trends in voter removals have evolved for those sixteen years.[63]

We first standardize the removal counts by calculating the "removal rate," or the percentage of voters originally registered in each county who were removed (for more information, refer to the Methodological Appendix). To examine this trend in covered and noncovered jurisdictions before and after *Shelby County*, we employ a difference-in-differences approach quite similar to the one we use in the previous two chapters. In brief, we compare the trend in voter removal rates in counties once covered by Section 4(b) of the Voting Rights Act to similar counties that were not covered in order to see whether the pattern shifted after *Shelby County* was decided. Because the structure of the EAVS data differs from the data we use in chapter 5, however, we do make some methodological adjustments here (which interested readers can learn more about in the Methodological Appendix).

We start by looking at all the covered counties together. Figure 7.1 depicts the time series of the voter removal rate for counties that were covered under Section 5 prior to *Shelby County* and those that were not. As the figure shows, both sets of counties moved more or less in parallel with one another prior to 2013.[64] The graph also makes clear that the covered and noncovered counties began to move in very different ways after *Shelby County* was handed down: Once jurisdictions were released from preclearance, the relative removal rate increased in the once-covered counties while it declined slightly in the noncovered ones. For the first three cycles following *Shelby County*, the median removal rate in the formerly covered counties hovered near 10%, substantially higher than the rate in the rest of the country. In other words, about one out of every ten voters registered for the 2012 election had been removed by the 2014 election in formerly covered areas.

The same was true for the following four years, too. While the removal rate has come back down in line with other, similar counties in recent years, these trend lines fit the pattern we would expect to see if states and localities took advantage of *Shelby County* to dramatically prune their voter registration lists. As with the annexations described in chapter 6, these outcomes can be accomplished quickly before returning to previous levels; once desired removals have been accomplished, there is little need to continue doing so at elevated levels.

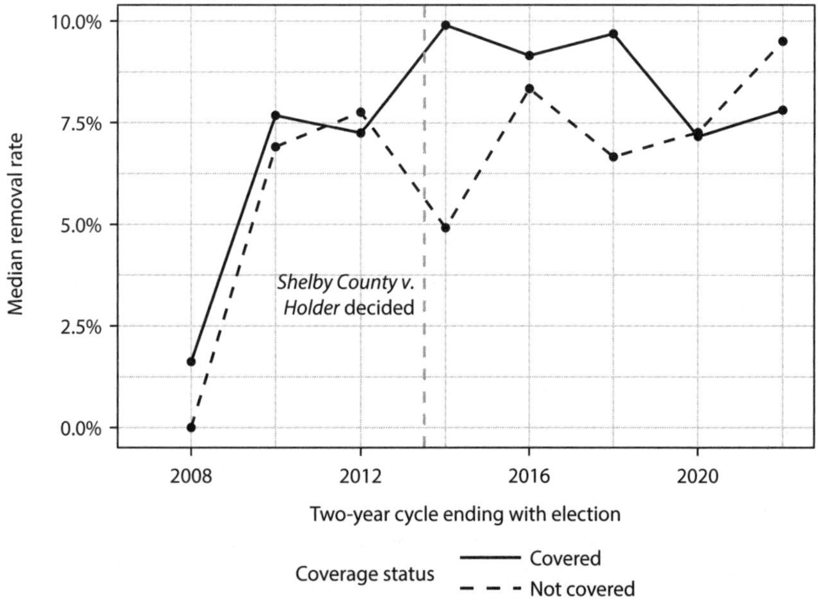

FIGURE 7.1. Removal Rates over Time Based on Section 5 Coverage Status
Note: For the purposes of presenting a time-series plot that accounts for differences between the covered and noncovered counties, this figure uses the same matching procedure described in chapter 5 to select control counties that look like the treated counties. See the Methodologicacl Appendix for further discussion.

Although figure 7.1 is consistent with the story that *Shelby County* led to at least an initial spike in registration removals in formerly covered counties, it does not account for an important nuance that must be considered in this analysis. With respect to list maintenance, it is especially key to investigate whether the effects of *Shelby County* were concentrated in the counties where preclearance constrained local practices (as opposed to noncovered counties in covered states). There is ample reason to suspect that this is the case. In chapter 3, we demonstrate that the overwhelming majority of policies that the DOJ blocked in preclearance were proposed at the local level. List maintenance is especially likely to be run at the local level; as political scientist Thessalia Merivaki puts it, "Local election administrators are mainly, if not exclusively, responsible for the day-to-day management of voter records, such as processing new voters, updating existing voter records, and *removing ineligible voter registrants from the rolls*."[65] Chapter 5 shows that, due to *Shelby County*, the turnout gap has grown most quickly in places where local practices were

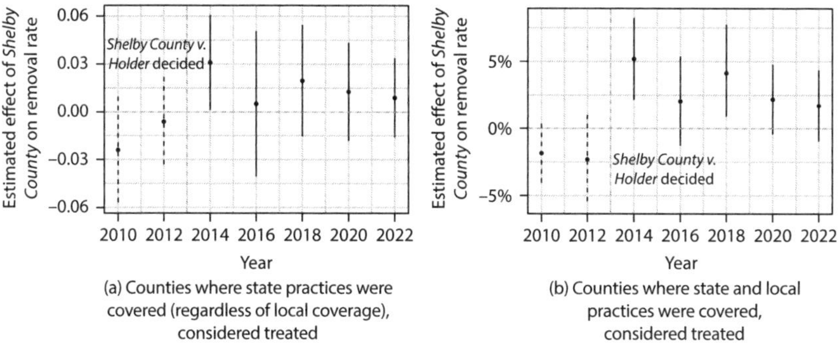

FIGURE 7.2. Estimated Effect of *Shelby County* on Voter Purge Rates by Coverage Status

previously constrained. We therefore want to examine how trends in the voter removal rate compare when we separately examine covered counties, as well as noncovered counties in covered states.

We also test the statistical significance of these relationships, as we have done thus far in other analyses we present in this book. To do so, we control for the same characteristics we used in the matching procedure described in chapter 5: the (logged) population; the share of the population that is non-Hispanic white and non-Hispanic Black; median income; median age; share of the population with at least a bachelor's degree; and Obama's vote share in 2012. To analyze voter purges specifically, however, we also add another important characteristic: the share of the population in each county that moved in the past year. We take this step because purge rates should be naturally higher where a larger share of the population is moving out of the county.[66]

In figure 7.2, we plot the statistical results analogous to those we present in chapters 5 and 6. By way of reminder, the dots in these figures indicate our best estimate of the effect of *Shelby County* on the removal rate in treated counties relative to matched controls consisting of comparable noncovered counties. Moreover, we can be 95% confident that the true effect is located somewhere within the confidence regions indicated by the vertical lines. When these lines do not cross zero, the model indicates a statistically significant difference between the relevant "treatment" group and the controls.

In the left-hand panel, we show models where counties are considered treated so long as they were in a state where statewide practices were covered under Section 5, regardless of whether their local practices were covered. On the right-hand side, we show the results from models where counties are considered treated only if their own local practices were subject to preclearance before *Shelby County*.[67] The black dashed lines in figure 7.2 give us important information: The fact that point estimates are relatively small prior to the *Shelby County* ruling in both panels—and that the confidence bars cross zero in that period—indicates that the purge rates in the treated and control counties were moving in parallel before 2013 after accounting for differences in their characteristics. This gives us confidence that if Section 5 had remained operative, we would likely have continued to observe no difference in purge rates between treated and control counties after 2014.

But we *do* see a difference emerge in 2014—especially in the right-hand panel, where we look only at counties where *Shelby County* had implications for local election administration. That makes sense: Since list maintenance is largely a local affair, freeing states to change their purge practices had little effect at the local level in counties where administrators could conduct maintenance without preclearance even before *Shelby County*. But, in the cycle in which *Shelby County* was handed down, the purge rate in the formerly locally covered counties jumped by more than 5 points relative to what we would have expected if preclearance had continued. Translating these effects back into hard numbers, we can therefore conservatively estimate that in the two years ending in 2014, *Shelby County* led to the removal of roughly 700,000 additional voters from the rolls above baseline expectations.[68]

Since 2014, the formerly covered counties have gradually come back in line with the rest of the country, though the estimates indicate that the difference remains slightly (if not statistically significantly) elevated. We estimate that across the post-*Shelby* era as a whole, the end of preclearance raised the purge rate in the formerly covered counties by about 3 percentage points. Using the same estimation approach indicates that in total, as many as 2 million voters have been removed from the rolls as a direct result of practices that sprang up after *Shelby County* was decided.

As in chapter 5, where we explore whether the turnout gap grew more quickly in formerly covered counties where a Section 5 objection letter had been issued, we next ask whether the purge rate also increased more in these counties than in other formerly covered counties. Again, the intuition underpinning this analysis is that counties engaged in problematic activity during the preclearance era might be especially likely to develop such practices when preclearance was removed. The results of these statistical models are presented in figure 7.3. Here, we run two separate models: one calculating the

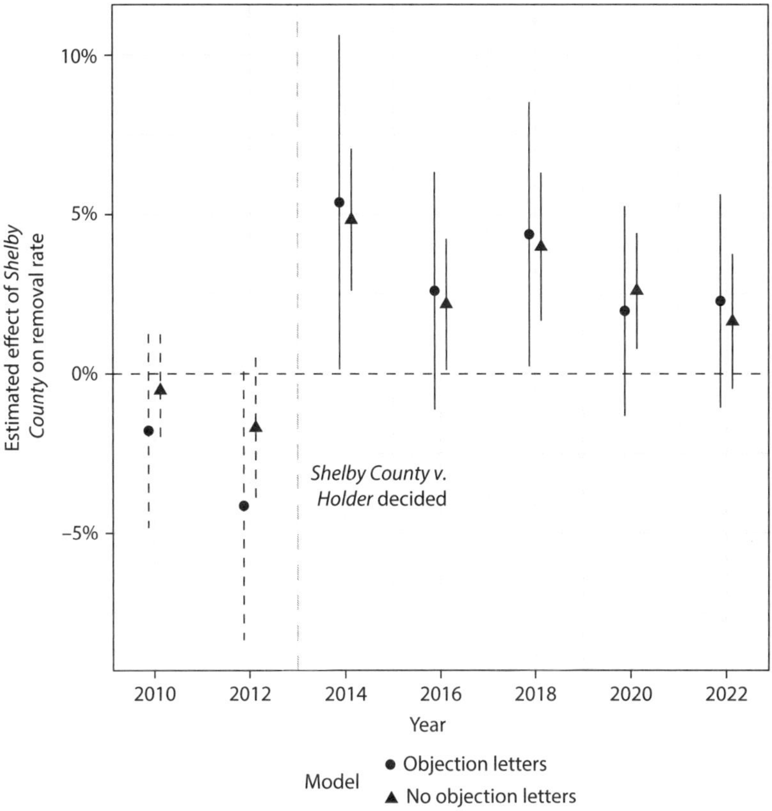

FIGURE 7.3. Estimated Effect of *Shelby County* on Voter Purge Rates by Objection Letter

difference-in-differences among covered counties *without* objection letters, and the other making the same calculation for counties *with* objection letters. We find that objection letters are less predictive of where voter purges increased than they were with regard to turnout gaps (chapter 5). The purge rates did increase slightly more in the covered counties with objection letters; the effect in both 2014 and over the period as a whole was about 10% higher in the counties with objection letters than in those without. However, these differences are not statistically significant.

Even so, in chapter 5 we show how the cumulative effect of *Shelby County* seems to be a growing turnout gap between white and nonwhite voters. Voter list maintenance is just one of the policies that administrators could use (intentionally or otherwise) in the aftermath of that ruling to shape the electorate.

It bears repeating that far from being a concern relegated to the dustbin of history, voter registration remains a central issue in election administration—and the fastest way for a single jurisdiction to declare thousands of voters ineligible at once. Our analysis indicates that local jurisdictions who were subject to preclearance prior to *Shelby County* began to purge more voters after the Court's ruling. And the momentum here may only be gathering.

January 3, 2025, was the first day of the 119th Congress, and Representative Chip Roy (R-TX) wasted no time reintroducing a piece of legislation that had twice passed the House of Representatives the year before, only to die in the Democratically controlled Senate. Now, with unified Republican control of Congress and, soon, the return of Donald Trump to the White House, Roy was better positioned. His bill, the Safeguard American Voter Eligibility (SAVE) Act, would require "individuals to provide documentary proof of U.S. citizenship when registering to vote in federal elections." Under the terms of the law, this proof would have to be furnished to state officials in person, which would effectively eliminate mail or online registration, voter registration drives by third parties, and most likely, automatic voter registration. It would in short dramatically curtail efforts by states, political parties, or even nonpartisan groups to register voters.

The SAVE Act has more in common with the Kansas SAFE Act than its name. For one, the SAVE Act's aims are utterly consistent with the narrative in *Fish v. Schwab* of rampant noncitizen voting in American elections. The bill also raises familiar concerns. While the SAVE Act would prevent few noncitizens from voting (since it is already illegal for them to do so), it would potentially disenfranchise more than 21 million Americans who do not have ready access to necessary documents—most of whom have actively participated in recent elections.[69] Also, this figure does not include other potential issues, such as the tens of millions of women who changed their name when they married—and therefore do not have a birth certificate that matches their identification.

We're not in Kansas anymore. The stakes are exponentially higher than in *Fish v. Schwab* when we consider the likely impact of a national proof of citizenship requirement, and the status of millions of eligible voters of *both parties* is hanging in the balance. What's more, the Supreme Court has recently signaled a willingness to tolerate proof of citizenship requirements—at least for a little while. That case came not from Kansas but Arizona, a state that was on the preclearance list prior to *Shelby County*.

In 2022 Arizona passed two laws regulating voter registration in that state. The first, HB 2492, was reminiscent of the Kansas SAFE Act in declaring that to be eligible to vote in a presidential election, voters had to furnish documentary proof of citizenship *and* residency. The second law (HB 2493) went even further in requiring local election officials to conduct periodic assessments of their voting rolls and to cancel registrations of anyone they have "reason to believe" are not citizens if the voter cannot furnish proof of citizenship. The program sounded eerily familiar to those who had watched the Georgia proposal from 2009 run afoul of preclearance before *Shelby County*.

The laws were swiftly challenged by a coalition of interest groups, Native nations, and Democratic Party organizations, whose argument was broadly similar to the one put forward in Kansas. Like the Kansas voters, the Arizona plaintiffs claimed that by requiring proof of citizenship in presidential elections, Arizona had illegally added a layer of registration beyond what was allowed by the National Voter Registration Act. Furthermore, the plaintiffs argued that the laws would disenfranchise far more citizens than the number of noncitizens they would prohibit from voting. As in Kansas, this possibility presented clear civil rights issues. Other than surname, race, or ethnicity, what would give election officials "reason to believe" that an existing voter was not a citizen?

These are strong arguments, to be sure, but the plaintiffs were further aided by the fact that HB 2492 was not Arizona's first attempt to require proof of citizenship. Indeed, the new law appeared to directly defy the Supreme Court's 2013 holding in *Arizona v. Inter Tribal Council of Arizona*.[70] There, the Court struck down a similar proof-of-citizenship requirement that had been passed by ballot initiative in Arizona. The Supreme Court held that the NVRA laid out clear requirements for registration in federal elections and that states could not go beyond them. Arizona was free to require proof of citizenship for voting in state and local elections, the Court ruled, but the state was not allowed to use failure to produce proof of citizenship as a means of preventing people from voting in presidential or congressional elections. In other words, Congress had exerted authority over federal elections that the Court had long held was within its power to do.[71] States could not add extra hurdles to registration on their own.

This decision and subsequent litigation led Arizona to maintain two parallel systems of voter registration until the passage of HB 2492:[72] Voters registering on the "federal only" list needed only to complete the NVRA form and supply no further proof of citizenship. Once registered, these voters were allowed to vote only in presidential and congressional elections. In contrast, to register as a "full ballot" voter, registrants had to complete the NVRA registration form *and* provide documentary proof of citizenship. They could then vote in federal, state, and local elections. In specifically mandating that voters show proof of citizenship to vote in *presidential* elections, HB 2492 shook up this arrangement, however. It seemed, then, that the plaintiffs held the high ground as they entered federal court.

In May 2024, following action in the Arizona US District Court, the plaintiffs prevailed.[73] The district court struck down nearly all of the two voting laws' provisions, including requirements for proof of citizenship in federal elections. What happened next, however, was at least a little surprising, given all that had taken place in Arizona before. The state went to the Supreme Court to request an emergency stay of the district court's decision. Here, the state invoked the *Purcell* Principle (explained in chapter 6). Arizona asked the Court to apply *Purcell* and let the entirety of both voting laws stand until it could appeal, so as not to disrupt the ongoing 2024 election.

In August the Supreme Court granted the state's request on just one aspect of HB 2492: the noncitizen voting requirement in presidential elections. Until the 9th Circuit Court of Appeals could decide on Arizona's appeal, the Supreme Court ruled that the state could continue requiring proof of citizenship for some voters hoping to register for the upcoming November election. *Purcell* notwithstanding, the Court's decision cut against its relatively recent *Inter Tribal Council* precedent.[74] Furthermore, the Court's order showed clear divisions among the justices.[75] Justices Alito, Gorsuch, and Thomas indicated that they would have reinstated all of the Arizona laws for the 2024 election. Justices Barrett, Jackson, Kagan, and Sotomayor would have left the district court's ruling fully in place, rescinding the citizenship requirement in 2024. Justices Kavanaugh and Roberts made no comment on their preferences, but given the stated views of the other justices, it is reasonable to infer that they wished to leave only the proof of citizenship requirement standing and that the other three took what they could get.

It is unclear whether these five justices would vote to overturn their *Inter Tribal Council* precedent and uphold a state requirement for proof of citizenship in federal elections—as opposed to a simple stay during an ongoing election to let appeals play out. The fact that it *is* unclear, however, might raise anxiety among observers watching the SAVE Act make its way through

Congress. To date, the Court has disallowed proof of citizenship requirements in federal elections mainly because they violate federal law. If federal law changes, there is little evidence from its actions in the Arizona case that the Supreme Court would move to stop the disenfranchisement of potentially millions of voters via the "first generation" method long thought to be a relic of the past: voter registration rules.

Throughout this period, Arizona's dual registration system has continued to provide insight into who proof-of-citizenship laws might affect the most, and we have examined the available data. Using data obtained via a public records request, Kevin T. Morris and Arlyss Herzig identified all Arizona voters who are registered as "federal only."[76] This analysis revealed that voters of color make up a far larger share of the federal-only electorate than the full-ballot electorate, suggesting that minority voters are disproportionately excluded from state and local elections because they lack proof of citizenship. The voters who lack proof of citizenship are also younger, more likely to identify as political independents, and tend to live in neighborhoods with lower incomes.

More litigation is likely to provide more data and perhaps a clearer picture of the stakes. We are also likely to find out soon exactly where the Supreme Court stands on proof-of-citizenship requirements. After Roy reintroduced it in January 2025, the SAVE Act began winding its way through Congress, passing the House of Representatives on April 10. In February of that year, a panel of 9th Circuit judges finally ruled on Arizona's appeal. It upheld the district court ruling and put the proof-of-citizenship requirement for presidential elections on ice,[77] though the state petitioned for the case to be reheard by the full 9th Circuit.[78] But in 2024 New Hampshire, Louisiana, and Indiana all passed laws requiring proof of citizenship that came into effect in 2025.

These laws are only part of a growing list of registration-related moves at the state and local level, as the years since *Shelby County* have seen several troubling trends in voter registration throughout the United States. Many policies enacted since 2013 have been initiated by formerly covered jurisdictions and would have had a difficult path (in our view) to approval in the preclearance process. One of these is the rise of a well-meaning but ill-fated program to help administrators track voters across state lines. Another is the increasingly widespread use of "voter challenge" laws like those that have garnered attention in Georgia,[79] allowing citizens to challenge the legality of other voters' registration status. And, although these new laws have received a tremendous amount of media attention, they are hardly the only threat: In the run-up to the 2024 election alone, activist groups sued more than 20 American states and counties, pressuring them to remove voters from the rolls. These trends suggest that registrations are under greater threat today than in 2013, when the prevailing viewpoint seemed to be that list maintenance practices no longer presented a menace to voting rights.

8

Almost Surgical Precision

VOTER ID

> A State may not burden the right to vote merely by invoking abstract interests—be they legitimate, or even compelling—but must make a particular, factual showing that threats to its interests outweigh the particular impediments it has imposed. The State has made no such justification here, and as to some aspects of its law, it has hardly even tried.
>
> —ASSOCIATE JUSTICE DAVID SOUTER, DISSENTING OPINION, *CRAWFORD V. MARION COUNTY ELECTION BOARD*[1]

THE SUPREME Court announced its decision in *Shelby County v. Holder* at 10 a.m. Eastern Time on the morning of June 25, 2013. Given the tone of the argument, the Court's ruling was not wholly unexpected, but it still sent shockwaves through American politics. Reporters raced to parse the decision and file stories conveying its expected impact. Journalists with National Public Radio, for instance, put a story online at 10:12 that morning with a headline that would soon be echoed in just about every American news outlet: "Supreme Court Strikes Down Key Provision of Voting Rights Law."[2]

One minute later, Texas attorney general Greg Abbott began making the public case for a dramatic change to his state's election laws. At 10:13, Abbott sent a tweet on the social media site then known as Twitter. The tweet was not legally binding, but it did clearly communicate Abbott's hope for new voting regulations in the Lone Star State. If we translate Abbott's communication from Twitter shorthand to fuller English, the attorney general's tweet read: "Texas' Voter ID law should go into effect immediately [because the Supreme Court] struck down Section 4 of [the] VRA today."[3]

Strictly speaking, a "voter ID" law was not wholly new to Texas. Prior to *Shelby County,* Texas voters had the option of presenting ID at the polling place, but all they were *required* to present was a voter registration card. What Abbott was advocating was significantly more stringent, however. He wanted Texas to execute a law that required Texas voters to show some kind of *photo* identification before they could cast their ballot. Prior to June 25, such a law would not have been implemented until the DOJ approved it after preclearance review. Freed from the burden of preclearance, Abbott wanted to make a significant change to voter procedures in his state, and he wanted it done immediately.

The state was happy to comply. Fewer than 24 hours after Chief Justice Roberts delivered the *Shelby County* opinion in Washington, Texas announced it would implement Senate Bill 14 (SB 14), which mandated that voters present photo identification at the polling place.[4] In enacting a voter ID law, Texas was not particularly unique among American states. Most states have long histories of requiring *some* kind of ID from voters—though historically a signature verification or showing a document, such as a utility bill, bearing the voter's name and address satisfied the requirement. Photo IDs were not usually required.

This protocol began to change in the mid-2000s. Arguing that requesting photo identification from voters was a crucial means of preventing election fraud, Indiana implemented a photo ID law in 2005. Indiana was not subject to Section 5 of the VRA, so its law avoided DOJ examiners' scrutiny. However, the statute was challenged in federal court under the 14th Amendment's guarantee of equal protection of all citizens, with plaintiffs arguing that the law created an undue burden for citizens without photo ID. In *Crawford v. Marion County Election Board,* the Supreme Court upheld Indiana's law.[5] While no majority opinion was issued in *Crawford,* Justice John Paul Stevens held that the state had a compelling interest in preventing election fraud, and even if fraud is rare, this rationale outweighs the harm to voters who did not possess state-issued photo identification.[6] So long as voter ID laws complied with the VRA, the Supreme Court was willing to allow them.

After the Court's ruling in *Crawford,* other states began enacting voter ID laws of their own; by the time Texas passed SB 14, such laws were fairly common.[7] Today, 11 states have strict photo ID laws that have not been softened or overturned by court rulings.[8] Although just four of these states were covered

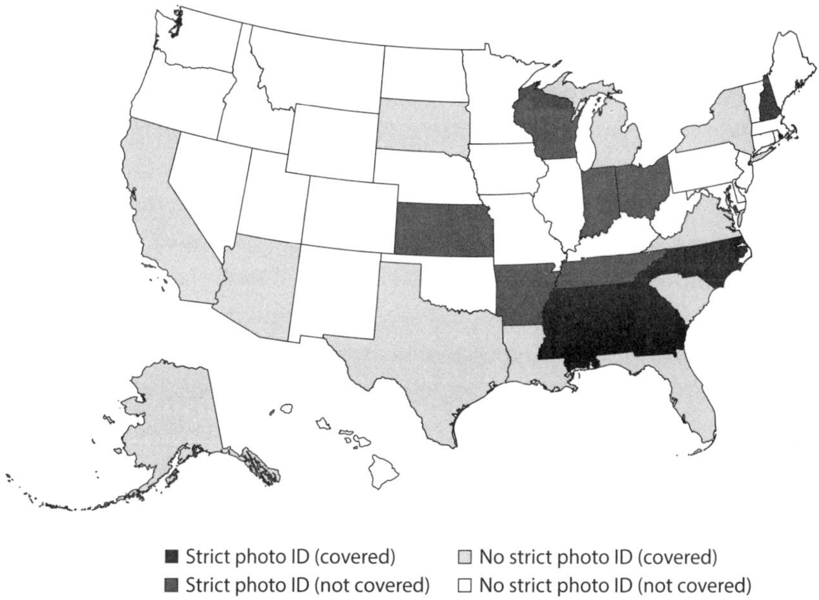

FIGURE 8.1. Strict Photo ID States by 2013 Coverage Status
Source: National Conference of State Legislatures.
Notes: Alabama classified as a strict voter ID state as a voter is required to provide photo identification unless two election officials swear an affidavit attesting they personally know the voter.

under Section 5 when *Shelby County* was struck down, three others had strict identification laws before they were stopped by preclearance (South Carolina), weakened by courts (Texas), or overturned by later state legislatures (Virginia) (see figure 8.1).

But in several respects, the case of Texas was unique. Political scientists characterize voter ID laws as "strict" if they bar voters from having their ballot counted until they produce photo identification from a predetermined list of acceptable IDs; the narrower this list, the stricter the law. One reason for the controversy surrounding SB 14 was that it was one of the strictest voter ID laws in American history. Under SB 14, election officials could accept only four types of state identifications, all of which were issued by the Texas Department of Public Safety. Acceptable state IDs included a photo-bearing Texas election identification certificate, a Texas ID, a Texas driver's license, or a license to carry a concealed handgun. Voters could also present one of three kinds of federal ID: a photo-bearing US citizenship certificate, a US military

ID, or a passport. Identification of any kind that was more than 60 days past expiration could not be accepted.

Like Indiana and other states, Texas's rationale for a strict photo ID law was to prevent voter impersonation fraud. This is a laudable goal, but SB 14's relatively restrictive list of acceptable identification led to some criticism. For one thing, the shorter the list of acceptable identification is, the longer the list of voters likely to be disenfranchised. At the time it passed SB 14, Texas was by far the most populous state to implement a voter ID law. In 2010 Texas estimated its voting age population at roughly 18.8 million people. With some back-of-the-envelope math, even if only one-half of 1% of voters lacked the identification that SB 14 required, nearly 100,000 people would be barred from casting a ballot. But this may be an extremely conservative estimate, given that existing work has found that up to 10% of white voters may lack ID of the sort required by voter ID laws, with substantially higher rates of nonpossession for minority voters.[9]

This was precisely the argument made by Stephen Ansolabehere, an expert who testified during litigation surrounding SB 14. Ansolabehere found that even if the universe of potential Texans lacking the required ID was restricted to registered voters—as opposed to the larger voting-age population—SB 14 could bar more than 600,000 people from the polls, or more than the entire population of Wyoming in 2010.[10] One reason this figure is so high is that SB 14 did not affect only voters who had for some reason never obtained ID. It would also disenfranchise those who had recently moved from out of state or other jurisdictions in Texas, those with expired ID, and those whose identification had been lost or stolen.

The possibility that a large number of Texans would be deterred from voting under SB 14 was clear enough. Some opponents of SB 14 pointed out that it seemed as though the legislature had tried to put its thumb on the scale in favor of certain voters when it crafted SB 14. Concealed-firearm carry permits were deemed acceptable for voting, but a student identification from a public Texas university was not. If the legislature was willing to disenfranchise students at a higher rate, might they have also been willing to do the same to other likely Democratic voters—and, especially, voters of color?

As it turns out, when Abbott sent his tweet calling for SB 14's immediate implementation, the law's discriminatory character had already been well documented. SB 14 was passed not in a flurry of activity in a single day after the Court's *Shelby County* decision, but as part of the usual legislative process way back in 2011—when Section 4(b) of the Voting Rights Act was still good law.

DOJ reviewers had already denied preclearance after Texas failed to prove that the law was racially neutral, and a federal court had affirmed this decision.[11] Until the morning of June 25, 2013, SB 14 was dead in the water. With the *Shelby County* ruling, it sprang back to life—and showed just how difficult protecting minority voting rights can be in the post-preclearance era.

By 2011, Republican legislators in Texas were frustrated. They had been trying to pass a voter ID law since the 2005 session. Their bill had died that year and again in 2007, and yet again in 2009. During the first two attempts to pass a voter ID law, Texas state senators had followed senate rules, which at that time required support from two-thirds of members to move a bill forward. Texas senators had historically cherished this rule, defending it against attack. When Dan Patrick, a freshman senator, pushed to change the two-thirds rule on his first day of service in 2007, his proposal was roundly defeated by a vote of 30 nays to his solitary aye.

But the rule had been responsible for the various voter ID bills' failure to advance in the Texas senate: In each session it seemed there were just enough Democrats to hold the opposition line. Sometimes, they cut it close. During the 2007 voter ID fight, Senator Mario Gallegos was suffering from complications due to a liver transplant four months earlier.[12] However, he knew that voter ID would pass if he were not present in the chamber, so the end of the legislative session found Senator Gallegos there, recording his dissent from a hospital bed on the senate floor.

Given this level of Democratic commitment to opposing voter ID, it was clear that if a bill was going to move in the senate, the two-thirds rule had to go. In 2009, senate Republicans suspended the rule specifically for voter ID, which allowed the bill to pass out of the chamber. It then fell prey to *house* rules, however. The bill was "chubbed" in the Texas house when Democrats used a dilatory tactic similar to the old US Senate talking filibuster that was then available and that allowed them to talk the bill to death.[13]

When the fourth opportunity to pass voter ID came around in 2011, its proponents resolved that they would not be defeated again. State legislators in 2011 designed extraordinary measures to lubricate the process for SB 14. The senate again suspended its two-thirds rule, and the house amended its chubbing rules so that voter ID would not die there either. Meanwhile, Governor Rick Perry declared voter ID an "emergency item," which sped up the legislative process.

Legislators also bypassed norms governing the role of committees and fiscal notes in passing legislation. When asked during the eventual trial over SB 14 whether there was "rigorous and fair debate in the senate" over the bill, Senator Rodney Ellis testified in the negative, noting that "this thing was on a spaceship" with Republicans trying "to rocket this bill out of there."[14] In March 2011, SB 14 passed along party lines.[15]

The contentious battle over SB 14 did not end with its passage, however. Texas was fully covered under Section 4(b) and therefore subject to Section 5 preclearance. Because it amended the state's elections code, SB 14 therefore fell squarely under the DOJ's preclearance purview. The state fulfilled its obligation, submitting the new law for preclearance on July 25, 2011. As with any preclearance request, Texas had to meet the burden of affirmatively showing that SB 14 would not discriminate against minority voters. On its initial review, the DOJ ruled that the state had not supplied enough evidence to meet this standard and requested that Texas send additional information regarding the race and ethnicity of registered voters who lacked compliant identification.

Texas provided the DOJ with two snapshots of the registered-voter file; one was from September 2011, and the other was from January 2012. In both snapshots, the state indicated whether it had been able to match the voter to the Department of Public Safety's database of Texans with a driver's license or personal ID card. The snapshots also flagged whether each voter had a Hispanic surname. As US assistant attorney general Thomas Perez noted during the preclearance review, these two lists were remarkably different. In the data from September, registered voters with Hispanic surnames were almost 50% more likely to lack an ID than those with non-Hispanic surnames. According to the January list, those with Hispanic surnames were more than *twice* (200%) as likely to lack an ID. "Significantly," Perez noted, "[Texas] declined to offer an opinion on which of the two data sets [was] more accurate."[16] It hardly mattered, though, since both sets of data showed that SB 14 would disproportionately harm Hispanics in Texas.

Perez also found that the state could not answer questions about how it would mitigate the disparity for Hispanic voters that the DOJ had identified, especially for voters who faced real obstacles—such as inability to secure transportation to the DMV. Nor, Perez wrote, had the state supplied sufficient data to determine whether Black and/or Asian American voters were similarly affected. "In conclusion," Perez wrote, "the state has not met its burden of proving that . . . the proposed requirement will not have a retrogressive effect, or that any specific features of the proposed law will prevent or mitigate that retrogression."[17] Preclearance was denied.

By the time it received the DOJ's objection in March, Texas had already initiated its right to review by the US District Court for the District of Columbia. The case, *State of Texas v. Holder*, was argued in July 2012.[18] In a unanimous decision, that court agreed with the DOJ, finding that SB 14 would likely have a retrogressive effect on minority voters. This decision mothballed SB 14. While its text had been added to Texas's election code in 2011, as long as preclearance remained the law of the land, Texas could not enforce SB 14's requirements. In response, and prior to the Supreme Court's ruling in *Shelby County*, Texas pushed forward in late 2012 with a new strategy. Rather than seek narrow permission for its voter ID bill, this time the state intended to ask the Supreme Court to negate Section 5 and kill preclearance once and for all.[19]

With the death of the coverage formula in *Shelby County*, however, this challenge was no longer necessary.[20] Texas had a voter ID law on the books and was instantly exempt from preclearance. Greg Abbott's tweet, then, was not advocating for legislative action; he was simply arguing that the state should immediately enforce a dormant law that had been part of its code for more than two years. That is precisely what happened. The day after *Shelby County* struck down preclearance, Texas began full implementation of its strict photo ID law for the 2014 election despite detailed and public evidence that it would undermine ballot access for minority voters. This was a controversial move: By refusing preclearance, the DOJ and the DC Circuit Court of Appeals had already opined that it would likely fall most heavily on voters of color—in clear violation of Section 2 of the VRA, which remained good law after *Shelby County*. Nevertheless, that was not the section of the statute under which the law had been blocked, and thus Abbott argued for its implementation.

Almost immediately, a group of citizens and the US Department of Justice challenged SB 14 in federal court, repeating the claims that had emerged from the preclearance process. This case, initially known as *Veasey v. Perry*, began a legal saga that would span several years.[21] Preclearance was not at issue in *Veasey*; rather, the plaintiffs leaned on Section 2 of the VRA in alleging that SB 14 would create barriers to voting that would dilute minority voters' political power. Moreover, by requiring voters with no compliant ID to obtain one, the plaintiffs also alleged that SB 14 amounted to an unconstitutional poll tax.

The case took some time to work through the courts; it was heard in September 2014 in the Southern District of Texas, after which, in early October, Judge Nelva Gonzales Ramos issued the court's opinion.[22] Ramos relied in part on Section 2 of the VRA, holding that SB 14 would discriminate against Black and Hispanic voters. Finding that SB 14 was an unconstitutional poll tax, the judge also declared that the state could not enforce the strict photo ID requirements in the 2014 election. In addition, the court ruled that the legislature *intended* to discriminate against voters of color when it passed SB 14, concluding that "proponents of SB 14 within the 82nd Texas Legislature were motivated, at the very least in part, *because of* and not merely *in spite of* the voter ID law's detrimental effects on the African-American and Hispanic electorate."[23]

Texas appealed, and days after the opinion was released, the 5th Circuit Court of Appeals issued an order that temporarily blocked Ramos's ruling. As chapter 6 points out, federal courts have since 2006 regularly allowed voting laws and district maps to stand under the *Purcell* Principle if the Court's opinion comes too close to an election—*even if* they are in violation of the VRA. Candidates, parties, and election officials had been preparing for an election with strict voter ID policies in place. While it considered the case further, the 5th Circuit left that framework in place under *Purcell*. This meant that the 2014 election would be conducted under SB 14's requirements, which two federal courts and the DOJ had already held to be discriminatory. For social scientists like us trying to understand how laws like SB 14 actually impact voters, this is where the saga of Texas's voter ID law gets particularly interesting.

Texas was not the only covered state entangled in preclearance over a voter ID law before the *Shelby County* ruling. Three months before objecting to SB 14, the DOJ had denied preclearance of the strict photo ID law South Carolina had passed in 2011—for largely the same reasons it would soon give Texas.[24] Like Texas, South Carolina sought to overrule the DOJ in the US District Court of the District of Columbia. Unlike Texas, however, South Carolina obtained a favorable verdict from that court in October 2012 after issuing new guidance regarding its law.[25] The key reason for the disparate results in the two states was that unlike Texas's, South Carolina's statute (as the state interpreted it following the DOJ's denial of preclearance) allowed voters without compliant identification to vote with a nonphoto ID instead, so long as they filed a "reasonable impediment declaration" stating why they did not have a photo ID. This potential escape hatch, in the mind of opinion author Judge Brett Kavanaugh, was a crucial feature that allowed South Carolina to convince the district court that no voter would be disenfranchised because they could not obtain identification.[26]

The preclearance process for new voter ID laws in other states was still pending when *Shelby County* was decided. In Mississippi a strict voter ID law was passed by ballot initiative in 2011 and enshrined in state law the following year. Although the law did not face major legal challenges outside the standard preclearance review, as of the spring of 2013, the DOJ had followed the same procedure it had employed in prior cases by requesting that Mississippi supply it with evidence that the law would not disenfranchise minority voters disproportionately. That query was still unanswered when the Supreme Court suspended preclearance and Mississippi then enacted voter ID.

Other formerly covered states faced challenges beyond preclearance. Virginia passed a strict photo ID law in February 2013, and was also in the process of preclearance review when the Supreme Court decided *Shelby County*. As with Mississippi and Texas, Virginia's new voter ID policy was therefore implemented immediately following the Supreme Court's ruling, but it still faced Section 2 and constitutional challenges in court from plaintiffs who alleged it would have discriminatory effects. At trial, however, the plaintiffs could not present any voters in Virginia who would be disenfranchised by the new law and, therefore, could not establish a sufficient burden on minority (or any) voters that would necessitate the law being overturned.[27]

Still, had Virginia and Mississippi gone through the full preclearance process, they would have had to meet the much different standard of needing to affirmatively show that the laws would not discriminate. The burden of proof, in other words, would be on the state to show evidence of a *lack* of discrimination rather than on plaintiffs to present *affirmative* evidence of discrimination. Unlike South Carolina, Mississippi and Virginia did not offer a way to cast a ballot for voters who did not possess compliant identification. If the case of Texas is instructive then, had preclearance proceeded, the DOJ would have likely looked at voter ID in Mississippi and Virginia with skepticism.

New strict photo ID statutes in still other formerly covered states were initiated after *Shelby County* was decided. These laws were therefore not subject to preclearance, but still faced legal challenges from voters alleging either that they would have discriminatory results or that a state legislature had intentionally sought to disenfranchise minority voters. North Carolina is a notable example of both. In 2013 the state legislature passed an omnibus election bill, HB 589, that made several key changes to election policies there, including shortening the early voting period, doing away with same-day voter registration, and implementing a strict photo ID requirement.[28] The strict photo ID component of HB 589 featured prominently in a series of legal challenges waged against the law by several groups, including the DOJ and the North Carolina chapters of the League of Women Voters and the NAACP. According to the state's own analysis, Black voters were twice as likely as white voters to fail to match to the state's DMV database—a fact that surely would have prevented it from being precleared.[29]

North Carolina won the first round in district court. In an exhaustive opinion spanning more than 450 pages (indicating the breadth of issues in the case), Judge Thomas Schroeder relied on the Supreme Court's *Crawford* precedent. Like Indiana in *Crawford*, North Carolina had not presented much evidence of voter impersonation fraud within its borders. Still, Schroeder held that, also like Indiana, North Carolina had a "legitimate state interest" in seeking to curb voter fraud. The voter ID component of the law, Schroeder wrote, simply provided the state with "a larger toolset with which to detect and deter voter fraud."[30] Schroeder allowed voter ID in North Carolina to stand.

The case ultimately landed in the 4th Circuit Court of Appeals, which overruled the district court. Judge Diana Gribbon Motz commended the district court for its thorough opinion, but criticized it for ignoring the very different political histories of North Carolina and Indiana—the latter of which had never been subject to VRA preclearance. "In holding that the legislature did not enact the challenged provisions with discriminatory intent," Motz wrote, "the court seems to have missed the forest in carefully surveying the many trees. This failure of perspective led the court to ignore critical facts bearing on legislative intent, including the inextricable link between race and politics in North Carolina."[31]

The court of appeals instead examined the legislative history of HB 589 and found what it deemed to be evidence of discriminatory intent. Motz noted the timing of the omnibus bill, coming hot on the heels of the *Shelby County* ruling, which had suspended preclearance. This fact alone might raise suspicion: If the law would pass muster with Section 5 of the VRA, why did the state wait until after *Shelby County* to enact it? Most damningly for the legislature, though, the 4th Circuit focused on evidence that North Carolina legislators had requested data on voting patterns by race, subsequently restricting methods of voting (such as early in-person voting on Sundays) favored by minority voters. Legislators had also researched the likelihood that voters of various races would have certain forms of identification, and then had tailored the list of acceptable IDs to be more favorable to white voters.[32]

Motz noted the difficulty of untangling political and racial discrimination, since "restriction of voting mechanisms and procedures that most heavily affect African Americans will predictably redound to the benefit of one political party and to the disadvantage of the other." Nonetheless, even if the intended result was to make it harder on average for *Democrats* (as opposed to Black voters) to vote, Motz found that when the entire evidentiary record was considered, the law had clear racial "discriminatory intent." Indeed, as Motz wrote in a line that has become rather famous among election lawyers and political scientists, HB 589 "target[ed] African-Americans with almost surgical precision."[33]

Coupled with events surrounding voter ID laws in Mississippi, South Carolina, and Virginia, the battle over North Carolina's HB 589 underscores the fact that Texas was hardly the only formerly covered state attempting to implement a voter ID law in the wake of *Shelby County*. Momentum behind voter ID laws had been building in noncovered states even before that ruling; states such as Ohio and Kansas had implemented strict photo ID laws prior to 2013, and many others would soon strengthen their identification requirements in some fashion. Even in these noncovered states, however, voter ID laws have been controversial. Opponents of the laws often worry that they will disenfranchise some voters who lack the resources to obtain compliant identification—and that this population is likely to be disproportionately nonwhite. On the other hand, voter ID advocates typically argue that requiring voters to present identification reduces the chances of election fraud and increases public confidence in elections, even though there is little evidence that this is the case.[34]

If we are to understand how *Shelby County* might have affected the roll-out of voter ID laws in formerly covered states, a good first step is to determine whether they depress turnout at all. Researchers began studying this question soon after the first voter ID laws were implemented. The bulk of this early research on the laws' effects typically found at most a negligible impact on overall turnout,[35] with few nonvoters reporting that a lack of identification kept them from the polls.[36] More recent work has employed administrative records to gain a finer-grained insight, but even when effects achieve statistical significance, they too usually find only the smallest effect of voter ID on turnout. For instance, Esposito, Focanti, and Hastings merge data from the

Department of Motor Vehicles and voter file data in Rhode Island and find that the state's voter ID law led to a decline in turnout of about 0.4 percentage points.[37] Similarly, Grimmer and Yoder find a small turnout decrease of about 0.7 points among voters who lacked identification when North Carolina's law took effect in 2016.[38] In an especially ambitious study, economists Enrico Cantoni and Vincent Pons constructed a national voter file to examine voting behavior at the individual level, and found little evidence that voter ID laws meaningfully decrease turnout.[39] Taken together, these studies suggest that voter ID laws do not seem to affect turnout all that much. Considering that more than 99% of would-be voters possess compliant identification, some analysts have pointed out, this conclusion should not be all that surprising.[40]

However, subsequent work has argued that these null results might mask more complicated forces surrounding voter ID laws. Some researchers have found that the apparently small effects of voter ID on turnout could stem from countermobilization efforts that help voters acquire the identification they need, in turn blunting demobilizing effects that might have been significantly larger in their absence.[41] Similarly, public information campaigns designed to educate voters about new identification requirements may also stem turnout declines after the polices are enacted.[42] Some evidence also suggests that these activities may be particularly concentrated in minority communities: In their paper showing that voter ID did not depress turnout, Cantoni and Pons also found that the likelihood of nonwhite voters being contacted by a campaign increased by nearly five percentage points following the implementation of voter ID laws.[43] In the absence of these concerted efforts to educate voters about new voter ID policies, we therefore might expect the voters least likely to possess identification—such as racial minorities, young voters, or people facing financial hardship[44]—to bear the brunt of their impact.

In short, while there are good theoretical reasons to expect that voter ID laws impose disproportionate burdens on minority voters, prior work tells us that the number of voters likely to be disenfranchised by these laws is probably quite small. Regardless of the raw number of voters lacking compliant identification, however, the potential for voter ID to affect minority voters more than white voters would have been central in any preclearance determination prior to *Shelby County*. Since striking down the coverage formula in that case, the Supreme Court has further narrowed the potential for successful Section 2 claims, signaling that it might not rule against an election law if only a very small number of voters was disenfranchised.[45] Nonetheless, during the preclearance era the DOJ would have certainly looked askance at a policy that resulted in a higher percentage of minority voters than white ones being turned away from the polls—even if the number of voters affected was ultimately small, and potentially even if they ultimately overcame the hurdles that a voter ID law placed between them and the ballot box. After all, the DOJ had historically objected to proposed changes that would make voting more onerous for minority voters relative to white voters.[46]

It is therefore essential to understand how voter ID laws affect white and nonwhite voters differently. In this regard, however, many researchers also recognize a particular challenge: We soon run into fairly significant data quality problems when we try to tackle this question. The effects of voter ID laws are difficult to untangle using traditional social science tools such as surveys, which are susceptible to measurement and other kinds of error.[47] This difficulty led to some disagreement about early, survey-based studies of voter ID. Some of this work found no disparate effects on minority turnout.[48] In contrast, Hajnal, Lajevardi, and Nielson used survey data to show that voter ID laws reduce minority voters' turnout significantly more than white voters'.[49] Subsequent work could not replicate these findings, however,[50] which has in turn generated substantial debate about the true impact of voter ID laws on minority voters.[51]

As with research on turnout overall, work since 2020 has used similar records to examine how voter ID laws affect minority voters specifically. As part of their study, Cantoni and Pons concluded that there was no differential turnout drop for minority voters compared to white voters, though as mentioned above, they also note that this may stem from efforts to organize in minority communities. Henninger, Meredith, and Morse employ administrative data from Michigan, whose nonstrict photo ID law is similar to South Carolina's in that it allows voters to cast ballots without presenting identification if they first complete an affidavit in which they assert that they do not have compliant identification.[52] Henninger and colleagues' analysis of these affidavits from a random sample of precincts revealed that while only about one-half of 1% of voters lacked identification, nonwhite voters were about five times more likely than white voters to fall into this category.

Henninger and colleagues' approach is especially insightful because it observes the very population we are interested in. Rather than discerning effects of voter ID by asking people on surveys about the identification they possess and their intention to vote (or even capturing their behavior from the voter file), the affidavits literally create a record of the entire population of voters who arrived at a polling place and affirmatively stated that they lacked identification. The potential of similar records to provide insight into the effects of voter ID laws in other states—including those formerly subject to preclearance—is clear. The problem is that in most states, no such records exist.

That is precisely why the judicial action surrounding Texas's SB 14 is so important: It led to the creation of new administrative records like those in Michigan. The 5th Circuit Court of Appeals had ordered SB 14 to remain in place for the 2014 election, but the legal battle over the new law was not yet over; the appeals court had merely forestalled the district court's ban of SB 14 while it considered the state's appeal. Texas's appeal was heard by a three-judge panel of the 5th Circuit in 2015. The case was now called *Veasey v. Abbott,* because Greg Abbott had been elected governor in 2014 and had become the chief named authority defending the law.[53] As the 4th Circuit had done with North Carolina's law, the 5th Circuit panel found that SB 14 had a discriminatory effect and would harm minority voters more than white voters, who were more likely to have one of the necessary forms of ID that the law required. The strict photo ID provisions in SB 14 could not continue.

This ruling was subsequently affirmed by the entire 5th Circuit Court in July 2016.[54] At this point, Texas's voter ID law had been ruled discriminatory and illegal *five times* under different provisions of the VRA by the Department of Justice, the DC district court, a judge in the Southern District of Texas, a three-judge panel of the US 5th Circuit, and the entire US 5th Circuit. Nevertheless, the law had been fully in effect for the 2014 election and the 2016 presidential primary.

As was the case two years before in the district court, the judges on the 5th Circuit Court of Appeals still faced a tough decision. They had decided that the voter ID component of SB 14 could not stand, but the calendar was quickly giving way to the 2016 election, which to that point had been conducted by all parties with strict voter ID in place. Now, the court had to find a way to terminate the strict photo ID law while complying with its duty under the *Purcell* Principle not to upset the dynamics of the election too much. The 5th Circuit Court sent the case back down to the district court, ordering it to find a legal remedy "that disrupts voter identification rules for the 2016 election season as little as possible, yet eliminates the discriminatory effect violation" of the Voting Rights Act.[55]

Judge Ramos followed the circuit court's directive in crafting a creative solution. In the 2016 election, Ramos ordered that Texas may request that voters produce photo identification in line with SB 14. If they possessed the necessary

ID, voters had to show it. But the judge also softened SB 14's requirements for expired ID, allowing voters to cast ballots with identification up to four years past its expiration date—as opposed to SB 14's original 60-day requirement.

For voters who had no compliant identification at all, the procedures in South Carolina, whose law had survived judicial preclearance prior to *Shelby County*, provided Ramos a way forward. The judge ordered Texas to allow voters who did not have compliant identification to vote anyway so long as they performed two tasks that mirrored the requirements in South Carolina's law: First, voters had to show supporting identification generally consistent with the kinds of ID that Texas would have accepted prior to SB 14, such as a utility bill, bank statement, pay stub, or some other government document. Second, voters in the 2016 presidential election would complete a form called a reasonable impediment declaration (RID) in which they swore under penalty of perjury that they did not have a valid photo identification and stated the reason why they lacked it. In an effort to maintain some continuity in the election's administration, the district court therefore effectively softened SB 14 from one of the strictest photo ID laws in the United States to a nonstrict voter ID law.

In mandating the usage of RIDs, however, Judge Ramos's order also created a windfall of data that facilitate insight into a population that is otherwise extremely difficult to observe. Like the voter affidavits that Henninger, Meredith, and Morse used their study of Michigan, Texas RIDs amount to a definitive list of voters who showed up to their polling place without identification.[56] The compiled RID records from a given election, however, provide only a rock-bottom estimate of the number of voters who are impacted by SB 14. It is possible that many voters heard about the voter ID law from family members, friends, or the press, but never heard about the court replacing strict voter ID with the RID process. If they lacked the required identification, these voters may not even have tried to vote out of a belief that they would not be allowed to do so. Other voters may have actually attempted to vote in 2014 or in the 2016 primaries when SB 14 was in full effect, only to be turned away. Still others might have shown up without an acceptable identification and opted against filling out an RID. There are, in short, certainly more voters whom SB 14 blocked from voting than the RIDs can reveal.

Despite these limitations, the RIDs still provide the best available record of Texans whom SB 14 would have blocked from voting had it remained unamended. The RIDs are especially useful because we can merge them with the Texas voter file and other data sources. This allows us to observe whether the group of voters who filed RIDs (and by definition could not produce ID at the polling place) differed in any observable way from voters who possessed compliant identification. If, say, the voters without ID are on average less white than those who have identification, we would have evidence that SB14 in its unamended form would have had discriminatory effects. But we can also look at any number of demographic attributes to compare those who have ID with those who do not.

Furthermore, we can analyze the reasons voters cited for lacking identification. Some voters may not be able to produce ID at the polling place because they simply misplaced it, while others may have an ongoing issue that could prevent them from *ever* obtaining compliant identification. These are quite different situations, with profound implications for the voters experiencing them under a strict photo ID law. Finally, by tracking RID filers through time, we can gain insight into how long their disenfranchisement lasts. The RIDs therefore provide greater insight into how Texas's law affected voters who lacked identification than any other data source of which we are aware.

In practice, Texas voters filing reasonable impediment declaration forms in the aftermath of the SB 14 fight reported the reason they lacked required ID during the check-in procedure at their polling place. Generally, once a voter stated that they did not have compliant identification, they would be provided with a paper form that they would complete by hand. These forms are the data source that fuels much of the analysis that follows. Shortly after the 2016 election, Michael G. Miller and his colleague Bernard Fraga began collecting reasonable impediment declaration forms from Texas via a series of requests under the Texas Public Information Act. Ultimately, the state turned over about 16,100 scans of the paper forms that RID filers had completed while voting in 2016.[57]

A typical top half of a scanned RID form from 2016 can be seen in figure 8.2 (the voter's printed name is visible on the original form, but we have redacted it from the figure). As was true of voters throughout the state, the voter who completed this form was directed to select at least one "reasonable impediment or difficulty that prevents me from getting an acceptable form of photo identification." The district court ruling mandated a number of choices here: among them lack of transportation, disability or illness, lack of birth certificate or other required documents, work conflicts, family responsibilities, lost or stolen ID, or a photo ID that had been applied for but not received, or some

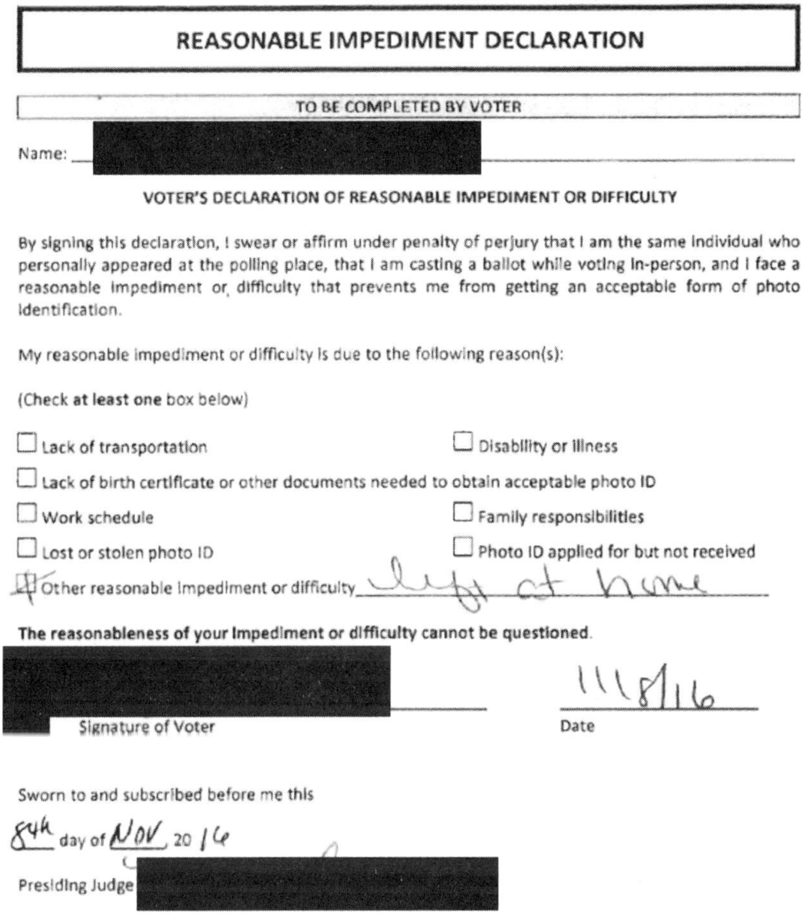

REASONABLE IMPEDIMENT DECLARATION

TO BE COMPLETED BY VOTER

Name: [redacted]

VOTER'S DECLARATION OF REASONABLE IMPEDIMENT OR DIFFICULTY

By signing this declaration, I swear or affirm under penalty of perjury that I am the same individual who personally appeared at the polling place, that I am casting a ballot while voting in-person, and I face a reasonable impediment or difficulty that prevents me from getting an acceptable form of photo identification.

My reasonable impediment or difficulty is due to the following reason(s):

(Check **at least one** box below)

- ☐ Lack of transportation
- ☐ Disability or illness
- ☐ Lack of birth certificate or other documents needed to obtain acceptable photo ID
- ☐ Work schedule
- ☐ Family responsibilities
- ☐ Lost or stolen photo ID
- ☐ Photo ID applied for but not received
- ☒ Other reasonable impediment or difficulty left at home

The reasonableness of your impediment or difficulty cannot be questioned.

Signature of Voter — Date 11/8/16

Sworn to and subscribed before me this

8th day of NOV, 20 16

Presiding Judge

FIGURE 8.2. Example RID Form, Top Pane

other reason. If they selected "other" (as the voter in figure 8.2 did), voters were prompted for an open-ended response describing the reason in their own words.

Once the voter made their selection, the election official would then verify the secondary identification that the voter had brought to the polls by checking a box on the same form. Again, the RID provided a range of options: an original birth certificate, utility bill, bank statement, government check, paycheck, or some other government document. The election official's selection options are shown in figure 8.3, which is a scan of the bottom half of the RID depicted in figure 8.2. After both halves of the RID were completed, the voter

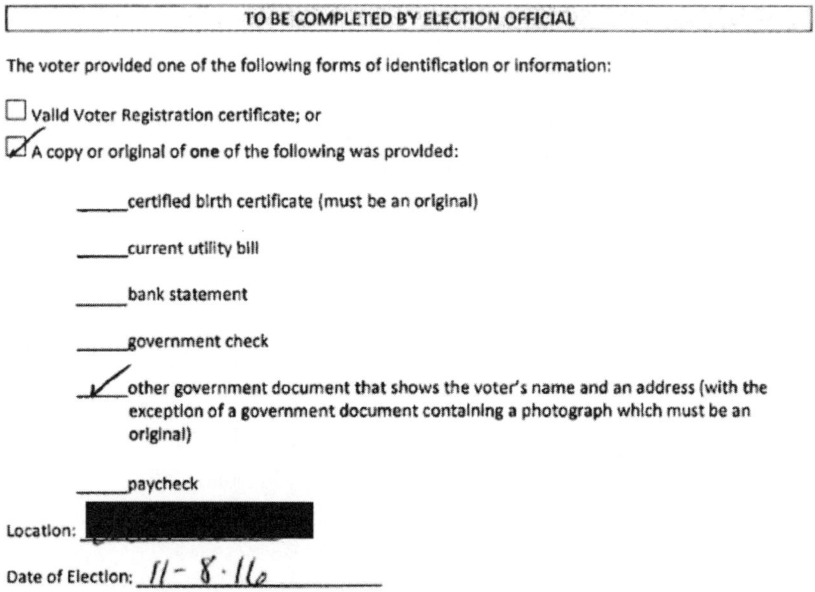

TO BE COMPLETED BY ELECTION OFFICIAL

The voter provided one of the following forms of identification or information:

☐ Valid Voter Registration certificate; or

☑ A copy or original of one of the following was provided:

_____certified birth certificate (must be an original)

_____current utility bill

_____bank statement

_____government check

✓ other government document that shows the voter's name and an address (with the exception of a government document containing a photograph which must be an original)

_____paycheck

Location: [redacted]

Date of Election: 11-8-16

FIGURE 8.3. Example RID Form, Bottom Pane

and official would sign the form, and the voter would receive a ballot. This was the procedure that was supposed to be employed throughout Texas in 2016 and, ultimately, in subsequent elections.

Due to the fact that each of Texas's 254 counties was responsible for determining how voters would complete the RIDs (with no standard statewide form), there was some variation not only in the data that the forms supply but also in how they were used. For instance, some counties wrote the voter's state voter identification number on the RIDs, while others did not. Counties also evidently applied different requirements for allowing voters to file RIDs at all. This is apparent in figure 8.2. The voter who completed that form did not actually meet the eligibility requirements; they selected "other" as their reason, and then wrote that they left their ID at home. Contrary to the district court's requirement, the election officials who accepted that form apparently saw RIDs as a way to allow anyone who arrived at the polling place without identification to vote—not just those who *could not obtain* compliant identification.

We can account for this in our analysis, however, and regardless of any county-to-county variation in how the forms were used, at minimum the RIDs give us the voter's name, their stated reason for lacking compliant identification, and the identification they *did* present. This is typically enough to merge the RID filers back into the voter file. Doing so provides insight into who they are, why they felt they needed to file an RID, and how they differ from voters who were able to present compliant identification.

This was the central goal that Fraga and Miller's initial research pursued. In their original analysis, Fraga and Miller hand coded the approximately 16,000 paper IDs into digital form and merged them with Texas voter files extending back four additional general elections to 2008.[58] Next, they estimated each voter's race using methods similar to those we describe in chapter 5. This step allowed them to estimate the share of RID filers that was white, Black, Hispanic, Asian, and "other," compared to voters in 2016 who presented compliant identification (and therefore did not need to submit an RID). The explanations that voters listed on their RIDs also afforded insight into whether people lacked identification for enduring reasons that would have made it difficult for them to overcome SB 14 in the absence of the federal court's intervention (such as lacking the necessary documents to get a state ID), or whether they were hindered by a less serious and likely temporary issue, such as a recent move.

Fraga and Miller's initial work yielded three important results. First, the population of voters filing RIDs was significantly less white than those who voted with identification. We have reproduced Fraga and Miller's findings in figure 8.4—though our findings are slightly different than theirs due to a different process used to estimate voters' race (our results are broadly consistent, however).[59] The figure shows that RID filers were about 5 percentage points less white than 2016 voters who produced identification. This difference is mostly accounted for by the fact that the RID population consists of substantially more Black voters (about 5 points) than the population who produced ID. The composition of Asian and Hispanic voters in our results are roughly the same among RID filers and voters who showed compliant ID.[60]

These findings are important with respect to the central inquiries we are concerned with in this book: One effect of SB 14 appears to be that it (would have) disenfranchised a higher proportion of minority voters than white voters. Moreover, because Fraga and Miller employ data from administrative records instead of surveys, we can be fairly confident in the accuracy of their findings. In short, this first analysis of voter ID in Texas vindicates the district court's finding that the unaltered law would likely have had discriminatory effects.

Voter race features prominently in Fraga and Miller, as well as in other work assessing the impact of voter ID. This is obviously important, but we want

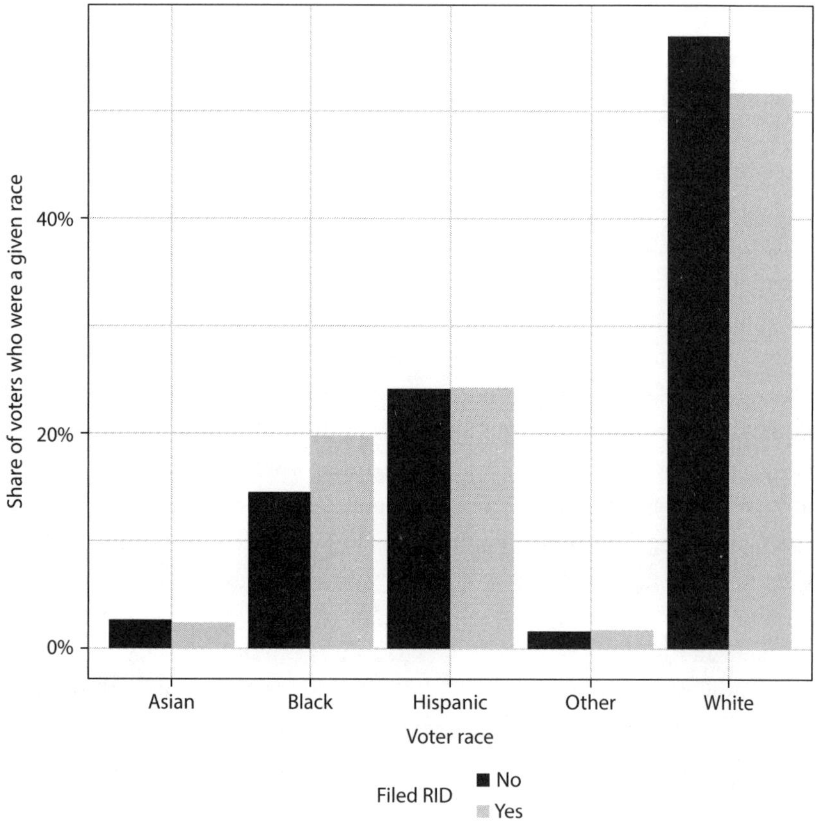

FIGURE 8.4. Voter Race by RID Filing Status, 2016 Texas General Election

to expand the scope of inquiry somewhat to areas that Fraga and Miller did not report in their analysis. For instance, if we use Fraga and Miller's data to examine voter age, we find that RID filers were almost twice as likely to be under 40 years of age as those who voted with identification. The pool of RID voters also contained substantially more women. These disparities are shown in figure 8.5.

We also consider each voter's partisan affiliation in figure 8.5. Since minority voters have traditionally been aligned with the Democratic Party, some have argued that voter ID laws are simply a way for Republican legislatures to chip away at their opponents' vote base.[61] In addition to comparing the racial composition of voters who filed RIDs to those who did not, we therefore also want to more explicitly examine how the *partisan* composition of RID filers differs from voters who presented ID. This procedure presents some methodological

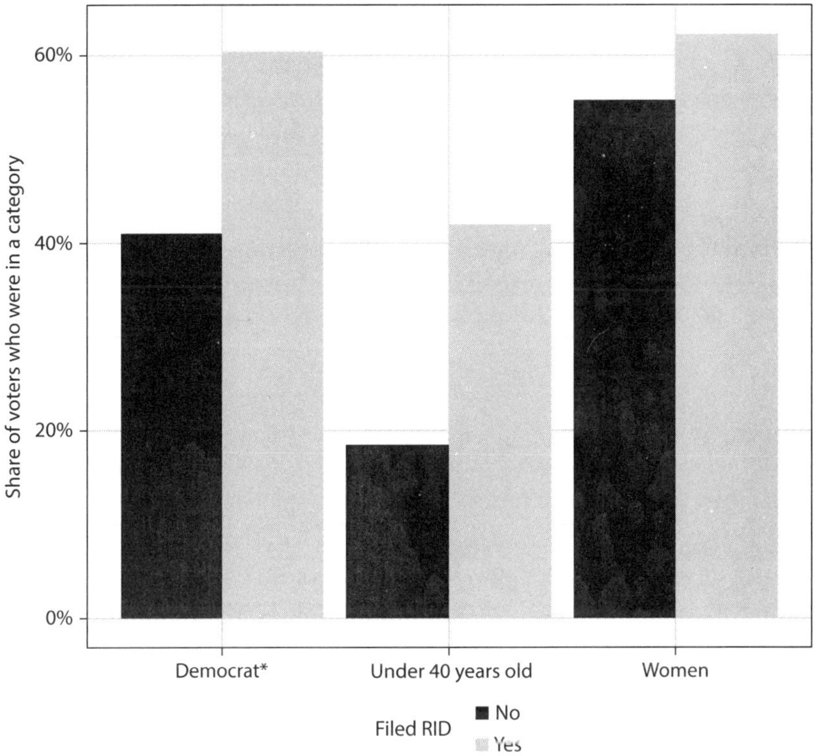

FIGURE 8.5. Voter Characteristics by RID Filing Status, 2016 Texas General Election
*Based on primary participation between 2008 and 2016.

challenges, however. Texas has open primaries, and voters do not declare a party affiliation when registering to vote. We must therefore estimate voters' partisanship.

To do so, we leverage voters' past primary participation to calculate what Dowling, Miller, and Morris call their "partisan loyalty score."[62] This score reflects how reliably people vote in partisan primaries, given the opportunity to do so. The intuition here is relatively simple: We assume that voters who typically voted in Democratic primaries in the past are more likely to be Democrats (and vice versa for Republicans). Interested readers can refer to the Methodological Appendix for more information on how we calculated these scores, but suffice it here to say that the scores generally indicate the percentage of their party's primaries that the voter participated in, assuming they had the opportunity. Our analysis reveals that the voters who filed RIDs in 2016 were far more likely to be Democrats. This disparity can be seen in figure 8.5, along with differences in the two groups' age and gender.

Fraga and Miller's second main contribution was their analysis of the reasons that voters cited in 2016 for not having identification. This investigation allowed them to distinguish between voters who had an enduring hardship that prevented them from obtaining compliant identification—such as lack of transportation, family obligations, lack of necessary documents, or work-related reasons—from voters they deemed "ID-capable." The voters in the "hardship" category are consistent with a common narrative surrounding voter ID laws, which stresses the presumably permanent barriers that some voters face when it comes to obtaining identification. If someone lacks reliable transportation or access to identifying documents like a birth certificate, we should expect that they are particularly likely to continue having difficulty obtaining identification in future elections. Only about one-third of RID filers in Fraga and Miller's analysis fell into the "hardship" category, however. This figure suggests that for most voters who lacked ID in the 2016 election, it should be possible to remedy the situation and obtain ID in the future. While this is good news for anyone hoping that voter ID laws have limited disenfranchising effects, it also underpins an important initial result of Fraga and Miller's analysis: Texas's voter ID law was ensnaring thousands of voters who could prove their identity—just not under the stringent rules of SB 14.

But *who* was most likely to have a hardship? Fraga and Miller do not provide a breakout of ID-capable and hardship voters by race. In table 8.1, we therefore show a summary from a reanalysis of Fraga and Miller's 2016 data. Because of the comparisons we want to make, we have narrowed the original data somewhat from the population of 16,000 RIDs. We use RIDs from about 14,000 voters who could be matched to the voter file, thereby allowing us to predict their race. All of the voters in table 8.1 also provided a reason for lacking ID that allowed them to be coded as either ID-capable or as having an enduring hardship preventing them from obtaining ID. We also simplify Fraga and Miller's classification scheme somewhat. Fraga and Miller binned voters into three categories: the two we describe above, and a "relocation" category that consists of voters who recently moved. We code recently relocated voters as ID-capable since according to their RIDs, nearly all of these voters could produce a photo ID—albeit one that had an incorrect address. This decision does not affect the designation of hardship voters.

These caveats aside, two patterns are notable in table 8.1. First, as Fraga and Miller found in their initial analysis, only a minority of RID filers cite

TABLE 8.1. Racial Distribution of ID-Capable and Hardship RID Filers, 2016 Texas General Election

	Count	% White	% Black	% Hispanic	% Asian	% Other	Total
ID-Capable Voters	8,432	57.5	15.5	21.4	2.9	2.7	100%
Hardship Voters	5,456	57.4	16.8	20.3	2.9	2.6	100%

Source: Author's reanalysis of data from Fraga and Miller (2022).
Note: Here we include data from RID filers who both cited a codable reason for not having identification and whom we could match with the voter file.

a hardship that would prevent them from getting a compliant ID. The 5,456 hardship voters compose less than 40% of RIDs in the sample. Second, a row-wise comparison reveals that there is effectively no difference in the racial composition of hardship and ID-capable voters. The percentages of white, Asian, and voters in the "other race" category in the two groups is more or less the same. There are slightly more (1.3 points) Black voters and slightly fewer (1.1 points) Hispanic voters in the hardship category, but these differences do not seem substantively significant. This said, as we showed above, voters of color were generally over-represented among voters who filed RIDs for any reason.

While there does not seem to be much racial difference between the two groups, the difference between hardship and ID-capable voters is an important theoretical distinction that informs the final key finding in Fraga and Miller's work. Fraga and Miller used difference-in-differences techniques to exploit an important wrinkle in the SB 14 story: While the district court ended the strict voter ID requirement prior to the 2016 election, it was fully in place in 2014. This allowed the authors to look backward to the 2014 election and compare trends in turnout among voters who filed an RID in 2016 to those that did not. The expectations here were twofold: Fraga and Miller theorized that the turnout trend among RID filers who could not produce compliant ID in 2016 would be significantly lower than for voters who showed ID in the 2016 election. However, because voters in the ID-capable category had proven themselves able to obtain identification in the past, Fraga and Miller anticipated that these effects would be muted for them—with a much larger decline in 2014 turnout among hardship voters.

Fraga and Miller's analysis found support for both of these hypotheses. Compared to voters who presented ID in 2016, RID filers displayed lower turnout in all three historical elections that Fraga and Miller examined: 2010, 2012, and 2014. However, the gap between the groups spiked noticeably in 2014, when SB 14 took effect. While the gap was about 10 percentage points in 2010 and 2012, it more than doubled in 2014. But there was also a clear division between ID-capable and hardship voters. Among ID-capable RID filers, turnout was 14 points lower than non-RID filers in 2014. That is a massive effect, but their turnout was still *10 points higher* in Fraga and Miller's analysis than among voters who reported an enduring hardship preventing them from obtaining identification.

In sum, Fraga and Miller's analysis painted a bleak picture of SB 14's effects. The law lowered turnout among voters without ID when it was fully implemented in 2014, and affected minority voters (especially Black voters) disproportionately. Our updated analysis of their data shows that SB 14 also fell harder on Democrats, younger voters, and women as well. Some might say that the 16,000 voters who filed an RID in 2016—and who presumably would have been disenfranchised in the absence of the federal court order—amounts to a small percentage of the 8.9 million ballots cast that year. Yet, turning away 16,000 people who clearly wanted to vote is a steep price to pay when we consider that Texas has presented no evidence of voter impersonation fraud in its elections.

And voters have continued to show up without ID. We have built on Fraga and Miller's analysis, collecting all RIDs from the 2018 and 2020 general elections in an effort to determine whether the patterns they identified have continued in subsequent Texas elections.[63] Many more of the 2018 and 2020 RID documents include each voter's unique voter ID number than the 2016 ones, which allows us to more easily identify each RID filer in the Texas voter file. As before, the later RIDs also contain a good deal of handwritten information. We manually coded these records into spreadsheet form, collecting all of the information included in each RID.

We began with the 16,104 RIDs from 2016 (coded by Fraga and Miller), then added another 8,778 from 2018 and 20,556 from 2020.[64] We also follow Fraga and Miller's approach in separating RID filers into "hardship" and "ID-capable" individuals, designating individuals who reported not having an ID because of family obligations, lack of transportation, lack of necessary documents to apply, work obligations, or a disability or illness as "hardship" users. These are the Texans who face substantial hurdles to obtaining a permitted ID. The ID-capable voters, meanwhile, are those who have (presumably) obtained an ID in the past: These individuals either had their ID stolen or lost it, had applied for (but not yet received) their ID, or had otherwise communicated a capacity to obtain identification in the past. As is our standard approach in this book, we join the RID records to the registered voter file using the voter ID numbers on the RIDs,[65] and use methods described in the Methodological Appendix to calculate the probability that voters are white, Black, Latino, Asian, or "other."

In total, the merged data include voters' racial probabilities, gender, partisan score, age, registration date, county of residence, and their turnout in the five most recent general elections prior to the one in which we observe their filing an RID (so, 2006–2014 for 2016, etc.). We also merge each set with later snapshots of the voter file to determine voters' turnout in subsequent federal elections. For 2016, of course, we have three posttreatment general federal elections (2018, 2020, and 2022); for 2018 and 2020, we have just two or one, respectively. To infer the causal relationship between RID usage and subsequent turnout, we use a difference-in-differences design similar to the setup we deploy elsewhere in this book. (See the Methodological Appendix for more specific information about our research design here.) This method, combined with extremely rich data, allows us to track how SB 14 shapes voters' participation over time.

Did the pool of voters using RIDs in the 2018 and 2020 elections look different from the 2016 RID filers? Figure 8.6 indicates some shifts occurring in the composition of voters using RIDs over the period in which the policy has been in effect: namely, the share of RID users who are Hispanic has dropped, while the share that is white has increased. By the time of the 2020 general election, white Texans made up an equal share of the RID and non-RID electorates (about 55%). Meanwhile, by 2020 Latinos made up just 20% of RID users, compared with 26% of the rest of the electorate. In all three elections, however, we see that Black Texans made up about 4 to 6 percentage points more of the RID electorate than the rest of the voting population. There is clearly something about voter ID that affects Black voters in Texas more than others. Figure 8.7 shows that Democrats, young voters, and women have also been consistently more likely to show up to the polling place without proper identification.

It is also worth repeating that the folks who filed an RID likely represent only the lower bound of voters who were affected. It is a safe assumption that many more voters, perhaps turned away in 2014, erroneously believed (and may continue to believe) that they must possess compliant photo identification to vote in Texas and simply stayed home. This begs some

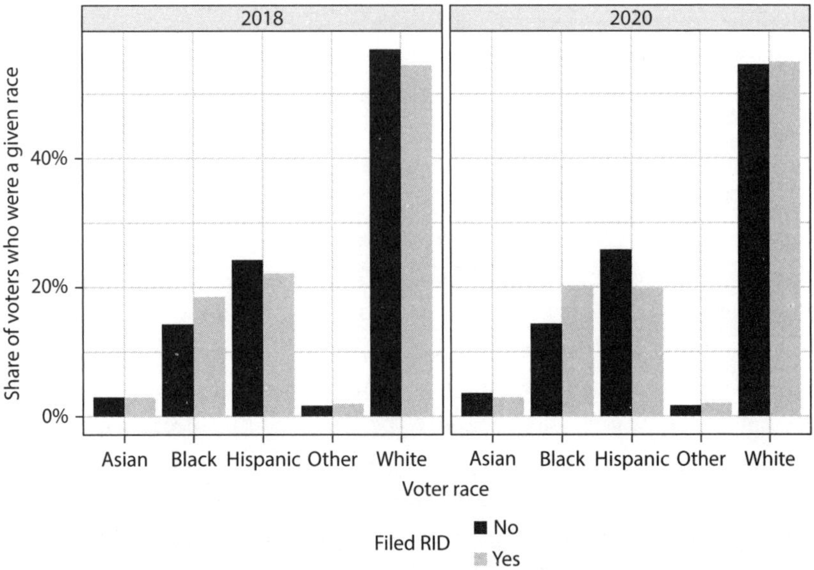

FIGURE 8.6. Voter Race by RID Filing Status, 2018 and 2020 Texas General Elections

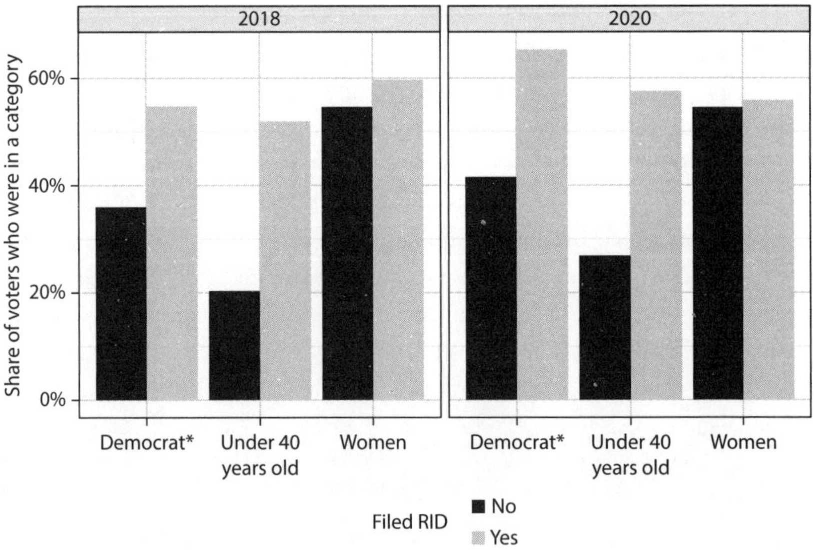

FIGURE 8.7. Voter Characteristics by RID Filing Status, 2018 and 2020 Texas General Elections
*Based on primary participation in ten years preceeding general election.

important final questions about SB 14. Namely, have the trends that Fraga and Miller observed continued in subsequent Texas elections? And how long do voters remain in the "no ID" category?

Recent work by Grimmer and Yoder finds that the negative turnout effects of voter ID laws can be "sticky";[66] that is, the laws can have lasting effects on citizens' likelihood of voting. Grimmer and Yoder use administrative records to follow voters in North Carolina from the 2016 primary election, when that state's voter ID law was in full effect, through to the 2018 general. Among the group of voters lacking identification (about 3% of voters), turnout declined in the primary election that required voters to show ID. That effect then remained for at least the next two general election cycles, even after North Carolina's law was struck down. Once dissuaded from voting, it seems that many voters without ID simply stopped trying.

It is conceivable that we would observe similar effects among Texas voters who were disenfranchised in 2014 or who, having seen news reports about SB 14's passage, may have assumed they needed photo ID to vote in 2016 and therefore never turned out at all. We do not have sufficient data to answer these exact questions, but we *can* look for long-term turnout effects among voters who filed an RID in 2016. Filling out a form is a much less negative voting experience than being turned away altogether, so we might expect that SB 14 does not cast such a long shadow over subsequent voting behavior. This said, RID filers still experience extra burdens in voting. They have to take time at the polling place to fill out the RID, and that assumes they have the required secondary identification. If voters do not have that secondary ID (or do not want to take the time to fill out an RID), they can be turned away.

Suboptimal voting experiences like these can shake voters' trust in elections and in turn affect their likelihood of turning out in the future.[67] For instance, voters who endure longer wait times in a given election are less likely to turn out in later ones.[68] These facts lead us to believe that even with the RID option, SB 14 may have enduring effects on turnout among voters who have at some point struggled to produce identification. Considering that these voters were less white than voters who could show ID, it is therefore possible that even though the district court reduced SB 14 to a much less severe shell of itself, the law continues to unduly shape minority voters' participation. This is the main question we engage in the remainder of this chapter.

TABLE 8.2. Subsequent Turnout Rates by 2016 RID Usage (Percent)

	2018			2020		
	Non-RID User	Non-Hardship	Hardship	Non-RID User	Non-Hardship	Hardship
Voted	75.8	54.8	48.5	82.2	60.3	54.0
Did Not Vote	24.2	45.2	51.5	17.8	39.7	46.0

Table 8.2 indicates that turnout was fairly low in elections following 2016 among RID filers, relative to that of voters who did not use an RID that year. For instance, while only about half of 2016 RID filers voted in 2018, that number was 76% for Texans who did not use an RID. That said, without accounting for other differences between these groups of voters, we cannot necessarily attribute this disparity to the experience of voting without ID. It is possible that RID filers had relatively low turnout in prior years, too; for whatever reason, they may simply be generally low-propensity voters. To infer any causal effect from RID usage on subsequent turnout, we therefore have to compare the turnout of RID users in the periods before and after they used an RID to similar voters who *never* used one. As in previous chapters where we match treated *counties* to similar untreated ones, we here facilitate this comparison by matching RID-using voters to other participants in the same year who did not use an RID (interested readers may refer to the Methodological Appendix for more information).

In figure 8.8 we plot RID voters' turnout and that of their matched "control" group (voters with similar attributes but who never used an RID) in the years before and after they were "treated" by filing an RID. As the figure makes clear, the treated and control voters moved in lockstep prior to the treatment election; this is not particularly surprising, however, given that pretreatment turnout was included in the matching procedure. Nevertheless, the pretreatment trendlines do indicate that our matched controls have baseline turnout propensities very much in line with the voters who would eventually use an RID to cast their ballot. Yet figure 8.8 also makes clear that in the years after the election in which treated voters had to use an RID to cast their ballot, their relative turnout declined. This was true in all three of the treatment years. Moreover, the effect appears to be sticky; even as late as 2022—*six years* after they had first used an RID—turnout among the voters who filed an RID in 2016 was lower than that of the matched control group.

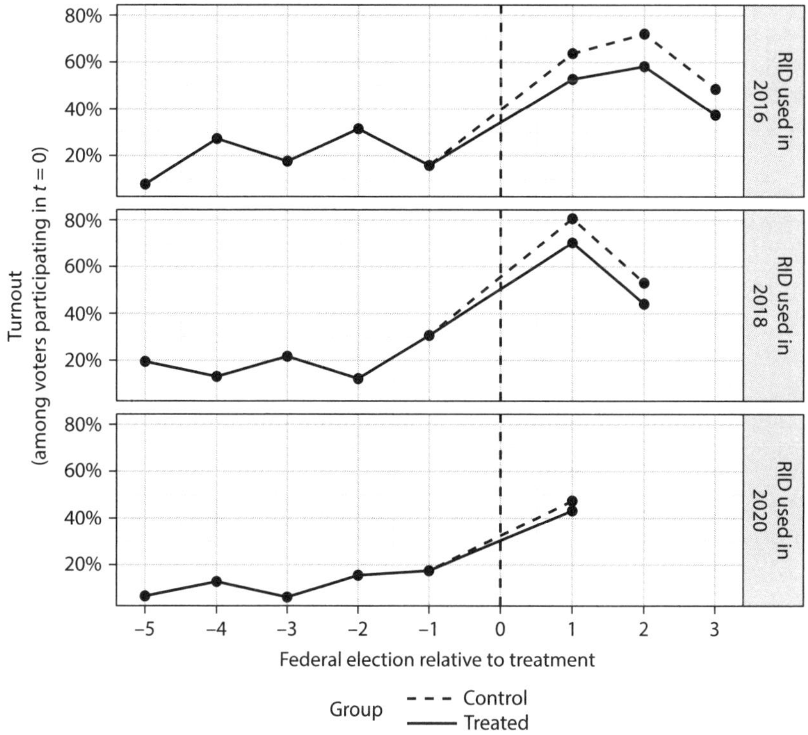

FIGURE 8.8. RID Usage and Subsequent Turnout

As previous chapters discuss, these time series plots can provide strong preliminary evidence of a potential effect, but we still want to precisely measure the magnitude of the effects and determine whether they are statistically significant. Remember from earlier chapters that testing statistical significance is a way to rule out that the apparent effect of filing an RID on subsequent turnout is due to random chance. In figure 8.9, we present the visualization of the statistical models testing these relationships (for those interested, we include the corresponding tables in the Methodological Appendix). By way of reminder, the dot at the middle of each line represents our best estimate of the effect of an RID usage in one year on turnout in the later year. We can be roughly 95% sure that the true effect is somewhere in the range indicated by the vertical lines, and if the range does not include zero, we can conclude there was a statistically significant effect. The figure shows how using an RID in one year impacted turnout in the following three elections; of course, for voters who used an RID in 2020 or 2018, we have only one or two (respectively)

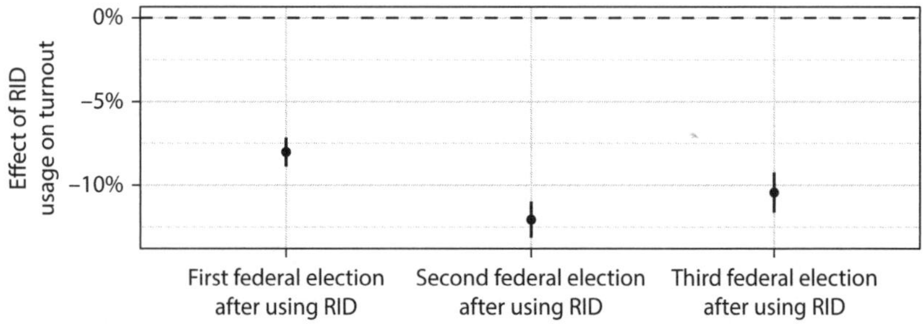

FIGURE 8.9. Effect of RID Usage on Subsequent Turnout

subsequent elections to examine. Figure 8.9 makes clear that using an RID reduces subsequent turnout by a considerable amount—more than 10 percentage points, we estimate, in the second and third federal elections after using one.

It is important to put these effect sizes in context. While only a few percentage points in turnout might not sound like a lot, in the world of election science, this is quite a large shift. Ryan Enos and Anthony Fowler, for instance, find that statewide presidential campaigns increase turnout in "highly targeted states" by 7–8 points.[69] In 2008 Alan Gerber, Donald Green, and Christopher Larimer experimentally treated individuals with social pressure to increase turnout; they noted that their "results in the 5% to 8% range [had] never before been observed."[70] And Kevin T. Morris and Peter Miller recently showed that closing almost *every single polling place* in Milwaukee—177 out of 182—in the 2020 primary reduced turnout by "only" 9 points.[71] Understood in this context, the fact that using an RID made voters as much as 10 percentage points less likely to vote is quite striking.

Were these effects larger for voters who indicated that they used an RID for a hardship-related reason in 2016? It seems possible. While the ID-capable voters would have likely replaced, renewed, or found their ID in the years following the 2016 election, it stands to reason that the hardship voters would be less likely to do so. These individuals faced material challenges to obtaining an ID—such as lack of income or transportation options—that could continue to prevent them from obtaining one in the future. Further, the RID process in 2016 might have sent different messages to voters in the two categories. While ID-capable voters might have faulted themselves for being required to fill out an RID in 2016, those for whom obtaining an ID was difficult might have heard something different; namely, that Americans like themselves were unwelcome

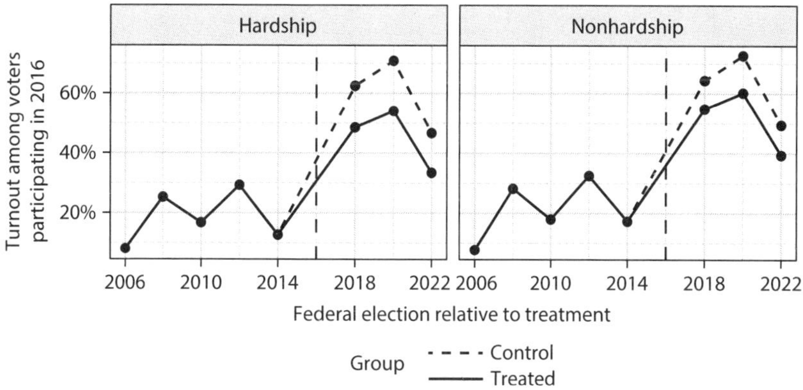

FIGURE 8.10. 2016 RID Usage and Subsequent Turnout, Hardship vs. Nonhardship

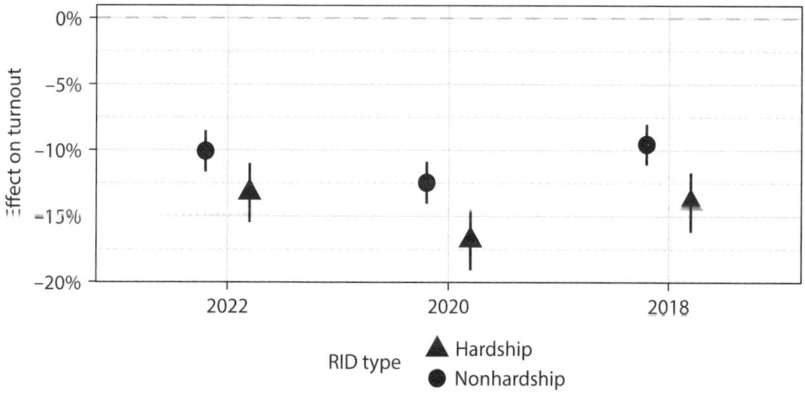

FIGURE 8.11. Effect of Hardship and Nonhardship RIDs on Subsequent Turnout

in the political process. Figure 8.10 provides visual evidence that the effects were indeed considerably larger for hardship voters.

We present the statistical estimates of these effects in figure 8.11. The figure makes two things clear: first, that hardship RIDs were especially detrimental to future turnout; but also, perhaps equally important, that *all* types of RIDs meaningfully reduced future turnout among 2016 Texas voters.

Table 8.3 provides additional evidence that voters with a hardship faced long-term obstacles to obtaining compliant identification. In both 2018 and 2020, voters who cited a hardship reason on their 2016 RID were more likely to continue using an RID than 2016 RID-filers who were ID-capable. We note,

TABLE 8.3. Subsequent RID Usage for 2016 RID Users (Conditional on Voting; Percent)

	2018		2020	
	Non-Hardship	Hardship	Non-Hardship	Hardship
Used RID	2.7	4.0	1.4	2.1
Did Not Use RID	97.3	96.0	98.6	97.9

however, that the overwhelming majority of individuals who used an RID in 2016 and voted in 2018 or 2020 did so without using an RID. This is in some respects good news: Most voters who were not able to show ID in 2016 apparently obtained identification before voting in the later elections.

When she complied with the 5th Circuit Court of Appeals's directive to alter SB 14 in a way that would reduce its impact on voters lacking identification, Judge Nelva Gonzales Ramos inadvertently created a rich dataset that allowed us to closely examine who arrives at Texas polling places without identification. We were also able to chart the reasons those voters gave for lacking ID and to follow their subsequent turnout behavior. Throughout the entirety of the period we examine, compared to voters who presented identification, those who had to file RIDs in order to vote were more likely to be Black, Democratic, young, and/or female. Moreover, SB 14's effects had long tails; voters who had to use an RID to vote in a given election were significantly less likely to turn out in subsequent ones. Ultimatley, the "fix" that Judge Ramos found in 2016 by mandating RIDs generated data that convincingly support her initial determination that SB 14 would discriminate against minority voters in Texas. We stress, however, that even the weakened voter ID law in Texas has been far from harmless: RID usage depresses turnout for years to come.

But even after Ramos's fix, the district court's job was not yet done. Although the 5th Circuit agreed with Ramos back in 2016 that Texas's voter ID law was illegal and required modification, it vacated her finding that SB 14 had been passed with discriminatory intent. To be sure, the circuit court did not necessarily disagree with Judge Ramos's finding here; in fact, the circuit court judges wrote that Ramos's opinion "contained evidence that could support a finding of discriminatory intent." But the 5th Circuit judges argued that the method Judge Ramos used to come to this conclusion was wrong; for that reason, they remanded this part of her opinion back to her court and asked it to reassess the question of intentional discrimination using a different methodology.

After the 2016 election, Judge Ramos reassessed the question of intentional discrimination. Using the circuit court's approved methodology, Ramos found in April 2017 that the state had intentionally discriminated in passing SB 14—just as she had three years earlier.[72] The State of Texas responded by passing Senate Bill 5 in June of that year, which codified the RID process into law beginning in 2018. Although Judge Ramos ultimately struck down SB 5 as well,[73] in April 2018 a divided panel of the 5th Circuit Court of Appeals eventually allowed Texas's voter ID policy—amended by SB 5 to allow for the RID process—to stand.[74] Just one month shy of its seventh birthday, the legal battle surrounding the Texas voter ID law was over. By the time the fight was done, Texas was on the hook for more than $10,000,000 in legal fees.[75] All this effort, to end up with a voter ID law that would likely have been upheld under preclearance, given that the scheme Texas ultimately enacted is functionally the same as the one that South Carolina had in place prior to *Shelby County*.

When *Shelby County* suspended the preclearance condition in 2013, strict voter identification laws were still fairly new. From the time they rose to prominence, political scientists and other scholars suspected that voter ID laws might fall harder on minority voters, even though these policies differed in important ways from the threats to the first-generation concerns that we discuss in chapter 7. In this sense, voter ID laws reflected the ongoing tension between covered states and the federal government going back to the 1960s, wherein states devised novel second-generation ways to undermine minority voters' political power. Nevertheless, Texas, North Carolina, Virginia, and Mississippi all provide examples of formerly covered states that had their voter ID laws stopped, amended, or not even introduced because of preclearance. Section 5 was clearly adaptable to the perceived threats that voter ID laws presented to minority voters. Like other work in political science, our analysis has shown that these laws do fall most heavily on voters of color—just as preclearance reviewers and federal judges suspected they would. Without preclearance, protecting minority voters' rights will undoubtedly be a longer and costlier process—if protection ever materializes at all.

9

Purity of the Ballot Box

MAIL VOTING

> The purpose of this Act is to exercise the legislature's constitutional authority under Section 4, Article VI, Texas Constitution, to make all laws necessary to detect and punish fraud and preserve the purity of the ballot box.
>
> —TEXAS SENATE, SENATE BILL 7, ENGROSSED VERSION, 87TH LEGISLATURE, REGULAR SESSION (2021).

> In no event shall a negro be eligible to participate in a Democratic party primary election held in the State of Texas. . . . The same precautions required by law to secure the purity of the ballot box in general elections . . . shall be observed in all primary elections.
>
> —*REVISED CIVIL STATUTES OF THE STATE OF TEXAS*, 1925, ARTICLES 3107 AND 3118.

AT NOON on January 6, 2021, President Donald J. Trump gripped a podium at the Ellipse in Washington, DC. From behind a sheet of protective glass, Trump addressed roughly 50,000 supporters for a little more than an hour. Trump had lost the 2020 election, but had been the first presidential candidate in American history who disputed the certified results and failed to concede. "You don't concede," Trump said near the outset of his remarks, "when there's theft involved." The Ellipse speech—timed to slightly precede congressional certification of the electoral certificates transmitted by the various states—was part of a broader effort to sow doubt in the election's integrity. If the allusion to "theft" left any doubt as to his intended talking points for the next 75 minutes, Trump offered a key signpost of where he wanted to go: "Today I will lay out just some of the evidence proving that we won this election and we won it by a landslide."

Mail ballots played a central role in Trump's claims of a stolen election. The COVID-19 pandemic had contributed to an extraordinary number of Americans seeking to cast their ballot using a method other than the traditional approach of voting at their precinct on Election Day. That fall, less than a third of voters cast a ballot in person on Election Day, while a record 43% completed a ballot they had received in the mail.[1] This allowed voters to return their ballot by placing it in a central drop box or by mailing it back to their election agency, limiting exposure to the COVID-19 virus.

The convenience and safety of mail voting made it a natural choice given the risks of an airborne global pandemic, but the process became a target of Trump and others who felt that the rise of mail voting had degraded electoral security. "This year," Trump said, "using the pretext of the China virus and the scam of mail-in ballots, Democrats attempted the most brazen and outrageous election theft." He repeated unfounded rumors of mail ballot fraud in key swing states, including Arizona, Georgia, Michigan, Nevada, Pennsylvania, and Wisconsin. In the case of Georgia, Trump railed against what he felt were lax policies to verify mail voters' identities. He noted that mail ballot rejection rates in Georgia were lower than in previous elections, which he took as evidence that the state had allowed the addition of "tens of thousands of illegitimate voters to the tally." Trump also levied a series of claims—most since debunked—about mail ballots being cast by Georgians who were incarcerated, who were unregistered or improperly registered, who had moved before the election, or who had died. Trump made similar allegations about other swing states as well, even though an agency within his Department of Homeland Security called 2020 "the most secure in American history."[2] The president's point was straightforward enough: Trump argued that when voting is done outside a secure precinct, the probability of election fraud is dramatically higher.

The president ended his speech with a call to action: "We're going to try and give our Republicans [in Congress] . . . the kind of pride and boldness that they need to take back our country. So let's walk down Pennsylvania Avenue [to the Capitol]." Shortly thereafter, a mob of his supporters—many of whom had been in the audience at the Ellipse—violently stormed the Capitol. Several Capitol Police officers were seriously injured, and one rioter was killed by police. The certification of the electoral count was briefly suspended as members of Congress sought temporary shelter at secure locations. Some rioters carried zip ties and weapons. Others held signs, and one of the more common slogans that appeared on them was by now familiar to anyone who even casually followed the aftermath of the 2020 election: "Stop the Steal." To many of Trump's supporters, the fix was in and mail ballots were to blame. Whether Trump believed the claims he made at the Ellipse or not, one thing was clear to him and affiliated political elites: A lot of Democrats had cast their vote by mail. Restricting mail ballots may then be seen as a viable means of gaining an electoral advantage, whether those votes were fraudulent or not.

Trump was right about one thing: The 2020 election saw the climax of a three-decade shift that political scientist Paul Gronke describes as a "quiet revolution" in election administration.[3] During this period, states have increasingly afforded voters an opportunity to cast their ballot before Election Day, and millions of voters have opted for so-called "convenience voting" methods. In 2016, nearly 24% of voters attempted to vote by mail,[4] which as noted, increased to more than 40% in 2020. A marked increase in early in-person voting that same year meant that in 2020, only about 30% of voters cast their ballots in-person on Election Day—the first time a minority of voters had done so.[5]

Voting by mail is usually a two-stage process: Voters first apply for a mail ballot (satisfying any state requirements for receiving one) and then, if approved, receive and return their ballot. Mailed "absentee" ballots were originally conceived as a way to help deployed military personnel vote, but after the First World War, they became available to civilians who could claim some reason they would be unable to vote on Election Day. As the twentieth century progressed, absentee voting expanded throughout the country.[6] While roughly one-quarter of the states maintained the excuse requirement well into the twenty-first century, most have now adopted no-excuse policies, which allow voters to request a mail ballot for any reason. Several states, mainly in the West, have gone even further. In these states, *all* ballots are transmitted to voters via the US Mail. Voters have the option of mailing them back, but for one reason or another, most opt to return them in person via special ballot drop boxes.[7] For voters in these places, the traditional Election Day, in-person voting experience is a relic of the past.

A substantial amount of previous research has found that increasing the prevalence of mail voting does not benefit the candidates of a particular party.[8] Democrats were approximately twice as likely as Republicans to vote by mail in 2020,[9] but available evidence suggests that rather than drawing new Democratic voters into the fold, mail voting mostly allowed Democrats who would

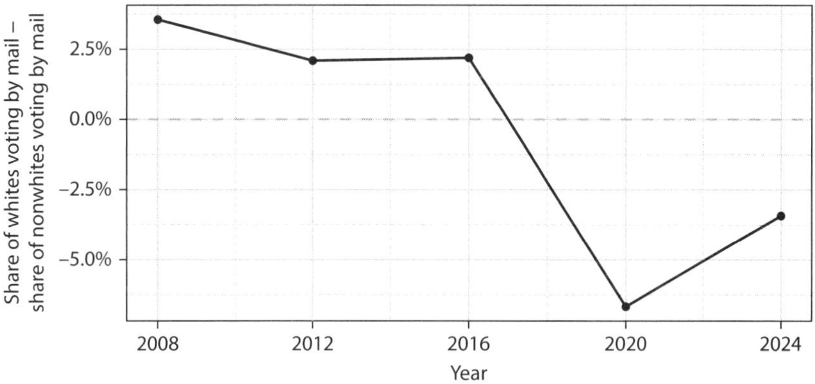

FIGURE 9.1. Difference in Mail Ballot Usage by Race
Note: Author calculations from the Cooperative Election Study.

otherwise have voted in person to avoid crowded polling places on Election Day during the pandemic. Still, President Trump—not to mention quite a few journalists and elites in both parties—certainly *believed* that expansive mail voting policies benefited Democrats that year, and they were not shy in saying so.[10]

Public expressions from sources like the president can exert a powerful pull on public opinion.[11] Since January 6, political scientists have discovered that a considerable swath of the public was susceptible to influence about election fraud both during and after the 2020 election.[12] Among people who accept the so-called Big Lie that Trump advanced in 2020, beliefs in election fraud are deeply held.[13] If the rhetoric emanating from the White House led them to believe that lax mail voting rules were contributing to Democratic victories in some way, Republican legislators might curtail mail voting if for no other reason than to make voting more difficult for their opponents. That sort of partisan advantage-seeking would be a tale as old as time.

Party is not all of the story, though. Demographic patterns in the ways Americans cast their ballots—what political scientists refer to as the vote *mode*—serve as an important backdrop to the rhetoric surrounding mail voting policies after 2020. Figure 9.1 shows a discernible shift in the use of mail voting by white and nonwhite voters in 2020 that continued into the 2024 election. Although a larger share of white voters (relative to minority voters) cast their ballots by mail in the three presidential elections prior to 2020, the pattern inverted that year, when minority voters were about 7 percentage points more likely than white voters to use a mail ballot. While this gap abated somewhat in 2024, a larger share of voters of color continued to vote by mail in that election as well.

Usage aside, there is also a fair amount of evidence that voters with certain characteristics are more likely to have their mail ballots *rejected* for reasons such as lateness or noncompliance with requirements. These traits include youth or inexperience with voting, military affiliation, and (most important for our purposes) being a racial minority or non-English speaker—two groups that the VRA explicitly seeks to protect.[14] Coupled with their already disproportionate rejection rate, minority voters' increased usage of mail voting in 2020 may have motivated some legislators to scrutinize mail ballots not because they were in reality less secure, but because restricting mail voting was a viable means to disenfranchise voters who skewed toward Democrats.[15] The racial disenfranchisement embedded in this decision would be a clear violation of the VRA, however, and one that preclearance certainly would have stopped in its tracks.

Race also played an important role in the way voters received important elements in the public conversation surrounding mail ballots. Recent research has shown that the national dialogue about voter fraud in the 2020 election was heavily racialized. For instance, at least one study has found that white Trump voters who held negative views of minority citizens believed lies about voter fraud more than other Trump voters, and white Republicans found accusations of voter fraud considerably more credible when they were levied against Black Americans.[16] Other research has shown that racially conservative white Americans were more supportive of the January 6 insurrection, even after accounting for other characteristics.[17]

There is growing evidence that in the aftermath of the 2020 election, a similar pattern was on display among legislators as well. To be sure, the 2021 legislative session saw virtually unprecedented activity to make voting more difficult.[18] Given Trump's apparent success in convincing his supporters of its potential for fraud, it is probably not surprising that this legislative flurry was especially focused on mail voting. In 2021 a total of 32 laws were passed in 14 states restricting mail voting in some way, such as shortening application or return deadlines or implementing stricter requirements for voter identification.[19] Three more states passed restrictive mail-voting laws in 2022.[20] These laws were not exclusive to states that had once been covered by preclearance, but those states certainly passed more than their share of mail ballot restrictions. By the time the 2024 election rolled around, 10 of the 15 states that would previously have been subject to preclearance had enacted restrictive mail-voting legislation (including 7 of the 9 fully covered states); the same was true for just 13 of the 35 noncovered states.[21]

Preclearance status aside, it is also true that not all Republican state legislators were equally likely to sponsor restrictive voting legislation. As it turns out, the most active lawmakers on this topic represented areas populated by a larger proportion of white Americans who held negative views of minorities.[22] In other words, although most of the efforts to restrict voting rights in 2021 were spearheaded by Republicans, racial considerations explain which Republicans were most likely to be especially active on this front. That these bills may well have risen out of racial animus implies that they might make voting disproportionately more difficult for Americans of color.

Limitations on drop boxes and enhanced identification requirements for mail voters were fairly typical among states changing their election laws after 2020, but others went even further. Take South Carolina, for instance. Voting "absentee" by mail has never been a straightforward proposition there. South Carolina is one of a handful of "excuse" states that have long refused to allow voters to request a mailed ballot unless they have a qualified reason—such as traveling out of the jurisdiction for work obligations on Election Day. South Carolina legislators eased the excuse requirement in 2020, allowing all voters to cast a mail ballot during the pandemic. In May 2022, however, the state enacted Senate Bill 108 (S108), which pulled back the permissive policy from two years before.

In one respect, S108 made voting easier for some South Carolinians. The new law established a 12-day early in-person period for the first time in South Carolina, allowing voters to cast their ballot prior to Election Day by presenting themselves and their identification in person at a designated polling place. But, while it expanded *early* voting, S108 dramatically narrowed the conditions in which *mail* voting would be allowed. S108 reinstituted the excuse requirement but made it even stronger than it had been prior to 2020. Rather than showing that they were away from home and would be unable to vote in person on just Election Day, S108 mandated that voters show they would be out of the jurisdiction for the *entire* 12-day early voting period.

The new law also required voters to supply the last four digits of their social security number and their voter registration number with their ballot application. Ballot drop boxes were explicitly banned under S108. Instead, voters could return their ballot by mail or by dropping it in person at an election office—where they were required to show photo identification that complied with the state's voter ID law. Thus, S108 erected significant hurdles for would-be mail voters. Following its passage, the excuse threshold in South Carolina became one of the strictest in the country, and the identification requirements could also thwart voters who did not have easy access to required documents. Our analysis in chapter 8 suggests that this population is disproportionately Black (at least in Texas).

New legislation in Georgia followed a similar playbook: In 2021 that state also passed a wide-ranging omnibus voting bill, Senate Bill 202 (SB202). As in South Carolina, the Georgia legislature made it considerably more difficult for voters to cast their ballots by mail. For one thing, local election officials were no longer allowed to send voters applications they could fill out to request a mail ballot. The law also shortened the window in which voters could request mail ballots and restricted both the number of ballot drop boxes and their operative hours.

Of course, we cannot know whether the Department of Justice would have objected to any of these restrictions on absentee voting, but at least in the case of the Georgia law, it seems likely: Shortly after the bill was passed into law, the DOJ sued the Peach State, arguing that the law "introduce[d] new impediments at every step of the absentee voting process: obtaining an application, completing and timely submitting the application, and timely returning a completed absentee ballot." The complaint continued, "The General Assembly adopted these changes after Black voters began disproportionately using absentee voting, and Black voters will be disproportionately impacted by each of these new obstacles." In concluding its complaint, the DOJ's summary of SB202 pulled no punches in characterizing legislative intent: "In enacting SB 202, the Georgia General Assembly intended to deny or abridge the right of Black Georgians to vote on account of race or color."[23]

The DOJ's efforts ultimately proved successful in part, though fleetingly. Federal judges temporarily enjoined components of the Georgia law in 2023.[24] However, like so many laws we have described that were ultimately struck down after litigation instead of being preempted by preclearance, a full election cycle passed with SB202 in effect. The DOJ's brief clearly indicates its belief that SB202 *intended* to discriminate against Black voters. It surely would therefore have failed preclearance. Absent the *Shelby County* ruling, the components of the law that the DOJ reasoned were discriminatory would never have been allowed to take effect in 2022.

Finally, there is Florida. In that state, a 2021 omnibus elections law known as Senate Bill 90 ended a policy allowing voters' mail ballot applications to cover a four-year period including two federal election cycles. Under SB90, voters would have to re-request mail ballots every two years. Another feature of SB90 was a requirement that Floridians supply identifying information on their ballot application, such as their driver's license number or the last four digits of their social security number. But perhaps the most controversial aspect of the law was a new limitation on ballot drop boxes. Under SB90, voters could drop mail ballots in drop boxes only during early in-person voting hours, and the boxes would be located only at a county's permanent voting location. However, the law also targeted a vote mode (returning mail ballots to drop boxes) that had recently surged in popularity among minority voters, who had heavily used ballot drop boxes outside business hours during the 2020 election. Thus, the drop box regulations in particular seemed potentially problematic.

SB90 was challenged in federal court on the grounds that these new regulations would create disproportionate harm for minority voters. The case landed in the US District Court for the Northern District of Florida. At the conclusion of the trial, district court judge Mark Walker ruled that SB90 was indeed discriminatory. Walker's ruling on this point was clear: "The Legislature enacted some of SB 90's provisions [including the restrictions to drop boxes] with the intent to target Black voters."[25] But Judge Walker did not end with simply overturning many of SB90's provisions: He went further, bailing the state into preclearance under Section 3(c) of the Voting Rights Act.

Bailed-in preclearance is often narrow in both scope and duration (see our discussion of this topic in part I). The same was true in this case, where Judge Walker bailed Florida into preclearance for 10 years, but only for any "law or regulation governing [third-party voter-registration organizations], drop boxes, or 'line warming' activities."[26] Judge Walker justified his decision using language that reads as though it could have been part of Attorney General Katzenbach's testimony to the Senate a half-century before:

> Without preclearance, Florida can pass unconstitutional restrictions . . . with impunity. Litigation takes time; here, it has taken a year. And so, before litigation can run its course, the Legislature can merely change the law—as it has done here. The result is that Floridians have been forced to live under a law that violates their rights on multiple fronts for over a year. Without preclearance, Florida could continue to enact such laws, replacing them

every legislative session if courts view them with skepticism. Such a scheme makes a mockery of the rule of law.[27]

Florida appealed Walker's decision to the 11th Circuit Court of Appeals. There, a split three-judge panel overruled the district court on nearly every point. The 11th Circuit not only overturned Walker's decision to bail Florida into preclearance but also allowed most of the provisions in SB90 to stand.[28]

The scope of new restrictions on mail voting after the 2020 election depended on the state in which they were enacted, and as we have seen, the new laws met various fates in federal court. However, plenty of evidence indicates that several of them harmed minority voters—in some cases, intentionally. In 2013, few observers would have predicted that we would be thinking of mail ballot procedures as a potentially widespread method of violating the Voting Rights Act, which is why this policy area merits close examination now: The procedures for accepting mail ballots are the sort of policy that Section 5 was designed to prevent—not because they were foreseen but precisely because preclearance was intended to guard against unforeseeable new devices. Thus, there is reason to scrutinize the effects of restrictive mail-voting laws in greater detail, especially when they are enacted in jurisdictions that were formerly covered by Section 5 of the Voting Rights Act. For the remainder of this chapter, rather than attempt a broad, multistate analysis of mail voting restrictions, we once again take a deep dive into one state where we have particularly rich data. It is time to return to Texas.

"Leave the chamber discreetly. Do not go to the gallery. Leave the building." This was the message that Texas house Democrats received from Chris Turner, the chair of the house Democratic caucus, on May 30, 2021.[29] Turner was playing legislative Democrats' final card. He was facing a Republican bill (SB7) that would enact sweeping changes to election rules in Texas. Democrats argued that the bill amounted to a package of restrictive policies that would imperil Democratic voters' rights. On Turner's order, they left the chamber to break legislative quorum, effectively forcing the house to shut down. Ultimately, Texas house Democrats would perform this maneuver twice, fleeing again in July to Washington, DC, in order to thwart a special session called to push the election bill forward.

The Democrats' flight to Washington paid off in the short term, allowing them to buy some additional negotiating time and a few concessions. In the long run, however, Republicans got most of what they asked for in another sweeping bill passed in that special session. That bill had a new name: SB1. The new law was passed in time to be implemented prior to the 2022 Texas primary elections. The contentious politics of its passage underscored just how clearly the two parties perceived the stakes of omnibus election legislation in Texas and elsewhere. Democrats certainly had reasons to be concerned, as SB1 diminished local election officials' ability to make decisions in response to emergencies. As we touch on in chapter 5, it also directly targeted voting methods that election administrators in Democratic-leaning Harris County had implemented, banning 24-hour and drive-through voting and restricting the allowable hours for in-person early voting.

A final area that SB1 affected—and the one we focus on here—was the distribution and submission of mail ballots. Texas did not have permissive policies with respect to mail ballots even prior to SB1. For instance, while people 65 or older were allowed to cast mail ballots with no documented hardship, all other voters had to demonstrate absence, illness, or disability to vote by mail. SB1 kept these rules in place but also added new ones. One change was that election officials risked felony charges if they encouraged mail voting or if they automatically sent voters mail ballot applications. Central to our analysis in this chapter, SB1 also added identification requirements for voters who chose to cast a mail ballot in 2022 and afterward. Beginning in 2022, voters were required to submit either their state identification number or a partial social security number on their application for mail ballots, and then again on the underside of the ballot envelope flap on submitting it. Failure to do so meant that either their application or their ballot would be rejected—and their vote would not count unless they could find another path to the ballot box.

This identification requirement drew the attention of journalists and others both before the election and in the early period of mail ballot processing; these observers were concerned that the enhanced ID requirements would lead to unusually high rejection rates for at least two reasons. First, SB1 required voters to write the number from the same identification included in the registration database, which in many cases the voter had provided years prior. If voters had only ever provided, say, a driver's license number to the state but submitted a partial social security number in 2022 instead, election officials were required to reject their application or ballot. Journalist Jessica Huseman noted the potential for this requirement to lead to high rejection rates more than six months prior to the primary election.[30]

The second issue was the location of the field that solicited identification numbers on the ballot submission envelope. The identification requirement was prominently featured on the application, immediately to the right of the fields requesting voters' name, address, and date of birth. If their application was approved—that is, if they met the requirements for casting a mail ballot *and* correctly completed the application—voters would receive a ballot in the mail, which they could complete and return. The identification field was less prominent when it came time to return mail ballots, however. Voters were required to write the correct identification number on the underside of the return envelope flap, a location that was easy to miss altogether. In fact, following the primary election, staff in the Texas secretary of state's office acknowledged that they did not think "it would be too much of a stretch to think that some people thought it was just an optional section."[31]

During the mail ballot period in advance of the primary, election officials noted high rates of ballots submitted without identification numbers, which were rejected following efforts to notify voters that they needed to "cure" those ballots by submitting complete information.[32] In response, good government groups like the Center for Civic Design began an early effort pushing the state to make changes to the envelope's design.[33] However, SB1 also attracted attention from the Department of Justice, which sued the state shortly after the law's passage, alleging that this identification provision violated federal law.[34] Unlike its complaint against Georgia's omnibus voting bill, the DOJ did not argue that Texas lawmakers intended to discriminate against voters of color when they passed SB1, and we therefore cannot know for sure whether the DOJ would have objected to the policy under the preclearance regime. Nevertheless, SB1's mail ballot provisions caught the DOJ's eye. Had Texas sought to implement SB1 while under preclearance, the state would have been required to affirmatively demonstrate that the law would not have fallen harder on minority voters. As it turns out, Texas would likely have failed in that effort.

To analyze rejection patterns under SB1, we largely follow the approach we have used for much of this book, utilizing data generated by the state itself. We conducted most of the work described in the remainder of this chapter with collaborators Ian Shapiro and Coryn Grange.[35] We started by obtaining

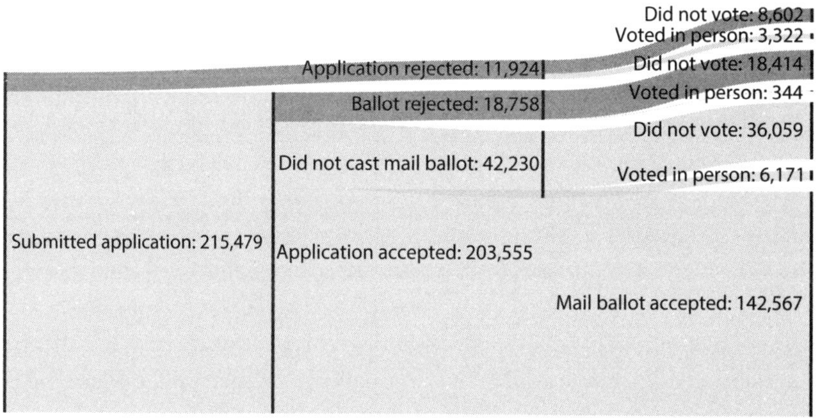

FIGURE 9.2. Distribution of Attempted Mail Voters in 2022 Primary

individual-level data on both mail ballot application forms and mail ballots in the 2022 Texas primary from a public records request to the Texas secretary of state, along with records obtained from the Brennan Center's lawsuit over SB1.[36] The records note whether each voter's application or ballot was accepted and, if not, the reason for the rejection. The "reason" codes in the records are especially important because they allow us to tell which applications and ballots would have been accepted had SB1 not been in place—that is, which applications and ballots were rejected only because the newly required identification number was incorrect or missing.[37]

To illustrate how this procedure works, in figure 9.2 we plot the different paths traveled by the roughly 215,000 Texans who requested a mail ballot for the 2022 primary election.[38] The figure makes clear that most voters did not have trouble voting; about two-thirds of voters who began the process eventually cast a mail ballot that was counted. But figure 9.2 also underscores that there were several potential trouble spots for voters intending to cast mail ballots. Of the remaining 70,000 voters in figure 9.2, about half received a mail ballot that they ultimately did not cast, either because they chose to vote in person instead or simply did not vote at all. The rest—some 30,000 voters, or one out of seven voters who started the process—attempted to cast their mail ballot but had either their application or their ballot rejected. Roughly 90% of these individuals did not find another way to participate in the 2022 primary.

To be sure, some of the individuals whose applications were rejected would not have cast a mail ballot had they successfully received one; about 20% of individuals who received a mail ballot did not cast it. Nevertheless, figure 9.2

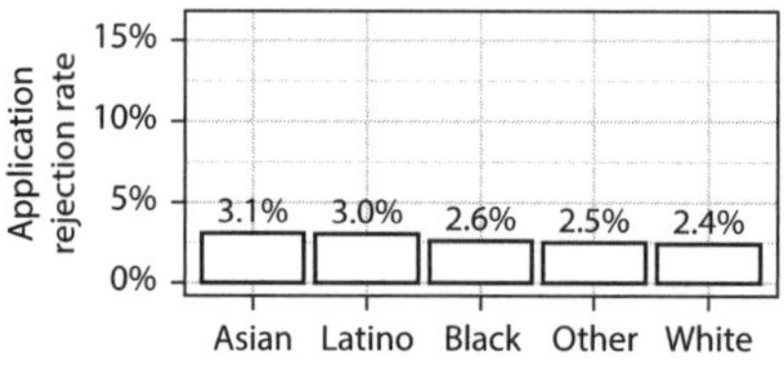

(a) Application rejections

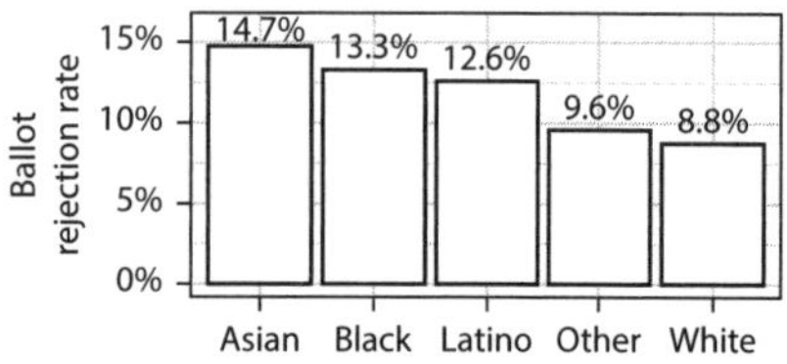

(b) Ballot rejections

FIGURE 9.3. SB1-Related Rejection Rates

reveals that as a result of mail application or ballot rejections, a large number of voters either did not vote at all or did not cast a vote by their preferred method. This fact implies that if we want to fully understand how SB1 impacted minority voters, we must look at both ballot *and* application rejections. And if we want to place the effects of SB1 in context with the *Shelby County* ruling, we need to look at whether minority voters were more likely than white voters to face rejection at either stage of their attempt to vote by mail.

To do so, we joined the rejection records to voter registration records from Texas (interested readers can refer to the Methodological Appendix for more information).[39] The voter file indicates whether and by which mode each voter participated in the primary, and includes sufficient information for us to determine where they live. We note in chapter 8 that the Texas voter file does not include fields for voters' self-reported race. We therefore use statistical procedures similar to those we employed there and elsewhere in this book to estimate the probability that each voter is white, Black, Latino, Asian, or "other" (see the Methodological Appendix for more information).

Figure 9.3 depicts the rate of both application and ballot rejections by voter race.[40] Several notable trends emerge in this figure. First, regardless of race, Texas voters appear to have had an easier time navigating the application process than successfully submitting a ballot; we can see that rates of ballot rejections are higher (by a factor of three or four times) than application rejections, on average. Second, rejection rates were substantially higher for minority voters than for white voters. For instance, the application rejection rates for Asian (3.1%) and Latino (3.0%) voters were more than 25% higher than for white voters (2.4%).

The differences are even starker when we look at ballot rejections, however. There, relative to white voters, Asian and Black voters were over 50% more likely to have their ballot rejected; for Latino Texans, the rejection rate exceeded that of white voters by about 43%. The pattern in the data is clear:

Relative to white voters, minority voters saw their applications and (especially) their ballots rejected at higher rates than white voters. While white voters experienced relatively lower rejection rates than minority voters, they still saw extraordinarily high ballot rejection rates. In the 2022 primary, one in eleven mail ballots cast by a white voter was discarded for an SB1-related reason. This observation underscores the dramatic impact that SB1 had on *all* Texas voters seeking to cast a mail ballot. Compare these figures with numbers from the previous general elections: Texas rejected just 1.8% of mail ballots in the 2018 general election,[41] and just 0.8% in 2020.[42] In fact, about as many mail ballots were rejected in the 2022 primary as in the 2018 and 2020 general elections *combined*.[43]

While these figures show that minority voters experienced higher rejection rates, they do not account for other voter traits that could affect our conclusions. For instance, if Black and Latino Texans are less frequent voters, they might, on average, be less certain about how to correctly complete mail voting paperwork. If this is the case, we might observe an apparent effect of voters' race or ethnicity when the result was actually driven by their familiarity with voting processes. To account for this and other factors that might confound our results if left unaccounted for, we estimate a series of statistical models that allow us to calculate the independent effect of several variables at once, avoiding the pitfall we just described. We can again distinguish between rejections that stemmed from SB1 and rejections that voters experienced for other reasons. The full results (which can be found in the Methodological Appendix) reveal some interesting correlates of rejection rates. Unsurprisingly, voters who had participated in previous primaries were less likely to have their ballots or applications rejected. Men had their ballots and applications rejected less frequently than women, and older voters had higher rejection rates, on average. Democrats also generally had lower rejection rates than Republicans or independents.

A number of takeaways are also clear from these models when it comes to voters' race and ethnicity. We show these results in figure 9.4, which depicts the rejection rates of minority voters relative to white voters after accounting for voters' other characteristics. Like other plots of statistical models we show throughout this book, the symbols represent the estimated relationship. These numbers can be interpreted as showing by how many percentage points voters of each group were more (or less) likely than white voters to have an application or ballot rejected. The horizontal lines represent our confidence in the estimate. That is, given inherent error in any statistical estimate, the

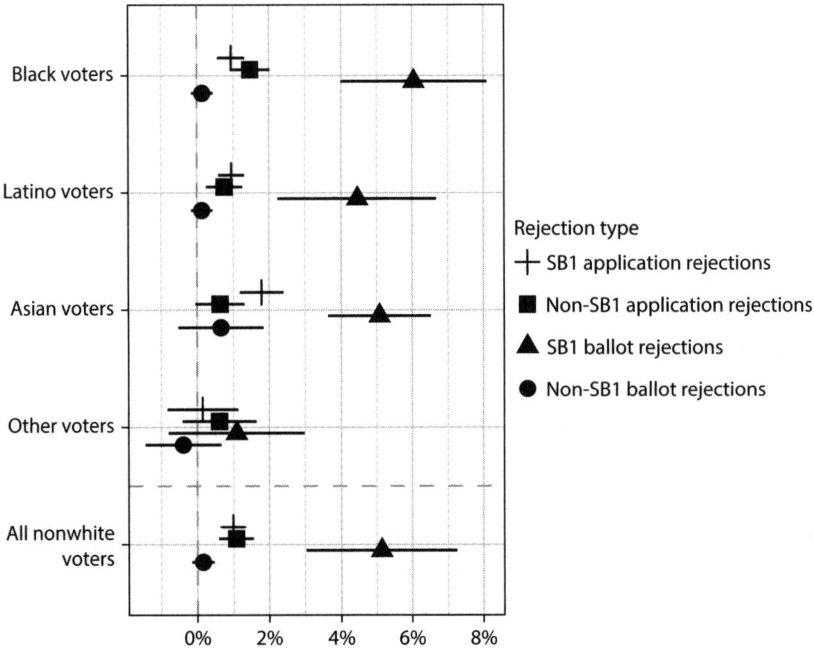

These relationships account for differences in age, gender, partisan affiliation, and past primary turnout.

FIGURE 9.4. Rejection Rates for Voters of Different Races, Relative to White Voters

lines may be interpreted as a zone in which we are 95% confident the relationship is located. If the confidence regions do not overlap with zero, we can conclude that there is a statistically significant difference in rejection rates between white voters and a given racial or ethnic group.

In figure 9.4, we can see that Black and Latino voters were about one percentage point more likely than white voters to have their application rejected, regardless of whether the reason for that rejection was related to SB1. The point estimates for SB1 and non-SB1 rejections are quite similar for both the Black and Latino groups. This suggests that while the hurdles presented by SB1 may not have been relatively more onerous for Black or Latino voters than the baseline difficulty of applying for a mail ballot, SB1 *did* add to the number of disenfranchised Black and Latino voters—and at a higher rate than white voters. For Asian voters, we see little difference from white voters with respect to non-SB1-related application rejections, but their SB1-related application rejection rate was 1.8 points higher than that of white voters. In short,

SB1 appears to have been relatively much more burdensome for Asian voters than the baseline difficulty of applying for a mail ballot. When it comes to application rejections, then, SB1 appears to have impacted Black, Latino, and (especially) Asian voters more than white voters.

The pattern for mail *ballot* rejections in figure 9.4 is even clearer. Looking at non-SB1-related ballot rejection rates, we see no meaningful differences between any of the racial or ethnic groups. For SB1 ballot rejections, however, the rates for Black, Latino, and Asian voters were 6.2, 4.5, and 5.1 points higher than for white voters, respectively. These differences are substantively large and statistically significant. Moreover, these effects are compounded: Due to racial disparities in application rejections, the pool of voters who have the opportunity to cast a mail ballot is already more white than the pool of *potential* mail voters. In total then, figure 9.4 provides strong support for the notion that, even after accounting for differences in things like gender and age, racial and ethnic minorities who voted by mail were disproportionately disenfranchised due to SB1 at both the application and ballot stage—with particularly strong effects for ballot rejections.

We have shown that minority voters were more likely to have both their mail ballot applications and mail ballots themselves rejected in the immediate aftermath of SB1. But what happens to these voters in subsequent elections? There are at least two reasons to think that having a ballot or application rejected in the 2022 Texas primary could have affected an individual's future voting behavior. First, rejections resulted in what we might refer to as a future "mechanical" disenfranchisement: In Texas, voters cannot join a "permanent" absentee list as voters in some other states can; instead, they are required to reapply for absentee ballots once every year (not once per election phase). Most individuals who have a mail ballot *application* accepted for a primary (regardless of whether their ballot is ultimately accepted) elect to have a mail ballot automatically sent for the general election as well. In contrast, voters whose ballot applications are rejected would not automatically receive a general election mail ballot. For voters whose application was rejected in the primary, the costs of voting in subsequent elections is likely to be higher in both information and time as they try to sort out why their mail ballot did not arrive, reapply for an absentee ballot, and seek out details about where to vote in person. This said, we should not expect the "mechanical" effect of a rejection in the 2022 primary to extend past the 2022 general election, since all voters would be required to re-request an absentee ballot in subsequent years anyway, even if their 2022 request was not rejected.

Second, some voters may also experience a more latent form of downstream disenfranchisement. Trying but failing to cast a ballot might decrease voters' sense that their voice matters, a concept that political scientists typically refer to as *political efficacy*. Lower efficacy can lead to less political participation.[44] In fact, we show a similar process at play in chapter 8: When voters in Texas showed up without one of the very few allowable voter ID options, they had the option to fill out a reasonable impediment declaration. While the RID allowed them to vote, these voters were less likely to return to the polling place in the years that followed. Application or ballot rejections might have similar ramifications for future turnout, but that might not be the only effect: Even when they *do* want to vote in the future, voters may recall their negative experience with mail voting and switch to an in-person option (early or on Election Day) as a result.

With these possibilities in mind, we compare the later voting behavior of would-be 2022 primary mail voters whose *application* was rejected, whose *ballot* was rejected, and who experienced no rejection. Examining the subsequent voting behavior of these voters can provide insight into the mechanism that might link rejections in 2022 and voting behavior in later elections. For instance, voters whose application was rejected experienced both a mechanical and latent disenfranchisement: They had a negative experience while voting, *and* did not receive an automatic mail ballot in the general election. They were also more likely to learn about their rejection early on, when they failed to receive the expected mail ballot for the primary.

Likewise, per Texas law we assume that voters who successfully submitted an application but had their primary ballot rejected still received mail ballots for the general election. If they still abstained in the general election at higher rates than comparable voters who experienced no rejection, we might conclude that any difference between them and the voters who experienced an application rejection is not attributable to the higher cost of seeking a ballot. It may instead stem from the decreased efficacy following a more difficult voting experience. The same mechanism would also apply for the 2024 primary.

While we anticipate that having an application or ballot rejected in the primary election reduced turnout in subsequent elections, we might therefore expect the effects of an application rejection in the primary on future voting behavior to be most substantial. We also expect that if they do decide to vote in elections after the 2022 primary, a larger proportion of rejected voters will choose to forego mail voting in favor of casting their ballot in person. Here again, we expect that rejected applications will have the largest effects. To examine these possibilities, we incorporate turnout information from two later voter file snapshots.[45] These records indicate whether a person voted and usually which mode they used to do so.[46] We use these records to examine voters' subsequent behavior in the 2022 *general* election as well as the 2024 *primary* election.

It is possible that individuals whose applications or ballots were rejected in March 2022 might have different underlying general election or presidential primary turnout propensities than other voters. In other words, voters "treated" by an application or ballot rejection in the spring of 2022 might have turned out at different rates in subsequent elections than "control" voters (who did *not* have an application or ballot rejected) even if they had not been disenfranchised by SB1. To account for this possibility, we turn again to a difference-in-differences framework similar to the one we have employed in numerous other places in this book.

Recall an important underlying premise in establishing difference in differences: We must assume that the treated and control groups would have moved in parallel had the treatment not occurred. This requires including information about each voter's turnout prior to the 2022 primary election, so that we can see how trends were moving in each group prior to SB1. To examine voting behavior in the 2022 general election, we incorporate each voter's turnout in the 2010–2018 general midterm elections as our base period, and assume that the gap between the treated and control groups would have been the same in 2022 as it had been historically if SB1 had not been not enacted.[47] Any deviance from this scenario may then be considered the causal effect on general election turnout of rejections in the 2022 primary election.

Figure 9.5 presents the turnout in each year among the individuals who requested an absentee ballot in 2022 in the left-hand panel, and among those who cast a mail ballot in the right-hand one. As this figure makes clear, although general election turnout prior to 2022 moved in parallel between those who did and did not experience a rejection (which is good news for our analysis), the same was not true in 2022.[48] As we expected, general election turnout declined precipitously for those whose application was rejected during the primary. This decline of about 16 percentage points was much deeper than the effect we see in the right-hand panel of figure 9.5, which depicts the trend

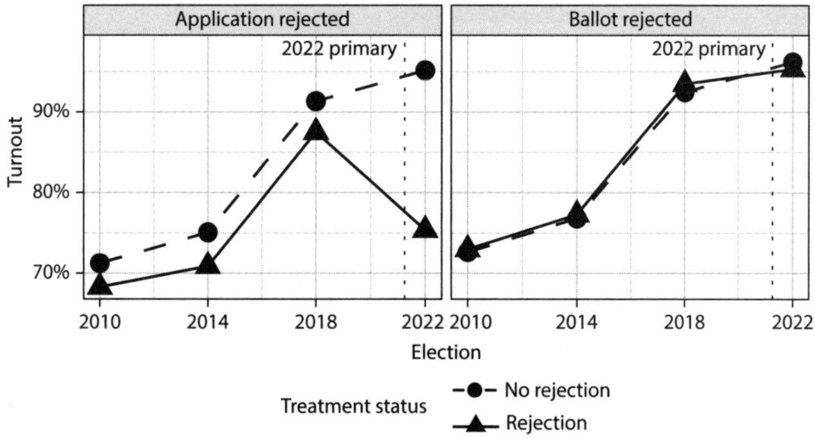

FIGURE 9.5. Midterm Election Turnout by 2022 Primary Status
Note: "Application Rejected" panel includes all individuals who submitted a mail ballot application for the 2022 primary. "Ballot Rejected" panel includes those who submitted a mail ballot in the 2022 primary. In all cases, "No Rejection" refers to voters who did not have an application or ballot rejected in the primary of 2022; the inverse is true for the "Rejection" voters. In other words, these groups remain constant across time.

among voters whose ballots were rejected. While there is a modest decline in general election turnout for voters whose ballot was rejected relative to those who experience no ballot rejection, figure 9.5 demonstrates much starker effects for application rejections. This finding is consistent with our theoretical expectations.

As we do elsewhere in this book, we follow these time series plots with models that return the causal effect of these rejections while also testing for statistical significance. As usual, we present the visual versions of these models here, but those who are interested can find the full tables in the Methodological Appendix (tables for the rest of the coefficient plots presented later in this chapter are there, too). One aim in using this approach is to determine whether the large, negative effect of mail ballot application rejections on 2022 general election turnout remains after more rigorous analysis. Figure 9.6 shows that it does. Relative to voters whose applications were accepted, application rejections in the primary caused voters' turnout to decrease by *16 percentage points* that fall. This is a massive effect. In chapter 8, we cite work by Ryan Enos and Anthony Fowler finding that presidential campaigns in highly targeted battleground states typically increase turnout by 7 or 8 points. In short, our

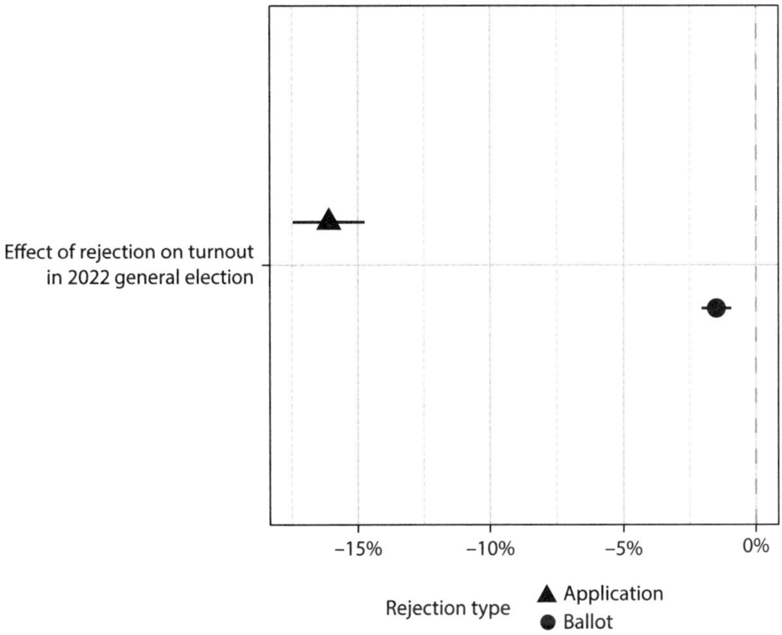

FIGURE 9.6. Effect of Rejections in the Primary on General Election Turnout

models find that the negative effect of ballot application rejection is double the effect of hundreds of millions of dollars in campaign spending going the other way.

While the effects of a ballot rejection were smaller, they still reduced turnout by about 1.5 percentage points. This seems small by comparison, but in the world of turnout analysis, a shift of this magnitude is still a meaningful effect in its own right. Moreover, there is little evidence that turnout for these voters was lower in the general election because they were ensnared anew by SB1-related rejections that fall. Only 1.2% of the individuals who had an application rejected in the primary were rejected again in the general; an even smaller share of voters (0.2%) had their ballot rejected in both stages of the 2022 election. Thus, the depressive effects of rejections on turnout for these voters do not seem to be tied to persistent hurdles; rather, it seems that the rejections in the primary altered future intentions to vote.

How about the voters who *did* cast a ballot in the fall of 2022, after having a mail application or mail ballot rejected in the primary? They shifted their mode of voting at very high rates. In the left panel of figure 9.7, we show that Texans who had their application rejected in the primary but voted in the

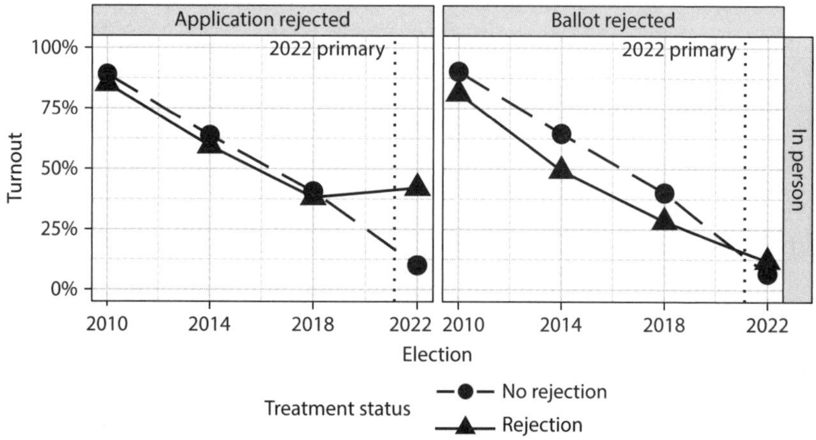

FIGURE 9.7. Share of Ballots Cast in Person, Midterm General Elections
Note: 'Application Rejected' panel includes all individuals who submitted a mail ballot application for the 2022 primary. 'Ballot Rejected' panel includes those who submitted a mail ballot in the 2022 primary. In all cases, 'No Rejection' refers to voters who did not have an application or ballot rejected in the primary of 2022; the inverse is true for the 'Rejection' voters. In other words, these groups remain constant across time.

general were far more likely to do so in person than other voters. This pattern may reflect that they were nervous about having their mail application or ballot rejected again and simply decided not to even try.

That the effects are apparent even for those whose mail *ballot* was rejected in the primary (right panel of figure 9.7) is of particular interest. Because they successfully applied for a mail ballot in the primary, most of these individuals would automatically have received a mail ballot for the general election as well. Many nevertheless shifted to in-person voting. While their in-person rates were 10 points *below* the control group in 2018, they were 5 points *more* likely to vote in person in 2022—a roughly 15-point swing in their propensity to vote in person relative to the controls, with whom they moved largely in parallel between 2010 and 2018.

When we estimate the causal effects of rejections on the probability of voting in-person in the general election (depicted in figure 9.8), we again find that rejections led to massive effects on subsequent voting behavior. Voters whose applications were rejected were more than 35 percentage points more likely to vote in person than similar voters whose application was accepted. For ballot rejections, the effect is more than 15 points. Clearly, primary election rejections

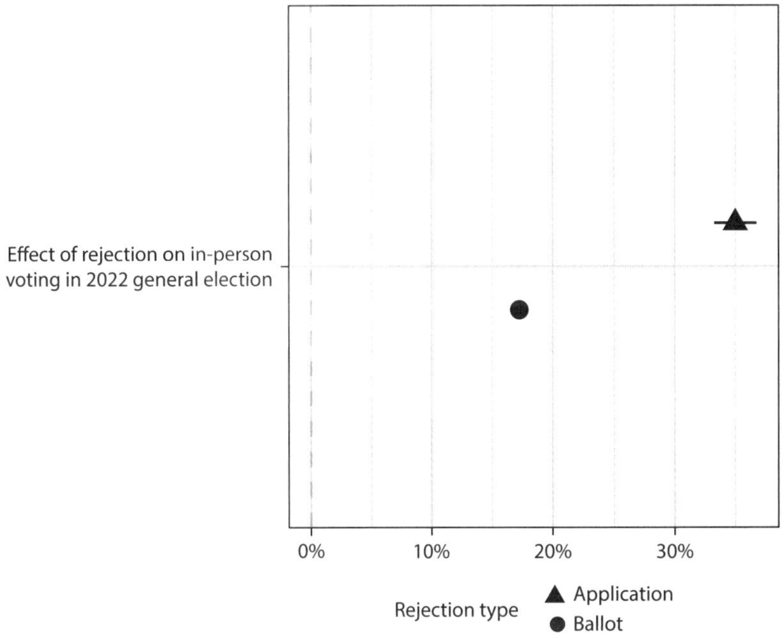

FIGURE 9.8. Effect of Rejections in the Primary on Vote Mode in 2022 General Election, Conditional on Voting

of both kinds had major implications for not only whether voters cast their ballots in the fall of 2022 but how they did so.

We have good reason to think that the voters who switched to voting in person in the 2022 general election would *rather* have voted by mail—after all, they tried to vote that way in the primary election. Political scientists might say that these voters switched to a voting method that was "costlier" for them. A voter with mobility issues may find it substantially more difficult to travel to a polling place than to request and complete an absentee ballot. Such voters may be willing to undergo a more onerous voting process when the election is perceived as important (as the 2022 general election undoubtedly was for most voters). But when the stakes are lower—such as, say, a presidential primary that had been effectively decided by the time Texans got a chance to vote—raising the costs of voting may have even larger consequences for how voters behave.

To find out, using the same approach we employ to look at the 2022 general election, we examine voting behavior in the 2024 Texas primary that occurred almost exactly two years after the voter's ballot or application was rejected in the wake of SB1's implementation. This approach allows us to examine voting patterns over a longer period, which provides insight into how substantial the effects of rejections might be on future voting. For instance, we might expect that the lower turnout and higher propensity to vote in person stemming from rejection that we observed in the 2022 general election may be less prevalent two years later. With more time to fade into the voter's memory, the negative feelings associated with the rejection might be a less powerful latent force. Moreover, the "mechanical" aspect of an application rejection in 2022 no longer applies in 2024, since voters must reapply for mail ballots every year regardless of previous status. Finally, with two more years to adapt to SB1—and with a rejection from which to learn—voters may have adjusted their behavior to avoid having their application or ballot rejected.

On the other hand, there are also good reasons to expect the downstream effects of a rejection in the 2022 primary to linger two years later. For example, voters may have felt that the 2024 primary mattered less than the 2022 general. In the 2024 primary, no statewide primaries were won with less than a 40 point margin (including the Republican and Democratic presidential primaries), and only a handful of congressional primaries were competitive. While we expect that many of the individuals who opted not to vote in the 2022 general might have failed to cast a ballot in 2024, it is also possible that some of the individuals motivated to vote in a "costly" way in 2022 (that is, in person) may have determined that the stakes of the 2024 primary were not high enough to justify the additional burdens they accepted for a general election. In short, even voters who did turn out in the 2022 midterm may have stayed home in a primary election they deemed unimportant.

Our analysis provides a clear answer: The effect of a ballot or application rejection was not confined to 2022. To the contrary, two years after the primary in which these voters experienced a rejection, they were *still* less likely to vote. Figure 9.9 illustrates that the turnout of these voters decreased more relative to 2020 than among those who were not prevented from voting by mail. The negative effect of an application rejection on turnout is slightly smaller in 2024 than in the 2022 general election, perhaps due to the absence of a mechanical disenfranchisement. However, as was the case for the 2022 general, the effect of an application rejection in 2024 is larger than that of a ballot rejection. The trend in figure 9.9 therefore strongly suggests that the downstream

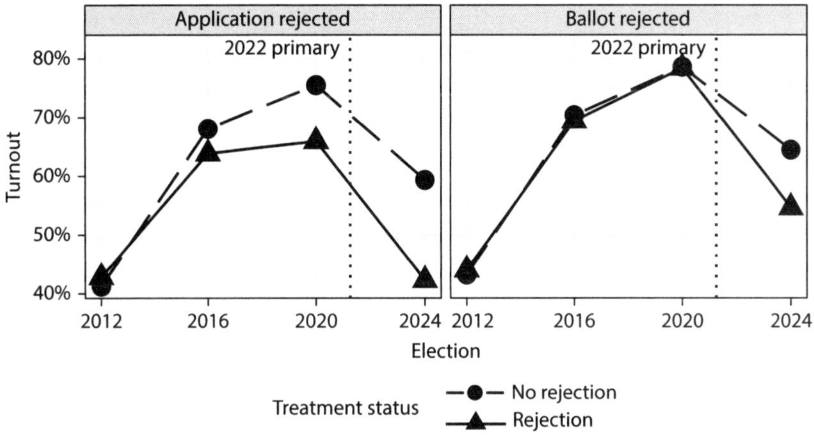

FIGURE 9.9. Primary Election Turnout by 2022 Primary Application Status
Note: 'Application Rejected' panel includes all individuals who submitted a mail ballot application for the 2022 primary. 'Ballot Rejected' panel includes those who submitted a mail ballot in the 2022 primary. In all cases, 'No Rejection' refers to voters who did not have an application or ballot rejected in the primary of 2022; the inverse is true for the 'Rejection' voters. In other words, these groups remain constant across time.

effects of rejections in the 2022 primary were quite durable, and in the manner we expected: Application rejections appear to be a more powerful force shaping subsequent voting behavior.

As usual, we next turn to models that return the causal effect of rejections on turnout in the 2024 primary.[49] Turnout in primary elections is somewhat more complicated to model than in general elections: a given primary might be competitive for only a single party, for instance. For a discussion of how we approach these challenges, interested readers can see the Methodological Appendix.

Figure 9.10 confirms the enduring power of rejections to shape future turnout decisions. Even two years after the primary election in which voters' mail application or mail ballot was rejected, they were still far less likely to participate than voters whose applications or ballots were accepted. Once again, application rejections had a generally stronger depressive effect on turnout in the 2024 primary. However, the effect of a ballot rejection on turnout in the 2024 primary was actually *larger* than the one we observed in the 2022 general election, growing to about 7 points (compared to about 1.5 points). Of course, this difference may be due to the fact that ballot rejections impact future

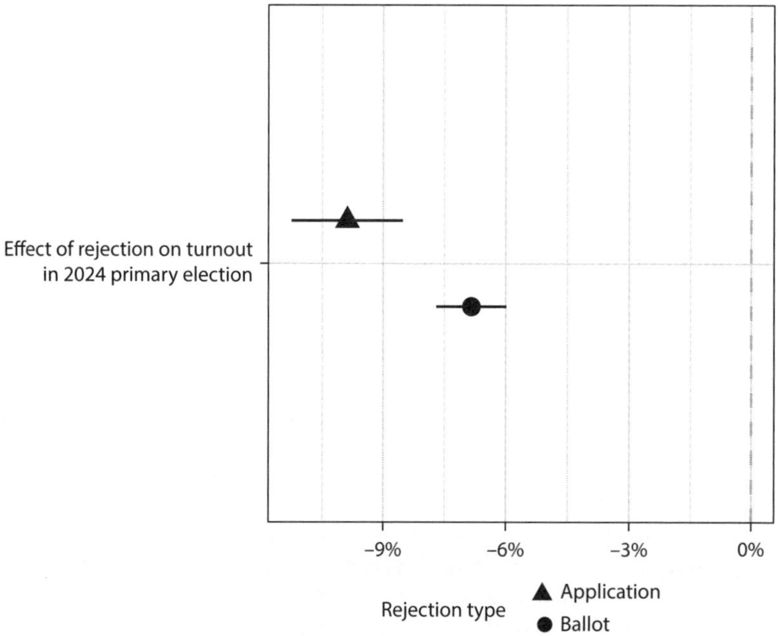

FIGURE 9.10. Effect of Rejections in the 2022 Primary on 2024 Primary Election Turnout

participation in primaries more than in generals. Nevertheless, this growth is striking.

Finally, we examine whether the effects of a rejection on *how* people vote lingered into the 2024 primary. Figure 9.11 depicts the trend in in-person voting rates from 2012 to 2024, broken out by whether the voter's application or ballot was rejected in the spring of 2022. As we show for the 2022 general election, both types of rejection pushed those who did participate away from mail voting and into their physical polling places. Here we see similar effects for application and ballot rejections on turnout. Figure 9.12 confirms that these results are indeed statistically significant. Voters whose mail applications and mail ballots were rejected in the spring of 2022 were about 14 points more likely to vote in person—if they voted at all.

What do these effects mean in real terms? In figure 9.13 we chart the turnout behavior of the approximately 5,500 voters whose application was rejected in the 2022 primary. Of these voters, a clear majority of 4,144 ultimately managed to vote in the 2022 general election, and a majority of *those* voters (2,170) cast ballots again in the 2024 primary. For the 1,354 voters who did not vote in the

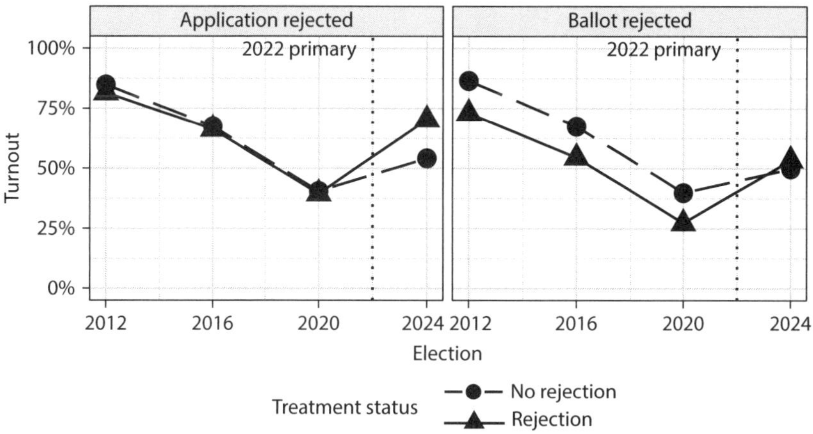

FIGURE 9.11. Share of Ballots Cast in Person, Presidential Primary Elections
Note: 'Application Rejected' panel includes all individuals who submitted a mail ballot application for the 2022 primary. 'Ballot Rejected' panel includes those who submitted a mail ballot in the 2022 primary. In all cases, 'No Rejection' refers to voters who did not have an application or ballot rejected in the primary of 2022; the inverse is true for the 'Rejection' voters. In other words, these groups remain constant across time.

2022 general election, however, there is a continued trend: Only 154 of these voters cast ballots in 2024. Put another way, roughly 22% of voters who unsuccessfully requested a mail ballot in the 2022 primary ultimately voted in *none* of the three elections we have examined here.

Savvy readers may note that in our discussion of the lingering effects of Texas's voter ID law in chapter 8, we found similar long-term implications for voters who have a negative experience in a given election. There is a crucial difference between that analysis and the one we present in this chapter, however: Voters who were ensnared in the voter ID law were often low-propensity voters who do not typically cast ballots in all elections. Here, we have shown effects for voters who attempted to vote in a partisan primary. Primary turnout is typically below 50%;[50] people looking to cast a primary ballot are among the most committed voters in the electorate. In fact, some 85% of these primary voters cast a ballot in *each* of the 2016, 2018, and 2020 general elections. The magnitude of depressive turnout effects we have observed following a mail ballot or application rejection is therefore especially concerning, and it speaks to the power that administrative decisions can have over the future voting decisions of even the most engaged citizens.

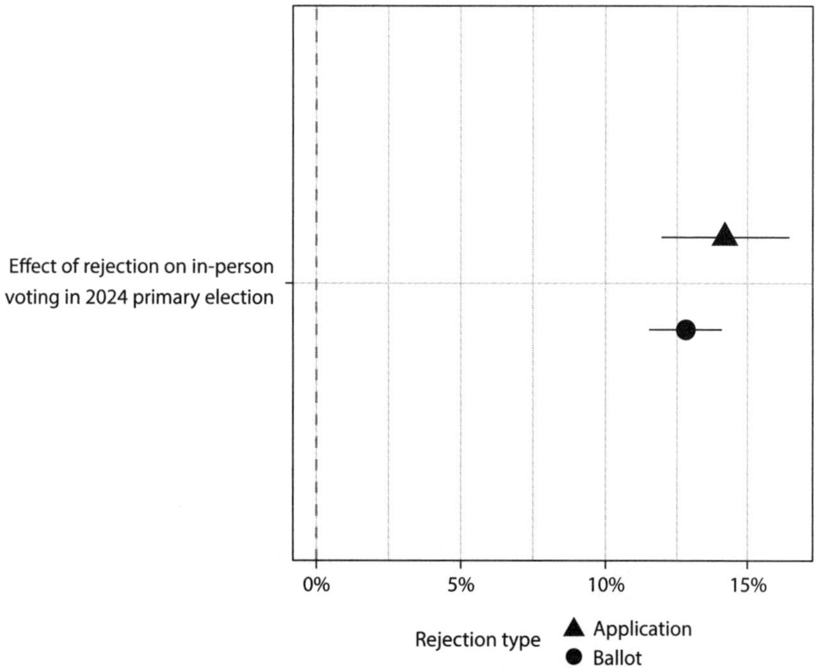

FIGURE 9.12. Effect of Rejections in the Primary on Vote Mode in 2024 Primary, Conditional on Voting

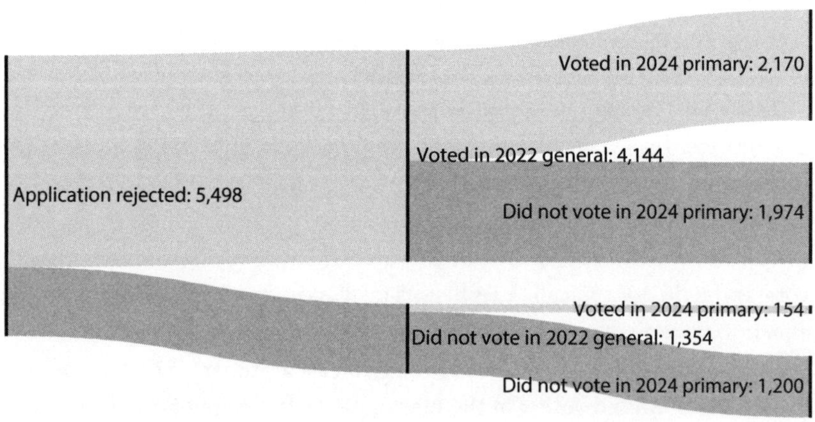

FIGURE 9.13. Subsequent Turnout for Voters with an SB1-Related Application Rejection

---

In the years leading up to the 2020 presidential election, white voters were a little more likely than minority Americans to vote by mail. This changed during the COVID-19 pandemic, which fueled unprecedented changes in American election administration. Suddenly, with a shift in who voted by mail, restrictions on absentee ballots offered a way to systematically increase the cost of voting for nonwhite citizens. This was not predicted in 2013, to say nothing of 1965. And yet, as we stress time and again, the emergence of these unforeseen devices with which to violate racial and ethnic minorities' access to the vote are exactly what Section 5 was designed to stop.

Taken together, the evidence from SB1 lays bare a number of facts about voting in Texas and raises broader concerns about administrative changes enacted in formerly covered states since the *Shelby County* ruling. First, there is still real concern about racially equitable access to the ballot box in the United States: Nonwhite voters had a ballot rejection rate roughly 5 points higher than white voters in Texas's 2022 primary election. And these effects lingered: Although the mechanical cost of voting in the 2024 presidential primary was not higher for voters who experienced a rejection in 2022, they nevertheless turned out at far lower rates than similar voters who were not disenfranchised. Finally, the clear mode shift among those who *did* cast a ballot indicates that studying turnout in isolation—without attending to voters incurring greater participation costs by switching from their preferred vote mode—underestimates the costs imposed by these new laws. Our results raise important questions about the effects of the recent wave of restrictive voting legislation in the United States, as well as their potential to linger.

These questions are especially important because by the time of the 2022 general election, Texas sorted out the ballot envelope issue and partially reduced rejection rates. But, in the 2022 general election, rejection rates were still extremely high: 3.4% of mail ballots were rejected—double the rejection rate in the 2018 general election. By comparison, the rejection rate for mail ballots in other states increased by less than 0.1% between 2018 and 2022.[51] While the 2022 primary's rejection rates in excess of 10% were not repeated in the general, mail ballots clearly continued to cause problems that fall.

This chapter makes clear that, despite the (relatively) lower rejection rates in the 2022 general election, the effects of SB1 were neither immaterial nor confined to a single primary election. Our analysis of state records shows that more than 10% of individuals who began the mail voting process in the

2022 primary were prevented from doing so by an SB1-related rejection. These numbers are enormous when put in national context. While the US Election Assistance Commission does not publish data about primaries (or about application rejections), its data can nonetheless provide context: Outside Texas, 98.9% of counties had rejection rates below 10% in the 2022 general election. The primary rejection rates from Texas were, then, an order of magnitude higher than national averages.

The effects of SB1 were also not limited to the 2022 primary. Individuals who had their application rejected in the primary were 16 percentage points less likely to vote that fall because of the rejection. The comparable figure for those whose ballots were rejected was about 1.5 points. Importantly, these effects were durable and, for those whose ballots were rejected, considerably larger two full years later. In the 2024 presidential primary, voters who had a rejection in 2022 were still between 7 and 10 points less likely to cast a ballot than they would have been absent SB1. It is important to stress (again) that these effect sizes are enormous. Our finding that an application rejection reduced turnout by more than 16 points is virtually unprecedented in the literature; that effects are as high as 10 points two years after the rejection is similarly striking.

SB1 continues to face challenges in court. On August 17, 2023, federal district court judge Xavier Rodriguez struck down the portion of SB1 requiring officials to reject applications and ballots when the voter's supplied identification number did not match the one listed on their registration form.[52] The State of Texas appealed this decision, and in December 2023 the US 5th Circuit stayed Judge Rodriguez's decision pending its full consideration of the ruling.[53] As of early 2026, despite weighing more heavily on minority voters, the requirement for the identification numbers on ballots and applications to match the registration database remains in effect.

Epilogue

THE SOUL OF AMERICA

> Ordinary people with extraordinary vision can redeem the soul of America by getting in what I call good trouble, necessary trouble. Voting and participating in the democratic process are key. The vote is the most powerful nonviolent change agent you have in a democratic society. You must use it because it is not guaranteed. You can lose it.
>
> —JOHN LEWIS, POSTHUMOUS ESSAY PUBLISHED IN *NEW YORK TIMES*, JULY 30, 2020

WHEN THE 117th Congress convened on January 3, 2021, it was a big day for Democrats. The 2020 election narrowed Democrats' majority in the House, but Nancy Pelosi still held the Speaker's gavel. In the Senate elections, Democrats had picked up three seats, drawing even with Republicans. Because Joe Biden had won the presidential election, Vice President Kamala Harris broke that tie. For the first time since *Shelby County,* Democrats held unified power over federal legislation.

Election law was literally the top item on their agenda. Democrats' first action was on a bill designed to make sweeping reforms to election administration: HR 1, which was ultimately dubbed the Freedom to Vote Act. Democrats had passed the bill in the House during the previous Congress, but it had died in the Senate. Now, with full control of the government, they were ready to make another attempt. Among other changes, H.R. 1 would require all states to implement automatic voter registration, same-day voter registration, and at least two weeks of early in-person voting. It also required states to allow 16- and 17-year-olds the opportunity to preregister (though they would still have to wait until they turned 18 to vote). HR 1 criminalized interfering with voter registration, intimidating voters, or disseminating misinformation about how to vote, and created new voter list maintenance procedures that states would be required to follow. The law would also make Election Day a national holiday and featured several campaign finance reforms as well. It was a far-reaching effort to expand ballot access and equity. The bill cleared its first hurdle in March, passing in the US House once more.

But HR 1 was not the only election bill on the Democrats' legislative docket. They soon followed with HR 4—also called the John R. Lewis Voting Rights Advancement Act of 2021 (VRAA)—in honor of Representative Lewis, who had died the year before. The VRAA revised Section 4(b) of the Voting Rights Act, updating the coverage formula and restoring preclearance. The proposed coverage formula was a direct response to the *Shelby County* decision, in which Chief Justice Roberts wrote that the formula used in the 2006 reauthorization kept "the focus on decades-old data relevant to decades-old problems, rather than current data reflecting current needs." Rather than rely on a static formula with 50-year-old criteria like the one the Court had rejected, HR 4 proposed a dynamic coverage formula that would use states' and sub-jurisdictions' recent conduct to determine whether they would be placed on the preclearance list.

The formula would count the number of voting rights violations within a jurisdiction over the previous 25 years. A "violation" would occur when a court ruled that racial disenfranchisement or vote dilution had taken place or when other administrative action revealed evidence of discrimination. States would be placed on the preclearance list for 10 years if jurisdictions therein committed 15 cumulative violations over the preceding 25-year period, but this threshold was reduced to 10 violations if the state itself was guilty of one. Individual jurisdictions such as counties or towns could be placed on the coverage list, too, if they committed three violations over the same time frame. Jurisdictions would then emerge from coverage as their violations receded into the past. In an important caveat, however, the bill also contemplated specific "known discriminatory practices"—such as redrawing electoral districts, implementing at-large elections, or moving polling places—that would be subject to preclearance for all jurisdictions so long as a racial or language minority group made up a sizable share of the jurisdiction's population, regardless of whether it had committed any recent violations.

The development of a dynamic coverage formula was a positive step toward addressing the concerns that the *Shelby County* majority justices had expressed. But when weighed against the formula that had been struck down in that decision, the proposed coverage formula demonstrated that perhaps things had not changed so dramatically in covered jurisdictions over the VRA's lifetime. As it turned out, the list of states that would be fully covered under the dynamic 2021 formula was remarkably similar to the old one. According to congressional testimony from Peyton McCrary, who served as the DOJ's in-house historian from 1990 until 2016, two states fully covered under the original formula (Alaska and Arizona) would not be covered under the new one, but six (Alabama, Georgia, Louisiana, Mississippi, South Carolina, and Texas) would retain their fully covered status.[1] Moreover, Florida and North Carolina—partially covered states where certain individual counties were covered prior to 2013—would switch to fully covered status, while Virginia would switch from fully covered to partially covered status.[2] McCrary further testified that four additional states would be partially covered, due to a single county being covered within them: California (Los Angeles County), Illinois (Cook County), New York (Westchester County), and Ohio (Cuyahoga County).

The House passed HR 4 along party lines in August 2021; the fight then moved to the US Senate, where it faced much longer odds. Readers may recall from chapter 1 that the Senate was known in the mid-twentieth century as the "graveyard" of civil rights because of the strength of the filibuster, which allowed a single senator to hold the floor indefinitely to "talk a bill to death." Only a cloture vote supported by 66 senators could break the filibuster. For decades, Senator Strom Thurmond held the record for the longest filibuster as he tried in vain to derail the 1957 Civil Rights Act.

But Thurmond's efforts did not lead to calls to reform the legislative filibuster. Indeed, in some key ways, the filibuster is even stronger today than it was back then. Until the 1970s, senators had to actually make good on their threat to filibuster; if they wanted to stall a bill, they had to stand until they could speak no longer. But the Senate changed its rules in 1974, ending the "talking filibuster" (but reducing the number of votes for cloture to 60). Today, so long as 41 Senators simply *threaten* to join a filibuster, the legislation is effectively dead; no debate actually occurs. This rule substantially reduces the costs of obstruction and means essentially that outside limited exceptions for things like judicial nominees and budget acts, virtually nothing can pass through the US Senate without the support of 60 members. Given the divisive political climate these days, that is a tall order. In November 2021, the VRAA and HR 1 (which had by this point been rolled into one large Senate bill) failed to garner the 60 votes necessary to move the bill forward, and things were looking pretty bleak.

To many Democrats, seeing HR 1 and the VRAA through the Senate was a matter of extreme urgency. Newly elected Democratic senator Raphael Warnock of Georgia described his state as "ground zero" for the fight over voting rights: "This is a defining moral moment. It is the most important thing we can do this Congress."[3] Warnock was not alone in his assessment of the bills' importance, but the voting rights legislation had little chance under the prevailing rules and—with the exception of Senator Lisa Murkowski (R-AK)[4]—unified Republican opposition in the Senate. President Joe Biden called for the Senate to hold a real debate on the merits of the bill, followed by a vote.

Biden's push was part of a growing effort to change filibuster rules for the voting rights bills, which many other Democrats joined. There was nothing particularly unusual about amending the filibuster in this way: Between 1969 and 2014, the majority party had made more than 150 exceptions to the filibuster rule.[5] In historical context, the Democrats' proposal was relatively modest. It did not involve eliminating the filibuster entirely, or even reducing the number of votes needed to end one. Instead, for consideration of the voting rights legislation, the Democrats wanted to bring back the talking filibuster. Senators opposed to the package of election reforms in the two bills would still be entitled to unlimited debate on the issue, but they would have to stand and have the debate—and when the debate ended, a vote would follow. Senator Bernie Sanders (I-VT) summarized the proposal this way:

> That is the vote to change Senate rules and establish a talking filibuster—a process which gives the minority an enormous amount of time to object to legislation and voice their concerns. The minority, whether it is a Democratic minority or a Republican minority, would have days and days and days to slow the process down and to rally the American people around their ideas, but they would not have forever. At the end of the time allotted, a majority vote would prevail, which, in my view, is what a democratic society is all about.[6]

It takes a simple majority of senators to change filibuster rules. In an evenly divided Senate, the Democrats could not afford to lose a single vote, but Senators Kyrsten Sinema (D-AZ) and Joe Manchin (D-WV) were reluctant to go along. Biden planned a personal visit to Capitol Hill in a last-ditch effort to bring them aboard. Shortly before that visit occurred, Senator Sinema surprised her party and the nation by unexpectedly taking to the floor of the Senate to oppose changing filibuster rules. While she supported the efforts to restore the Voting Rights Act, Sinema claimed, she would not support changing the rules to require Senators opposed to the effort to publicly debate it. According to Sinema, doing so would "worsen the underlying disease of division infecting our country."[7] Both Sinema and Manchin voted against the rules change the following week. Still lacking the 60 required votes to move ahead, the Democrats' voting rights package died again.

Throughout this book, we focus largely on the birth, life, and death of the coverage formula made operational in Sections 4(b) and 5 of the Voting Rights Act. Today, more than a decade after the Supreme Court's ruling in *Shelby County v. Holder*, Section 5's preclearance power remains mothballed. The John R. Lewis Voting Rights Advancement Act was reintroduced in the 118th and 119th Congresses, but failed to move forward. To date, the Supreme Court's suggestion that Congress "draft another formula based on current conditions" remains unheeded. We present ample evidence in this book that the results of this delay have been disastrous, leading to negative impacts for minority voters in terms of ballot access and vote dilution—the two chief concerns that the VRA has long sought to address. Relative to white voters, turnout rates among Americans of color have declined dramatically in the places once subject to strict oversight of their elections. We also show that in many of the same places, minority voters' power was often diluted via district maps that federal courts or the DOJ ultimately judged as at least "likely" to be discriminatory. The annexation practices of formerly covered cities further fuel this problem. We find, in other words, little evidence that threats to minority voters' ballot access or their ability to elect candidates of their choosing have disappeared in the formerly covered jurisdictions.

Section 5 reflected an understanding that far from withering away, the forces that had fueled discriminatory voting practices were likely to drive new and ever-innovative practices. All the way back in 1965, Attorney General Nicholas Katzenbach testified that preclearance was designed to proactively combat the decades-long pattern in which states and localities continually "devise[d] whole new methods of discrimination."[8] In *Shelby County*, however, the Supreme Court reasoned that this kind of nefarious policy innovation was no longer so substantial that ongoing monitoring was warranted. The Court could therefore not justify the continued disparate treatment of covered and noncovered jurisdictions.

In many ways, Section 5 was a policy well tailored for the uniquely localized nature of election administration in the United States. Preclearance allowed local actors to draw their own school board districts, site their own polling places, and maintain their own voter rolls so long as it was not done in a discriminatory way. Preclearance thus was faithful to both America's long history of local control over elections and to the Fifteenth Amendment. *Shelby County* upended this balance, increasing the authority delegated to localities with histories of discrimination—and at a time when institutions like local media are less capable of aiding accountability than ever before. As much as state-level policies can weaken democratic institutions,[9] the threats arising from a system in which a huge majority of administrative changes happen at the substate level are potentially an order of magnitude greater.

The analyses presented in this book support this troubling conclusion. We have found consistent evidence that, once more, the absence of preclearance has led to the rise of discriminatory practices. This is true with respect to so-called first-generation practices that even liberal justices in the *Shelby County* minority thought had been relegated to history—such as voter registration and removals. However, we also find that the decision has allowed for the implementation of other policies whose results have raised higher hurdles for minority voters. Our analysis of data from Texas suggests that this is the case not only for voter ID laws (which were common but relatively new at the time *Shelby County* was decided) but also for practices that few would have seen in 2013 as an obvious trouble spot, such as mail voting procedures.

As we show in chapters 5 and 6, the cumulative effects of these policies have been to reduce minority representation in our political system, relative to what would have happened in these regions had *Shelby County* never been handed down. In most counties, the share of the electorate made up of minority voters has decreased; if preclearance were still in effect, we estimate that Americans of color would have made up a majority of voters in 15 more lower-house state legislative districts throughout the fully covered states in 2022. And the maps that have been drawn have made the votes cast by voters of color less meaningful, given vote dilution tactics at levels ranging from congressional maps to local offices.

But the baseline we measure the effects of *Shelby County* against is not a rosy one. When we say that the end of preclearance made the situation for minority

Americans worse, we do not mean to imply that things would have been excellent otherwise. As we show in chapter 5, the turnout gap has grown much more quickly in formerly covered counties; but it has also grown alarmingly even in parts of the country that were not released from preclearance in 2013. As Kevin T. Morris and Coryn Grange show in a recent report from the Brennan Center, Americans of color would have cast an additional 9 million more ballots in the 2020 election if they had turned out at the same rate as white voters—and the gap is only growing.[10] And, while we show that discriminatory practices and policies have become especially prevalent in formerly covered states, democratic backsliding is not confined to these regions. For instance, states like Wisconsin and Indiana have also passed voter ID laws in recent years similar to that of Texas. Kansas and other states have led the way in purging voters from the rolls, as chapter 7 reveals. More broadly, 29 states passed restrictive voting laws between the 2020 and 2024 presidential elections.[11] While the once-covered states were overrepresented in this group (11 of the 15 states required to preclear state policies enacted at least one restrictive policy), 18 out of 35 noncovered states—more than half—made voting more difficult. From school board districts in Ferguson, Missouri,[12] to the state of Nevada,[13] more than three dozen policies in noncovered states have been challenged since *Shelby County* was handed down.[14] We are thus forced to conclude not just that *Shelby County* caused retrogression in the formerly covered regions but also that it *accelerated* the backsliding we likely would have seen anyway.

Nearly everywhere we have looked, we have consistently found that *Shelby County* allowed old problems to reappear and new ones to emerge. Preclearance could have headed off these problems; instead, the Court's action has introduced a new generation of Americans to the limitations of the litigation-first Whac-a-Mole game that DOJ lawyers from the mid-twentieth century knew all too well. With Section 5 no longer available, the only course of action available to minority voters seeking relief from discriminatory policies is the slow grind of Section 2 litigation.

Section 2 is a poor substitute for Section 5, to be sure, but that does not mean that we should ignore its power to negate discriminatory voting practices. Recall the image of Section 2 as a sword to Section 5's shield. That sword has been well used. Legal researcher Peyton McCrary identified some 139 adjudicated Section 2 violations during the quarter century ending in 2021.[15] We stress that these are likely quite conservative estimates of the number of policies stopped or overturned by Section 2, since they do not include policies (like the closure of polling places we discuss in chapter 5 in Randolph County, Georgia) that were changed after lawyers merely *threatened* to bring a Section 2 lawsuit. Section 2 has therefore clearly been crucial for protecting minority voters in its own right.

But Section 2 of the Voting Rights Act has also come under tremendous attack from federal courts (including the Supreme Court) in recent years. The most substantial of these came in *Brnovich v. Democratic National Committee.*[16] In *Brnovich,* the justices considered an appeal of the 9th Circuit Court's ruling that two Arizona policies were racially discriminatory. The first required ballots cast in the wrong precinct to be wholly discarded, including votes for offices like president or governor that showed up on every ballot in every precinct in the state. The 9th Circuit judges held that this practice violated Section 2 because it had a racially disparate effect, falling more heavily on Native, Black, and Latino voters. The second policy barred community members from collecting their neighbors' mail ballots and returning them, a practice common on Native American reservations where citizens often live far from polling places and have limited mail services. The 9th Circuit struck down this law as well, finding that it had been enacted with racially discriminatory intent.[17]

In a 5–4 decision, the Supreme Court overruled both of the 9th Circuit's rulings. In so doing, the Court also rewired how Section 2 functions in at least two important ways. Recall from chapter 4 that during the 1982 reauthorization of the VRA, Congress amended the statute's language to render illegal any voting policy that "*resulted in* a denial or abridgment of the right . . . to vote on account of race or color" (emphasis added). This results test was added in direct response to the Supreme Court's opinion in *City of Mobile v. Bolden* that only *intentionally* discriminatory policies violated the VRA. Writing for the majority in *Brnovich* however, Justice Samuel Alito offered an extremely narrow interpretation of Section 2, signaling that the Court would tolerate election policies that resulted in worse outcomes for nonwhite voters, so long as the gap between them and white voters was not very large.

Justice Alito held that in considering whether a Section 2 violation occurred, "the size of any disparity matters." In Alito's view, the racial disparities resulting from Arizona's policies were simply too small to warrant judicial intervention. Roughly 1% of ballots cast by nonwhite voters were thrown out by the out-of-precinct rule, compared to a rate of 0.5% for white voters. Although nonwhite voters were twice as likely to be affected, Alito was much more focused on the voter counts in each category than the rate. Alito went so far as to say that anyone characterizing the rejection rate among minority voters as double that of white voters (despite relatively simple underlying math) was engaging in "statistical manipulation." At the same time, Justice Alito referred to the dissenting justices' focus on disparate impact as a "radical project."

The Voting Rights Act does not include an exemption for "small" racially disparate impacts; with *Brnovich*, the Court appears to have created one. This distinction is important in more than just a legal sense. Readers will note that in several of the policy areas we explore in part II, even though we show racially disparate effects, it could be argued that the raw number of affected voters is small. In the first Texas election where federal courts required voters to file paperwork when they lacked compliant identification, roughly 16,000 people did so. In some annexations, only a few hundred residents might be added. Likewise, a voter purge in a small county could affect a relatively small number of people in absolute terms. But, as we show in chapter 5, the cumulative effect of thousands of policy changes—many affecting so small a number of voters that they might escape attention entirely—amount to a massive aggregate effect. If the federal judiciary is willing to overlook voting practices that disadvantage "just" a small number of minority voters, this problem will only grow, and Section 2's power will continue to wither.

The Supreme Court's opinion in *Brnovich* also undermined Section 2 in another way. When considering Section 2 claims, Justice Alito wrote, "the degree to which a voting rule departs from what was standard practice when Section 2 was amended in 1982 is a relevant consideration." Although more than 75% of Arizonans typically use no-excuse absentee voting today, the practice was not widely utilized in 1982. Applying this logic, Alito therefore concluded that Arizona's restrictions on mail ballot collection merited less protection under Section 2. Alito's framework substantially constrains the universe of policies subject to future Section 2 litigation.

At the same time, Section 2 is needed now more than ever. Section 2 could never have fully repaired the breach left by *Shelby County*, but it is difficult to overstate how important it can be in slowing the spread of discriminatory election policies in formerly covered jurisdictions since the Court ended preclearance. In the 12 years prior to *Shelby County*, just a third of Section 2 cases that were decided by federal judges arose from covered jurisdictions. Since the Court's ruling, that number has jumped to more than 54%.[18] Similarly, two-thirds of Section 2 cases brought by the DOJ since *Shelby County* have originated in formerly covered jurisdictions.[19] The *Brnovich* decision came at just the moment when Section 2 was already groaning under the increased weight imposed by *Shelby County*. By limiting Section 2's scope, *Brnovich* will further reduce the VRA's ability to thwart vote denial discrimination in voting practices.

In the years since *Shelby County*, the Court has also made it considerably more difficult to bring vote dilution claims under the Voting Rights Act through a series of other cases. The first of these, *Rucho v. Common Cause*,[20] did not appear to have much to do with the Voting Rights Act at first glance. The case turned on whether *partisan* (not racial) gerrymandering violated the Constitution. After a partisan gerrymander in North Carolina, Republican congressional candidates there were likely to win 10 of 13 seats, despite winning just 55% of votes cast in congressional races in 2014 and 49% in 2012.[21] Democratic plaintiffs brought suit in federal court, arguing that the decided partisan lean of North Carolina's districts violated their constitutional right to equitable representation.

A similar case was brought in Maryland by Republican voters; in that state, just one of eight congressional districts was won by a Republican in 2012, despite Republican candidates winning 33% of the votes. The district courts agreed with the plaintiffs in both cases,[22] but the states appealed the decisions to the US Supreme Court. While the Court had expressed an openness to adjudicating the constitutionality of partisan gerrymanders the previous year,[23] the retirement of Associate Justice Anthony Kennedy shifted the balance of the Court, fueling uncertainty about how it would view partisan gerrymandering in the new cases.[24] In a 5–4 decision, the Supreme Court neither affirmed nor overturned the lower courts' finding that the partisan gerrymanders violated voters' constitutional rights. Instead, in an opinion authored by Chief Justice Roberts, the Court held that the problem of partisan gerrymandering is inherently "political" in nature and, thus, beyond the jurisdiction of federal courts. The federal judiciary, the majority argued, has no role to play in overturning even the most flagrant partisan gerrymanders.[25]

The upshot of *Rucho* was that addressing the harms of partisan gerrymanders was beyond the reach of federal courts, even while racial gerrymanders remained illegal under the Voting Rights Act. But of course, race and party cannot be separated neatly, especially in the Southern United States. Social scientists have known for decades that racial identity and partisan identity are tightly linked.[26] Put differently, most racial gerrymanders also have partisan effects, since minority voters tend to prefer Democratic candidates. *Rucho* thus introduced a powerful incentive for states to cloak racial gerrymanders as partisan ones: If a state could convince a court that a map that favored Republicans was purely partisan—and not driven by racial considerations—the federal court would have no say over its constitutionality.

It was out of this context, from once-fully-covered South Carolina, where racially polarized voting is higher than just about anywhere else in the United States, that the next attack on Section 2 of the VRA would arise. After it was narrowly won by Democrat Joe Cunningham (Black voters' preferred candidate) in the 2018 midterms, South Carolina sought to tilt the balance of its 1st Congressional District in favor of Republicans. To do so, during the redistricting process following the 2020 census, mapmakers in South Carolina split Charleston County across the 1st and 6th Congressional Districts. White Democratic voters remained behind in the old 1st District, while the heavily Black and Democratic cities of Charleston and North Charleston were drawn into the 6th District.

The NAACP and other groups sued the state, arguing that Black voters had been targeted during the redistricting fight in violation of their constitutional rights. The federal district court unanimously agreed, finding that the state had improperly relied on racial data when determining which voters to draw into which district,[27] and the state appealed to the US Supreme Court. In a surprising move, the High Court overturned the district court's ruling in 2024. Writing for the six-justice majority, Associate Justice Samuel Alito held that because South Carolina's argument that it was merely pursuing *partisan* ends was plausible, the state deserved deference. To find that a state engaged in racial gerrymandering, Alito wrote, is to accuse the state of "offensive and demeaning conduct,"[28] and courts ought therefore to avoid such a conclusion if at all possible. In other words, if a state's actions *might* have been driven by partisan considerations alone, the court *must* find that they were—even if the Court considers other explanations for the state's behavior more compelling. And should the Court find that a state engaged in partisan and not racial gerrymandering, there is no remedy to provide because of the *Rucho* decision handed down in 2019. Especially in the states once covered by Section 5 of the VRA, the tight links between race and partisanship will mean that states and localities can claim that partisanship guided their actions in most cases of racial gerrymandering in the years to come, leaving federal courts incapable of providing remedies for voters of color.

Eleven years after *Shelby County*, the standards in South Carolina and other covered jurisdictions have been flipped on their head. No longer is the federal government examining changes to elections in places with a history of racial discrimination under the presumption that old poison might be in new bottles. Instead, the opposite is true: The federal government is required to begin from the presumption that these states are operating in good faith—a far cry indeed from the principles of the preclearance regime.

Other threats abound, and not just in the recent decision in *Louisiana v. Callais*, which, as previously noted, dramatically limited Section 2's protections against racially discriminatory districting. Following the 2020 redistricting cycle, the Arkansas State Conference of the NAACP and the Arkansas Public Policy Panel brought a lawsuit alleging that the new Arkansas state house district map discriminated against Black citizens. As in the cases in Alabama, Georgia, Louisiana, and Texas discussed in chapter 6, the plaintiffs argued that the plan diluted Black political power: 16.5% of the state's population was Black, but Black voters constituted an "effective majority" in just 11 of Arkansas's 100 house districts. The plaintiffs argued that the state should create five more majority-Black districts, bringing the proportion of opportunity seats in line with their share of the population.[29]

The State of Arkansas, however, seized on an aside from Justice Neil Gorsuch in a concurring opinion in *Brnovich* that had been joined by Justice Clarence Thomas. There, Gorsuch had addressed an issue that had not even been raised in the case. In Gorsuch's words, he wanted to "flag one thing" that the majority opinion had failed to take up: whether the plaintiffs in *Brnovich* were allowed to be there in the first place.[30] Private citizens and affiliated groups had brought Section 2 suits to challenge discriminatory practices for decades. To Gorsuch, however, whether anyone other than the US attorney general was allowed to sue states and localities for violating Section 2 of the Voting Rights Act was actually "an open question."

This opinion signaled that at least two justices were willing to revisit what had been to that point a bedrock principle of the Voting Rights Act. Since the first days of the 1960s, it has been clear that a litigation-only approach relying on the Department of Justice to bring suits was not enough. As the US

Commission on Civil Rights wrote in 1961, "Although the Civil Rights Division has been repeatedly increased in size and budget, and has concentrated its efforts in the voting field, it has not been able to prepare and file all the suits that appear warranted."[31] In chapter 2 we describe how the Supreme Court subsequently validated this view in its 1969 opinion in *Allen v. State Board of Elections*. In that case, the Court ruled that the VRA allowed a "private right of action" allowing citizens to sue the government for circumventing Section 5 (though the case was silent on the private right of action in Section 2 claims). Writing for the majority in *Allen*, Chief Justice Earl Warren recognized how important it was to maintain this avenue: "The achievement of the Act's laudable goal could be severely hampered . . . ," he wrote, "if each citizen were required to depend solely on litigation instituted at the discretion of the Attorney General." Warren continued, "The Attorney General has a limited staff, and often might be unable to uncover quickly new regulations and enactments passed at the varying levels of state government."[32]

We make this point countless times throughout the book in underscoring how difficult it is to enforce the VRA without preclearance. Coupled with the resources required for litigation, the sheer volume of election policies that jurisdictions enact each cycle makes it effectively impossible for a single outside entity to monitor them all—not to mention bringing all necessary claims to enforce Section 2. This is of course doubly true today, since litigation is now the only way to root out discriminatory voting policies. Since at least 1968—a year before the Supreme Court ruled in *Allen*—private plaintiffs have filed many hundreds of suits alleging Section 2 violations.[33] Many of them have been successful and have resulted in the termination of discriminatory election practices.

In short, the right to private action had been fully accepted for more than half a century when Gorsuch opened the door a crack. In defending its districting plan, Arkansas now tried to kick that door in. In addition to trying to convince the federal judiciary that its maps were not in fact illegal, Arkansas endeavored to throw the case out entirely by claiming that the VRA actually did *not* allow a right to private action. The plaintiffs could not win their case, the state said, because they were not allowed to bring a claim under Section 2 in the first place.

History and case law notwithstanding, the US District Court for the Eastern District of Arkansas agreed with the state at trial, reading the VRA as not allowing a private right of action. A split three-judge panel of the 8th Circuit affirmed this decision on appeal, and the entire 8th Circuit Court refused to rehear it en banc. This settles the matter in the 8th Circuit for now. There are 22 million Americans living in the seven states that compose the 8th Circuit: Arkansas, Iowa, Minnesota, Missouri, Nebraska, North Dakota, and South Dakota. These states are home to more than 10% of the nation's Native American population as well. With the 8th Circuit's ruling, none of these states' citizens can initiate Section 2 claims to assert electoral discrimination; only the US attorney general can.[34]

This ruling contradicts not only Supreme Court precedent and decades of tradition but also the explicit stated intention of Congress. During the 1982 reauthorization of the Voting Rights Act—the same one that made clear that proving racially discriminatory *intent* was not necessary to overturn a discriminatory voting law—Congress also affirmed the private right of action under Section 2. Indeed, the legislative record leaves little doubt as to Congress's intent. As a Senate Judiciary Committee report from that reauthorization states, "The Committee reiterates the existence of the private right of action under Section 2, *as has been clearly intended by Congress since 1965*" (emphasis added).[35] None of that matters for 8th Circuit voters today. Legal action on this question is ongoing. Coupled with its decisions in other recent cases we describe throughout this book, Gorsuch's apparent willingness to revisit the private right of action leaves its fate in the Supreme Court anything but certain.[36] If the Court does rule that private citizens cannot bring Section 2 suits, the VRA's sword might be best considered a museum piece.

While we focuse extensively on the role of federal courts in undermining the power of the Voting Rights Act, the threats to the law's enforcement expanded even further in the opening months of 2025. With the beginning of Donald Trump's second term as president, the Department of Justice has all but walked away from protecting ballot access for minority voters. This move is no mere reflection of simple partisanship: Between 2001 and 2007, for instance, Republican president George W. Bush's DOJ objected to some 50 policies under Section 5 and brought 15 suits under Section 2. The DOJ in Democratic president Barack Obama's subsequent administration brought just five Section 2 suits—despite preclearance no longer being available for most of Obama's final term in office (which led to a greater necessity for Section 2 litigation). While there is some historical evidence that DOJ attorneys under both Republican and Democratic presidents strategically enforced the VRA in ways helpful to their party over the years,[37] the Civil Rights Division has largely been staffed by career attorneys committed to enforcing the Voting Rights Act and other federal civil rights legislation. Collectively, they have kept up this work more or less uninterrupted since Selma. That is, until now.

The new actions undertaken by the second Trump administration in early 2025 are entirely unprecedented. On the new administration's third day in office—two weeks before Attorney General Pam Bondi was confirmed by the Senate—the Department of Justice directed the Civil Rights Division to freeze all new and ongoing litigation.[38] The DOJ later removed all managers from the Voting Section and directed lawyers to dismiss all active cases.[39] As of May 2025 the Voting Section reportedly had just three lawyers working for it—a mere 10% of the staffing level just four months earlier, at the end of the Biden administration.[40] The DOJ has little capacity to initiate *any* Section 2 cases in the second Trump administration, not that it has expressed an interest in doing so: In May 2025 the DOJ dropped all pending Section 2 challenges. Given that private citizens in the 8th Circuit can longer bring suits against states and localities for violating Section 2 of the VRA, it is no exaggeration to say that the Voting Rights Act is effectively a dead letter for citizens living in the 8th Circuit's seven states.

However, it would be inaccurate to imply that the second Trump administration's DOJ has been *entirely* inactive on voting issues. The DOJ attorneys who remained on staff spent the early part of 2025 defending President Trump's executive order titled "Preserving and Protecting the Integrity of American Elections."[41] Among other things, the order would have required voters to demonstrate citizenship by showing a US passport, an Enhanced REAL ID, or an official military identification card to register to vote. A birth certificate would not suffice, because, the administration has argued elsewhere, being born on American soil does not itself confer citizenship.[42] A federal judge blocked this order via a preliminary injunction issued in April 2025, but litigation is ongoing.[43] Even so, this effort demonstrates a commitment to so-called reforms that, as we and others have argued, would disenfranchise far more eligible voters than the number of noncitizens they would keep from voting.

On May 28, 2025, the DOJ voting section finally brought the first lawsuit of the new Trump administration. This one was atypical, to say the least. In nearly every voting rights suit the DOJ had filed since 1965, the federal government had sought to block states from pursuing restrictive policies. Here, the federal government sued North Carolina not to protect the rights of minority voters but in an attempt to compel the state to kick voters off its rolls because their registrations were missing information the state had inadvertently failed to collect.[44] In stark contrast to its historical position in such cases, the DOJ wanted fewer voters in North Carolina.

In some ways, the United States is substantially more democratic today than it was when we begin our story, at the Colfax Courthouse on that fateful Easter Sunday of 1873. The time of mob lynchings has ended, and the Ku Klux Klan no longer engages in organized terror against Black Americans who simply wish to exercise their basic rights. The nefarious Jim Crow voting practices—literacy tests, grandfather clauses, white primaries, and the like—have been relegated to the dustbin of history. And over nearly 50 years, the Voting Rights Act and its subsequent reauthorizations ensured that neither they nor newer, novel policies could create conditions in which racial disenfranchisement or vote dilution would take root in any corner of America's political system. Since the VRA's passage, millions of previously disenfranchised voters have registered, and minority candidates have won office in city, state, and federal government—including the top executive offices in the land. We have made undeniable progress toward multiracial democracy.

But we have not reached the mountaintop. Indeed, over the past decade, it seems that goal is moving farther away, because if we look just a bit closer, there are signs that we have begun running downhill. Freed from the proactive review and deterrent effect of preclearance, formerly covered jurisdictions have for the past decade enjoyed free reign over their own election policies. We here provide overwhelming evidence that the net effect of their actions has been a wider racial turnout gap and worse outcomes for minority voters in just about every policy area we examine. The same places that once engaged in first-generation voter suppression have apparently returned to practices that weigh more heavily on minority voters. Over roughly the same period of time, political assassinations (or attempts)—long vanishingly rare—have grown more common, and we need look no further than January 6, 2021, for a startlingly similar example of just the sort of partisan political violence that occurred at Colfax.

For those seeking to preserve the voting rights for which so many have struggled for so long, it might therefore be difficult to summon much optimism these days. The Voting Rights Act was passed and reauthorized after a powerful social movement found a willing partner in a president and the Congress; along the way, the Supreme Court largely blessed their actions. It was never reasonable (to us, at least) to expect jurisdictions that have been violating the Voting Rights Act for decades to stop doing so when federal oversight was removed. These behaviors are a constant in our story. What has changed, however, is the utter erosion throughout the federal government of any willingness to combat them: The Justice Department in the second Trump administration has shown little interest in defending minority voters' rights, and after striking down preclearance, the federal judiciary has subjected Section 2 to a death by a thousand cuts. Congress, hamstrung by the Senate's countermajoritarian rules, seems paralyzed to act. We live today in a wildly different time than in 1965, and with leaders whose commitment to restoring the VRA is a mere shadow of that moment.

With the leadership vacuum at the federal level, some states have taken matters into their own hands. Since *Shelby County* was handed down, seven states have enacted state voting rights acts (SVRAs), though only two (partially covered New York and fully covered Virginia) were subject to preclearance prior to the Court's ruling.[45] These SVRAs are intended to provide protections above and beyond those in the federal VRA. They typically make it easier for plaintiffs to bring claims of vote dilution, and allow voters to challenge policies like at-large elections. Three of the SVRAs also include some sort of preclearance: In New York and Connecticut, the state attorney general must approve all changes to election policies originating from election jurisdictions with a history of racial discrimination; Virginia has a somewhat more complicated preclearance system.[46] As was the case when Section 5 of the federal VRA was in effect, the preclearance systems in the SVRAs require a set of skeptical eyes on all election practices.

Given the substantial effort that many covered states devoted to getting off of the coverage list prior to *Shelby County,* it is extraordinary that both New York and (especially) Virginia have effectively opted back into the legal regime from which they were freed by the Court's decision. We might take this as a sign of recognition that preclearance helped them to ensure an equitable democracy for their citizens. Regrettably, until preclearance is restored to *all* jurisdictions willing to implement discriminatory voting practices, the SVRAs will likely do little to stem the retrogressive tide we have described again and again in the preceding pages. With the voluntary coverage of Virginia and the three formerly covered New York State counties, just 16% of the population living in areas covered under preclearance prior to *Shelby County* are now covered by a state regime. We are not particularly sanguine that the worst offenders—states like Alabama, Georgia, Mississippi, and Texas, not to mention thousands of counties and municipalities—will voluntarily stop violating their minority citizens' voting rights. History has made clear the limitations of a state-by-state approach to securing voting rights for all Americans. Today, there is little reason to hope that offending jurisdictions will respond to anything other than powerful federal action, including the reinstatement of a Voting Rights Act with the power to push back against the retrogression we identify in this book.

We know that because federal action is the only force that ever *has* worked. Vigorous enforcement of the VRA and its subsequent amendments is responsible for correcting centuries of injustice in just a single generation. In an irony not lost on *Shelby County*'s critics, including Justice Ruth Bader Ginsburg in her famous dissent, the effectiveness of the VRA itself laid the groundwork for the majority justices to claim that preclearance was no longer justified. Skeptics of the decision feared that, absent a duty to disclose their policies and subject them to federal scrutiny, the old forces of discrimination in the American states—however novel or subtle—would soon return. Having now spent years examining all evidence available to us, we can only conclude that they have.

It is not impossible to move forward from here. The Voting Rights Act of 1965 was passed after steadfast leadership in the Civil Rights Movement, and with a commitment from a bipartisan coalition of federal politicians summoned by the enormous outpouring of sympathy for those who were attacked on the Edmund Pettus Bridge. Citizens, elected officials, and judges recognized the urgency of the moment in 1965, setting partisan or other allegiances aside because the problem confronting them had become too enormous to ignore. Over the howls of the Old South, America aspired to realize the promise of its founding documents, to finally confront the "American problem," and to create a democracy that serves all of its citizens. We are now drifting away from that goal. If Americans wish to correct our trajectory once more, the effort will require bravery, dedication, and cooperation in Congress. The best—indeed, perhaps the only—way to facilitate this endeavor is for the public to demand it. For, as John Lewis wrote in his final message to the American public, published shortly after his death, "Ordinary people with extraordinary vision can redeem the soul of America."[47]

NOTES

Introduction

1. *Dred Scott v. Sandford*, 60 U.S. 393 (1856).

2. For a full description, see Alexander (2012).

3. Martin Luther King Jr., Address Delivered at the Prayer Pilgrimage for Freedom, Washington D.C., May 17, 1957, Martin Luther King Jr. Research and Education Institute, Stanford University, https://kinginstitute.stanford.edu/king-papers/documents/give-us-ballot-address-delivered-prayer-pilgrimage-freedom.

4. Bullock, Gaddie, and Wert (2016, pg. 62).

5. Ibid.

6. As we discuss in the following chapter, the Voting Rights Act had a *second* preclearance condition embedded in Section 3(c). Federal judges could—and still can—require individual jurisdictions to submit policies for preclearance as an outcome of litigation. Preclearance imposed under Section 3(c) is generally time limited, and judges typically require only certain classes of policy to be submitted for preclearance.

7. *Alexander v. South Carolina State Conference of the NAACP*, 602 U.S. 1 (2024).

8. Dombrowski et al. (2025).

9. For instance, decentralized administration may hamper efforts to manipulate election results nationwide (Kreis, 2025) and may have contributed to the accurate counting of election results in 2020 (Landau, Wiseman, and Wiseman, 2021).

10. Grumbach (2022, pg. 14, emphasis in the original).

11. We describe this concept further and in accessible terms in Chapter 5.

12. See Fraga (2018).

Chapter 1

1. John Lewis (2014), "An Oral History of Selma and the Struggle for the Voting Rights Act," *Time* Magazine, December 25.

2. Brim's account is described in Keith (2009, pgs. 104, 106–108), where his name is spelled "Brimm," and in Lane (2008, pg. 106-107).

3. Keyssar (2008, pg. 84).

4. Foner (2014, pg. 426).

5. Ibid., pg. 342.

6. "The New-Orleans Riot: Its Official History," *New York Tribune*, 1866.

7. Kousser (1999).

8. Foner (2014, pg. 342).

9. 60 U.S. 393 (1856).

10. US Constitution, Article 1, Section 4.

11. Keyssar (2008, pg. 84).
12. 17 Stat. 13, §2.
13. Lane (2008, pg. 40).
14. Keith (2009, pg. 60).
15. Lane (2008, pg. 41).
16. Keith (2009, pg. 63).
17. Lane (2008, pg. 24).
18. Keith (2009, pg. 63).
19. Lane (2008, pg. 65).
20. Allegations of fraud clouded the results of the presidential elections as well; Congress rejected Louisiana's electoral votes.
21. Lane (2008, pg. 13).
22. Ibid., pgs. 93–95.
23. Ibid.
24. Ibid., pg. 102.
25. Ibid.
26. Keith (2009, pg. 82).
27. Lane (2008, pg. 106–107).
28. Ibid., pg. 20.
29. "Military Report on Colfax Riot," 1875, Grant Parish, Louisiana.
30. Lane (2008, pg. 97).
31. Ibid., pgs. 124–126.
32. Ibid., pgs. 170–171.
33. Ibid., pg. 203.
34. Until the 1890s, in addition to hearing cases with the full Supreme Court in Washington, DC, justices also spent roughly half of each year "riding the circuit," adjudicating cases in geographic circuits for which they shared responsibility with a local judge and one other fellow Supreme Court justice. This practice is the predecessor of the modern United States Courts of Appeals, still known as "circuit courts."
35. Lane (2008, pg. 208).
36. 92 U.S. 542 (1876).
37. Lemann (2007, pg. 174).
38. Bateman, Katznelson, and Lapinski (2018).
39. Richard Rubin, "The Colfax Riot," *Atlantic Monthly* (July–August 2003).
40. The Civil Rights Cases, 109 U.S. 3 (1883).
41. Keyssar (2008, pg. 182).
42. Epperly et al. (2020).
43. Gray and Jenkins (2025).
44. Keele, Cubbison, and White (2021).
45. Keyssar (2008, pg. 92).
46. Williams v. Mississippi, 170 U.S. 213 (1898).
47. 238 U.S. 347 (1915).
48. Guinn v. United States, 238 U.S. 347 (1915), at 357–358.
49. Kousser (1999, pg. 49).
50. Valelly (2004, pg. 157).
51. 256 U.S. 232 (1921).
52. Nixon v. Herndon, 273 U.S. 536 (1927).
53. The Supreme Court had long held that it would avoid adjudicating purely political questions, such as interbranch disputes. This tradition goes back at least to *Marbury v. Madison* (5 U.S. 137 [1803]). In *Baker v. Carr* (369 U.S. 186 [1962]), the Court clarified the contours

of political questions, identifying circumstances in which courts should avoid ruling, and, by contrast, when they could weigh in.

54. 273 U.S. 536 (1927).

55. Klarman (2001).

56. 286 U.S. 73 (1932).

57. Dr. Lawrence Nixon, a Black physician from El Paso, was the plaintiff in both cases.

58. 295 U.S. 45 (1935).

59. 313 U.S. 299 (1941).

60. 321 U.S. 649 (1944).

61. Kousser (1999, pg. 53).

62. Terry v. Adams, 345 U.S. 461 (1953).

63. C. Parker (2009).

64. Sterling (n.d.).

65. Dan Berry, "Killing and Segregated Plaque Divide Town," *New York Times*, March 18, 2007, pg. A20.

66. After *Smith*, a federal court also struck down Georgia's white primary in *Chapman v. King*, 154 F.2d 460 (5th Cir., 1946).

67. Bernd (1982).

68. Quoted in Bernd (1982, pg. 494).

69. Berry, "Killing and Segregated Plaque Divide Town."

70. "Bullets, Vote Not Connected in Taylor Death," *Atlanta Constitution*, July 26, 1946, pg. 4.

71. Sterling (n.d.).

72. Martin Luther King Jr., "Letter to the Editor," *Atlanta Constitution*, August 6, 1946.

73. Martin Luther King Jr., "'Kick Up Dust,' Letter to the Editor, *Atlanta Constitution*," August 6, 1946, Martin Luther King Jr. Research and Education Institute, Stanford University, accessed December 18, 2025, https://kinginstitute.stanford.edu/king-papers/documents/kick-dust-letter-editor-atlanta-constitution.

74. 347 U.S. 483 (1954).

75. Myrdal (1944, pg. 1004).

76. Skrentny (1998); Dudziak (2011).

77. Dudziak (1988).

78. Goldfield (2014).

79. "The Atlantic Report on the World Today: Washington," *The Atlantic* (March 1957).

80. Arthur Krock, "In the Nation: Mr. Russell Lands on Both Horns of a Dilemma," *New York Times*, July 18, 1952, pg. 18.

81. Caro (2002, ch. 36).

82. *United States v. Raines*, 362 U.S. 17 (1960).

83. Quoted in Caro (2002, pg. 991).

84. Civil Rights Act of 1957, §104(a)(1).

85. United States Commission on Civil Rights, "Report of the United States Commission on Civil Rights" (1959), pg. 135, Thurgood Marshall Law Library, Francis Key Carey School of Law, University of Maryland, https://www2.law.umaryland.edu/marshall/usccr/documents/cr11959.pdf.

86. Ibid., pg. 143.

87. United States Commission on Civil Rights, "1961 U.S. Commission on Civil Rights Report Book 1: Voting," (1961), pg. 5, https://www2.law.umaryland.edu/marshall/usccr/documents/cr11961bk1.pdf.

88. United States Commission on Civil Rights, "1963 Report of the United States Commission on Civil Rights," (1963), pg. 15, Civil Rights Movement Archive, https://www.crmvet.org/docs/ccr_63_civil_rights.pdf.

89. Civil Rights Act of 1960, §301.

90. Civil Rights Act of 1960, §601(a).

91. Ibid.

92. 380 U.S. 145 (1965).

93. *Louisiana v. United States*, 380 U.S. 145 (1965), at 145.

94. Ibid. at 150.

95. Ibid. at 152.

96. Ibid. at 154.

97. Ibid. at 155.

98. Derfner (1973, pg. 550). See also *Alabama v. United States*, 304 F.2d 583 (5th Cir. 1962).

99. Valelly (2004, pg. 189).

100. Testimony of Nicholas Katzenbach, U.S. Congress, Senate, Committee on the Judiciary, *Voting Rights Hearings on S. 1564 to Enforce the 15th Amendment to the Constitution of the United States*, 89th Cong., 1st sess., March 23–April 5, 1965, part 1 (Washington, DC: Government Printing Office, 1965), pg. 123.

101. US Commission on Civil Rights, "1961 U.S. Commission on Civil Rights Report Book 1: Voting," pg. 100.

102. US Commission on Civil Rights, "Voting in Mississippi," United States Commission on Civil Rights (1965), pg. 1, https://www2.law.umaryland.edu/marshall/usccr/documents/cr12v94.pdf.

103. John Lewis, "An Oral History of Selma and the Struggle for the Voting Rights Act," *Time Magazine*, December 25, 2014.

104. Adam Bernstein, "Alabama Sheriff James Clark: Embodied Violent Bigotry," *Washington Post*, June 7, 2007.

105. Vivian with Fiffer (2021, pg. 84).

106. May (2013).

107. Memo from Reverand B. L. Tucker, September 16-24, 1963, Civil Rights Movement Archive, https://www.crmvet.org/lets/630916_selma_tucker.pdf.

108. Quoted in Alvin Benn, "Sheriff Jim Clark Died Believing He Did Right Thing," *Montgomery Advertiser*, March 1, 2015.

109. Quoted in Garrow (2004, pg. 391).

110. John Herbers, "Woman Punches Alabama Sheriff," *New York Times*, January 26, 1965, pg. 1. For a discussion of Cooper's tussle with Sheriff Clark, see May (2013, pgs. 64–65).

111. Robert D. McFadden, "C.T. Vivian, Martin Luther King's Field General, Dies at 95," *New York Times*, July 17, 2020.

112. May (2013, pgs. 75–80).

113. Garrow (2004); May (2013).

114. Caro (2012, pg. 568).

115. Gallup Organization, Gallup Poll Number 1960-0626: 1960 Presidential Election (Version 3) [dataset], Roper Center for Public Opinion Research: Cornell University, Ithaca, NY, doi:10.25940/ROPER-31087610; Gallup Organization, Gallup Poll Number 701 (Version 4) [dataset], Roper Center for Public Opinion Research. Cornell University, Ithaca, NY, doi:10.25940/ROPER-31087684.

116. "Lyndon B. Johnson and Martin Luther King Jr. on 15 January 1965," Conversation WH6501-04-6736-6737, Presidential Recordings Digital Edition (Lyndon B. Johnson and Civil Rights, vol. 2, ed. Kent B. Germany) (Charlottesville: University of Virginia Press, 2014–), http://prde.upress.virginia.edu/conversations/4005068.

117. Califano (2015).

118. King (1998, pg. 271).

119. Quoted in May (2013, pg. 48).

120. John D. Pomfret, "President Promises Dr. King Vote Move," *New York Times*, February 10, 1965, pg. 1.

121. See, where it is ranked number 10, "Top 100 American Speeches of the 20th century," University of Wisconsin–Madison and Texas A & M University, https://news.wisc.edu/archive/misc/speeches/.

122. President Lyndon Johnson's Speech to Congress on Voting Rights, March 15, 1965.

123. Ibid.

124. Ibid.

125. Ibid.

126. Garrow (2004, pg. 408).

127. Nicholas Katzenbach Interview, November 29, 2005, Edward M. Kennedy Oral History Project, Miller Center, University of Virginia.

128. Ibid.

129. *Voting Rights: Hearings Before Subcommittee No. 5 of the Committee on the Judiciary, House of Representatives, Eighty-Ninth Congress, First Session on H.R. 6400, and Other Proposals to Enforce the 15th Amendment to the Constitution of the United States* (Washington, DC: Government Printing Office, 1965).

130. P.L. 89-110.

131. As we have seen, however, Section 4(e) is a general provision.

132. P.L. 89-110 §4(b).

133. "Determination of the Director of the Census Pursuant to Section 4(b)(2) of the Voting Rights Act of 1965 (Public Law 89–110)," *Federal Register* 30, no. 152 (August 6, 1965): 9897 "Determination of the Director Pursuant to Section 4(b)(2) of the Voting Rights Act of 1965 (Public Law 89-110)," *Federal Register* 30, no. 224 (November 18, 1965): 14505.

134. P.L. 89-110§4(c).

135. To the best of our knowledge, the Supreme Court neither affirmed nor overturned under the Civil Rights Act of 1960 this practice of disparate federal intervention, though it would become an important part of the fight over Section 4(b) in *South Carolina v. Katzenbach* in 1966 (see Chapter 2).

136. United States v. Manning, 215 F. Supp. 272 (W.D. La. 1963).

137. U.S. Congress, House, *Voting Rights Act of 1965*, H.R. Rep. No. 89–439, 89th Cong., 1st sess. (1965).

138. Landsberg (2007, pg. 64).

139. Landsberg (2007, pg. 155).

140. *Voting Rights*, pg. 60.

141. Pub.L. No. 89–110 §4(a).

142. Pub.L. No. 89–110 §3(c).

143. As of 2025, three jurisdictions are covered under Section 3(c) preclearance: City of Pasadena, Texas (until January 13, 2027); Town of Newbern, Alabama (until January 1, 2030); and Jefferson County Board of Education, Alabama (until December 31, 2031).

144. Pub.L. 89–110 §6. As with preclearance, other jurisdictions could be bailed in to observer coverage under Section 3(a). Originally called "examiners," they were renamed "observers" in the 2006 reauthorization of the Voting Rights Act. The 2006 also combined the coverage determinations and role of federal observers into Section 8, removing Section 6.

145. Pub.L. 89–110 §3(a).

146. Pub.L. No. 89–110 §4(a).

147. Some jurisdictions were able to bail out between 1965 and 1970, including the State of Alaska and five total counties across three states: Arizona (three counties), Idaho, and North Carolina (one each).

148. Ewald (2009, ch. 1).
149. Bateman, Katznelson, and Lapinski (2018, pg. 398).
150. Hale, Montjoy, and Brown (2015, pg. 28).
151. President Lyndon Johnson's Speech to Congress on Voting Rights.
152. *Voting Rights*, 5.
153. Ibid., 440.
154. Ibid., 5.
155. Landsberg (2007, pg. 150).
156. Landsberg (2007, pgs. 157–158).
157. May (2013).

Chapter 2

1. 393 U.S. 544 (1969).
2. E. W. Kenworthy, "Capitol Is Scene: Room in Which Lincoln Freed Some Slaves Is Used," *New York Times*, August 7, 1965.
3. John Herbers, "U.S. Voting Aides Depart for South," *New York Times*, August 7, 1965.
4. Tulani Salahu-Din, "Hidden Herstory: The Leesburg Stockade Girls," National Museum of African American History and Culture, accessed January 7, 2026, https://nmaahc.si.edu/explore/stories/hidden-herstory-leesburg-stockade-girls.
5. Aelony v. Pace, 32 U.S.L.W. 2215 (M.D. Ga., Nov. 1, 1963).
6. Gene Roberts, "Americus Names Negroes to Jobs as Polling Clerks," *New York Times*, August 7, 1965.
7. United Press International, "700 at Klan Rally Honor Youth Slain in Americus Strife," *New York Times*, August 8, 1965. , pg. 1.
8. New York would not be covered under Section 4(b) until the 1970 reauthorization, but Section 4(e) outlawed English literacy tests nationwide beginning in 1965.
9. Crawford (1925).
10. Ibid.
11. US Census Bureau, 1920 Census, Volume 3: Population, Composition, and Characteristics of the Population by States, 678.
12. Lee (2020).
13. *Statistical Abstract of the United States* (Washington, DC: Government Printing Office, 1929), no. 106.
14. Leibowitz (1969).
15. Ibid.
16. Camacho v. Rogers (199 F. Supp. 155 (S.D.N.Y. 1961).
17. 360 U.S. 45 (1959).
18. Avins (1969).
19. Ben A. Franklin, "New Voting Law Attacked in Suit," *New York Times*, August 7, 1965.
20. 383 U.S. 301 (1966).
21. Berman (2015, pg. 46).
22. South Carolina v. Katzenbach, 383 U.S. 301 (1966), brief of plaintiff, pg. 41.
23. *Katzenbach*, oral argument, US Supreme Court, January 17, 1966.
24. Ibid.
25. Ibid.
26. Ibid.
27. Ibid.
28. Ibid.
29. Ibid.

30. Ibid.

31. *Katzenbach*, brief of plaintiff, pg. 7.

32. *Katzenbach*, oral argument, US Supreme Court, January 17, 1966.

33. Amicus briefs on file with authors.

34. National Opinion Research Center (NORC), *NORC Poll: Amalgam Study # 160 (Version 3)* [Dataset]. Cornell University, Roper Center for Public Opinion Research, 1963, https://doi.org/10.25940/ROPER-31095174.

35. Gallup Organization. Gallup Poll # 708 (Version 3) [Dataset], Cornell University, Roper Center for Public Opinion Research, 1965, https://doi.org/10.25940/ROPER-31087689.

36. Louis Harris & Associates, Louis Harris & Associates Poll: April 1965 (Version 1) [Dataset], Cornell University, Roper Center for Public Opinion Research, 1965, https://doi.org/10.25940/ROPER-31103175.

37. Louis Harris & Associates, Louis Harris & Associates Poll: May 1965 (Version 1) [Dataset], Cornell University, Roper Center for Public Opinion Research, 1965, https://doi.org/10.25940/ROPER-31103177.

38. Louis Harris & Associates, Louis Harris & Associates Poll: December 1965 (Version 1) [Dataset], Cornell University, Roper Center for Public Opinion Research, 1965, https://doi.org/10.25940/ROPER-31103167

39. *Katzenbach*, oral argument, US Supreme Court, January 18, 1966.

40. *Katzenbach*.

41. Ibid.

42. Ibid.

43. Ibid.

44. Ibid.

45. Ibid.

46. We describe the relevant sections of the Constitution authorizing congressional oversight of election practices in Chapter 1.

47. Morgan v. Katzenbach, 247 F. Supp. 196 (D.D.C. 1965).

48. 384 U.S. 641 (1966).

49. Katzenbach v. Morgan, 384 U.S. 641 (1966).

50. Ibid.

51. Ibid. Brennan's opinion in *Morgan* is often credited with establishing the "one-way ratchet" theory of 14th Amendment protections: Congress may go beyond minimum 14th Amendment protections established by judicial precedent, but may not weaken these protections past minimums that courts establish. This understanding lasted more than thirty years, until the Court deviated from it in *City of Boerne v. Flores* (521 US 507 [1997]).

52. US Census Bureau, "1960 Census of the Population: Supplementary Reports—Race of the Population of the United States, by States: 1960," https://www.justice.gov/crt/section-4-voting-rights-act

53. F. Parker (2011, pg. 38).

54. US Commission on Civil Rights, "Political Participation: A Report of the United States Commission on Civil Rights," (1968), Pg. 22.

55. For a detailed discussion of the elimination of elected offices throughout the covered jurisdictions, see Komisarchik (2026).

56. F. Parker (2011, pg. 40).

57. US Commission on Civil Rights, "Political Participation," pg. 23.

58. 393 U.S. 544 (1969).

59. Allen v. State Board of Elections, 393 U.S. 544 (1969).

60. Ibid.

61. Ibid.

62. Berman (2015, pg. 77).

63. F. Parker (2011, pg. 179).

64. Quoted in John W. Finney, "House Approves Nixon Bill to End Voting Rights Act," *New York Times*, December 12, 1969.

65. Berman (2015, pg. 84).

66. "Determination Regarding Literacy Tests," *Federal Register*, 35, no. 149 (July 24, 1970): 12354; "Determination of Director Regarding Voting Rights," *Federal Register*, 36, no. 60 (March 15, 1971): 5809; "Determination of Director Regarding Voting Rights," *Federal Register*, 39, no. 92 (May 9, 1974): 16912–16913.

67. US Commission on Civil Rights. "Summary and Text: The Voting Rights Act," Clearinghouse Publication 32 (September 1971).

68. Berman (2015, pg. 85).

69. 400 U.S. 112 (1970).

70. Oregon v. Mitchell, 400 U.S. 112 (1970).

71. Ibid.

72. 400 U.S. 379 (1971).

73. "Justice Department Revises The Civil Rights Division," *New York Times*, September 25, 1969.

74. Berman (2015, pg. 92).

75. "Ford Still Backs Voting Rights Act," *New York Times*, January 15, 1975, pg. 15.

76. Berman (2015, pg. 105).

77. White v. Regester, 412 U.S. 755 (1973).

78. Voting Rights Act Amendments of 1975, Pub. L. No. 94-73, § 203, 89 Stat. 400, 401 (1975).

79. 52 U.S.C. § 10503.

80. Over the course of 1975 and 1976, the Census Bureau and DOJ posted the jurisdictions brought into coverage due to discrimination against language minorities. See "Voting Rights Act Amendments of 1975: Partial List of Determinations," *Federal Register*, 40, no. 185 (September 23, 1975): 43746; "Voting Rights Act Amendments of 1975: Partial List of Determinations," *Federal Register*, 40, no. 205 (October 21, 1975): 49422; "Voting Rights Act Amendments of 1975: Partial List of Determinations Made Pursuant to Section 4(b) of the Voting Rights Act of 1965, as Amended," *Federal Register*, 41, no. 2 (December 29, 1975): 784; "Voting Rights Act Amendments of 1975: Partial List of Determinations Made Pursuant to Section 4(b) of the Voting Rights Act of 1965, as Amended," *Federal Register*, 41, no. 158 (August 10, 1976): 34329.

81. The numerosity requirement is met if the single-language minority group "is more than 10,000, or is more than five percent of all voting age citizens, or, on an Indian reservation, exceeds five percent of all reservation residents." See US Department of Justice, Civil Rights Division, "About Language Minority Voting Rights," accessed June 12, 2025, https://www.justice.gov/crt/about-language-minority-voting-rights.

82. Ibid.

83. Alt (1994); Bullock, Gaddie, and Wert (2016, pg. 22); Fresh (2018).

84. Ang (2019); Bernini et al. (2025).

85. Bernini et al. (2025); Bullock, Gaddie, and Wert (2016, pg. 65), Greenberger and Smith (2025); Grofman and Handley (1991); Handley and Grofman (1994); May (2013, pg. 191), Shah, Marschall, and Ruhil (2013).

86. Schuit and Rogowski (2017).

87. Cascio and Washington (2014).

88. Aneja and Avenancio-Leon (2019).

89. Rushovich et al. (2024).

90. For instance, Eubank and Fresh (2022) demonstrate that in response to growing Black political power, Southern state governments became more likely to imprison Black defendants.

Chapter 3

1. 570 U.S. 529 (2013).

2. City of Richmond v. United States, 422 U.S. 358 (1975).

3. Hayter (2014).

4. Harper v. Virginia Board of Elections, 383 U.S. 663 (1966).

5. Holt v. City of Richmond, 334 F. Supp. 228 (E.D. Va. 1971).

6. Hayter (2014).

7. Ibid.

8. Ibid.

9. Ibid.

10. *Holt.*

11. Ibid.

12. Hayter (2014).

13. U.S. Department of Justice, Civil Rights Division, "Letter to C.S. Mattox, City Attorney of Richmond, Virginia," May 7, 1971, https://www.justice.gov/sites/default/files/crt/legacy/2014/05/30/VA-1010.pdf.

14. 422 U.S. 358 (1975).

15. We submitted a Freedom of Information Act request for the Section 5 submissions from 1965 to 1998 in January 2021. That request remains open at this writing, more than five years later.

16. These proposed actions take the form of fairly standardized descriptions, which allow us to scan the records for important keywords that reveal the nature of each request.

17. Per Section 5, covered jurisdictions could also submit their proposals to the US District Court for the District of Columbia. While we do not have access to those submissions, the "overwhelming majority of the covered jurisdictions [submitted] their redistricting plans to the Attorney General." See: US Department of Justice, "Guidance Concerning Redistricting Under Section 5 of the Voting Rights Act," January 2011, *Federal Register*, Notice, https://www.federalregister.gov/documents/2011/02/09/2011-2797/guidance-concerning-redistricting-under-section-5-of-the-voting-rights-act-notice.

18. The DOJ objected to New Mexico's state senate plan in 1991. US Department of Justice, Civil Rights Division, "Letter to Manny M. Aragon, President Pro Tempore of the New Mexico Senate, and Raymond G. Sanchez, Speaker of the New Mexico House of Representatives," December 10, 1991, https://www.justice.gov/sites/default/files/crt/legacy/2014/05/30/NM-1000.pdf). The DOJ objected to the county commission districts in Charles Mix County, South Dakota, in 2008, along with the county's plan to reduce the number of commissioners from five to three. US Department of Justice, Civil Rights Division, "Letter to Sara Frankenstein of Charles Mix County, South Dakota," February 11, 2008, https://www.justice.gov/sites/default/files/crt/legacy/2014/05/30/l_080211.pdf. The objection letter incorrectly indicates that the county was covered under Section 5, not Section 3(c).

19. Donald M. Wright, General Counsel, North Carolina State Board of Elections, Statement before the Subcommittee on the Constitution, Civil Rights, and Property Rights, Committee on the Judiciary, U.S. Senate, *Reauthorizing the Voting Rights Act's Temporary Provisions: Policy Perspectives and Views from the Field*, 109-822, 109th Cong., June 21, 2006.

20. Donald M. Wright, "Statement of Donald M. Wright, General Counsel, North Carolina State Board of Elections," Hearings Before the Subcommittee on the Constitution, Civil Rights and Property Rights, Senate Committee on the Judiciary, *Reauthorizing the Voting Rights Act's Temporary Provisions: Policy Perspectives and Views from the Field*, June 21, 2006.

21. Given the wording of the DOJ's objection letter and an apparently missing supplementary document, we cannot be be certain of this figure. In this case, the number should be

interpreted as the ceiling of the number of rejected annexations. See United States Department of Justice, Civil Rights Division, Objection Letter 84-3316, Issued to the City of Summerville, South Carolina, October 10, 1986.

22. United States Department of Justice, Civil Rights Division, Objection Letter LA-2210, Issued to the City of Shreveport, Louisiana, September 6, 1994.

23. Although these are the only instances in Figure 3.3 where we have estimated the number of blocked policies, if our estimate for the Summerville objection is wrong, it is too high; for Shreveport, our estimate could be wrong in either direction.

24. If we calculate the rejection rate as the number of policies receiving an objection divided by the number of policies proposed, the rejection rate is essentially the same, at 0.14%.

25. Fraga and Ocampo (2007).

26. These data were obtained via a public records request for all policies in the STAPS database for which the Department of Justice requested more information. We consider a policy "changed" due to the request if a postrequest action included any of the following codes: "No determination—change superseded," "No determination—change not finally adopted," or "No determination—change not implemented." A policy was considered withdrawn or abandoned if it was tagged with any of the following codes: "No determination—change withdrawn," "Notice of withdrawal," "Administratively closed,"; or if the jurisdiction never responded to the information (that is, if the final action was "Additional information requested," "Additional information request follow-up," or "Please submit").

27. Grumbach (2022).

28. Ferrier, Sinha, and Outrich (2016).

29. These provisions subsequently became part of Section 8 of the VRA. See also 52 U.S.C. § 10305.

30. Federal observers could also be assigned to Section 4(b) jurisdictions if the attorney general "received written meritorious complaints from residents, elected officials, or civic participation organizations that efforts to deny or abridge the right to vote under the color of law on account of race or color" (see Section 8(a)(2)(A)), though Tucker (2007, pg. 236) reports that in 2007, "nearly all" of the recent action under Section 8 occurred after a determination from the attorney general. Even now, after *Shelby County*, federal observers can be assigned as part of a judicial order under Section 3(a) of the VRA. However, like the bail-in provisions found in Section 3(c), they are rarely used: for the 2024 presidential election, federal observers were authorized under Section 3(a) in just five local jurisdictions in the nation. See US Department of Justice, Civil Rights Division, "About Federal Observers and Election Monitoring," accessed June 17, 2025, https://www.justice.gov/crt/about-federal-observers-and-election-monitoring.

31. Tucker (2007, pg. 230).

32. Ibid.

33. US House Committee on the Judiciary, *Fannie Lou Hamer, Rosa Parks, and Coretta Scott King Voting Rights Act Reauthorization and Amendments Act of 2006*, H.R. Rep. No. 109–478, 109th Cong. (2006), 44, https://www.govinfo.gov/content/pkg/CRPT-109hrpt478/pdf/CRPT-109hrpt478.pdf.

Chapter 4

1. 557 U.S. 193 (2009).

2. US Census Bureau, *Fourteenth Census of the United States: 1920 Bulletin—Population: Alabama, Number of Inhabitants, by Counties and Minor Civil Divisions.*

3. Bolden v. City of Mobile, Ala., 542 F. Supp. 1050 (S.D. Ala. 1982).

4. *Journal of the Proceedings of the Constitutional Convention of the State of Alabama, Held in the City of Montgomery, Commencing May 21st, 1901* (Brown Printing Company, 1901), Second Day, pg. 9.

5. *Bolden.*

6. Quoted in *Bolden.*

7. Quoted in *Bolden.*

8. 412 U.S. 755 (1973).

9. This view was clearly articulated by Justice Byron White (who authored the opinion of the Court in *White v. Regester*) in his dissenting opinion in *City of Mobile v. Bolden*, 446 U.S. 55 (1980).

10. Martin and Quinn (2002).

11. Although his appointment does not appear to have immediately shifted the median justice's ideal point as shown in Figure 4.1 (partially due to shifts among other justices), the addition of John Paul Stevens was also important for the dynamics of voting rights cases. He began as more of a centrist than either Blackmun or Powell, but Stevens replaced William O. Douglas—one of the most reliably liberal votes in history.

12. 163 U.S. 537 (1896).

13. Qtd. in Berman (2015, pg. 146).

14. Jenkins (2012, pg. 69).

15. Wang (2012, pgs. 46–49).

16. This standard was required by the Court's precedent in *Reynolds v. Sims* (377 U.S. 533 (1964)) and subsequent cases.

17. Beer v. United States, 425 U.S. 130 (1976), at 136.

18. 425 U.S. 130 (1976).

19. See *City of Rome v. United States*, 446 U.S. 156 (1980).

20. Berman (2015, pg. 133).

21. 446 U.S. 55 (1980).

22. *Bolden.*

23. Berman (2015, pg. 135).

24. U.S. Congress, House, *Voting Rights Act Extension, Report to Accompany H.R. 3112*, H.R. Rep. No. 227, 97th Cong., 1st sess. (1981), 29–30.

25. "Reagan Is Said to Shift on Voting Rights Act," *New York Times*, August 6, 1981, pg. 17.

26. "Reagan Takes Flexible View on Voting Rights Extension," *Washington Post*, November 7, 1981.

27. Robert, Pear. "Justice Department Aide Warns Senators on Passing the Voting Rights Bill," *New York Times,* March 2, 1982, sec. A, pg. 11.

28. Robert, Pear. "Compromise Likely on Voting Rights," *New York Times,* May 1, 1982, sec. 1, pg. 12.

29. S. Rep. No. 97-417 (1982), reprinted in 1982 U.S.C.C.A.N. 177, pg. 28.

30. Ibid.

31. Ibid.

32. Rogers v. Lodge, 458 US 613 (1982).

33. Berman (2015, pg. 149).

34. Ibid. pg. 151.

35. Memo from John Roberts to the Attorney General, "Section 2 of the Voting Rights Act and *City of Mobile v. Bolden,*" November 6, 1981, pg. 2, Correspondence Files of Ken Star, 1981–83, Acc. 60-88-0498, Box 2, US Department of Justice.

36. Memo from John Roberts to the Attorney General, "Why Section 2 of the Voting Rights Act Should Be Retained Unchanged," December 22, 1981, pg. 3, from Correspondence Files of Ken Star, 1981–83, Acc. 60-88-0498, Box 22, US Department of Justice.

37. Ibid.

38. Memo from John Roberts to the Attorney General, "Talking Points for White House Meeting on Voting Rights Act," January 26, 1982, pg. 1, Correspondence Files of Ken Star, 1981–83, Acc. 60-88-0498, Box 22, US Department of Justice.

39. Memo from John Roberts to the Attorney General, "Voting Rights Act," January 25, 1982, pg. 4, Correspondence Files of Ken Star, 1981–83, Acc. 60-88-0498, Box 22, US Department of Justice.

40. Colegrove v. Green, 328 U.S. 549 (1946).

41. Ibid.

42. 369 U.S. 186 (1962).

43. 377 U.S. 533 (1964).

44. See, for instance, *Gaffney v. Cummings*, 412 U.S. 735 (1973); *Karcher v. Daggett*, 462 U.S. 725 (1983); and *Evenwel v. Abbott*, 136 S. Ct. 1120 (2016).

45. Ansolabehere, Gerber, and Snyder (2002).

46. 478 U.S. 30 (1986).

47. We note that in *Louisiana v. Callais*, issued in April 2026, the Court substantially reworked the Gingles framework, making it considerably more difficult to prove that racial vote dilution had in fact occurred.

48. Quoted in Davis (1989).

49. Davidson and Grofman (1994, pg. 83).

50. Bullock, Gaddie, and Wert (2016, pg. 30).

51. Ibid. pg. 31.

52. 509 U.S. 630 (1993).

53. Shaw v. Hunt, 517 U.S. 899 (1996).

54. See *United Jewish Organizations of Williamsburgh, Inc. v. Carey*, 430 U.S. 144 (1977).

55. 515 U.S. 900 (1995).

56. 517 U.S. 952 (1996).

57. 528 U.S. 320 (2000).

58. 539 U.S. 461 (2003).

59. Bullock, Gaddie, and Wert (2016, Ch. 5).

60. Ibid., pg. 108.

61. Ibid.

62. Berman (2015, pg. 242).

63. Bullock, Gaddie, and Wert (2016, pg. 122).

64. For a more thorough discussion, see Jones (2018).

65. Qtd. in Daley (2024, pg. 147).

66. Qtd. in Bullock, Gaddie, and Wert (2016, pg. 124).

67. Persily (2007).

68. U.S. Senate, Committee on the Judiciary, *Fannie Lou Hamer, Rosa Parks, Coretta Scott King, and Cesar E. Chávez Voting Rights Act Reauthorization and Amendments Act of 2006: Report Together with Additional Views to Accompany S. 2703*, S. Rep. 109-295, 109th Cong., July 26, 2006, pg. 30.

69. Persily (2007).

70. Berman (2015, pg. 251).

71. 557 U.S. 193 (2009).

72. See *Escambia County v. McMillan*, 466 U.S. 48 (1984).

73. New York Public Radio, "The Imperfect Plaintiffs," *More Perfect*, June 28, 2016, https://www.wnycstudios.org/podcasts/radiolabmoreperfect/episodes/imperfect-plaintiff.

74. Scammon and McGillivray (1993, pg. 474).

75. SCOTUSblog on Camera, "Edward Blum (Complete)," YouTube, August 18, 2014, https://www.youtube.com/watch?v=xZyR3Ty35Og.

76. Ibid.

77. Ibid.

78. US Department of Justice, Civil Rights Division, "Letter to Dan Head of Columbiana, Alabama," August 25, 2008, https://www.justice.gov/crt/voting-determination-letter-48.

79. Ibid.

80. US Department of Justice, Civil Rights Division, "Letter to [Illegible]," July 7, 1975, https://www.justice.gov/sites/default/files/crt/legacy/2014/05/30/AL-1230.pdf; US Department of Justice, Civil Rights Division, "William T. Harrison of Columbiana, Alabama," December 27, 1977, https://www.justice.gov/sites/default/files/crt/legacy/2014/05/30/AL-1360.pdf; US Department of Justice, Civil Rights Division, "Letter to Gladys D. Prentice, City Clerk of Leeds, Alabama," May 4, 1987, https://www.justice.gov/sites/default/files/crt/legacy/2014/05/30/AL-1720.pdf; US Department of Justice, Civil Rights Division, "Letter to J. Frank Head of Columbiana, Alabama," August 16, 2000, https://www.justice.gov/crt/voting-determination-letter-46.

81. Bullock, Gaddie, and Wert (2016, pg. 154).

82. 570 U.S. 529 (2013).

83. 811 F. Supp. 2d 424 (D.D.C. 2011); 679 F.3d 848 (D.C. Cir. 2012).

84. New York Public Radio, "The Imperfect Plaintiffs."

85. Colby (2016, pg. 1087).

86. Cantu (2015, pg. 275).

87. Richard Posner, "The Supreme Court and the Voting Rights Act: Striking Down the Law Is All About Conservatives' Imagination," *Slate*, June 26, 2013.

Chapter 5

1. 383 U.S. 301 (1966).

2. Mark Joseph Stern, "Brian Kemp's Bid for Governor Depends on Erasing the Black Vote in Georgia," *Slate*, August 17, 2018.

3. ACLU of Georgia, "Letter to Randolph County Board of Elections and Registration," August 14, 2018, https://www.acluga.org/sites/default/files/field_documents/aclu-ga-ltr-re-randolph-polling-place-closures-8-14-18.pdf.

4. Brinely Hineman, "ACLU of Georgia Slams Plan to Close Many of County's Polls," Associated Press, August 15, 2018.

5. Stern, "Brian Kemp's Bid for Governor."

6. WJBF (Augusta, GA), "Randolph County Defends Voting Precinct Closures, Claims to Help People with Disabilities." YouTube, August 21, 2018, https://www.youtube.com/watch?v=VC1lRmTC6qY.

7. Stern, "Brian Kemp's Bid for Governor."

8. "Black Voters Energized amid Outcry over Georgia Polling Places," Associated Press, August 23, 2018.

9. Congressional Black Caucus, "Letter to Randolph County Board of Elections and Registration," August 23, 2018, https://cbc.house.gov/news/documentsingle.aspx?DocumentID=940.

10. "Black Voters Energized amid Outcry over Georgia Polling Places."

11. Ferrier, Sinha, and Outrich (2016).

12. Snyder and Strömberg (2010); Hayes and Lawless (2015, 2018); Meeks (2020); Rubado and Jennings (2020).

13. Posner-Ferdman and Cuillier (2025).

14. *Shelby County v. Holder: Brief for the States of New York, California, Mississippi, and North Carolina as Amici Curiae in Support of Respondents*, Supreme Court records on *Shelby County v. Holder* (Government Printing Office, Washington, DC, 2013), 12, Supreme Court Insight, ProQuest.

15. Jasleen Singh and Sara Carter, "States Have Added Nearly 100 Restrictive Laws Since SCOTUS Gutted the Voting Rights Act 10 Years Ago," Brennan Center for Justice, June 23, 2023.

16. United States v. Houston County (M.D. Ga. 2025); NAACP v. Reeves (S.D. Miss. 2023); United States v. Galveston County, TX (S.D. Tex. 2022); United States v. State of Texas (W.D. Tex. 2021) (challenging the state's congressional and house districting place); United States v. State of Texas (W.D. Tex. 2021) (challenging the state's omnibus voting bill titled "SB1"); United States v. State of Georgia (N.D. Ga. 2021); United States v. City of West Monroe, LA (W.D. La. 2021); United States v. State of North Carolina (M.D.N.C. 2013), United States v. State of Texas (W.D. Tex. 2013), United States v. State of Texas (S.D. Tex. 2013).

17. Allen v. Milligan, 599 U.S.__(2023).

18. Moore v. Harper 600 U.S.__(2023).

19. Grimmer and Hersh (2023).

20. Fraga and Miller (2022); Grimmer and Yoder (2022); Grumbach and Hill (2022).

21. Gerken (2007); Kimball and Baybeck (2013); Hale, Montjoy, and Brown (2015); Brown, Hale, and King (2019); Merivaki (2020).

22. Kropf, Vercellotti, and Kimball (2013); Mohr et al. (2019); McBrayer, Williams, and Eckelman (2020).

23. Shepherd et al. (2021); Ferrer, Geyn, and Thompson (2023).

24. White, Nathan, and Faller (2015); Porter and Rogowski (2018).

25. Leadership Conference on Civil and Human Rights (2019).

26. McInerney et al. (2020, pg. 166).

27. Willis, Merivaki, and Ziogas (2022); Dara Gold, "Election Data Is Vital to Voting Rights, So Why Is It So Hard to Track Down?" *Election Law Blog*, April 12, 2024.

28. North Dakota is the only state without formal voter registration. Nevertheless, the state does make available a list of the individuals who participated in any given election, which is functionally equivalent for our purposes.

29. Ansolabehere, Fraga, and Schaffner (2022); Enamorado and Imai (2019).

30. Kim and Fraga (2022).

31. We compare our ballot counts to the number of ballots cast for the highest office in each state and year. Michael P. McDonald, "Voting Statistics: 2008–2022," United States Elections Project, https://www.electproject.org/election-data/voter-turnout-data, accessed April 11, 2024.

32. Fraga (2018).

33. Self-reported race is available in the Alabama, Florida, Georgia, Louisiana, North Carolina, and South Carolina files.

34. Imai and Khanna (2016).

35. See, for example, Fraga (2018).

36. The number of "Non-white" ballots (citizen voting age population, or CVAP) is calculated by subtracting the number of white ballots (CVAP) from the total number of ballots (CVAP).

37. This assumption relies on researchers demonstrating that turnout in the two groups moved in a similar fashion in elections *prior* to Time 1—which researchers usually describe as the groups exhibiting "parallel trends."

38. Our test is potentially conservative, however, as it is at least theoretically possible that *Shelby County* increased the racial turnout gap in areas that were *not* covered under Section 5. If

the increased reliance on Section 2 litigation in formerly covered jurisdictions shifted resources away from litigation in places that were *not* formerly covered, it is possible that this shift could have led to worsening conditions for minorities in these noncovered areas. To the extent this is true, our empirical approach *underestimates* the effects of *Shelby County v. Holder* on the racial turnout gap.

39. As is typical these days in social science research, we test these hypotheses using a variety of methods and after weighting the data in a number of ways. Here, we present results from methods similar to those we employ in subsequent chapters, though we note here that the key findings we present below do not depend on our methodological decisions. Interested readers can find more information about our methodological approach—as well as several alternate analyses—in the Methodological Appendix.

40. These are two-way fixed-effects models, with fixed effects for years and counties.

41. Strictly speaking, the models provide an "average treatment effect on the treated" counties (ATT).

42. Nine states were "fully covered" at the time of the decision in 2013: Alabama, Alaska, Arizona, Georgia, Louisiana, Mississippi, South Carolina, Texas, and Virginia. New Hampshire was covered until March 2013. In the Methodological Appendix, we show that our estimates are not affected if we consider New Hampshire covered, though we note that the state's successful appeal to be bailed out of preclearance means it sufficiently proved a relative lack of racial discrimination in their voting policies.

43. California, Florida, Michigan, New York, North Carolina, and South Dakota.

44. See *Lopez v. Monterey County*, 525 U.S. 266 (1999).

45. Of course, local counties were still constrained by the threat of litigation under Section 2 of the Voting Rights Act, but this litigation could move forward only once a policy or practice had been effectuated.

46. Here we are estimating the conditional average treatment effects (CATEs).

47. While this analysis considers whether a county *ever* received an objection letter, our results are consistent if we instead consider whether a county received an objection letter between 2000 and 2013.

48. See, e.g., Gibson (2020); and Raze (2022).

49. Billings et al. (2024).

50. Komisarchik and White (2025).

51. Jolie McCullough, "Nearly 127,000 Harris County Drive-Thru Votes Appear Safe After Federal Judge Rejects GOP-Led Texas Lawsuit," *Texas Tribune*, November 2, 2022.

52. Madeleine Greenberg, "Harris County Sues Texas over New Law Targeting How It Runs Elections." *Democracy Docket*, July 6, 2023, https://www.democracydocket.com/news-alerts/harris-county-sues-texas-over-newlaw-targeting-how-it-runs-elections/.

53. Ferrier, Sinha, and Outrich (2016).

54. Voris and Trantham (2024).

55. *Shelby County*, 570 U.S. at 531.

56. Jasleen Singh and Sara Carter, "States Have Added Nearly 100 Restrictive Laws Since SCOTUS Gutted the Voting Rights Act 10 Years Ago," *Brennan Center for Justice*, June 23, 2023.

Chapter 6

1. Nos. 2:21-cv-1291-AMM and 2:21-cv-1530-AMM (N.D. Ala. filed May 8, 2025).

2. Baker v. Carr, 369 U.S. 186 (1962); Reynolds v. Sims, 377 U.S. 533 (1964).

3. See Kyle Whitmire, "Ambushed in Eufaula: Alabama's Forgotten Race Massacre." *Speakin' Out News* (Huntsville, AL), January 16, 2022, https://speakinoutweeklynews.net/2022/02/11/ambushed-in-eufaula-alabamas-forgotten-race-massacre/.

4. Singleton v. Merrill, No. 2:21-cv-1291-AMM (N.D. Ala. Jan. 24, 2022) (three-judge court), consolidated with Milligan v. Merrill, No. 2:21-cv-1530-AMM, Memorandum Opinion and Order, at 6. The case originally included Alabama secretary of state John Merrill's name in its title, until he was succeeded by Wes Allen.

5. The *Purcell* Principle comes from the majority opinion in *Purcell v. Gonzalez*, 549 U.S. 1 (2006).

6. 599 U.S. 1 (2023).

7. Joint Stipulated Facts for Remedial Proceedings, Caster v. Allen, No. 2:21-cv-01530-AMM (N.D. Ala. Aug. 10, 2023).

8. Singleton v. Allen, Nos. 2:21-cv-1291-AMM, 2:21-cv-1530-AMM, and 2:21-cv-1536-AMM (N.D. Ala.), Transcript of Motion Hearing, August 14, 2023, before Judges Anna M. Manasco, Terry F. Moorer, and Stanley Marcus, filed August 18, 2023, ECF No. 184, pg. 138.

9. Ibid., pg. 72.

10. Ibid., pgs. 163–164.

11. Singleton v. Allen, No. 2:21-cv-1291-AMM (N.D. Ala. Sept. 5, 2023) (three-judge court), consolidated with Milligan v. Allen, No. 2:21-cv-1530-AMM, Injunction, Opinion, and Order, pgs. 8–9.

12. The 2021 Alabama map was similar to the 2011 Alabama map that, in theory, the DOJ could have objected to in the aftermath of the 2006's reauthorization granting them power to block plans that would fail a Section 2 analysis. However, Eric Holder's DOJ did not exercise this new power it had been granted under the 2006 reauthorization, likely to avoid drawing undue attention to the VRA in the aftermath of the *NAMUDO* case. This is one example of why we can never be certain whether a given policy would have been definitely blocked by the DOJ if *Shelby County* had not been handed down.

13. US Department of Justice, Civil Rights Division, "Letter to Jimmy Evans, Alabama Attorney General," March 27, 1992, https://www.justice.gov/sites/default/files/crt/legacy/2014/05/30/AL-1880.pdf.

14. Alpha Phi Alpha Fraternity Inc. v. Raffensperger, Nos. 1:21-cv-05337-SCJ, 1:21-cv-05339-SCJ, and 1:22-cv-00122-SCJ (N.D. Ga.), Order Following Coordinated Hearing on Motions for Preliminary Injunction, filed February 28, 2022, pg. 221.

15. *Alpha Phi Alpha Fraternity Inc. v. Raffensperger*, Opinion and Memorandum of Decision, filed October 26, 2023.

16. Robinson v. Ardoin, No. 3:22-cv-00211-SDD-SDJ (M.D. La. June 6, 2022), ECF No. 173.

17. Ardoin v. Robinson, 597 U.S. ____ (2022) (granting stay and cert. before judgment), Order List, June 28, 2022.

18. Robinson v. Ardoin, No. 22-30333 (5th Cir. filed Nov. 10, 2023), ECF No. 336-1.

19. Molly Ryan, "After a Court Fight, Louisiana's New Congressional Map Boosts Black Political Power," *All Things Considered*, NPR, January 23, 2024.

20. Complaint, Callais v. Landry, No. 3:24-cv-00122 (W.D. La. Jan. 31, 2024).

21. Callais v. Landry, No. 3:24-cv-00122-DCJ-CES-RRS (W.D. La.), Injunction and Reasons for Judgment, filed April 30, 2024.

22. United States v. Texas, No. 3:21-cv-299 (W.D. Tex. filed Dec. 3, 2021).

23. Natalia Contreras, "DOJ Drops Fight Against Texas Political Maps as Trump Administration Retreats from Voting Rights Cases," *Texas Tribune*, March 13, 2025.

24. South Carolina v. Katzenbach, 383 U.S. 301 (1966).

25. Ibid., pg. 5.

26. General Order 3 of Major General Gordon Granger, Military District of Texas, June 19, 1865, National Archives and Records Administration, https://catalog.archives.gov/id/182778372.

27. 840 F.2d 1240, 1244 (5th Cir. 1988).

28. Campos v. City of Baytown, 840 F.2d 1240, 1244 (5th Cir. 1988).

29. US Department of Justice, Civil Rights Division, Letter to Ray Holbrook, Galveston County Judge, March 17, 1992, https://www.justice.gov/sites/default/files/crt/legacy/2014/05/30/TX-2450.pdf.

30. Petteway v. Galveston Cnty., 698 F. Supp. 3d 952 (S.D. Tex. Oct. 13, 2023).

31. U.S. Department of Justice, Civil Rights Division, "Letter to Ray Holbrook, Galveston County Judge," March 17, 1992, https://www.justice.gov/sites/default/files/crt/legacy/2014/05/30/TX-2450.pdf.

32. Hoskins v. Hannah, Civil Action No. G-92-12 (S.D. Tex. Aug. 19, 1992).

33. US Department of Justice, Civil Rights Division, "Letter to James E. Trainor III of Galveston County, Texas," March 5, 2012, https://www.justice.gov/crt/voting-determination-letter-38.

34. Emergency Application to Vacate the Fifth Circuit's Stay of the Order Issued by the United States District Court for the Southern District of Texas, Terry Petteway, et al., Applicants, v. Galveston County, Texas, et al., Respondents., 2023 WL 8586330 (Dec. 8, 2023).

35. US Department of Justice, Civil Rights Division, "Letter to James E. Trainor III of Galveston County, Texas," March 5, 2012, https://www.justice.gov/crt/voting-determination-letter-38.

36. Petteway v. Galveston Cnty., 698 F. Supp. 3d 952 (S.D. Tex. Oct. 13, 2023).

37. Petteway v. Galveston Cnty., No. 3:13-cv-308, at 1 (S.D. Tex. Aug. 31, 2022).

38. In May, 2022, the incumbent Precinct 4 commissioner, Ken Clark, died after winning his primary two months earlier. County judge Mark Henry filled his vacancy with Robin Armstrong, a Black Republican. Armstrong was elected to a full term that fall. See Andrew Schneider, "Galveston County's Redistricting Plans Go to Trial next Month, in a Major Test of the Voting Rights Act," *Texas Standard*, July 18, 2023.

39. *Petteway*, 698 F. Supp. 3d 952. The account that follows is drawn from the trial transcript and opinion.

40. *Petteway*, No. 3:22-cv-00057 (order).

41. See, for instance, section II.A of defendant's closing brief for the district court trial, in *Petteway*, No. 3:22-cv-00057.

42. Petteway v. Galveston Cnty., No. 23-40582 (5th Cir. Aug. 1, 2024).

43. Ibid. at 71.

44. Nixon v. Kent Cnty., 76 F.3d 1381, 1387 (6th Cir. 1996).

45. Ibid. at 1401–2.

46. US Department of Justice, Civil Rights Division, "Letter to Gary W. Smith, Galveston City Attorney," December 14, 1992, https://www.justice.gov/sites/default/files/crt/legacy/2014/05/30/TX-2600.pdf.

47. U.S. Department of Justice, Civil Rights Division, "Letter to Barbara E. Roberts, Galveston City Attorney," December 14, 1998, https://www.justice.gov/crt/voting-determination-letter-33.

48. U.S. Department of Justice, Civil Rights Division, "Letter to C. Robert Heath of Galveston City, Texas," October 3, 2011, https://www.justice.gov/crt/voting-determination-letter-39.

49. Patino v. City of Pasadena (S.D. Tex. 2017); Jones v. Jefferson County Board of Education (N.D. Ala. 2019); Alabama State Conference of NAACP v. City of Pleasant Grove (N.D. Ala. 2019); Wright v. Sumter County Board of Elections and Registration (M.D. Ga. 2020); Whitest v. Crisp County School District (M.D. Ga. 2021); Dixon v. Lewisville Independent School District (E.D. Tex. 2022); Elizondo v. Spring Branch Independent School District (S.D. Tex. 2023). See also Ellen D. Katz et al., "To Participate and Elect: Section 2 of the Voting Rights Act Since 1982," University of Michigan Law School Voting Rights Initiative (2025), https://voting.law.umich.edu.

50. Lee and Velez (2024).

51. De Benedictis-Kessner et al. (2023).

52. Ibid., pg. 1.

53. For this chapter, we identify "municipalities" as places identified by the Census Bureau using the following legal/statistical area description codes: 25 (city); 37 (municipality); 43 (town); 47 (village).

54. This is a conservative estimate in that it counts only the proposals that contained a request to annex at least one outlying tract, and ignores how many tracts may have been part of a single request.

55. See, for example, Aiken (1987); Lichter et al. (2007).

56. Baumle, Fossett, and Waren (2008).

57. Durst (2018).

58. Ibid., pg. 938.

59. Durst (2019).

60. I. Zhang (2024).

61. Throughout, we weight bloc groups by their population.

62. This time, however, because racial characteristics form a component of our outcome variable, they are not included as covariates.

63. Aiken (1987).

Chapter 7

1. 570 U.S. 529 (2013).

2. *Fish v. Kobach*, 309 F. Supp. 3d 1048, 1053 (D. Kan. 2018), aff'd sub nom; *Fish v. Schwab*, 957 F.3d 1105 (10th Cir. 2020). The account that follows is drawn from the trial transcript and opinion.

3. *Fish v. Kobach*, bench trial transcript, pgs. 159–160.

4. Opening statement of Dale Ho., *Fish v. Kobach*.

5. Richman, Chattha, and Earnest (2014).

6. The CCES has since changed its name to the Cooperative Election Study.

7. See Donald J. Trump (@realDonaldTrump), "In addition to winning the Electoral College in a landslide, I won the popular vote if you deduct the millions of people who voted illegally," Twitter (now X), November 27, 2016, https://x.com/realDonaldTrump/status/802972944532209664.

8. Nate Cohn, "Illegal Voting Claims, and Why They Don't Hold Up," *New York Times*.

9. "Presidential Executive Order on the Establishment of Presidential Advisory Commission on Election Integrity," White House, Office of the Press Secretary, May 11, 2017, archived on Internet Archive Wayback Machine, https://web.archive.org/web/20170511232125/https://www.whitehouse.gov/the-press-office/2017/05/11/presidential-executive-order-establishment-presidential-advisory.

10. Spencer S. Hsu and John Wagner, "Trump Voting Commission Bought Texas Election Data Flagging Hispanic Voters," *Washington Post*, January 22, 2018.

11. Joseph P. Williams, "Trump Panel Finds No Voter Fraud," *US News and World Report*, January 10, 2018. Multiple independent studies similarly failed to produce any evidence of widespread fraud in the 2016 election. See Cottrell, Herron, and Westwood (2018); Keith, Pérez, and Famighetti (2017).

12. *Fish v. Kobach*, bench trial transcript, pg. 1072.

13. This claim is also based on Minnite's academic work, which finds that most instances that might be characterized as fraud are in fact simple administrative mistakes. See Minnite (2011).

14. *Fish v. Kobach*, bench trial transcript.

15. Ibid., pg. 1452.
16. Ibid., pg. 1453.
17. Ibid., pg. 1453.
18. Ansolabehere, Luks, and Schaffner (2015).
19. This letter was cowritten by Michael G. Miller and Brian Schaffner.
20. US Department of Justice, Civil Rights Division, "Letter to Antonio Garza, Texas Secretary of State," January 16, 1996, https://www.justice.gov/sites/default/files/crt/legacy/2014/05/30/TX-2860.pdf.
21. Ibid.
22. Ibid.
23. US Department of Justice, Civil Rights Division, "Letter to Thurbert E. Baker, Georgia Attorney General," May 29, 2009, https://www.justice.gov/crt/voting-determination-letter-58.
24. Ibid.
25. Merivaki (2021).
26. See Husted v. A. Philip Randolph Institute, 584 U.S. ____ (2018).
27. Von Mises (1939).
28. February 29 provides an extra option in leap years.
29. Interstate Voter Registration Data Crosscheck, "2014 Participation Guide," December 2013, archived on Internet Archive Wayback Machine, https://web.archive.org/web/20181207145620/https://wei.sos.wa.gov/agency/osos/en/press_and_research/weekly/Documents/Participation%20Guide%20with%20Comments.pdf.
30. Greg Palast, "The GOP's Stealth War Against Voters," *Rolling Stone*, August 24, 2016.
31. Goel et al. (2020).
32. Ibid., pg. 456.
33. Virginia State Board of Elections, "Annual Report on Voter Registration List Maintenance Activities," January 6, 2014, https://www.elections.virginia.gov/media/formswarehouse/maintenance-reports/2013SBEListMaintenancereport.pdf.
34. Jim Nolan, "Chesterfield Registrar Delays Purge of Voter Rolls," *Richmond Times-Dispatch*, November 20, 2013.
35. Virginia Department of Elections, *Annual List Maintenance Report, July 1, 2016 - June 30, 2017*, archived on Internet Archive Wayback Machine, https://web.archive.org/web/20171218031200/https://www.elections.virginia.gov/Files/maintenance-reports/2017SBEListMaintenancereport.pdf, page 4.
36. "Interstate Crosscheck Program Grows," *Canvassing Kansas* (December 2013), archived on Internet Archive Wayback Machine, https://web.archive.org/web/20140726103354/http://www.kssos.org/forms/communication/canvassing_kansas/dec13.pdf.
37. Arcia v. Florida Secretary of State, 772 F.3d 1335 (11th Cir. 2014).
38. N.C. State Conference of the NAACP v. N.C. State Bd. of Elections, 1:16CV1274 (M.D.N.C. Nov. 4, 2016).
39. Mark Joseph Stern, "North Carolina Is Engaging in 'Insane' Jim Crow–Style Voter Suppression, Says Federal Judge," *Slate*, November 3, 2016.
40. Moore v. Kobach, No. 18-2329-DDC-KGG (D. Kan. filed 2018).
41. Huseman and Willis (2017).
42. ERIC (Electronic Registration Information Center, "How ERIC Works, accessed January 14, 2026, https://ericstates.org/how-does-it-work/.
43. Mark Kasler, "LaRose Says Ohio May Drop out of Voter Registration Program He Praised Last Month," *Statehouse News Bureau*, March 7, 2023.
44. Marozzi (2023).
45. Combs (2023).
46. Alabama, Florida, Iowa, Louisiana, Missouri, Ohio, Texas, Virginia, and West Virginia.

47. EIP (2021).

48. Jim Hoft, "Who's 'Cleaning' Our Voter Rolls? Soros Funded ERIC Is Now Used In 31 States," *Gateway Pundit*, January 20, 2022, https://www.thegatewaypundit.com/2022/01/cleaning-voter-rolls-soros-founded-fundederic-now-used-31-states/.

49. Jessica Huseman, "The Texas Election Bill Contains a New Obstacle to Voting That Almost No One Is Talking About," *Votebeat Texas*, July 26, 2022, https://texas.votebeat.org/2021/7/26/22627685/texas-election-bill-voter-id-number-matching-problem.

50. ERIC, "Statistics," accessed January 15, 2026, https://ericstates.org/statistics/. See also Steve Lohr, "Another Use for A.I.: Finding Millions of Unregistered Voters," *New York Times*, November 5, 2018.

51. Miles Parks, "3 More GOP States Announce They're Leaving a Key Voting Data Partnership," *Morning Edition*, NPR, March 7, 2023.

52. These numbers come from our analysis of the Louisiana L2 voter file following the 2020 election.

53. ERIC, "Statistics."

54. Bergin and Ye (2016).

55. Bergin (2016).

56. Bergin et al. (2016).

57. Bergin and Ye (2017).

58. Common Cause New York et al. v. Board of Elections in the City of New York et al., No. 1:16-cv-06122-NGG-RML (E.D.N.Y. filed Nov. 2, 2016).

59. 52 U.S.C. § 20503 et seq.

60. US Department of Justice, Civil Rights Division, "Letter to Dennis R. Dunn, Georgia Senior Assistant Attorney General," October 24, 1994, https://www.justice.gov/sites/default/files/crt/legacy/2014/05/30/GA-2570.pdf; US Department of Justice, Civil Rights Division, "Letter to Joyce Hazeltine, South Dakota Secretary of State," June 19, 1995, https://www.justice.gov/sites/default/files/crt/legacy/2014/05/30/SD-1020.pdf. The DOJ objected to these policies because it determined that they likely violated the National Voter Registration Act. That said, given the US Supreme Court's cramped reading of the NVRA in *Husted v. A. Philip Randolph Institute* (584 U.S. ___ [2018]), such practices might not have been blocked by Section 5 after 2018.

61. Versions of the following analyses, which focus only on the first few election cycles post–*Shelby County*, were published in Brater et al. (2018), Morris (2019), and Feder and Miller (2020).

62. US EAC, "Election Administration and Voting Survey (EAVS) Comprehensive Report," December 23, 2025, https://www.eac.gov/research-and-data/studies-and-reports.

63. Some local election officials provided these data in the 2006 version of the survey as well.

64. Recall from Chapter 5 that this is an important precondition for assessing whether the end of preclearance might have had a *causal* effect on our outcome of interest—here, of course, the voter removal rate.

65. Merivaki (2020, pg. 561; emphasis added)).

66. While we cannot tell how many people moved *out* of a county, we expect that the figure is highly correlated with overall mobility rates. With the exception of Obama's 2012 vote share (which comes from the MIT Election Lab), all these characteristics are five-year ACS estimates, ending in the same year as the relevant electoral cycle.

67. In these models, uncovered counties in partially covered states are included among the controls (along with the fully noncovered counties).

68. In 2014, 797 covered counties reported their data to the EAVS. Among these, the median county had just under 17,000 registered voters at the time of the 2014 election and removed about 1,800 voters. Applying the average treatment effect of 5.19 points across these counties

indicates that 764,000 fewer voters would have been removed. Given that a model in which we weight counties by their logged population returns nearly identical point estimates, we are not especially concerned about heterogeneous effects driven by county size. Nevertheless, we use the median counts, rather than the means, in this calculation to err on the side of being highly conservative. The mean county had nearly 60,000 registered voters and removed more than 6,000.

69. Kevin, Morris, and Cora Henry, "Millions of Americans Don't Have Documents Proving Their Citizenship Readily Available," Brennan Center for Justice, June 11, 2024, https://www.brennancenter.org/our-work/analysis-opinion/millions-americans-dont-have-documents-proving-their-citizenship-readily; Kevin, Morris, and Cora Henry, "The SAVE Act Would Hurt Americans Who Actively Participate in Elections," Brennan Center for Justice, February 20, 2025, https://www.brennancenter.org/our-work/analysis-opinion/save-act-would-hurt-americans-who-actively-participate-elections.

70. 570 U.S. 1 (2013).

71. Burroughs & Cannon v. United States, 290 U.S. 534 (1934).

72. League of United Latin American Citizens of Arizona v. Reagan, No. CV17-4102 PHX DGC, 2018 WL 5983009 (D. Ariz. Nov. 14, 2018).

73. Mi Familia Vota v. Fontes, No. CV-22-00509-PHX-SRB, 2024 WL 2244338 (D. Ariz. May 2, 2024), aff'd in part, vacated in part, remanded, 129 F.4th 691 (9th Cir. 2025).

74. The Supreme Court allowed Arizona to require voters registering using the *state* form to prove their citizenship if they wanted to vote for president. Voters could register using the *federal* form without proving citizenship, however, and vote for president.

75. Republican National Committee v. Mi Familia Vota, 145 S. Ct. 108, 219 L. Ed. 2d 1355 (2024).

76. Kevin, Morris, and Arlyss Herzig, "Arizona's Show-Your-Papers Requirement Hurts Voters," Brennan Center for Justice, February 19, 2025, https://www.brennancenter.org/our-work/analysis-opinion/arizonas-show-your-papers-requirement-hurts-voters.

77. Mi Familia Vota v. Fontes, 129 F.4th 691 (9th Cir. 2025).

78. As of this writing, that case is still pending.

79. Garber (2025).

Chapter 8

1. 553 U.S. 181 (2008).

2. Eyder Peralta, Scott Neuman, and Mark Memmott "Supreme Court Strikes Down Key Provision of Voting Rights Law," NPR, June 25, 2013.

3. Gregg Abbott, @gregabbot, "Texas #VoterID law should go into effect immediately b/c #SCOTUS struck down section 4 of VRA today," Twitter (now X), June 25, 2013, https://x.com/gregabbott_tx/status/349532390336643075.

4. Texas Election Code § 63.001 et seq.

5. 553 U.S. 181 (2008).

6. Indeed, in *Crawford*, Indiana could not show any evidence of voter impersonation fraud in that state, nor could the voters who brought suit find anyone who would be barred from voting for lack of a compliant ID.

7. "Summary of Voter ID Laws Passed," Brennan Center for Justice, November 12, 2013.

8. "Strict" identification laws are ones that do not allow a voter to cast a ballot without presenting such an identification. In other states, voters are requested but not required to present such an identification.

9. See, for example, Barreto et al. (2019).

10. Ansolabehere (2014).

11. State of Texas v. Holder, 888 F. Supp. 2d 113 (D.D.C. 2012).

12. Gary Scharrer, "Ailing Gallegos Risks Health to Stop Voter ID Bill," *Chron. (Houston Chronicle)*, May 22, 2007.

13. Andrew Weber, "Texplainer: What Is Chubbing?," *Texas Tribune*, February 2, 2011.

14. Testimony of Rodney Ellis, Veasey v. Perry, No. 2:13-cv-00193 (S.D. Tex. Sept. 5, 2014) (trial transcript, day 4), 172.

15. Julián Aguilar, "Voter ID Passes House After Long, Emotional Debate," *Texas Tribune*, March 23, 2011.

16. US Department of Justice, Civil Rights Division, "Letter to Keith Ingram, Texas Director of Elections," March 12, 2012, https://www.justice.gov/sites/default/files/crt/legacy/2014/05/30/l_120312.pdf.

17. Ibid.

18. 888 F. Supp. 2d 113 (D.D.C. 2012).

19. Texas v. United States, No. 12:496 (S.D. Tex. 2012).

20. Ultimately, the Supreme Court would affirm its *Shelby County* precedent; with no need to consider the Section 5 question, the case was remanded to the district court, which dismissed it.

21. 71 F. Supp. 3d 627 (S.D. Tex. 2014).

22. Veasey v. Perry, 71 F. Supp. 3d 627 (S.D. Tex. 2014).

23. Ibid. (emphasis in original).

24. US Department of Justice, Civil Rights Division, "Letter to C. Havird Jones, Jr., South Carolina Assistant Deputy Attorney General," December 23, 2011, https://www.justice.gov/crt/voting-determination-letter-65.

25. State of South Carolina v. United States, No. 1:12-cv-00203 (D.D.C. Oct. 10, 2012), ECF No. 299. See the concurring opinion of Judge John D. Bates, joined by Judge Colleen Kollar-Kotelly: "To state the obvious, Act R54 as now pre-cleared is not the R54 enacted in May 2011. It is understandable that the Attorney General of the United States . . . would raise serious concerns about South Carolina's voter photo ID law as it then stood. But now, to the credit of South Carolina state officials, Act R54 as authoritatively interpreted does warrant pre-clearance."

26. Ibid.

27. Lee v. Virginia State Board of Elections, 155 F. Supp. 3d 572 (E.D. Va. 2015). Virginia ultimately repealed its voter ID law in 2020, making it the only state to date to have done so by legislative action.

28. Initially, the voter ID component was the only election law change in HB 589. After *Shelby County*, however, the legislature decided to expand the scope of HB 589, adding other provisions that likely would never have survived preclearance.

29. North Carolina State Board of Elections, "April 2013 SBOE-DMV ID Analysis," April 17, 2013.

30. North Carolina State Conference of the NAACP v. McCrory, 182 F. Supp. 3d 320, 275 (M.D.N.C.).

31. North Carolina State Conference of the NAACP v. McCrory, 831 F.3d 204 (4th Cir. 2016).

32. Ibid.

33. Ibid.

34. Cantoni and Pons (2021).

35. Highton (2017).

36. Ansolabehere (2009); Hershey (2009); Mycoff, Wagner, and Wilson (2009).

37. Esposito, Focanti, and Hastings (2019).

38. Grimmer and Yoder (2022).

39. Cantoni and Pons (2021).

40. E. Zhang (2022).

41. Valentino and Neuner (2017).

42. Citrin, Green, and Levy (2014); Hopkins et al. (2017).

43. Cantoni and Pons (2021).

44. See, for example, Barreto, Nuño, and Sanchez (2009); Barreto et al. (2018); Stewart (2013); Ansolabehere (2014); Highton (2017).

45. As Justice Alito put it in *Brnovich v. Democratic National Committee* (594 U.S. 647 [2021]), "A policy that appears to work for 98% or more of voters to whom it applies—minority and non-minority alike—is unlikely to render a system unequally open."

46. The DOJ objected to numerous such policies during the preclearance era. Take, for instance, its 1975 objection to proposed polling place relocations in Warren County, Mississippi (V8673). In its objection, the DOJ preclearance reviewer noted that the proposed polling place for Black voters was "5 miles from the predominantly Black areas in the Jonestown precinct, (and) that there is no public transportation to the polling place," rendering the act of voting substantially less convenient on average for Black residents of Warren County compared to white residents.

47. Erikson and Minnite (2009); Grimmer et al. (2018).

48. Hood and Bullock (2012); Rocha and Matsubayashi (2014).

49. Hajnal, Lajevardi, and Nielson (2017).

50. Grimmer et al. (2018).

51. Hajnal, Kuk, and Lajevardi (2018); Burden (2018).

52. Henninger, Meredith, and Morse (2021).

53. 796 F.3d 487 (5th Cir. 2015).

54. Veasey v. Abbott, 796 F.3d 487 (5th Cir. 2015), on rehearing en banc, 830 F.3d 216 (5th Cir. 2016).

55. Ibid.

56. Henninger, Meredith, and Morse (2021).

57. Fraga and Miller (2022).

58. The process for merging is described in much greater detail in Fraga and Miller (2022). In 2016, far fewer RIDs contained the unique voter identification numbers than in subsequent elections. Fraga and Miller used voter counties, names, and other available information from the RIDs to make matches.

59. Our numbers are slightly different than those that Fraga and Miller (2022) report, largely because of differences in the use of BISG. To keep our approach here consistent with that reported in the rest of the book, we use census block groups and CVAP as the inputs for the BISG algorithm.

60. Fraga and Miller (2022) found that the percentage of Hispanic voters in the RID pool was about 1 percentage point higher in the RID pool than the ID pool, whereas Asian voters were about 0.7 points less represented in the RID pool.

61. Bentele and O'Brien (2013); Rocha and Matsubayashi (2014); Hicks et al. (2015); Biggers and Hanmer (2017); Highton (2017).

62. Dowling, Miller, and Morris (2025).

63. While the 2020 general election was held during the COVID-19 pandemic, when many voters cast mail ballots—and thus would not have been "eligible" to use an RID—this was less common in Texas, where mail voting rules were not altered in response to the pandemic. As in earlier years, voters under 65 needed a (non-COVID) excuse in order to cast a mail ballot. Thus, we are less concerned about "missing" RIDs here than we might be in the cases of other states in 2020.

64. In this effort, we are grateful to our colleagues Bernard Fraga, Phoebe Henninger, and Marc Meredith, as well as their research assistants.

65. We use snapshots from L2 Political from shortly following each of the 2016 (March 12, 2017), 2018 (February 24, 2019), 2020 (March 25, 2021), and 2022 (March 12, 2023) elections to measure turnout in each election. See Kim and Fraga (2022) for a discussion of voter file timing.

66. Grimmer and Yoder (2022).

67. Alvarez, Cao, and Li (2021).

68. Pettigrew (2021).

69. Enos and Fowler (2018).

70. Gerber, Green, and Larimer (2008, pg. 38).

71. Morris and Miller (2022).

72. Veasey v. Abbott, No. 2:13-CV-193 (S.D. Tex. Apr. 10, 2017).

73. Veasey v. Abbott, No. 2:13-CV-193 (S.D. Tex. Aug. 23, 2017).

74. Veasey v. Abbott, No. 17-40884 (5th Cir. Apr. 27, 2018).

75. Jim Malewitz and Lindsay Carbonell, "Texas' Voter ID Defense Has Cost $3.5 Million," *Texas Tribune*, June 17, 2016; Alexa Ura, "Texas on the Hook for $6.8 Million After Long Voter ID Fight," *Texas Tribune*, May 27, 2020.

Chapter 9

1. United States Election Assistance Commission (EAC), *Election Administration and Voting Survey 2020 Comprehensive Report*, August 2021, https://www.eac.gov/sites/default/files/document_library/files/2020_EAVS_Report_Final_508c.pdf.

2. Cybersecurity and Infrastructure Security Agency, *Joint Statement from Elections Infrastructure Government Coordinating Council & the Election Infrastructure Sector Coordinating Executive Committees*, last modified November 12, 2020, https://www.cisa.gov/news-events/news/joint-statement-elections-infrastructure-government-coordinating-council-election-infrastructure.

3. Gronke (2012).

4. EAC, *The Election Administration and Voting Survey, 2016 Comprehensive Report*, 2016, figure obtained from Overview Table 2, U.S. Total, https://www.eac.gov/sites/default/files/eac_assets/1/6/2016_EAVS_Comprehensive_Report.pdf.

5. EAC, *The Election Administration and Voting Survey, 2020 Comprehensive Report*, pg. 1.

6. Gronke (2012).

7. Menger and Stein (2020).

8. Amlani and Collitt (2022); Barber and Holbein (2020); Berinsky, Burns, and Traugott (2001); Hassell (2017); McGhee, Paluch, and Romero (2022); Southwell and Burchett (2000); Thompson et al. (2020); Yoder et al. (2021).

9. Pew Research Center, "The Voting Experience in 2020," November 20, 2020, https://www.pewresearch.org/politics/2020/11/20/the-voting-experience-in-2020/.

10. Yoder et al. (2021).

11. Zaller (1992).

12. Berlinski et al. (2023); Calvillo, Rutchick, and Garcia (2021); Enders et al. (2021).

13. Graham and Yair (2024).

14. Alvarez, Hall, and Sinclair (2008); Baringer, Herron, and Smith (2020); Cottrell, Herron, and Smith (2021); Shino, Suttmann-Lea, and Smith (2022).

15. The Trump campaign lost 60 of the 61 lawsuits it brought alleging fraud in the 2020 election. See William Cummings, Joey Garrison, and Jim Sergent, "By the Numbers: President Donald Trump's Failed Efforts to Overturn the Election," *USA Today*, update January 6, 2021.

16. Morris and Shapiro (Forthcoming).

17. Rush et al. (2025).

18. Amy Gardner, Kate Rabinowitz, and Harry Stevens, "How GOP-Backed Voting Measures Could Create Hurdles for Tens of Millions of Voters," *Washington Post*, March 11, 2021.

19. Brennan Center for Justice, "Voting Laws Roundup: December 2021."

20. Brennan Center for Justice, "Voting Laws Roundup: December 2022."

21. Brennan Center for Justice, "Voting Laws Roundup: September 2024."

22. Morris (2023).

23. United States v. Georgia, No. 1:21-cv-02575-JPB (N.D. Ga. June 25, 2021).

24. In re Georgia Senate Bill 202, No. 1:21-mi-55555-JPB (N.D. Ga.), Georgia State Conference of the NAACP v. Raffensperger, No. 1:21-cv-01259-JPB, ECF No. 131 (Aug. 18, 2023), and Georgia State Conference of the NAACP v. Raffensperger, No. 1:21-cv-01229-JPB, ECF No. 144 (Aug. 18, 2023).

25. League of Women Voters of Florida, Inc. v. Lee, Nos. 4:21cv186-MW/MAF, 4:21cv187-MW/MAF, 4:21cv201-MW/MJF, 4:21cv242-MW/MAF (N.D. Fla. Mar. 31, 2022), pg. 135.

26. Ibid., pg. 281.

27. Ibid., pg. 279.

28. League of Women Voters of Florida Inc. v. Florida Secretary of State, 66 F.4th 905 (11th Cir. 2023).

29. Qtd. in Alexa, Ura, "Texas Democrats Abandon House Floor, Blocking Passage of Voting Bill Before Final Deadline," *Texas Tribune*, May 30, 2021.

30. Jessica Huseman, "The Texas Election Bill Contains a New Obstacle to Voting That Almost No One Is Talking About," *Votebeat Texas*, July 26, 2021, https://texas.votebeat.org/2021/7/26/22627685/texas-election-bill-voter-idnumber-matching-problem.

31. Qtd. in Ashley Lopez, "How Texas Officials and Voting Groups Are Trying to Limit Mail Ballot Rejections," *Morning Edition*, NPR, May 24, 2022, https://www.npr.org/2022/05/24/1100796467/texas-primary-texas-runoff-mailballot-rejections.

32. Alexa ura, "Hundreds of Mail-In Ballots Are Being Returned to Texas Voters Because They Don't Comply with New Voting Law," *Texas Tribune*, February 10, 2022, https://www.texastribune.org/2022/02/10/texas-mail-voting-rejections/.

33. Lopez, "How Texas Officials and Voting Groups Are Trying to Limit Mail Ballot Rejections."

34. The DOJ did not challenge SB1 on Section 2 grounds, but argued instead that the law ran afoul of a provision of the 1964 Civil Rights Act that outlaws rejecting ballots for "[im]material" reasons. See United States v. Texas, No. 5:21-cv-1085 (W.D. Tex. filed Nov. 4, 2021), complaint.

35. Much of this work appears in Miller et al. (Forthcoming).

36. About 5% of Texans live in one or another of the 91 counties that reported no application rejections to the state. While we exclude the large counties with no reported rejections in the primary analyses—under the assumption that they did not truly have a 0% rejection rate—we show in the Methodological Appendix that our central results about the characteristics of the disenfranchised voters hold if we assume that these counties did in fact reject no mail applications.

37. If a voter fixed (or "cured") their application or ballot, they are not considered to have been rejected.

38. As discussed above, some counties failed to provide data on application and ballot rejections. Large counties with zero reported application rejections are excluded. See the Methodological Appendix for more detailed discussion.

39. We exclude the 2–3% of rejections that we cannot match to the registered voter file.

40. We calculate these rates in much the same way as we do elsewhere in this book: The numerators are the summed racial probabilities that voters whose applications or ballots were rejected were members of each racial category, while the denominators are the summed racial probabilities for the full set of potential voters. Panel (a) includes as the denominator all

individuals who requested an absentee ballot, while the denominator in Panel (b) includes only the individuals who cast a mail ballot after successfully requesting one. While this method leads to noninteger voter "counts," it allows us to incorporate uncertainty surrounding voters' predicted race. These numbers differ slightly from Miller et al. (Forthcoming) because, for the sake of consistency, we here use the same BISG modification discussed in Chapter 5. The conclusions are unchanged.

41. EAC, *Election Administration and Voting Survey 2018 Comprehensive Report*, 2019, pg. 30.

42. EAC, *Election Administration and Voting Survey 2020 Comprehensive Report*, 2021, pg. 36.

43. Ibid.

44. See, for example, Finkel (1985); Valentino, Gregorowicz, and Groenendyk (2009).

45. One from March 12, 2023 (with turnout data from the 2022 general election) and another from April 10, 2024 (indicating participation in the March 5, 2024, primary election).

46. About 4% of individuals marked as participating are missing information about their vote mode.

47. We use a different set of elections to analyze voting behavior in the 2024 primary. Rather than incorporate historical information about turnout in midterm general elections, we look to presidential primary turnout in 2012, 2016, and 2020 for the base period. We similarly employ these same contests with respect to vote mode conditional on participation.

48. The timing of the treatment is not staggered; all treated voters were treated by a disenfranchisement in early 2022. Because we do not condition the parallel trends assumption on covariates, we therefore do not need to implement the recent advances in difference-in-differences models. See: Roth et al. (2023).

49. We note that Figure 9.9 indicates that the turnout of voters whose applications were rejected was not moving in parallel to that of voters whose application was accepted in the pretreatment period. In the Methodological Appendix, we show that accounting for differences between these groups using entropy balancing results in a plausible parallel trends assumption; this model indicates that an application rejection in 2022 reduced turnout in the 2024 primary by about 9.9 points, consistent with the other estimates here.

50. Hirano and Snyder (2019, pg. 213).

51. EAC, "Election Administration and Voting Survey," 2018, 2022, https://www.eac.gov/research-and-data/studies-and-reports.

52. La Unión del Pueblo Entero et al. v Abbott et al., 5:21-CV-0844-XR (2023).

53. La Unión del Pueblo Entero et al. v Abbott et al., USDC No. 5:21-CV-844 (2023).

Epilogue

1. Peyton McCrary, *Testimony before the Subcommittee on the Constitution, Civil Rights and Civil Liberties of the U.S. House Committee on the Judiciary, Oversight of the Voting Rights Act: Potential Legislative Reforms*, 117th Cong., August 16, 2021, https://www.congress.gov/117/meeting/house/114010/witnesses/HHRG-117-JU10-Wstate-McCraryJ-20210816.pdf.

2. This is due to the coverage of Northhampton County.

3. Qtd. in Sam Levine, Joanna Walters, and Joan E. Greve, "Sinema Says No to Filibuster Reform to Scuttle Democrats' Voting Rights Hopes," *The Guardian*, January 13, 2022, https://www.theguardian.com/us-news/2022/jan/13/kyrsten-sinema-democrats-filibuster-voting-rights.

4. Liz Ruskin, "Murkowski Is the Only Senate Republican Who Voted to Advance Voting Rights Bill," Alaska Public Media, November 4, 2021.

5. Reynolds (2017).

6. Bernie Sanders, *Congressional Record*, 117th Cong., 2nd sess., vol. 168, no. 12 (January 19, 2022): S331.

7. Qtd. in Levine, Walters, and Greve, "Sinema Says No to Filibuster Reform."

8. *Voting Rights*, pg. 5.

9. Grumbach (2022).

10. Morris and Grange (2024).

11. Brennan Center for Justice, Voting Laws Roundup: September 2024.

12. Missouri State Conference of the NAACP v. Ferguson-Florissant School District, 201 F. Supp. 3d 1006 (E.D. Mo. 2016).

13. Sanchez v. Cegavske, 214 F. Supp. 3d 961 (D. Nev. 2016).

14. Author analysis of Ellen D. Katz, Brian Remlinger, Andrew Dziedzic, Brooke Simone, and Jordan Schuler, *To Participate and Elect: Section 2 of the Voting Rights Act at 40*, University of Michigan Law School Voting Rights Initiative (2022), https://voting.law.umich.edu.

15. McCrary, *Testimony before the Subcommittee on the Constitution, Civil Rights and Civil Liberties*. Kevin T. Morris helped Dr. McCrary compile the data used in his testimony.

16. 594 U.S. 647 (2021).

17. Democratic Nat'l Comm. v. Hobbs, 948 F.3d 989 (9th Cir. 2020).

18. Author analyses of Katz et al., *To Participate and Elect*.

19. See "Cases Raising Claims Under Section 2 of the Voting Rights Act," Civil Rights Division, US Justice Department, accessed January 21, 2026, https://www.justice.gov/crt/cases-raising-claims-under-section-2-voting-rights-act-0.

20. Rucho v. Common Cause, 588 U.S. 684 (2019).

21. *Common Cause v. Rucho*, Complaint for Declaratory Judgment and Injunctive Relief, No. 1:16-CV-1026 (M.D.N.C. Aug. 5, 2016), pg. 12.

22. Common Cause v. Rucho, Nos. 1:16-cv-1026 & 1:16-cv-1164 (M.D.N.C. Jan. 9, 2018) (mem. op.); Benisek v. Lamone, No. 1:13-cv-03233 (D. Md. Nov. 7, 2018) (mem. op.).

23. Gill v. Whitford, 585 U.S. 48 (2018).

24. Justice Kennedy had long believed that the Court could come up with manageable standards for assessing partisan gerrymanders. See, for instance, his concurring opinion in *Vieth v. Jubelirer*, 541 U.S. 267 (2004).

25. The North Carolina congressional maps were later struck down by *state* courts which determined that the partisan gerrymander violated the state constitutional guarantee to free elections. See Harper v. Lewis, No. 19 CVS 012667 (N.C. Super. Ct. Wake Cnty. Oct. 28, 2019).

26. Giles and Hertz (1994); Hutchings and Valentino (2004); Mangum (2013); White and Laird (2020).

27. NAACP v. Alexander, No. 3:21-cv-03302 (D.S.C. Jan. 6, 2023).

28. Internal quotations omitted.

29. Arkansas State Conference NAACP v. Arkansas Board of Apportionment, No. 4:21-cv-1239-LPR (E.D. Ark. filed Dec. 29, 2021).

30. Brnovich v. Democratic National Committee, 594 U.S. 647 (2021).

31. US Commission on Civil Rights, "1961 U.S. Commission on Civil Rights Report Book 1: Voting," pg. 100.

32. Allen v. State Board of Elections, 393 U.S. 544 (1969), at 556.

33. Brown v. Post, 279 F. Supp. 60 (W.D. La. 1968).

34. Arkansas State Conference NAACP et al. v. Arkansas Board of Apportionment et al., No. 4:21-cv-01239-LPR (E.D. Ark. Feb. 17, 2022), Document 100, pg. 16.

35. U.S. Senate, *Report of the Senate Committee on the Judiciary on the Voting Rights Act Amendments of 1982*, 97th Cong., 2d sess., 1982, S. Rep. 97-417, 30.

36. The debate continued over the ensuing years, with later private plaintiffs arguing that they could bring a Section 2 suit under 42 U.S. Code § 1983, which allows Americans to hold the government accountable for violating their federal rights. On May 14, 2025, a split three-judge panel held that the Voting Rights Act of 1965 did not "unambiguously confer" a right to

vote and, thus, plaintiffs could not bring suits under Section 1983. Turtle Mountain Band of Chippewa Indians et al. v. Howe, No. 23-3655 (8th Cir. 2025), pg. 14. On May 28, 2025, plaintiffs petitioned for an en banc hearing by the full 8th Circuit.

37. Katz (2012).

38. Sarah N. Lynch, "US Justice Department Freezes Its Civil Rights Litigation," Reuters, January 22, 2025.

39. Sam Levine, "Trump's Justice Department Appointees Remove Leadership of Voting Unit," *The Guardian*, April 28, 2025.

40. Chiraag Bains, "What Just Happened: The Trump Administration's Dismissal of Voting Rights Lawsuits," *Just Security*, May 27, 2025.

41. Donald J. Trump, "Preserving and Protecting the Integrity of American Elections," Executive Order, March 25, 2025, White House, https://www.whitehouse.gov/presidential-actions/2025/03/preserving-and-protecting-the-integrity-of-american-elections/.

42. Donald J. Trump, "Protecting the Meaning and Value of American Citizenship," Executive Order, January 20, 2025, White House, https://www.whitehouse.gov/presidential-actions/2025/01/protecting-the-meaning-and-value-of-american-citizenship/.

43. League of United Latin American Citizens v. Executive Office of the President, 1:25-cv-00946 (D.D.C. Apr 24, 2025), ECF No. 104. The Brennan Center served as litigants in this case.

44. United States v. North Carolina State Board of Elections, No. 5:25-cv-00283-FL (E.D.N.C. May 27, 2025) (complaint).

45. California and Illinois passed SVRAs prior to *Shelby County* in 2002 and 2011, respectively. The states that have enacted one since *Shelby County* are Washington (2018); Oregon (2019); Virginia (2021); New York (2022); Connecticut (2023); Minnesota (2024); and Colorado (2025).

46. Virginia's jurisdictions can either seek approval from the state attorney general for any change or post the change publicly and receive comments for 30 days, followed by a further 30-day waiting period to allow citizens to challenge the proposal.

47. John Lewis, "Together, You Can Redeem the Soul of Our Nation," *New York Times* July 30, 2020.

BIBLIOGRAPHY

Aiken, Charles S. 1987. "Race as a Factor in Municipal Underbounding." *Annals of the Association of American Geographers* 77(4):564–579.

Alexander, Michelle. 2012. *The New Jim Crow: Mass Incarceration in the Age of Colorblindness.* The New Press.

Alt, James E. 1994. "The Impact of the Voting Rights Act on Black and White Voter Registration in the South." In *Quiet Revolution in the South: The Impact of the Voting Rights Act*, edited by Chandler Davidson and Bernard Grofman. Princeton University Press.

Alvarez, R. Michael, Jian Cao, and Yimeng Li. 2021. "Voting Experiences, Perceptions of Fraud, and Voter Confidence." *Social Science Quarterly* 102(4):1225–1238.

Alvarez, R. Michael, Thad E. Hall, and Betsy Sinclair. 2008. "Whose Absentee Votes Are Returned and Counted? The Variety and Use of Absentee Ballots in California." *Electoral Studies* 27(4):673–683.

Amlani, Sharif, and Samuel Collitt. 2022. "The Impact of Vote-by-Mail Policy on Turnout and Vote Share in the 2020 Election." *Election Law Journal: Rules, Politics, and Policy* 21(2). https://doi.org/10.1089/elj.2021.0015.

Aneja, Abhay, and Carlos F. Avenancio-Leon. 2019. "The Effect of Political Power on Labor Market Inequality: Evidence from the 1965 Voting Rights Act." Unpublished working paper.

Ang, Desmond. 2019. "Do 40-Year-Old Facts Still Matter? Long-Run Effects of Federal Oversight Under the Voting Rights Act." *American Economic Journal: Applied Economics* 11(3):1–53.

Ansolabehere, Stephen. 2009. "Effects of identification requirements on voting: Evidence from the Experiences of Voters on Election Day." *PS: Political Science and Politics* 42(1):127–130.

Ansolabehere, Stephen. 2014. "Corrected Supplemental Report." Marc Veasey, et al. v. Rick Perry, et al. United States District Court, Southern District of Texas, Corpus Christi Division, 2:13-cv-193. Document 600-1, September 16, 2014.

Ansolabehere, Stephen, Alan Gerber, and Jim Snyder. 2002. "Equal Votes, Equal Money: Court-Ordered Redistricting and Public Expenditures in the American States." *American Political Science Review* 96(4):767–777.

Ansolabehere, Stephen, Bernard L. Fraga, and Brian F. Schaffner. 2022. "The Current Population Survey Voting and Registration Supplement Overstates Minority Turnout." *Journal of Politics* 84(3):1850–1855.

Ansolabehere, Stephen, Samantha Luks, and Brian F. Schaffner. 2015*a*. "The Perils of Cherry Picking Low Frequency Events in Large Sample Surveys." *Electoral Studies* 40:409–410.

Avins, Alfred. 1969. "School Segregation and History Revisited." *Catholic Lawyer* 15(4).

Bains, Chiraag. 2025. "What Just Happened: The Trump Administration's Dismissal of Voting Rights Lawsuits."

Barber, Michael, and John B. Holbein. 2020. "The Participatory and Partisan Impacts of Mandatory Vote-by-Mail." *Science Advances* 6(35):eabc7685.

Baringer, Anna, Michael C. Herron, and Daniel A. Smith. 2020. "Voting by Mail and Ballot Rejection: Lessons from Florida for Elections in the Age of the Coronavirus." *Election Law Journal: Rules, Politics, and Policy* 19(3):289–320.

Barreto, Matt A., Stephen A. Nuño, and Gabriel R. Sanchez. 2009. "The Disproportionate Impact of Voter-ID Requirements on the Electorate—New Evidence from Indiana." *PS: Political Science and Politics* 42(1):111–116.

Barreto, Matt A., Stephen Nuño, Gabriel R. Sanchez, and Hannah L. Walker. 2018. "The Racial Implications of Voter Identification Laws in America." *American Politics Research* 47(12).

Barreto, Matt A., Stephen Nuño, Gabriel R. Sanchez, and Hannah L. Walker. 2019. "The Racial Implications of Voter Identification Laws in America." *American Politics Research* 47(2):238–249.

Bateman, David A., Ira Katznelson, and John S. Lapinski. 2018. *Southern Nation: Congress and White Supremacy After Reconstruction*. Princeton Studies in American Politics. Princeton University Press.

Baumle, Amanda K., Mark Fossett, and Warren Waren. 2008. "Strategic Annexation Under the Voting Rights Act: Racial Dimensions of Annexation Practices." *Harvard Blackletter Law Journal* 24:81.

Bentele, Keith G., and Erin E. O'Brien. 2013. "Jim Crow 2.0? Why States Consider and Adopt Restrictive Voter Access Policies." *Perspectives on Politics* 11(4):1088–1116.

Bergin, Brigid. 2016. "AG Launches Investigation into NYC Board of Elections." New York Public Radio, Podcasts, Live Streaming Radio, News. WNYC, April 20.

Bergin, Brigid, John Keefe, Jenny Ye, and Clarissa Diaz. 2016. "The Brooklyn Voter Purge: By Age, Registration, and Sanders Districts." New York Public Radio, Podcasts, Live Streaming Radio, News. WNYC, June 22.

Bergin, Brigid, and Jenny Ye. 2016. "60,000 Fewer Democrats in Brooklyn and No Clear Reason Why." New York Public Radio, Podcasts, Live Streaming Radio, News. WNYC, April 18.

Bergin, Brigid, and Jenny Ye. 2017. "A Year After Brooklyn Voter Purge Scandal, a Timeline of Action and Inaction." New York Public Radio, Podcasts, Live Streaming Radio, News. WNYC, April 19.

Berinsky, Adam J., Nancy Burns, and Michael W. Traugott. 2001. "Who Votes by Mail?: A Dynamic Model of the Individual-Level Consequences of Voting-by-Mail Systems." *Public Opinion Quarterly* 65(2):178–197.

Berlinski, Nicolas, Margaret Doyle, Andrew M. Guess, Gabrielle Levy, Benjamin Lyons, Jacob M. Montgomery, Brendan Nyhan, and Jason Reifler. 2023. "The Effects of Unsubstantiated Claims of Voter Fraud on Confidence in Elections." *Journal of Experimental Political Science* 10(1):34–49.

Berman, Ari. 2015. *Give Us the Ballot: The Modern Struggle for Voting Rights in America*. Farrar, Straus and Giroux.

Bernd, Joseph L. 1982. "White Supremacy and the Disfranchisement of Blacks in Georgia, 1946." *Georgia Historical Quarterly* 66(4):492–513.

Bernini, Andrea, Giovanni Facchini, Marco Tabellini, and Cecilia Testa. 2025. "Black Empowerment and White Mobilization: The Effects of the Voting Rights Act." *Journal of Political Economy* 133(10).

Biggers, Daniel R., and Michael J. Hanmer. 2017. "Understanding the Adoption of Voter Identification Laws in the American States." *American Politics Research* 45(4):560–588.

Billings, Stephen B., Noah Braun, Daniel B. Jones, and Ying Shi. 2024. "Disparate Racial Impacts of *Shelby County v. Holder* on Voter Turnout." *Journal of Public Economics* 230:105047.

Brater, Jonathan, Kevin Morris, Myrna Pérez, and Christopher Deluzio. 2018. "Purges: A Growing Threat to the Right to Vote." Brennan Center for Justice.

Brown, Mitchell, Kathleen Hale, and Bridgett King. 2019. *The Future of Election Administration: Cases and Conversations*. Palgrave Macmillan.

Bullock, Charles S., Keith Gaddie, and Justin J. Wert. 2016. *The Rise and Fall of the Voting Rights Act*. University of Oklahoma Press.

Burden, Barry C. 2018. "Disagreement over ID Requirements and Minority Voter Turnout." *Journal of Politics* 80(3).

Califano, Joseph A. 2015. *The Triumph and Tragedy of Lyndon Johnson: The White House Years*. Simon and Schuster.

Calvillo, Dustin P., Abraham M. Rutchick, and Ryan J. B. Garcia. 2021. "Individual Differences in Belief in Fake News About Election Fraud After the 2020 US Election." *Behavioral Sciences* 11(12):175.

Cantoni, Enrico, and Vincent Pons. 2021. "Strict ID Laws Don't Stop Voters: Evidence from a US Nationwide Panel, 2008–2018." *Quarterly Journal of Economics* 136(4): 2615–2660.

Cantu, Edward. 2015. "The Roberts Court and Penumbral Federalism." *Catholic University Law Review* 64(2):271–316.

Caro, Robert A. 2002. *The Years of Lyndon Johnson*, Volume 3: Master of the Senate New York: Alfred A. Knopf.

Caro, Robert A. 2012. *The Years of Lyndon Johnson*, Volum 4: *The Passage of Power*. Alfred A. Knopf.

Cascio, Elizabeth U., and Ebonya Washington. 2014. "Valuing the Vote: The Redistribution of Voting Rights and State Funds Following the Voting Rights Act of 1965." *Quarterly Journal of Economics* 129(1):379–433.

Citrin, Jack, Donald P. Green, and Morris Levy. 2014. "The Effects of Voter ID Notification on Voter Turnout: Results from a Large-Scale Field Experiment." *Election Law Journal* 13(2):228–242.

Colby, Thomas. 2016. "In Defense of the Equal Sovereignty Principle." *Duke Law Journal* 65(6):1087–1171.

Combs, Cory. 2023. "Withdrawals from ERIC Are the Result of Politics That Hurt the Integrity and Security of U.S. Elections, Say Current and Former Election Officials." Press release. Issue One, March 8.

Cottrell, David, Michael C. Herron, and Daniel A. Smith. 2021. "Vote-by-Mail Ballot Rejection and Experience with Mail-In Voting." *American Politics Research* 49(6):577–590.

Cottrell, David, Michael C. Herron, and Sean J. Westwood. 2018. "An Exploration of Donald Trump's Allegations of Massive Voter Fraud in the 2016 General Election." *Electoral Studies* 51:123–142.

Crawford, F. C. 1925. "New York State Literacy Test." *American Political Science Review* 19(4):788–790.

Daley, David. 2024. *Antidemocratic: Inside the Far Right's 50-Year Plot to Control American Elections*. Erscheinungsort nicht ermittelbar. HarperCollins.

Davidson, Chandler, and Bernard Grofman. 1994. *Quiet Revolution in the South: The Impact of the Voting Rights Act, 1965–1990*. Princeton University Press.

Davis, Martha S. 1989. "Attorney Fee Awards in Voting Rights Litigation." *South Dakota Law Review* 34:303.

de Benedictis–Kessner, Justin, Diana Da In Lee, Yamil R. Velez, and Christopher Warshaw. 2023. "American Local Government Elections Database." *Scientific Data* 10(1):912.

Derfner, Armand. 1973. "Racial Discrimination and the Right to Vote." *Vanderbilt Law Review* 26(3):523.

Dombrowski, Diana, Alex Ebert, Kimberly Strawbridge Robinson, Jon Meltzer, K. Sophie Will, and Umar Farooq. 2025. "Voting Rights Claims Plunge in Wake of Supreme Court Decision."

Bloomberg Law, February 12. https://news.bloomberglaw.com/litigation/voting-rights-claims-plunge-in-wake-of-supreme-court-decision.

Dowling, Conor M., Michael G. Miller, and Kevin T. Morris. 2025. "Crossover Voting Rates in Partisan and Nonpartisan Elections: Evidence from Cast Vote Records." *Political Research Quarterly* 78(2):720–737.

Dudziak, Mary L. 1988. "Desegregation as a Cold War Imperative." *Stanford Law Review* 41(1):61–120.

Dudziak, Mary L. 2011. *Cold War Civil Rights: Race and the Image of American Democracy*. Politics and Society in Twentieth-Century America. Princeton University Press.

Durst, Noah J. 2018. "Racial Gerrymandering of Municipal Borders: Direct Democracy, Participatory Democracy, and Voting Rights in the United States." *Annals of the American Association of Geographers* 108(4):938–954.

Durst, Noah J. 2019. "Race and Municipal Annexation After the Voting Rights Act." *Journal of the American Planning Association* 85(1):49–59.

EIP (Election Integrity Partnership). 2021. *The Long Fuse: Misinformation and the 2020 Election*. Technical report. https://www.eipartnership.net/report.

Enamorado, Ted, and Kosuke Imai. 2019. "Validating Self-Reported Turnout by Linking Public Opinion Surveys with Administrative Records." *Public Opinion Quarterly* 83(4):723–748.

Enders, Adam M., Joseph E. Uscinski, Casey A. Klofstad, Kamal Premaratne, Michelle I. Seelig, Stefan Wuchty, Manohar N. Murthi, and John R. Funchion. 2021. "The 2020 Presidential Election and Beliefs About Fraud: Continuity or Change?" *Electoral Studies* 72:102366.

Enos, Ryan D., and Anthony Fowler. 2018. "Aggregate Effects of Large-Scale Campaigns on Voter Turnout." *Political Science Research and Methods* 6(4):733–751.

Epperly, Brad, Christopher Witko, Ryan Strickler, and Paul White. 2020. "Rule by Violence, Rule by Law: Lynching, Jim Crow, and the Continuing Evolution of Voter Suppression in the U.S." *Perspectives on Politics* 18(3):756–769.

Erikson, Robert S., and Lorraine C. Minnite. 2009. "Modeling Problems in the Voter Identification–Voter Turnout Debate." *Election Law Journal* 8(2):85–101.

Esposito, Francesco Maria, Diego Focanti, and Justine S. Hastings. 2019. "Effects of Photo ID Laws on Registration and Turnout: Evidence from Rhode Island." National Bureau of Economic Research (January). https://www.nber.org/papers/w25503.

Eubank, Nicholas, and Adriane Fresh. 2022. "Enfranchisement and Incarceration After the 1965 Voting Rights Act." *American Political Science Review* 116(3):791–806.

Ewald, Alec C. 2009. *The Way We Vote: The Local Dimension of American Suffrage*. Vanderbilt University Press.

Feder, Catalina, and Michael G. Miller. 2020. "Voter Purges After *Shelby*: Part of Special Symposium on Election Sciences." *American Politics Research* 48(6):687–692.

Ferrer, Joshua, Igor Geyn, and Daniel M. Thompson. 2023. "How Partisan Is Local Election Administration?" *American Political Science Review* 118(2):1–16.

Ferrier, Michelle, Gaurav Sinha, and Michael Outrich. 2016. "Media Deserts: Monitoring the Changing Media Ecosystem." In *The Communication Crisis in America, and How to Fix It*. Palgrave Macmillan.

Finkel, Steven E. 1985. "Reciprocal Effects of Participation and Political Efficacy: A Panel Analysis." *American Journal of Political Science* 29(4):891–913.

Foner, Eric. 2014. *Reconstruction: America's Unfinished Revolution, 1865–1877*. Updated ed. Harper Collins.

Fraga, Bernard L. 2018. *The Turnout Gap: Race, Ethnicity, and Political Inequality in a Diversifying America*. Cambridge University Press.

Fraga, Bernard L., and Michael G. Miller. 2022. "Who Do Voter ID Laws Keep from Voting?" *Journal of Politics* 84(2):1091–1105.

Fraga, Luis, and Maria Ocampo. 2007. "More Information Requests and the Deterrent Effect of Section 5 of the Voting Rights Act." In *Voting Rights Act Reauthorization of 2006: Perspectives on Democracy, Participation, and Power*, ed. Ana Henderson. Berkeley Public Policy Press.

Fresh, Adriane. 2018. "The Effect of the Voting Rights Act on Enfranchisement: Evidence from North Carolina." *Journal of Politics* 80(2):713–718.

Garber, Andrew. 2025. "New Georgia Law Spurs Bogus Challenges to Voter Eligibility." Technical report. Brennan Center for Justice.

Garrow, David J. 2004. *Bearing the Cross: Martin Luther King, Jr., and the Southern Christian Leadership Conference*. New York: William Morrow.

Gerber, Alan S., Donald P. Green, and Christopher W. Larimer. 2008. "Social Pressure and Voter Turnout: Evidence from a Large-Scale Field Experiment." *American Political Science Review* 102(1):33–48.

Gerken, Heather. 2007. *The Democracy Index: Why Our Election System Is Failing and How to Fix It*. Princeton University Press.

Gibson, Nadine Suzanne. 2020. "Moving Forward or Backsliding: A Causal Inference Analysis of the Effects of the *Shelby* Decision in North Carolina." *American Politics Research* 48(5):649–662.

Giles, Micheal W., and Kaenan Hertz. 1994. "Racial Threat and Partisan Identification." *American Political Science Review* 88(2):317–326.

Goel, Sharad, Marc Meredith, Michael Morse, David Rothschild, and Houshmand Shirani-Mehr. 2020. "One Person, One Vote: Estimating the Prevalence of Double Voting in U.S. Presidential Elections." *American Political Science Review* 114(2):456–469.

Goldfield, David. 2014. "Border Men: Truman, Eisenhower, Johnson, and Civil Rights." *Journal of Southern History* 80(1):7–38.

Graham, Matthew H., and Omer Yair. 2024. "Expressive Responding and Belief in 2020 Election Fraud." *Political Behavior* 46:1–26.

Gray, Thomas R., and Jeffery A. Jenkins. 2025. "Estimating Disenfranchisement in US Elections, 1870–1970." *Perspectives on Politics* 23(1):55–75.

Greenberger, Michael, and Jasmine Carrera Smith. 2025. "Federal Enforcement and Black Political Representation: Evidence from Reconstruction and the Voting Rights Act." *Journal of Race, Ethnicity, and Politics* 10: 742–765.

Grimmer, Justin, and Eitan Hersh. 2023. "How Election Rules Affect Who Wins" (working paper), Eitan Hersh, June 29, https://www.eitanhersh.com/uploads/7/9/7/5/7975685/effectslaws_062923.pdf.

Grimmer, Justin, Eitan Hersh, Marc Meredith, Jonathan Mummolo, and Clayton Nall. 2018. "Obstacles to Estimating Voter ID Laws' Effect on Turnout." *Journal of Politics* 80(3).

Grimmer, Justin, and Jesse Yoder. 2022. "The Durable Differential Deterrent Effects of Strict Photo Identification Laws." *Political Science Research and Methods* 10(3):453–469.

Grofman, Bernard, and Lisa Handley. 1991. "The Impact of the Voting Rights Act on Black Representation in Southern State Legislatures." *Legislative Studies Quarterly* 16(1): 111–128.

Gronke, Paul. 2012. "Early Voting: The Quiet Revolution in American Elections." In *Law and Election Politics: The Rules of the Game*, edited by Matthew Justin Streb. Routledge.

Grumbach, Jacob. 2022. *Laboratories Against Democracy: How National Parties Transformed State Politics*. Princeton Studies in American Politics. Princeton University Press.

Grumbach, Jacob M., and Charlotte Hill. 2022. "Rock the Registration: Same Day Registration Increases Turnout of Young Voters." *Journal of Politics* 84(1).

Hajnal, Zoltan, John Kuk, and Nazita Lajevardi. 2018. "We All Agree: Strict Voter ID Laws Disproportionately Burden Minorities." *Journal of Politics* 80(3).

Hajnal, Zoltan, Nazita Lajevardi, and Lindsay Nielson. 2017. "Voter Identification Laws and the Suppression of Minority Votes." *Journal of Politics* 79(2):363–379.

Hale, Kathleen, Robert Montjoy, and Mitchell Brown. 2015. *Administering Elections*. Palgrave Macmillan.

Handley, Lisa, and Bernard Grofman. 1994. "The Impact of the Voting Rights Act on Minority Representation: Black Officeholding in Southern State Legislatures and Congressional Delegations." In *Quiet Revolution in the South: The Impact of the Voting Rights Act*, ed. Chandler Davidson and Bernard Grofman. Princeton University Press.

Hassell, Hans J. G. 2017. "Teaching Voters New Tricks: The Effect of Partisan Absentee Vote-by-Mail Get-Out-the-Vote Efforts." *Research and Politics* 4(1):2053168017694806.

Hayes, Danny, and Jennifer L. Lawless. 2015. "As Local News Goes, So Goes Citizen Engagement: Media, Knowledge, and Participation in US House Elections." *Journal of Politics* 77(2):447–462.

Hayes, Danny, and Jennifer L. Lawless. 2018. "The Decline of Local News and Its Effects: New Evidence from Longitudinal Data." *Journal of Politics* 80(1):332–336.

Hayter, Julian Maxwell. 2014. "From Intent to Effect: Richmond, Virginia, and the Protracted Struggle for Voting Rights, 1965–1977." *Journal of Policy History* 26(4):534–567.

Henninger, Phoebe, Marc Meredith, and Michael Morse. 2021. "Who Votes Without Identification? Using Individual-Level Administrative Data to Measure the Burden of Strict Voter Identification Laws." *Journal of Empirical Legal Studies* 18(2):256–286.

Hershey, Marjorie Randon. 2009. "What We Know About Voter-ID Laws, Registration, and Turnout." *PS: Political Science and Politics* 42(1):87–91.

Hicks, William D., Seth C. McKee, Mitchell D. Sellers, and Daniel A. Smith. 2015. "A Principle or a Strategy? Voter Identification Laws and Partisan Competition in the American States." *Political Research Quarterly* 68(1):18–33.

Highton, Benjamin. 2017. "Voter Identification Laws and Turnout in the United States." *Annual Review of Political Science* 20:149–167.

Hirano, Shigeo, and James M. Snyder Jr. 2019. *Primary Elections in the United States*. Cambridge University Press.

Hood, M. V., and Charles S. Bullock. 2012. "Much Ado About Nothing? An Empirical Assessment of the Georgia Voter Identification Statute." *State Politics and Policy Quarterly* 12(4):394–414.

Hopkins, Daniel J., Marc Meredith, Michael Morse, Sarah Smith, and Jesse Yoder. 2017. "Voting but for the Law: Evidence from Virginia on Photo Identification Requirements." *Journal of Empirical Legal Studies* 14(1):79–128.

Huseman, Jessica, and Derek Willis. 2017. "The Voter Fraud Commission Wants Your Data—But Experts Say They Can't Keep It Safe." *ProPublica*, October 23. https://www.propublica.org/article/crosscheck-the-voter-fraud-commission-wants-your-data-keep-it-safe.

Hutchings, Vincent L., and Nicholas A. Valentino. 2004. "The Centrality of Race in American Politics." *Annual Review of Political Science* 7:383–408.

Imai, Kosuke, and Kabir Khanna. 2016. "Improving Ecological Inference by Predicting Individual Ethnicity from Voter Registration Records." *Political Analysis* 24(2):263–272.

Jenkins, John A. 2012. *The Partisan: The Life of William Rehnquist*. PublicAffairs.

Jones, M. Adrienne. 2018. "When Yes Means No: GOP Congressional Strategy and the Reauthorization of the VRA in 2006." *The Forum* 16(2):289–312.

Katz, Ellen. 2012. "Democrats at DOJ: Why Partisan Use of the Voting Rights Act Might Not Be So Bad After All." *Stanford Law and Policy Review* 23(2):415–430.

Keele, Luke, William Cubbison, and Ismail White. 2021. "Suppressing Black Votes: A Historical Case Study of Voting Restrictions in Louisiana." *American Political Science Review* 115(2):694–700.

Keith, Douglas, Myrna Pérez, and Christopher Famighetti. 2017. "Noncitizen Voting: The Missing Millions." Technical report. Brennan Center for Justice, May 5. https://www.brennancenter.org/our-work/research-reports/noncitizen-voting-missing-millions.

Keith, LeeAnna. 2009. *The Colfax Massacre: The Untold Story of Black Power, White Terror, and the Death of Reconstruction*. Oxford University Press.

Keyssar, Alexander. 2008. *Right to Vote: The Contested History of Democracy in the United States*. Perseus (Hachette).

Kim, Seo-young Silvia, and Bernard Fraga. 2022. "When Do Voter Files Accurately Measure Turnout? How Transitory Voter File Snapshots Impact Research and Representation" (working paper). American Political Science Association (APSA) Preprints. September 13.

Kimball, David C., and Brady Baybeck. 2013. "Are All Jurisdictions Equal? Size Disparity in Election Administration." *Election Law Journal: Rules, Politics, and Policy* 12(2):130–145.

King, Martin Luther Jr. 1998. *The Autobiography of Martin Luther King, Jr.* Ed. Clayborne Carson. Intellectual Properties Management in association with Warner Books.

Klarman, Michael J. 2001. "The White Primary Rulings: A Case Study in the Consequences of Supreme Court Decisionmaking." *Florida State University Law Review* 29(1):55–107.

Komisarchik, Mayya. 2026. "Democrats Versus Democracy: The Southern Response to the Voting Rights Act." *Journal of Politics* 88(1).

Komisarchik, Mayya, and Ariel White. 2025. "Throwing Away the Umbrella: Minority Voting After the Supreme Court's *Shelby* Decision." *Quarterly Journal of Political Science* 20(2):269–305.

Kousser, J. Morgan. 1999. *Colorblind Injustice: Minority Voting Rights and the Undoing of the Second Reconstruction*. University of North Carolina Press.

Kreis, Anthony Michael. 2025. "Coups and Punishment in the Constitutional Order." *Wisconsin Law Review* pp. 459–481.

Kropf, Martha, Timothy Vercellotti, and David C. Kimball. 2013. "Representative Bureaucracy and Partisanship: The Implementation of Election Law." *Public Administration Review* 73(2):242–252.

Landau, David, Hannah Jacobs Wiseman, and Samuel R. Wiseman. 2021. "Federalism, Democracy, and the 2020 Election." *Texas Law Review* 99:96–121.

Landsberg, Brian K. 2007. *Free at Last to Vote: The Alabama Origins of the 1965 Voting Rights Act*. University Press of Kansas.

Lane, Charles. 2008. *The Day Freedom Died: The Colfax Massacre, the Supreme Court, and the Betrayal of Reconstruction*. Henry Holt.

Leadership Conference on Civil and Human Rights. 2019. *Democracy Diverted: Polling Place Closures and the Right to Vote*. Technical report. September.

Lee, Diana Da In, and Yamil Ricardo Velez. 2024. "Rising Tides or Political Ripcurrents? Gentrification and Minority Representation in 166 Cities." *Urban Affairs Review* 60(3):956–982.

Lee, Erika. 2020. "America First, Immigrants Last: American Xenophobia Then and Now." *Journal of the Gilded Age and Progressive Era* 19(1):3–18.

Leibowitz, Arnold H. 1969. "English Literacy: Legal Sanction for Discrimination." *Notre Dame Law* 45:7.

Lemann, Nicholas. 2007. *Redemption: The Last Battle of the Civil War*. Macmillan.

Lichter, Daniel T., Domenico Parisi, Steven Michael Grice, and Michael Taquino. 2007. "Municipal Underbounding: Annexation and Racial Exclusion in Small Southern Towns." *Rural Sociology* 72(1):47–68.

Mangum, Maruice. 2013. "The Racial Underpinnings of Party Identification and Political Ideology." *Social Science Quarterly* 94(5):1222–1244.

Marozzi, Collin. 2023. "In Their Own Words: ERIC Improves Election Integrity." Technical report. ACLU Ohio.

Martin, Andrew D., and Kevin M. Quinn. 2002. "Dynamic Ideal Point Estimation via Markov Chain Monte Carlo for the US Supreme Court, 1953–1999." *Political analysis* 10(2):134–153.

May, Gary. 2013. *Bending Toward Justice: The Voting Rights Act and the Transformation of American Democracy*. New York: Basic Books.

McBrayer, Markie, R. Lucas Williams, and Andrea Eckelman. 2020. "Local Officials as Partisan Operatives: The Effect of County Officials on Early Voting Administration." *Social Science Quarterly* 101(4):1475–1488.

McGhee, Eric, Jennifer Paluch, and Mindy Romero. 2022. "Vote-by-Mail Policy and the 2020 Presidential Election." *Research and Politics* 9(2):20531680221089197.

McInerney, Taylor C., Kayla Z. Thompson, Kimberly K. Shackelford, Felicia J. Tuggle, and Jennifer F. Jettner. 2020. "Alabama After *Shelby v. Holder*: Polling Place Changes and Access to Polling Place Information." *Journal of Policy Practice and Research* 1(4):165–177.

Meeks, Lindsey. 2020. "Undercovered, Underinformed: Local News, Local Elections, and U.S. Sheriffs." *Journalism Studies* 21(12):1609–1626.

Menger, Andrew, and Robert M. Stein. 2020. "Choosing the Less Convenient Way to Vote: An Anomaly in Vote by Mail Elections." *Political Research Quarterly* 73(1):196–207.

Merivaki, Thessalia. 2020. "'Our Voter Rolls Are Cleaner than Yours': Balancing Access and Integrity in Voter List Maintenance." *American Politics Research* 48(5):560–570.

Merivaki, Thessalia. 2021. *The Administration of Voter Registration: Expanding the Electorate Across and Within the States*. Elections, Voting, Technology. Palgrave Macmillan.

Miller, Michael G., Kevin T. Morris, Ian Shapiro, and Coryn Grange. Forthcoming. "The Disparate and Durable Effects of Mail Voting Restrictions: Evidence from Texas." *Journal of Politics*.

Minnite, Lorraine C. 2011. *The Myth of Voter Fraud*. Cornell University Press.

Mohr, Zachary, JoEllen V. Pope, Martha E. Kropf, and Mary Jo Shepherd. 2019. "Strategic Spending: Does Politics Influence Election Administration Expenditure?" *American Journal of Political Science* 63(2):427–438.

Morris, Kevin. 2019. Voter "Purge Rates Remain High, Analysis Finds." Brennan Center for Justice.

Morris, Kevin T. 2023. "A Right Restricted: Racial Threat and the Sponsorship of Restrictive Voting Laws." *Journal of Race, Ethnicity, and Politics* 8(3):421–445.

Morris, Kevin T., and Ian Shapiro. Forthcoming. "On Fertile Ground: How Racial Resentment Primes White Americans To Believe Fraud Accusations." *Political Behavior*.

Morris, Kevin T., and Peter Miller. 2022. "Voting in a Pandemic: COVID-19 and Primary Turnout in Milwaukee, Wisconsin." *Urban Affairs Review* 58(2):597–613.

Morris, Kevin, and Coryn Grange. *Growing Racial Disparities in Voter Turnout, 2008–2022*. New York: Brennan Center for Justice; New York University School of Law, 2024.

Mycoff, Jason D., Michael W. Wagner, and David C. Wilson. 2009. "The Empirical Effects of Voter-ID Laws: Present or Absent?" *PS: Political Science and Politics* 42(1):121–126.

Myrdal, Gunnar. 1944. *An American Dilemma: The Negro Problem and Modern Democracy*. New York: Pantheon Books.

Parker, Christopher S. 2009. *Fighting for Democracy: Black Veterans and the Struggle Against White Supremacy in the Postwar South*. Princeton Studies in American Politics. Princeton University Press.

Parker, Frank R. 2011. *Black Votes Count: Political Empowerment in Mississippi After 1965*. University of North Carolina Press.

Persily, Nathaniel. 2007. "The Promise and Pitfalls of the New Voting Rights Act." *Yale Law Journal* 117:174.

Pettigrew, Stephen. 2021. "The Downstream Consequences of Long Waits: How Lines at the Precinct Depress Future Turnout." *Electoral Studies* 71:102188.

Porter, Ethan, and Jon C. Rogowski. 2018. "Partisanship, Bureaucratic Responsiveness, and Election Administration: Evidence from a Field Experiment." *Journal of Public Administration Research and Theory* 28(4):602–617.

Posner-Ferdman, Brett, and David Cuillier. 2025. "Dark Deserts: Newspaper Decline and Its Relation to Government Non-Compliance with Public Records Laws." *News Research Journal* 46(3):427–445.

Raze, Kyle. 2022. "Voting Rights and the Resilience of Black Turnout." *Economic Inquiry* 60(3):1127–1141.

Reynolds, Molly E. 2017. *Exceptions to the Rule: The Politics of Filibuster Limitations in the U.S. Senate.* Brookings Institution Press.

Richman, Jesse T., Gulshan A. Chattha, and David C. Earnest. 2014. "Do Non-Citizens Vote in U.S. Elections?" *Electoral Studies* 36:149–157.

Rocha, Rene R., and Tetsuya Matsubayashi. 2014. "The Politics of Race and Voter ID Laws in the States: The Return of Jim Crow?" *Political Research Quarterly* 67(3):666–679.

Roth, Jonathan, Pedro H. C. Sant'Anna, Alyssa Bilinski, and John Poe. 2023. "What's Trending in Difference-in-Differences? A Synthesis of the Recent Econometrics Literature." *Journal of Econometrics* 235(2):2218–2244.

Rubado, Meghan E., and Jay T. Jennings. 2020. "Political Consequences of the Endangered Local Watchdog: Newspaper Decline and Mayoral Elections in the United States." *Urban Affairs Review* 56(5):1327–1356.

Rush, Tye, Chelsea Jones, Michael Herndon, and Matt A. Barreto. 2025. "Catalysts of Insurrection: How White Racial Antipathy Influenced Beliefs of Voter Fraud and Support for the January 6th Insurrection." *Journal of Race, Ethnicity, and Politics* 10(1):5–25.

Rushovich, Tamara, Rachel C. Nethery, Ariel White, and Nancy Krieger. 2024. "1965 US Voting Rights Act Impact on Black and Black Versus White Infant Death Rates in Jim Crow States, 1959–1980 and 2017–2021." *American Journal of Public Health* 114(3):300–308.

Schuit, Sophie, and Jon C. Rogowski. 2017. "Race, Representation, and the Voting Rights Act." *American Journal of Political Science* 61(3):513–526.

Shah, Paru R., Melissa J. Marschall, and Anirudh V. S. Ruhil. 2013. "Are We There Yet? The Voting Rights Act and Black Representation on City Councils, 1981–2006." *Journal of Politics* 75(4):993–1008.

Shepherd, Michael E., Adriane Fresh, Nick Eubank, and Joshua D. Clinton. 2021. "The Politics of Locating Polling Places: Race and Partisanship in North Carolina Election Administration, 2008–2016." *Election Law Journal: Rules, Politics, and Policy* 20(2):155–177.

Shino, Enrijeta, Mara Suttmann-Lea, and Daniel A. Smith. 2022. "Determinants of Rejected Mail Ballots in Georgia's 2018 General Election." *Political Research Quarterly* 75(1): 231–243.

Skrentny, John David. 1998. "The Effect of the Cold War on African-American Civil Rights: America and the World Audience, 1945–1968." *Theory and Society* 27(2):237–285.

Snyder, James M., and David Strömberg. 2010. "Press Coverage and Political Accountability." *Journal of Political Economy* 118(2):355–408.

Southwell, Priscilla, and Justin Burchett. 2000. "Does Changing the Rules Change the Players? The Effect of All-Mail Elections on the Composition of the Electorate." *Social science quarterly* 81(3):837–845.

Sterling, Erica. N.d. "A Man Whose Death Inspired the Teenager Who Led the Movement." Technical report. Georgia Civil Rights Cold Cases Project, Emory University, Atlanta.

Stewart, Charles. 2013. "Voter ID: Who Has Them; Who Shows Them." *Oklahoma Law Review* 66:21.

Thompson, Daniel M., Jennifer A. Wu, Jesse Yoder, and Andrew B. Hall. 2020. "Universal Vote-by-Mail Has No Impact on Partisan Turnout or Vote Share." *Proceedings of the National Academy of Sciences* 117(25):14052–14056.

Tucker, James. 2007. "The Power of Observation: The Role of Federal Observers Under the Voting Rights Act." *Michigan Journal of Race and Law* 13(1):227–276.

Valelly, Richard M. 2004. *The Two Reconstructions: The Struggle for Black Enfranchisement.* American Politics and Political Economy. University of Chicago Press.

Valentino, Nicholas A., and Fabian G. Neuner. 2017. "Why the Sky Didn't Fall: Mobilizing Anger in Reaction to Voter ID Laws." *Political Psychology* 38(2):331–350.

Valentino, Nicholas A., Krysha Gregorowicz, and Eric W. Groenendyk. 2009. "Efficacy, Emotions and the Habit of Participation." *Political Behavior* 31(3):307–330.

Vivian, C. T., with Steve Fiffer. 2021. *It's in the Action: Memories of a Nonviolent Warrior.* NewSouth Books.

Von Mises, Richard. 1939. "Über aufteilungs-und besetzungswahrscheinlichkeiten." *Revue de la Faculté des Sciences de l'Université d'Istanbul* 4:145–163

Voris, Ryan E., and Austin Trantham. 2024. "Oh, the Places They'll Go: A Geographic Analysis of Gubernatorial Campaigns." *American Politics Research* 52(4):389–402.

Wang, Tova Andrea. 2012. *The Politics of Voter Suppression: Defending and Expanding Americans' Right to Vote.* Cornell University Press.

White, Ariel R., Noah L. Nathan, and Julie K. Faller. 2015. "What Do I Need to Vote? Bureaucratic Discretion and Discrimination by Local Election Officials." *American Political Science Review* 109(1):129–142.

White, Ismail K., and Chryl Nicole Laird. 2020. *Steadfast Democrats: How Social Forces Shape Black Political Behavior.* Princeton Studies in Political Behavior. Princeton University Press.

Willis, Derek, Thessalia Merivaki, and Ioannis Ziogas. 2022. "Election Data Transparency: Obtaining Precinct-Level Election Returns." *Public Integrity* 24(2):162–178.

Yoder, Jesse, Cassandra Handan-Nader, A. Wu Jennifer, et al. 2021. "How Did Absentee Voting Affect the 2020 US Election?" *Science Advances* 7(52):eabk1755.

Zaller, John. 1992. *The Nature and Origins of Mass Opinion.* Cambridge University Press.

Zhang, Emily Rong. 2022. "Questioning Questions in the Law of Democracy: What the Debate over Voter ID Laws' Effects Teaches About Asking the Right Questions." *UCLA Law Review* 69(2022):1028–1074.

Zhang, Iris H. 2024. "The Limits of Preclearance: Municipal Annexations Before and After *Shelby County v. Holder*." *Du Bois Review: Social Science Research on Race* 21(1):24–49.

INDEX

NOTE: Page numbers in *italics* refer to figures and tables. Note information is indicated by n and note number following the page number.